TEACHING DIFFICULT TOPICS

MUSIC AND SOCIAL JUSTICE

Series Editors: William Cheng and Andrew Dell'Antonio

TITLES IN THE SERIES

Hold Me Down [Online Resource]
Ben Lauren

Teaching Difficult Topics: Reflections from the Undergraduate Music Classroom
Olivia R. Lucas and Laura Moore Pruett, Editors

*Improvising Across Abilities: Pauline Oliveros and the
Adaptive Use Musical Instrument*
The AUMI Editorial Collective

Rape at the Opera: Staging Sexual Violence
Margaret Cormier

Jamming the Classroom: Musical Improvisation and Pedagogical Practice
Ajay Heble and Jesse Stewart

On Music Theory, and Making Music More Welcoming for Everyone
Philip Ewell

For the Culture: Hip-Hop and the Fight for Social Justice
Lakeyta M. Bonnette-Bailey and Adolphus G. Belk, Jr., Editors

Sonorous Worlds: Musical Enchantment in Venezuela
Yana Stainova

Singing Out: GALA Choruses and Social Change
Heather MacLachlan

Performing Commemoration: Musical Reenactment and the Politics of Trauma
Annegret Fauser and Michael A. Figueroa, Editors

Sounding Dissent: Rebel Songs, Resistance, and Irish Republicanism
Stephen R. Millar

Teaching Difficult Topics

Reflections from the Undergraduate Music Classroom

Olivia R. Lucas and Laura Moore Pruett, Editors

University of Michigan Press
Ann Arbor

Copyright © 2024 by Olivia R. Lucas and Laura Moore Pruett
Some rights reserved

This work is licensed under a Creative Commons Attribution-NonCommercial 4.0 International License. *Note to users:* A Creative Commons license is only valid when it is applied by the person or entity that holds rights to the licensed work. Works may contain components (e.g., photographs, illustrations, or quotations) to which the rightsholder in the work cannot apply the license. It is ultimately your responsibility to independently evaluate the copyright status of any work or component part of a work you use, in light of your intended use. To view a copy of this license, visit http://creativecommons.org/licenses/by-nc/4.0/

For questions or permissions, please contact um.press.perms@umich.edu

Published in the United States of America by the
University of Michigan Press
Manufactured in the United States of America
Printed on acid-free paper
First published October 2024

A CIP catalog record for this book is available from the British Library.

Library of Congress Cataloging-in-Publication Data

Names: Lucas, Olivia R., editor. | Pruett, Laura Moore., editor. | Michigan Publishing (University of Michigan), publisher.
Title: Teaching difficult topics : reflections from the undergraduate music classroom / Olivia R. Lucas and Laura Moore Pruett, Editors.
Other titles: Music and social justice.
Description: Ann Arbor : University of Michigan Press, 2024. | Series: Music and Social Justice | Includes bibliographical references and index.
Identifiers: LCCN 2024023132 (print) | LCCN 2024023133 (ebook) | ISBN 9780472056965 (paperback) | ISBN 9780472076963 (hardcover) | ISBN 9780472904594 (ebook other)
Subjects: LCSH: Music in universities and colleges. | Music—Instruction and study. | Music and race. | Antisemitism in music | Anti-racism.
Classification: LCC MT18 .T36 2024 (print) | LCC MT18 (ebook) | DDC 780.71—dc23/eng/20240604
LC record available at https://lccn.loc.gov/2024023132
LC ebook record available at https://lccn.loc.gov/2024023133

DOI: https://doi.org/10.3998/mpub.12837931

The University of Michigan Press's open access publishing program is made possible thanks to additional funding from the University of Michigan Office of the Provost and the generous support of contributing libraries.

We dedicate this volume to all those who brave the depths.

Contents

List of Illustrations	ix
List of Appendices	xi
List of Tables	xiii
Acknowledgments	xv
Preface: Navigating Deep Waters	xvii

Introduction	1

PART I: MUSIC AND DYNAMICS OF POWER

Chapter 1: Success and Music Education: Teaching the Value of Art in the Neoliberal University *John R. Pippen*	13
Chapter 2: Teaching Music and the Holocaust: Facilitating Discussions and Trust in an Undergraduate Seminar *Jessica Grimmer*	33
Chapter 3: Teaching Difficult Topics in Large Enrollment Classes *Kelsey Klotz*	45
Chapter 4: Decentering Whiteness in the Music Appreciation Classroom: An Anti-Racist Approach *Everette Scott Smith*	61
Chapter 5: Opera and Masculinity *Sean M. Parr*	77

PART II: SOCIAL JUSTICE, ACTIVISM AND DECOLONIZATION, AND BUILDING RESILIENCE

Chapter 6: Beyond the Canon: Using Contemporary Works to Address Sexual Violence in the Music Drama *Annalise Smith*	95

viii   CONTENTS

Chapter 7: Asking Non-Majors to Music in Reclamation and Remix
Projects: Challenging Topics, Collaborative Learning, and
Creative Assignments   112
April L. Prince

Chapter 8: "Decolonizing" the Music in Canada Course   131
Colette Simonot-Maiello

Chapter 9: Reimagining Indigenous Existence in Period Performance
Practice in the Academic Classroom   148
Breana H. McCullough

Chapter 10: Less Is More: Opportunity for Deeper Dialogue through
the Jesuit Examen   167
Trudi Wright

PART III: CRITICAL RACE STUDIES

Chapter 11: Transdisciplinary Antiracism Research and Teaching as a
Foundation for Revising Music Coursework   185
John Spilker-Beed

Chapter 12: Discussing White Nationalist Music in the Shadow of the
Christchurch Mosque Shootings: The Importance of Reflecting
on Race and Racism with Students in Aotearoa New Zealand   212
Olivia R. Lucas

Chapter 13: Don't You Cry for Me: A Critical-Race Analysis of
Undergraduate Music Theory Textbooks   226
Philip Ewell and Megan Lyons

Chapter 14: Stephen Foster and Slavery in Music Textbooks: A Case
Study Outlining the Benefits of Using Class Time to Enrich
Textbook Narratives about American Slavery   252
Christopher Lynch

Chapter 15: The Jazz of a Black Ethnographer: A Memoir of Pedagogy,
Improvisation, and Reflexivity at a Liberal Arts College   278
Whitney Slaten

Contributors   297
Index   301

Digital materials related to this title can be found on the Fulcrum platform
via the following citable URL: https://doi.org/10.3998/mpub.12837931

List of Illustrations

Figure 6.1: Musical depiction of the rape in *Thumbprint* 102
Figure 9.1: *Les Sauvages* as seen in the manuscript of *Nouvelles Suites de Pieces de Clavecin* 155
Figure 9.2: *Inoca War Chief in 1701*, Gilcrease Museum 156
Figure 10.1: *The Ignatian Pedagogical Paradigm* 173
Figure 13.1: Composers of Color in the most common music theory textbooks 234
Figure 14.1: Cover art for "Oh! Susanna," Courtesy of the Center for American Music, University of Pittsburgh 267
Figure 14.2: Early printing of "Oh! Susanna" 268
Figure 14.3: Early printing of "Oh! Susanna" 269
Figure 14.4: Early print of "Jeanie with the Light Brown Hair," published by Firth, Pond & Co. 270
Figure 14.5: Early print of "Jeanie with the Light Brown Hair," published by Firth, Pond & Co. 271

List of Appendices

Appendix 2.1: Course Content · 42

Appendix 5.1: Selected Primary Source Excerpts on the
Voices of Castrati · 85

Appendix 7.1: Reclamation Project · 116

Appendix 7.2: Remix Project · 122

Appendix 10.1: The Examen in Five Steps from James Martin's
The Jesuit Guide to (Almost) Everything · 175

Appendix 10.2: *Examen* to Prepare for a Difficult Conversation/
Class Discussion · 176

Appendix 13.1: Women Composers and Composers of Color
in Benward and Saker, 9th ed. (2015) · 240

Appendix 13.2a: Women Composers and Composers of Color
in Burstein/Straus (2016) · 241

Appendix 13.2b: Women Composers and Composers of Color
in Burstein/Straus (2019) · 241

Appendix 13.3: Women Composers and Composers of Color
in Clendinning/Marvin (2016) · 243

Appendix 13.4: Women Composers and Composers of Color
in Kostka/Payne/Almén (2018) · 245

Appendix 13.5: Women Composers and Composers of Color
in Laitz (2015) · 246

Appendix 13.6: Women Composers and Composers of Color
in Roig-Francoli (2010) · 246

List of Tables

Table 13.1: Musical examples by composers of color and women
in the most common music theory textbooks 228

Table 13.2: Percentages of musical examples by Bach, Beethoven, and
Mozart 229

Table 13.3: Racial and gender data of composers for the most common
music theory textbooks 229

Table 13.4: Burstein/Straus first edition and second edition data 230

Table 13.5: Stephen Foster examples in the most common music
theory textbooks 233

Table 13.6: Popular music examples from the most common music
theory textbooks 236

Table 13.7: Popular music composers from the most common music
theory textbooks 237

Table 14.1: Well-Known Examples of Foster's Songs 259

Acknowledgments

This project has been the work of several years and has been lovingly supported by many. We are forever grateful to anyone who has contributed to this book in any way at any stage.

We are deeply grateful to all of the contributing authors, who have been generous, patient, and committed to what turned out to be a long project timeline. Their chapters continued to evolve as our situations, and the world around us, evolved. Their writings are inspiring, sobering, thought-provoking, and elevating, and encourage all of us to be better, more empathetic teachers.

We are also grateful to the editors and editorial staff at the University of Michigan Press, who have been similarly patient with and committed to the project. Andrew Dell'Antonio, Annie Carter, Sara Cohen, and Will Cheng have been supportive shepherds through the entire process. Samantha Bassler skillfully indexed the entire manuscript. We would also like to thank Anna Nekola for her careful reading of the first versions of many of the chapters, as well as the two anonymous reviewers who offered engaged and supportive suggestions for revisions.

Olivia offers special thanks to Andrew, Ivy, and feline friends Yevgeny, Squid, and Mr. Cheddar, for their silliness, support, affection, and love. Love y'all!

Laura tenders her inexpressible gratitude for the unwavering support of her family, and astonished reverence for their enduring resilience through years of difficulty. Christy, Alexander, and Althea, you will always strengthen me; I love you.

Preface

Navigating Deep Waters

It's a beautiful summer day in New England. Fluffy clouds waft through a sky so blue there's no choice than to hear Irving Berlin's lyrics in your mind. I walked down to the water this morning, to the lake I can glimpse from my home office window. I felt the sunshine, warm on my back; I felt the cool breeze blowing across the water and ruffling the hair across my forehead, causing my loose pantlegs to flutter. The warmth and the coolness, both welcome in the moment, the delicious pleasure of each balanced against each other in a perfect moment of physical enjoyment as I looked out over the little blue waves toward the distant shore.

Today, the death toll from the Hawaii fire rises.[1]

Today, my hometown in Louisiana enters a second week of daily high temperatures over 100 degrees Fahrenheit.[2]

Today, I reflect on and write about a metaphor, one that represents much I love about this world and provided the inspiration for this volume's cover: navigating deep waters. The phrase conjures a scene, at least for me, of diving into the deepest blues, of quiet yet unceasing movement, of coolness; it evokes a sense of profundity, and feelings of both uncertainty and exhilaration.

It feels ironic to write about water at a time when our planet is on fire.[3]

Earlier this summer, before scientists began rescuing corals from the heating ocean,[4] my partner and I traveled to the Florida coast, between Destin, where my family of origin has vacationed since my infancy, and Tallahassee, where I earned my master's and doctoral degrees in the 2000s. We spent a day on the public beach of St. George Island, alone on a patch of sand far enough from anyone else we couldn't overhear conversations. Behind us was the bay; before us a shallow beach where the ocean waves invited us into deepening blue depths before washing up and over what seemed to be an aquamarine sandbar, perhaps a hundred yards out from shore. Since the water felt so joyfully balmy after the chilly lakes of a Massachusetts spring, I proposed that we swim out that far and see if we could touch. I am not a strong swimmer, and halfway there I almost lost my nerve and turned back. But I knew my

xviii   PREFACE

partner was right next to me, I knew that other people were out on the shore who would hear and help us if we needed it, and—most importantly of all—I knew and honored the limits of my own physical capabilities in this potentially hazardous situation.[5] We arrived at the sandbar, where it was wonderfully clear and indeed shallow enough for us to stand and catch our breaths before heading back to shore to bake in the July sun, tired but exhilarated and proud of the little adventure we'd embarked on, without knowing exactly how it might end.

I often feel similarly tired, exhilarated, and proud after teaching a challenging class session. When I enter a classroom, ready to discuss a difficult topic like the racist history of blackface minstrelsy or rap lyrics being used as evidence in murder trials, I can imagine myself jumping off a high-dive, or setting sail from a dock into the open water, or—more recently—confidently setting out to swim to a turquoise sandbar. I know that I will get to the end of the class session time physically, mentally, and emotionally intact, as will my students; I know that we will navigate difficult topics I feel very self-assured discussing with them; I know that we will also likely talk about artists, cases, songs or incidents I might know nothing about, or that they may know—and *feel*—way more about than me. These are deep waters, but I have points of navigation, perhaps some already-mapped sandbar in mind; a place to land, maybe, halfway through class, and a return to shore before we part ways. When we meet again, we're all a little more prepared for another dive into the sea, and navigate the waves together progressively more adeptly and adaptively throughout the semester. By the end of fifteen weeks, my hope is that they each feel confident enough in this particular cove to both navigate its waters on their own in individual and group final projects, but also to take the skills they've learned during our collective explorations out of the classroom and into whatever other oceans, lakes, rivers they might find themselves: hard subjects, difficult workplaces, challenging family dynamics, complicated human existence. I hope they know, when I wish them a happy, restorative break, both that they are better equipped to navigate difficult waters on their own *and* that seeking and embracing guidance or help along the way isn't a sign of weakness, but one of wisdom.

Over the past five years, a thoughtful, generous, and skilled cohort of individuals has come together to share experiments in navigating the deeper waters of teaching. Our contributors are a group invested in making change both within our classes, with our students, but also at our institutions, within academia, even in response to national and international events. We seek to navigate the deep waters. These waters are both inviting and forbidding; we should approach them with both profound, deep caution and reverence, but also with the confidence in one's abilities to dive in, to explore, and at least get back to shore, if not out to the sandbar or beyond.

These chapters were all written by teachers who dove into the deep waters ahead of many of the global and personal troubles we've all had to learn to navigate in the past five years: before the pandemic, before losing loved ones, before divorces and job firings and school closings and war and climate catastrophes. The book represents work, learning, and progress already made as we watched others dip their toes in the shallows from the shore, just as everyone could see the waves really beginning to roil. We were in the water already.

Every step of the process of creating this book has meant navigating some new challenge: as every day of life brings new challenges for all of us to navigate, does it not? Navigation, or spatial intelligence, is a skill set I possess rather little of, and I rely on the help and guidance of others (and GPS) to make my way throughout my lived world.[6] Navigating the teaching of "difficult topics" can be intimidating, too. Not only are we as teachers swimming in the waters ourselves, we're keeping watch on our students, calling out directions as they keep pressing on, pointing out the undertows, both those they can anticipate and those unseen. We teach them to navigate, to steer their boats, to swim with foresight and buoyancy in uncharted waters.

People have cycled off and on this project. It has changed as our teaching has changed, as we have changed and learned and grown. At times it has felt like we were in over our heads. Why press on? Because we know that teaching and learning in the music classroom is indeed difficult. I come to teaching with a simple dictum from the first day of each semester: *Meet them where they are*. This is not a pedagogically transformative statement for our discipline; I know many of you hold similar tenets already, and practice them in your own ways in your classrooms and your lives. But when I meet students in September or January, the very first thing I want to know about them, what I often ask even before I've introduced myself, is what kind of music they're listening to, right then, that very week—on the way to class, or at sunrise lift or practice with their team, or last night in a club with friends, or beside their pillow as they dropped off to sleep. What music do these humans presently *love*?[7]

And they do love music, in a way that they don't necessarily love their majors of chemistry, or business, or even nursing or education—not as what they want to *do* after graduation, but as a part of who they *are* right now, both how they see themselves, on an intimate, vulnerable, inward-focused level, and also how they represent themselves in the world, in society, among

xx PREFACE

friends and in public spaces and as a means to join and form communities. Our relationship with music is special, ineffable, and ever-evolving for each one of us, whether student or teacher; it feels difficult for me to teach without swimming alongside, pointing out the sandbars, buoying my students as they learn from the place of strength of my own confidence and assurance. I don't want to stand on the shore. Hence, this book: an invitation, a call to join us in navigating these deep, difficult waters, even though they may be unfamiliar or untested.

Our contributors range from adjunct or contingent to full professors. Some are graduate students, and some completed their degrees while the book was in progress. Most are from the US. Some identify as LGBTQ+, BIPOC or Latinx, or Indigenous. We teach at public institutions in the deep south and Canada, at progressive religious colleges in the northeast and conservative ones in the Midwest. We teach in difficult situations, and we teach in difficult contexts—during semesters with catastrophes happening near and far that unfolded in our news feeds and that we have had to navigate as the leaders, the guides in and of our classrooms. It reminds me of the heavy additional burden spiritual leaders and therapists face, of being called ever more loudly and often to bear others' emotional and spiritual pain and helping them process it while also more acutely aware of and feeling their own agonies. How do you lead a flock or support a sick teenager, especially amid a global health or political or climate crisis? How, as a college educator, do you do both at the same time, and without any kind of training to do either? And still try to "teach"—whatever that might mean to us, our students, our administrators?

We profess no concrete answers for "how to teach and learn difficult topics in the music classroom." Instead, we offer specific stories of moments we've experienced that felt difficult, most often and for many of us in ways that layer upon one another—topically, geographically, institutionally, politically, departmentally. We offer some suggestions of exercises, activities, syllabi, and course revisions and new frameworks for music programs and courses of study. But in the end, what I think we perhaps offer here which is of most value is the continued shaping of a pedagogically supportive community in music.

I am filled with hope by what I see and hear at the Teaching Music History Conference, in the Composers of Color Resource Project, and by the fact of pedagogy panels proliferating at co-organized in-person conferences such as the 2022 AMS/SEM/SMT meeting in New Orleans. I see this volume as an additional layer of community building bridges among the Venn diagrams of our contributors' lives and trajectories and reaching additional young people passionate about both studying and music who have somehow stumbled their way into the beginnings of an academic career. These early-career professionals, post-grads, ABDs, Ph.D. and master's students, and even the undergraduate music majors and non-majors who populate our classes—this is who I want to touch and help to grow. We must share whatever wisdom we do gain along the way with one another; it's the only way we have, given the confines and difficulties of academia, to hold onto our humanity and return to the love that brought us to these classrooms in the first place.

After a half hour or so of roasting in the heat on the beach, my partner and I noticed some commotion in the water nearby. Dolphins! They weren't far away, and we watched them frolic, dorsal fins surfacing, and even leaping fully out of the water. Without much discussion, we headed back into the water, swimming confidently back out to the sandbar, to be rewarded with an astonishingly close encounter with a pair of friendly, if somewhat intimidating, large and joyful pink-bellied dolphins. We held hands and gripped our toes in the sand of the bar, backing away just enough to show our respect for the creatures in their own environment, and finally floated back, dazed, to the beach, exhilarated by the experience. We had to decide to swim out, had to be assured of our capabilities and strengths and flexibilities, to experience the encounter. We'd made the swim once and we knew we could return again, feeling even stronger and braver the second time, and ready for the spiritually profound experience of watching the dolphins play. And if we ever visit that beach again, we'll stride confidently into the water, arms strong and grins wide, as we start swimming toward the sand bar, in search of our slippery friends.

Navigating deep waters can be intimidating, even frightening. But my hope is that, equipped with the reports of some who have traversed such waters—or similar ones—as the ones you are facing, equipped with a community supporting and cheering one another on, the network we've sought to build in this volume amid the many complicated conversations on undergraduate music teaching, you too will feel excited and ready to navigate difficult teaching, to traverse and map these fathoms. Join us in the deep—the water's just fine.

Laura Moore Pruett

Notes

1. Jonathan Oatis, "Maui fires: What to know about Hawaii's deadliest disaster, damage, and death toll," *Reuters*, August 21, 2023, https://www.reuters.com/

xxii   PREFACE

world/us/how-did-hawaii-wildfires-start-what-know-about-maui-big-island-blaz-es-2023-08-11/

2. Adam Olivier, "More Days at 100 Degrees," *KADN News15*, August 7, 2023, https://www.kadn.com/weather/forecast/more-days-at-100-degrees/article_5f09491a-350f-11ee-89dc-ab4ae96b068c.html

3. I am inspired here by the work and writing of Ayisha Siddiqa, especially "On Another Panel About Climate, They Ask Me to Sell the Future and All I've Got is a Love Poem," *The Eco Justice Project*, https://www.theecojusticeproject.com/submissions/all-ive-got-is-another-love-poem, accessed August 15, 2023. Siddiqa's poem was read as part of the *On Being* project on June 10, 2022: https://onbeing.org/poetry/on-an-other-panel-about-climate-they-ask-me-to-sell-the-future-and-all-ive-got-is-a-love-poem/. For more on Siddiqa, see the recent Women of the Year profile by Kyla Mandel, "Ayisha Siddiqa Is Making the World Think Differently About Climate Action," *Time*, March 2, 2023, https://time.com/6259119/ayisha-siddiqa/

4. Catrin Einhorn, "A Desperate Push to Save Florida's Coral: Get it Out of the Sea," *New York Times*, July 31, 2023, https://www.nytimes.com/2023/07/31/climate/coral-reefs-heat-florida-ocean-temperatures.html

5. Megan VerHelst, "12 Die at Gulf Beaches in 2 Weeks," *Patch*, June 28, 2023, https://patch.com/florida/across-fl/12-die-gulf-beaches-2-weeks-including-ex-nfl-qb

6. Howard Gardner outlines and differentiates among eight distinct intelligences, including spatial, bodily-kinesthetic, and musical, among others. As an undergraduate, I researched and wrote a thesis on his theory that ultimately aided my entrance into a master's program in musicology. See "The Components of MI" at the *Multiple Intelligences Oasis*, https://www.multipleintelligencesoasis.org/the-components-of-mi

7. I build here on the work of William Cheng's *Loving Music Till It Hurts* (New York: Oxford University Press, 2020), especially his Prelude, "Loving Music and Loving People," 1–10.

Introduction

What is a difficult topic, and how should we approach them as teachers and learners in our music classrooms? To ask this question amid the challenges of 21st century life feels almost absurd; our very human existence is being challenged in "difficult" ways on a daily basis. This book was drafted amid a horrifying global pandemic with a tremendous, ongoing death toll. Out-of-control climate change is generating unprecedentedly massive natural disasters. Racism (both institutional and overt), sexism, homophobia and transphobia, sexual and gender-based violence, ableism, xenophobia, mass shootings, and longstanding patterns of colonial violence and oppression, means that everyone sitting in a classroom, whether teacher or student, musician or non-major, musicologist or theorist or singer or composer, has been intimately and recently impacted by challenges and losses that make living and learning difficult. Teaching and learning can be hard in general these days; when our selected content is inherently fraught or when the inescapable news cycle is impossible to divorce from our daily labors, the additional stress of approaching such material sensitively and while holding grace for all our students (and ourselves as educators) might feel insurmountable.

The music classroom in particular has often been considered (sometimes, regretfully, by music teachers themselves) as a depoliticized and "neutral" space. We believe this also ties in with the belief that many students (and potentially, professors) still hold, that music has an innate moral goodness and positivity that transcends any moral ills associated with its circumstances. Discussing the realities of music's social contexts prepares students to consider the question of whether art can be separated from the artists—a question of considerable public debate—with more than a knee-jerk reaction. We must consider when, why, and how to incorporate not only the events that happen on a near-daily basis, but our own and our students' reactions and responses as we process them both individually and as a society. This book acknowledges that the space of the music classroom can and should be a place to have these conversations.

Simultaneously, however, the collected chapters in this volume demonstrate that the idea of a "difficult topic" for the music classroom is both diffuse

TEACHING DIFFICULT TOPICS

and a matter of intuition, making the whole enterprise problematic and worrisome. If teachers can sense that a topic they are bringing into the classroom is difficult, what is it they are feeling and responding to? Is it their own discomfort with the content? Are they worried about student reactions, or that they or a student might (accidentally, or on purpose) say something offensive or hurtful? Difficult topics bring out anxieties about administrative surveillance, "customer satisfaction" (evinced in student evaluations), and the fundamental purposes of teaching and learning; these anxieties can then in turn impact the learning experience itself. As Lori Patton Davis reflected in her foreword to the 2018 publication *Difficult Subjects: Insights and Strategies for Teaching about Race, Sexuality, and Gender,*

> [T]here is no such thing as a difficult dialogue without feelings of fragility that prompt individuals to retreat from confrontation in hopes of maintaining comfort. Fragility and discomfort are also fueled in classroom spaces where learners (especially those with privileged identities) attempt to manage discomfort by attempting to dictate the depth of conversations about race and racism. . . . And while fragility in classrooms is quite challenging and daunting, there are instructors committed to unpacking [difficult topics such as] race, sexuality, and gender through intersectional lenses and courageous questioning of self, students, and oppressive structures.[1]

The authors in this volume have demonstrated this "courageous questioning" and meditated on its impacts in their varied music classroom situations. These experiences have led them to write about "difficult teaching" in ways that fall into three main categories: topics that instructors sense to be controversial or emotionally challenging to discuss, topics that derive from or intersect with real-world events that are difficult to process or traumatic, and bigger-picture discussions of how music studies centers dominant narratives and ignores other perspectives.[2]

Are personal identity topics such as gender or race, both addressed by writers in this volume, inherently difficult? Or is it that they can quickly become personal, and thus potentially difficult to both students and teachers? It is also not always obvious for whom such discussions of race and gender are difficult. Some of the chapters in this volume remind us that it is often white students who struggle with discussions of race; unlike their classmates of color, they have lived lives where their race is unmarked, default, and easily set aside—a difficult topic that mainly impacts others, but not themselves. This disparity suggests that for topics centered on personal identity, it may be students who are unlearning previous thought patterns (e.g., "racism was

Introduction 3

solved by the civil rights movement"), or who are resisting unlearning such thoughts, for whom the issue feels difficult.

On the other hand, study of historical collective trauma (such as the Holocaust) can provide what feels like distance to some course members (although perhaps not all). Does the passage of time make discussion of collective trauma easier? There's an adage about the difference between a horrifying mass grave and a fascinating archeological find being a thousand years. But findings in epigenetics suggest that traces of trauma remain in the DNA for generations.[3] What some students might unemotionally experience as the distant past, others might find raw and painful.

Many instructors have grown accustomed to notifying students in advance of "difficult content," particularly around issues of sexual and racial violence. The chapters in this book go far deeper than the so-called "trigger warning," investigating ways that we, as teachers, can better prepare ourselves, our students, and even our administrations for the necessity, challenge, and opportunity of studying systems, events, and people that have caused harm.

We seek to explore multiple dimensions of teaching difficult topics in the music classroom. We have included essays on specific "hows" of teaching a set of issues or questions as well as reflections on the "whys" of doing this significant work within music programs / departments and more broadly within liberal arts curricula. Authors also share how they are working among and with the diverse levels of curricula and institutional frameworks, exploring practices that create and hold space for courses that engage these subjects. We urged our contributors to keep in mind the specific nature of addressing such topics within the music classroom: what is it about music that gives us as educators and learners a singular position from which to do this brave and necessary work?

We have also encouraged the authors to consider how their held identities impact the contents of their chapters. In some chapters, the author's positionality is a central thread; in others, its influence is more peripheral, but never wholly absent. In keeping with the contributors' generous self-disclosures, we, the co-editors, should also introduce ourselves.

Olivia R. Lucas: Professionally, I am Assistant Professor of Music Theory at Louisiana State University. I've also taught at Te Herenga Waka—Victoria University of Wellington and the University of Iowa, and I received my PhD from Harvard University. My research has centered primarily on extreme metal music, though it has touched on other areas of popular music as well. Personally, I am a white, European-American, cisgender woman from a middle-class background, and these intersecting facets of my identity have shaped my experiences as a member of classroom communities, both as student and teacher. I became interested in ongoing conversations about supportive pedagogy and teaching viscerally challenging subject matter the first time I taught about my research area—extreme metal and other forms of transgressive popular music. I found that it was impossible to responsibly teach about the sound of early Norwegian black metal without also discussing its ties to white supremacy. It also felt irresponsible to go flinging the idea of "white supremacy in music" into a group of young adults of varying backgrounds and identities without some form of preparation for that conversation. I have always valued empathy and responsiveness in teaching, but I discovered that I needed more deliberateness in the way I approached and scaffolded difficult issues into my teaching. With a background and a majority of my teaching experience in music theory, I am also conscious of the way that whiteness and maleness have shaped and propped up that field's existence, and the way that race, gender, and nationality (often the explicit "difficult topics" of musicology classrooms) shape music theory syllabi without ever being openly mentioned. It has been a privilege to educate myself about these issues from the relative safety of a tenure-track position, and I remain humbled by the opportunity to continue to improve my teaching.

Laura Moore Pruett: I have been teaching music at Merrimack College for over a decade, and at MTSU and FSU before that. With intensifying enthusiasm and urgency over the years, I have made my classrooms the site of scholarly inquiry. As part of a robust and growing community of musicologists currently attuned to music history pedagogy, I have explored "difficult teaching" in a variety of pedagogical scenarios: I co-teach a class on music and politics with a political scientist (our sixth iteration is fall 2024); I developed syllabi for and have taught several additional interdisciplinary courses, both on my own and with department and school colleagues; I worked under internal grant funding to co-develop a cross-school general education course on music and mathematics until halted by COVID; and I currently collaborate on an additional grant-funded project for faculty development on contemplation in and outside the classroom. My radical experiments in teaching began in the classroom, but they continue in hallway conversations on campus, in e-mails and catch-up lunches at conferences, and in collaborative publications such as this one, all crucial shared spaces for reflection. I identify as a queer, white, cisgender woman. I am the middle-aged mother of two t(w)eenagers, recently divorced and newly engaged; I am a cradle Catholic from Louisiana; I was first diagnosed with panic disorder, depression, and anxiety when I was nineteen and a sophomore in college. As co-editor of this volume, I sought to bring thoughtful musicians together to reflect on difficult teaching of all kinds—to facilitate and participate in a stimulating, expansive, and hopefully galvanizing conversation.

Introduction 5

As the subdisciplines of music studies continue to confront the idea that there can be no art forms free of their social and political contexts, this volume moves discussion of music pedagogy into the realm of public cultural consciousness. Not only does it encourage teacher-scholars and their students to engage in critical forms of interdisciplinary study and analysis in music classrooms, it also seeks to offer practical ideas for how to do this more and to do it better.

We also want to acknowledge the limitations of this volume. These chapters are predominantly first-hand reports—a collection of on-the-ground experiences, reflections, and iteratively developed approaches to challenges frequently faced by academic music teachers at the post-secondary level.[4] We are also aware that it is not possible, in a single volume, to address every difficult topic that comes up in music classrooms. It is our hope that the chapters in this volume will inspire others to write on areas and topics we have missed, including issues of dis/ability and xenophobia. We would further be thrilled to see additional work on teaching difficult topics in other higher education contexts, such as the studio teaching environment, ensembles, and composition lessons. The overwhelming majority of our authors and both co-editors are based in the United States, and the resulting chapters reflect this educational context, with limited emphasis in two chapters on Canadian and Aotearoa New Zealand contexts.

The idea for this volume originated at a session for the Pedagogy Interest Group at the 2018 Annual Conference of the Society for American Music. In the intervening years, the importance of navigating the pedagogy of challenging issues with sensitivity, integrity, and what Cheng calls an "ethic of care" has only become more clear. Some difficult topics—especially those related to race and gender—have become even more difficult and politically charged. The scholars in this volume represent a wide range of teaching experiences, from large non-major lectures to small seminars, and from graduate student and contingent to tenured faculty. Their collective experience and wisdom offers a variety of both approaches to the practical issues of teaching difficult topics in music classes and reflections on why this teaching is important for us, our students, and our communities.

STRUCTURE

We have organized the volume into three thematically linked sections: 1) music and dynamics of power; 2) social justice, activism and decolonization, and building resilience; and 3) critical race studies.

6   TEACHING DIFFICULT TOPICS

Music and Dynamics of Power

The idea that historical and current power structures shape music cultures has influenced much musicology of the last generation, and has become an important pedagogical anchor across many U.S. and Canadian music curricula. Teaching informed by this knowledge, however, remains challenging, because classroom dynamics and pedagogical techniques afforded by the current university environment tend themselves to rely on explicit and implicit power structures, and because students may resist these concepts due to encultured beliefs about music's aesthetic and moral purity. The impact of power structures on music teaching touches every chapter of this book, but the authors in this opening section focus their work on processing the power dynamics that impact not only their teaching of emotionally challenging material, but also those that impact their lived realities in their university roles.

At the broadest level of the section, John Pippen considers the power dynamics that shape the contemporary university and push instructors and even entire degree programs toward teaching music as an entrepreneurial path. In doing so, he strives to offer ways that instructors can help students find balance among the capitalist exigencies they face, the realities of musical labor, and their valuing of music as art. On a more granular level, Jessica Grimmer and Kelsey Klotz offer experiential advice on the power dynamics of the classroom, especially in the face of content that students may find traumatic (Grimmer) or challenging to their worldview (Klotz). Despite common themes, their accounts diverge in the face of vastly different teaching circumstances. Grimmer finds ways to productively question and dismantle certain classroom hierarchies in a small, upper-level seminar on music and the Holocaust. Klotz's general education class, by contrast, is by necessity a more anonymous environment for its hundreds of students, and she must balance her power to shape course content with the students' power to make her feel unsafe in the classroom by reacting negatively or harassingly to content they deem too "liberal" or "activist." Klotz's and Grimmer's chapters are further linked by the (unrelated) shooting incidents that impacted the course of their semesters—a shared experience on which Olivia Lucas also reflects in her chapter (see chapter 12 in the Critical Race studies section). That three chapters in this volume deal at least in part with the impacts of gun violence on teaching speaks to the unfortunate, numbing regularity of such incidents, especially in the United States, and reminds us that our classrooms can never be isolated from external events. The section concludes with chapters that

Introduction   7

make productive use of exposing power dynamics to student discussion. Everette Scott Smith's chapter makes this issue a central focus, and discusses how he pushes students to reconsider preconceived notions about the value of discussing race and intersectionality in music appreciation classes in an overwhelmingly conservative region of the United States. Sean Parr explores how thoughtful classroom consideration of gender norms can help students see how these expectations have the power to shape their ideas of musicality.

Social Justice, Activism and Decolonization, and Building Resilience

As the title of the book suggests, all of its chapters in some way concern themselves with how students learn about and in the face of difficult topics. These explorations of learning generally deal with how students may best be able to confront, discuss, and absorb material that may stir up strong emotions or challenge deeply held, and possibly previously unexamined, beliefs. The chapters in this section, however, propose ways that students and teachers can move through learning to activism. In addition to confronting, discussing, and absorbing, the students in these chapters are doing, shaping, and making change. As one of two specific, actionable examples of using course activities that encourage an activist stance, Annalise Smith finds that including Kamala Sankaram and Susan Yankowitz's *Thumbprint* in her opera course provides a context for discussing sexual violence in opera in which the reality of rape cannot be avoided or glossed over. The story's confronting nature, and her teaching of it, leads students to more deeply consider their own beliefs about consent and the impact of sexual assault on victims and their communities. April L. Prince, on the other hand, offers assignments that enable non-majors to connect with both music-making and activism. Her "reclamation" and "remix" projects ask students to attend to the political significance of music (and sound more broadly) and participate in this significance by creating their own pieces of activist music.

Throughout the book, the authors write about teaching experiences that took place in former (British) colonies—the United States, Canada, and Aotearoa New Zealand. This shared postcolonial experience, whether explicitly addressed in the chapters or not, forms an important contextual foundation for many of the challenging topics that arise in our classrooms. Two additional chapters in this section address the powers claimed by colonizers and their heirs, and offer suggestions for resisting these legacies. For the authors, this work begins in context-specific ways, but yields broad insights about how colonial legacies impact educational structures, content, and research pathways. Colette Simonot-Maiello offers a map, structure, and critical framework for instructors seeking to decolonize an existing course. The course she describes focuses on music in Canada, but the teaching strategies she offers show how to make the colonizing structures of grand historical narratives more readily apparent even to early undergraduate students, and are widely applicable. Breana McCullough combines personal perspectives with Indigenous epistemologies to open paths for students to engage with "alter-Native" histories of musical works that were written by European composers about Indigenous peoples.

The section concludes with Trudi Wright's chapter, in which change-making happens within the students themselves, as they use mindfulness and self-examination techniques to prepare space for and reflect on difficult topics that come up in class. Wright emphasizes the importance of taking time—even deliberately reducing content—to create opportunities for students to actively learn practices that can build resilience; she reminds us that good pedagogy encompasses far more than coverage and exhorts us to make proper space for difficult topics.

Critical Race Studies

Several contributing authors write about the importance of and challenges inherent in teaching about race and racism in the music classroom. Such writing is important and illuminating in the face of both the increased urgency of such discussions as well as the increasing hostility to these topics that many U.S.-American instructors face. On the one hand, our classrooms are becoming more diverse, such that racial issues can no longer be ignored via a preponderance of white students and instructors who take their racial "un-markedness" for granted. On the other hand, several states have moved to ban the teaching of "critical race theory" and other "divisive topics," whatever the legislators believe those to be.

John Spilker-Beed's chapter opens the section with an autoethnographic approach that is simultaneously broad and specific, examining the process by which a (white) professor can work toward building an anti-racist classroom. A chapter by Olivia Lucas confronts some of the challenges that arise in doing this work. Specifically, both address an observed dynamic in which classroom discussions about race often present greater challenges to white students, as they frequently do not understand their everyday experiences to be racialized, whereas students of color have typically understood this for a long time. Lucas's chapter expands the context beyond the United States to Aotearoa New Zealand, and considers forces beyond the classroom (administrations, collective trauma, outsider status) that can impact the shape of class discussions. Chapters by Philip Ewell/Megan Lyons and Christopher Lynch analyze how textbooks contribute to building and maintaining white supremacist narratives and frameworks. On the surface, the two chapters seem to take disparate positions on the inclusion of Stephen Foster in music textbooks, with Ewell and Lyons advocating dropping him altogether and Lynch advocating for presenting a more complicated view of the man and his music. The two agree, however, that current presentations of Foster in widely used textbooks are unacceptable, and the solutions they propose have as much to do with the differing needs of the music theory (Ewell and Lyons) and music history (Lynch) classrooms as they do with the authors' personal opinions. Finally, Whitney Slaten uses his experiences as a Black ethnographer to frame his pedagogical engagement with reflexivity and improvisation, calling for a disciplinary reawakening to respond to the contemporary moment by connecting ethnographic learning with student agency.

We hope that readers will interact with this volume in ways they find useful: as a source of concrete pedagogical ideas, as a sounding board for their own ideas on teaching, or as a way of observing how some of their colleagues understand today's music classroom.

Olivia R. Lucas and Laura Moore Pruett

Notes

1. Badia Ahad-Legardy and OiYan A. Poon, eds., *Difficult Subjects: Insights and Strategies for Teaching About Race, Sexuality, and Gender* (Sterling, VA: Stylus, 2018), x.

2. We are grateful to the anonymous reviewer who enumerated these categories.

3. Andrew Curry, "Parents' Emotional Trauma May Change Their Children's Biology: Studies in Mice Show How," *Science*, July 18, 2019, https://www.science.org/content/article/parents-emotional-trauma-may-change-their-children-s-biology-studies-mice-show-how

4. Readers looking for more theoretical discussions of difficult topics in higher education might look at Adams and Bell 2016, Ahad-Legardy and Poon 2018, Ahmed 2012, Bhambra, Gebrial, and Nişancıoğlu 2017, Cheng 2016, Cheng 2019, Crenshaw, Harris, Martinez HoSang, and Lipsitz 2019, Dolmage 2017, Freebody, Goodwin, and Proctor 2019, Grosfoguel, Hernández, and Rosen Velásquez 2016, among others.

Works Cited

Adams, Maurianne, and Lee Anne Bell, eds. *Teaching for Diversity and Social Justice*, 3rd edition. New York: Routledge, 2016.

Ahad-Legardy, Badia, and OiYan A. Poon, eds. *Difficult Subjects: Insights and Strategies for Teaching About Race, Sexuality, and Gender*. Sterling, VA: Stylus, 2018.

Ahmed, Sara. *On Being Included: Racism and Diversity in Institutional Life*. Durham: Duke University Press, 2012.

Bhambra, Gurminder K., Dalia Gebrial, and Kerem Nişancıoğlu, eds. *Decolonising the University*. London: Pluto Press, 2017.

Cheng, William. *Just Vibrations: The Purpose of Sounding Good*. Ann Arbor: University of Michigan Press, 2016.

Cheng, William. *Loving Music Till It Hurts*. Oxford: Oxford University Press, 2019.

Crenshaw, Kimberlé Williams, Luke Charles Harris, Daniel Martinez HoSang, and George Lipsitz, eds. *Seeing Race Again: Countering Colorblindness across the Disciplines*. Berkeley: University of California Press, 2019.

Curry, Andrew. "Parents' Emotional Trauma May Change Their Children's Biology: Studies in Mice Show How." *Science*, July 18, 2019, https://www.science.org/content/article/parents-emotional-trauma-may-change-their-children-s-biology-studies-mice-show-how. Accessed July 13, 2023.

Dolmage, Jay Timothy. *Academic Ableism: Disability and Higher Education*. Ann Arbor: University of Michigan Press, 2017. https://library.oapen.org/handle/20.500.12657/47415

Freebody, Kelly, Susan Goodwin, and Helen Proctor, eds. *Higher Education, Pedagogy and Social Justice: Politics and Practice*. Cham, Switzerland: Palgrave Macmillan, 2019.

Grosfoguel, Ramón, Roberto Hernández, and Ernesto Rosen Velásquez, eds. *Decolonizing the Westernized University: Interventions in Philosophy of Education from Within and Without*. Lanham, MD: Lexington Books, 2016.

PART I

Music and Dynamics of Power

CHAPTER 1

Success and Music Education

Teaching the Value of Art in the Neoliberal University

John R. Pippen

What is the value of music? What counts as "success" in music? How do we, as teachers, help students negotiate the vicissitudes of working in the arts? This chapter engages these questions by critiquing an educational literature sweeping through musical higher education: arts entrepreneurship.[1] While this literature appears in both academic and public-facing genres, here I focus largely on its public manifestation. It often operates in a didactic "how-to" capacity and purports to instruct readers, especially students, about "success stories" from the music industry. However, I argue here that it uncritically circulates capitalist labor ideologies—namely neoliberalism—that reduce music's value to economic productivity. This literature also universalizes a middle-class position while hiding the processes that produce class. In my second section, I show this position as intended to critique a romantic ideology that positions art as best when it seems to be somehow beyond market exchange. Such ideologies have, in fact, been part of the ways that musicians reproduced bourgeois class values while simultaneously masking their efforts as "natural" to art. In my third section, I develop a case study from the how-to literature to demonstrate how a critical arts entrepreneurship might provide a more accurate account of musical labor. By providing students with critical perspectives on labor, we can move beyond either overly economic or simplistic anti-economic rationalizations for music and begin to encourage a more imaginative engagement with what art could be.

I. ARTS ENTREPRENEURSHIP AND NEOLIBERAL IDEOLOGIES

While not all arts entrepreneurship publications embrace a neoliberal ideal, many do. In sum, neoliberalism privileges the marketplace as the primary indicator of value and the autonomous "rational" individual as the most important agent of social change. Arts entrepreneurship texts uncritically reproduce middle-class notions of work that emphasize "marketspeak" which naturalize financial profit as an indicator of general value.[2] This naturalization is common to the masking of class boundaries that help constitute the middle class in general.[3] Neoliberalism, as an ideology, a mode of governance, and a set of policies, has had widespread impact upon the shape of contemporary life, especially in the discourses of labor across numerous industries. Along such lines, arts entrepreneurship largely analyzes the efforts of individuals or small groups, seeking to create and teach "a management process through which cultural workers seek to support their creativity and autonomy, advance their capacity for adaptability, and create artistic as well as economic and social value."[4] The creative self is here rendered as the result of proper "management" of "assets." How, exactly, one is meant to acquire such assets in the first place is not considered. This stance omits persistent structural characteristics of musical life, especially the precarity faced by musicians working within capitalist societies. I critique here prominent examples of what I call the "how-to" genre of musical arts entrepreneurship that espouse neoliberal ideologies uncritically.[5] These include books aimed primarily at music instructors and students, written in a relatively accessible style, and with many compelling examples of successful musicians. Titles announce the "how-to" approach, as in Jeffrey Nytch's *The Entrepreneurial Muse: Inspiring Your Career in Classical Music* and Angela Myles Beeching's *Beyond Talent: Creating a Successful Career in Music*.[6] Though many of their central claims appear in academic writings, the "how-to" literature is less nuanced and less well-researched than the academic literature found in peer-reviewed journals. Such books are, nevertheless, published by major academic presses. By focusing on individual actors and economic value, they obscure the social relations that produce musical value and inequality. This obfuscation takes the form of intersecting discourses of entrepreneurship and "do what you love" (DWYL), both of which reproduce neoliberal ideology.

While brief acknowledgments of the widely precarious nature of arts labor abound, authors portray this precarity as a solution to be solved by individuals, rather than resulting from systemic inequality. To naturalize this stance, authors theorize cases of "successful arts entrepreneurs," people who are in fact the least precarious of arts workers.[7] The literature extends the definition of entrepreneurship so broadly as to apply to any type of worker. In the field of music, such figures are often virtuoso performers, though they can be almost anything. Flutist Claire Chase, ensembles such as Pittsburgh New Music Ensemble, major companies such as Spotify, or individuals who have otherwise attained a significant amount of economic prosperity serve as examples.[8] While often told in a narrative style that portrays success as somewhat surprising, the literature consistently omits crucial details such as the ways that educational networks provide access to professional work.[9] As Izabela Wagner has demonstrated in her study of violin virtuoso competitions,

> high-mobility and international activity is organized by networks of teachers who are powerful people in the classical music world. Without their support, no one could achieve a high-quality soloist education and embark on a soloist career.[10]

Such networks often reinforce barriers of race, class, gender, and physical ability. Christina Scharff notes, "The reliance on networks, however, tends to disadvantage women, as well as working-class and black and minority ethnic workers."[11] Overlooking the importance of informal labor networks is but one way that the how-to literature obscures precarity and instead naturalizes the experiences of elite musicians as if they were possible for all musicians.

Much arts entrepreneurship literature incorrectly describes the history of arts labor as only recently precarious, thus only recently in need of the tools of entrepreneurship.[12] This lack of rigor extends to in-text definitions, as seen in Astrid Baumgardner's *Creative Success Now: How Creatives Can Thrive in the 21st Century*.[13] Baumgardner is chair of the board for the virtuosic ensemble Sō Percussion and adjunct faculty at the Yale School of Music. She routinely holds workshops for students hosted by educational institutions. Baumgardner loosely defines "creative" work to mean nearly any job with some degree of mental labor, but most especially white-collar professions that require specialist education. Baumgardner points to the economic size of the creative industries to incorrectly assert that precarity does not pervade, though empirical research on creative economy workers, musical and otherwise, clearly demonstrates a high degree of precarity.[14] Rather, Baumgardner asserts that creativity requires "inspired hard work that creatives dive into, fueled by a sense of purpose and meaning with the potential for well-being and happiness—and a job that pays."[15]

By focusing on such elites, authors seem to evidence the promises of entrepreneurship as delivering a life where one can "do what you love" (DWYL). Marisol Sandoval has situated this discourse as central to neoliberal work ideologies.[16] DWYL, according to its believers, is an amazing union of individual fulfillment, social reform, and enhanced productivity. The DWYL discourse pervades the "how-to" literature and is a central rationale for the

16 TEACHING DIFFICULT TOPICS

theorizations presented to readers. Jeffrey Nytch, director of the University of Colorado's Entrepreneurship Center for Music, employs DWYL constantly in his above-cited book as a way to empower readers. He defines entrepreneurship as "unlocking value for a product by connecting it to a need in the marketplace."[17] While deriving his definition from literature on for-profit companies, Nytch argues that entrepreneurship can be applied to non-profit endeavors. He views entrepreneurship as a "mind-set" that facilitates both personal authenticity and profitability: "entrepreneurship is never about 'selling out.' In fact, your artistic integrity is your most valuable asset—to compromise that makes no sense in an entrepreneurial context."[18] Here DWYL is used to rationalize for-profit endeavors while seeming to simultaneously reproduce allegedly altruistic action.

Nytch's argument exemplifies a common refrain in the "how-to" literature that seeks to reconfigure the value of artistic labor. In nineteenth-century philosophy and musical aesthetics, artistic integrity was positioned as a reconciliation between notions of truth and subjective interiority. True "artists" had to engage a canon of masterworks, which was created over time through debates that aspired to broad social consensus. These values were increasingly prized by bourgeoisie seeking to distinguish themselves from both aristocrats and the growing working class.[19] Well into the twentieth century, artistic integrity was positioned as antithetical to market-oriented musical practices, as famously theorized by sociologist Pierre Bourdieu.[20] In contrast, Nytch and others reconfigure artistic integrity as originating from the synthesis of the individual and the marketplace.

Mark Rabideau similarly reconfigures the value of authenticity as derived solely from the individual. His *Creating the Revolutionary Artist: Entrepreneurship for the 21st-Century Musician* builds on his experience teaching arts entrepreneurship courses at the DePauw University School of Music.[21] The book is designed to help instructors at other institutions design courses. He argues for the "artist revolutionary," a dynamic figure modeled on virtuoso musicians such as Melissa Snoza of Fifth House Ensemble and superstar cellist Yo-Yo Ma. Musicians are natural "agents of change," Rabideau argues, but he bemoans that a musician's "list of career options hasn't expanded much since the Middle Ages."[22] As in much arts entrepreneurship literature, Rabideau fails to account for the structural and cultural forces that have changed over time and that have devalued musical labor.[23] Instead, he encourages readers to "embrace a willingness to invent our own most promising futures and craft an excitedly uncertain future for our music."[24] Here precarity is explicitly the-

Success and Music Education   17

orized as possibility via exciting writing. The labor market is not precarious; it is full of potential for individuals to find meaning for themselves and find a way to commodify that meaning through their musical work. Within the "how-to" literature, the DWYL discourse facilitates a broader conflation of personal fulfillment with economic success. One feeds the other, in this line of reasoning. Capitalize your source of fulfillment, and you *will* find economic success. Rabideau misleads readers by masking the unstable labor of the cultural industries.

Though writers acknowledge social value, most draw heavily on approaches from arts administration, business administration, and marketing, omitting those arguments that conflict with core neoliberal tenets. This approach imbues writings with the appearance of academic rigor. An example of such theoretical appropriation can be seen in David Bruenger's *Making Money, Making Music: History and Core Concepts.*[25] Bruenger directs the Music, Media and Enterprise Program at The Ohio State University, one of the only schools to offer the Ph.D. in Arts Management. Like others in the "how-to" genre, he advocates for the "artist/entrepreneur," though Bruenger provides a sort of history of musical labor. With the "artist/entrepreneur" figure he describes how various individuals negotiate copyright and venues. In this, he draws on historian William Weber's argument for a similar approach but omits crucial issues core to theorizations of historical or contemporary creative industries.[26] Bruenger's analysis consistently reduces all systems—laws, social statuses, aesthetic values, history—to economic value: "There is . . . one system of measurement—a metric—that can quantify musical value objectively and consistently, and that supports comparative analysis across styles and contexts. Money."[27] This claim conflates money's status—an embodiment of value that renders commodities commensurate—with the broader notion of "objective" as meaning above the influence of society. Money *is* objective in the sense that it is a thing you can hold, but it is not free of social influence. Rather, money's value fluctuates all the time.

In an attempt to acknowledge the nuances of value, Bruenger employs Bourdieu's theorization of capital to account for the contrasting value forms generated by musical labor. However, he jettisons the attendant notions of field and habitus, both of which are central to situating the actions of individuals within larger social systems of value. This omission erases Bourdieu's stringent critiques of artistic labor as a form of class formation. The result is that Bruenger fails to account for the interactions of social class, historical change, economics, and the labor of musical production. In the end, Bruenger only alleges to acknowledge contrasting value forms, while in fact portraying musical enterprises as "successful" only when they provide enduring economic value:

> musical value is synergistic. Without the presence of all three forms—artistic, social, economic—a musical venture rarely succeeds and is never sustainable. With powerful artistry, social impact, and economic stability, the art lasts longer, more people enjoy and benefit from it, and more economic value is created for the artist and the larger economy.[28]

Bruenger ultimately bases his notion of success on economic productivity. The result is a tautology: Art is valuable because people pay for it, and people pay for art because it is valuable. Social value is as valuable as its price on the market. Economic value reigns supreme, in keeping with neoliberal ideology.

II. MAKING IDEOLOGY VISIBLE

The "how-to" literature erases the enduring precarity of contemporary life within capitalism. These authors have extended a core feature of neoliberal ideology—the valorization of the artist—into musical discourses. Academics such as César Graña, Peter Fussell, and Richard Florida positioned the life of the artist as an ideal for all people on the grounds that living thusly would resolve enduring forms of alienation within late capitalism.[29] Though touted as providing freedom, these policies and discourses reinforce and expand the power of higher economic classes and global corporations and naturalize the mobility of middle classes as if available to all people in all settings.[30] Social inequality persists in the United States, resulting in part from the outsourcing of manufacturing and tax structures that favor corporations and a global elite, and as seen in the growth of a migrant underclass.[31] Rather than flourishing, white-collar jobs that accommodate this artistic ideal are highly competitive and demanding.[32] White collar jobs in all sectors often go to highly accomplished workers who can manage access to elite educational and labor networks, "virtuosos" of sorts in their own respective fields. As a result, Sarah Brouillette argues, the potential for social change once located in the labor of the artist and her work have "disappeared with its generalization" into many domains of labor.[33] The arts entrepreneurship literature has built upon faulty arguments to the effect of misleading readers and our students.

Despite flaws, the literature's refutation of older bourgeois anti-economic notions of art can draw attention to the conflicting ways that people value music. Drawing on the arts entrepreneurship literature provides useful ways to teach music by helping us critique dominant narratives that mask social class, racism, or other forms of oppression. This literature attempts to debunk the historical antagonism between economics and art. This critique stems from the neoliberal DWYL discourse, but it does usefully suggest a way toward a revaluation of oft overlooked or devalued labor practices. While music has often been laborious, various discourses—notions of "genius," gendered policing of physical display, and comparisons to other forms of labor—have positioned music as non-laborious, as somehow not work.[34] Furthermore, the labor of everyday musicians, teachers, music shop owners and others hidden from the limelight has been consistently undervalued, especially in musical higher education. Correctly then, arts entrepreneurship vehemently rebuts notions of the "starving artist" that seek to value music only so long as it is created for non-economic reasons. Such notions have long alleged to protect art from the "corrupting" influence of the marketplace.[35] This is a much-needed revaluation. By accounting for the ways that people in capitalist societies must sell their labor to survive, we can better prepare students for the vicissitudes of life in a musical profession. To do otherwise simply reproduces and naturalizes the discourses that separate art from labor.

Part of the literature's frustration with the lack of music business skills is warranted, but it requires some historicization. For too long, conservatory-style institutions of musical higher education have excluded practical business skills necessary to the precarious working life of an artist. Rabideau's polemic that "schools of music and conservatories across the nation [have been] exclusively training excellence" directly confronts the disconnect often found between performance training and business training.[36] Despite historical calls for greater curricular engagement with such topics, a general antipathy toward teaching musical labor skills, especially in elite conservatories, persisted.[37] Only unevenly over the past thirty years have arts entrepreneurship courses and degree programs grown that address this exclusion.[38]

However, the literature overlooks the teaching of music business skills in non-conservatory music education settings. Music business degrees have been offered in various guises throughout the twentieth century, and authors have published numerous didactic texts intended to outline the economic components of music.[39] The "how-to" genre largely ignores these to the effect that it erases less prestigious forms of musical education. But part of the spirit of Rabideau's criticism is correct. As Dawn Bennett has argued, "Stu-

20   TEACHING DIFFICULT TOPICS

dents learning in the conservatorium tradition are unlikely to be immersed in the [profession's] cultural environment or exposed to its complexities and opportunities."[40] Many schools have focused on craftsmanship, individual expression as balanced against the will of the composer, and the concepts of masterwork and talent, even as they acknowledged the difficulty of securing stable employment in the arts. For many decades, graduates of prestigious institutions floundered once they left school, and criticized their alma maters for failing to prepare them for working life.[41] Angela Beeching's how-to book is much more rigorous in this sense, though she also fails to account for the systems of prestige that shape labor networks.[42] As music educators teaching students who face an uncertain labor market, we ought to provide students with honest descriptions of the business of music and encourage the study of business skills.

III. WHAT MIGHT A CRITICAL ARTS ENTREPRENEURSHIP LOOK LIKE?

Untangling the strengths and weaknesses of the arts entrepreneurship literature is complicated, though I offer here some possible ways to negotiate this tension. An arts entrepreneurship literature that accounts for unequal access to power should engage economic, social, and aesthetic value. This is not to reinvoke an art versus business binary, but to advance a richer engagement of music, one that facilitates critique, including critiques of capitalism itself. This would present educators and community leaders with a special opportunity: we can de-invest in the notion of music as either antithetical to economic profit or necessarily economically productive and instead emphasize music's potential for collectivity, critical thinking, compassion, and empathy.[43] We can help students create musical work, works, settings, and collaborations that highlight the complexities of our world. We can teach our students how those works are created, the challenges involved, and the setbacks, failures, and successes that result from people working together.

What might a critically oriented arts entrepreneurship look like? First, it would do a better job of interrogating underlying ideology. Take, for example, the pervasive biases toward individualism—a core value of neoliberalism. Bruenger's analysis, for example, leads him to explain Scott Joplin's struggles in producing his operas as an individual failure: "This was, in part, a consequence of his race and then-current social attitudes, but also a result of the difficulty inherent in securing funds to produce theatrical performances."[44]

Success and Music Education   21

Bruenger argues that Joplin failed as an "artist/entrepreneur" because he was African American and because he was not able to master the skills needed to raise money. Problems like racism may exist, but in Bruenger's logic Joplin bears at least some responsibility for his economic woes. This analysis incorrectly places the burden of success on an individual working in a complex field of production. In this, Bruenger repeats a consistent failure of the literature: its focus on individual actors and inconsistent accounting of systemic conditions.

Second, an arts entrepreneurship literature more focused on power would clearly articulate the ways musical labor is shaped by broader issues of race, gender, class, and ability. I cannot engage all these here, but I want to briefly consider some of the ways race and class shaped Joplin's work as a way to correct Bruenger's analysis. Throughout the history of the United States, the place generally afforded most public African American musicians was shaped by racist stereotypes. Dehumanizing notions of African Americans plagued the popular sphere, as Nina Sun Eidsheim and Ronald Radano have each demonstrated.[45] Many African American musicians were severely constrained in their choices of genre, performing for minstrel shows, other popular domains, or required to develop a repertoire of spirituals.[46] Minstrelsy and persistent blackface performances created powerful stereotypes that taught audiences that bodies marked as Black could only produce a certain kind of music. These stereotypes, as Jenifer Barclay has shown, reinforced notions of disability that fueled racist arguments about a lack of intellectual acumen among African Americans.[47] The influence of minstrelsy persisted and informed later genres such as vaudeville, ragtime, and musicals. Even when singers broke through such systemic barriers, "nineteenth-and early twentieth-century audiences dealt with the shocking phenomenon of black classical singers by, mentally or in practice, relegating the singers to stereotypical black roles."[48] A critical arts entrepreneurship literature would consider how Joplin faced a national audience with racist expectations in an industry created on racist terms. To imply that a lack of entrepreneurial skill was the cause of Joplin's struggles is, at best, an incomplete analysis. We, as educators, must demonstrate to our students the ways that race and racism were and are a systemic barrier. Race creates labor struggles, and sidelining race only reinforces an implicitly racist status quo.

Third, an arts entrepreneurship engaged with a broader history of musical labor would consider struggle as well as success. Examining Joplin's struggles presents us with a richer consideration of musical labor than that provided by the arts entrepreneurship literature. It connects Joplin with historical debates about race and class common to his period. In Bruenger's telling, Joplin's actions can seem rather ridiculous. How could an African American man in early 1900s America think he could break into opera? In fact, this was Joplin's second opera and there were many such musicians widely engaged in similar efforts. Joplin himself was active in the New York City scene that was interested in supporting his opera *Treemonisha* (1911).[49] Joplin's early previews of music for the opera were received with great enthusiasm, but his reputation as a composer of rags and his opera's use of rag music discouraged publishers and financiers from investing in productions.[50] Ragtime had a reputation as a minstrel genre of African American lower classes that belonged in saloons and was thus considered unfit for the hallowed halls of art music.[51] Joplin himself worked tirelessly to create performances of the opera, networking with backers, publicizing the piece, self-publishing, and pursuing his passion, all strategies advocated for in the "how-to" literature. Lacking proper funding to hire and adequately rehearse singers, his attempts failed to garner backing for a run of the opera.[52] The content of the opera also considers the racial barriers faced by early twentieth century African Americans. *Treemonisha* itself directly advocated for education and hard work as ways of overcoming systemic racism.[53] The notion that education would improve the lives of African Americans, commonly described as the "uplift narrative," pervaded in Joplin's lifetime. It was commonly espoused by influential leaders such as W. E. B. Dubois and invoked by public intellectuals such as Zora Neale Hurston. Joplin sought to overcome the racist stereotypes that shaped his working environments, and the opera can be interpreted as a direct challenge to the idea that African American music was unsuited to operatic treatment.[54] Joplin's struggles are consistent with racial and classist barriers faced by musicians across the United States, regardless of the level of fame or "success" they enjoyed. As numerous scholars have demonstrated, the stereotypes faced by musicians and the legal barriers of segregation persisted within the music industry and presented Black musicians with unequal access to music labor markets.[55] Joplin's opera is an example of the ways things could have been different.

A critical arts entrepreneurship literature demonstrates crucial lessons for our students. The power of the white majority over legal and entertainment systems created a deeply segregated work environment for musicians in Joplin's lifetime. Teaching this lack of success does not disservice Joplin's work. Rather, it demonstrates how social systems minoritize individuals and groups. It also serves as a powerful counterpart to the conventional canon of music history, which, I would argue, repeats the mistaken overemphasis on "success stories" by privileging the work of small numbers of white men.[56]

Success and Music Education   23

Only through sustained, difficult, contentious, and dangerous action have African American musicians and allies been able to begin to overcome barriers of musical labor.[57] As Amy Absher demonstrates in her study of the Chicago Black musician union, "The Black musician is still fighting to emancipate Black music from the racist imagination of the white audience and white employers."[58] Teaching these histories and examining both the successes and the struggles of musicians illustrates the power of collective action. Musicians have long been central to the struggle for equality in the United States Civil Rights Movement.[59] Considering persistent forms of oppression shows our students that even talented and hardworking individuals, such as Joplin, may encounter social systems that they cannot overcome on their own. But collective action can produce meaningful change.

The critiques I level here are not meant simply as part of a fault-finding mission. Rather, they stem from my pedagogical concern with how we teach musical labor. If the goal is to help students find "success" on economic terms, then we will probably only justify the elimination of music from pedagogical settings. Most of our students will be professional "failures," fools for believing that they could contribute to society via art. For most people throughout history, musical labor has not been a stable profession. The notion of simply educating our young adults into financial security has been a promise never fully delivered.[60] Instead of justifying our existence by our ability to provide economic prosperity, we should prioritize the ways music is shaped by, critiques, resists, and accommodates social power. We can teach students to build empathy and community and foster imaginative alternatives to current realities.

Notes

1. This chapter originated from the differences between my experiences working as a young musician and the ways early careers were discussed in professional music circles. As a young musician, I struggled to piece together performance work and eventually transitioned to academic research. Once there, I was frustrated to see a persistent optimism about musical work that did not match the tenuous life I had lived as a working musician. I was especially bothered by how race was omitted from discussions of working in classical music. I hope this chapter can serve to enhance the critical conversations occurring in classical music about race and labor.

2. Thomas Frank, *One Market Under God: Extreme Capitalism, Market Populism, and the End of Economic Democracy* (New York: Random House, 2001).

3. Beverley Skeggs, *Class, Self, Culture* (New York: Routledge, 2004). Hadas Weiss, *We Have Never Been Middle Class* (Brooklyn, NY: Verso, 2019).

4. Woong Jo Chang and Margaret Wyszomirski, "What Is Arts Entrepreneurship? Tracking the Development of its Definition in Scholarly Journals," *Artivate: A Journal of Entrepreneurship in the Arts* 4, no. 2 (2015): 24.

5. Angela Beeching's "how-to" book foregrounds precarity to a far greater extent than most other sources I critique here. See Angela Myles Beeching, *Beyond Talent: Creating a Successful Career in Music*, 2nd ed. (New York: Oxford University Press, 2010). In contrast with the "how-to" literature I critique here, two edited volumes attempt to address these issues for music educators. Neither, however, addresses neoliberal ideology. See Dawn Bennett, ed., *Life in the Real World: How to Make Music Graduates Employable* (Champaign, IL: Common Ground Publishing, 2012); Gary D. Beckman, ed., *Disciplining the Arts: Teaching Entrepreneurship in Context* (Lanham, MD: Rowman & Littlefield Education, 2011). Bennett offers an excellent overview of related issues, though without theorizing neoliberal ideology. See also Dawn Bennett, *Understanding the Classical Music Profession: The Past, the Present and Strategies for the Future* (Burlington, VT: Ashgate, 2008).

6. Jeffrey Nytch, *The Entrepreneurial Muse: Inspiring your Career in Classical Music* (New York: Oxford University Press, 2018). Beeching, *Beyond Talent*.

7. Gary D. Beckman, "'Adventuring' Arts Entrepreneurship Curricula in Higher Education: An Examination of Present Efforts, Obstacles, and Best Practices," *The Journal of Arts Management, Law, and Society* 37, no. 2 (2007): 91, https://doi.org/10.3200/JAML .37.2.87-112

8. Jeffrey Nytch, "The Case of the Pittsburgh New Music Ensemble: An Illustration of Entrepreneurial Theory in an Artistic Setting," *Artivate: A Journal of Entrepreneurship in the Arts* 1, no. 1 (2012); David Bruenger, *Making Money, Making Music: History and Core Concepts* (Oakland, CA: University of California Press, 2016); Astrid Baumgardner, *Creative Success Now: How Creatives Can Thrive in the 21st Century* (Oceanside, CA: Indie Books International, 2019).

9. Doris Ruth Eikhof and Chris Warhurst, "The promised land? Why social inequalities are systemic in the creative industries," *Employee Relations* 35, no. 5 (2013)., https://doi.org/10.1108/ER-08-2012-0061, https://www.emeraldinsight.com/doi/abs /10.1108/ER-08-2012-0061.

10. Izabela Wagner, *Producing Excellence: The Making of Virtuosos* (Rutgers, NJ: Rutgers University Press, 2015), 4.

11. Christina Scharff, *Gender, Subjectivity, and Cultural Work: The Classical Music Profession* (New York: Routledge, 2018), 60.

12. See, for example, the conversation in Gary D. Beckman and Linda Essig, "Arts Entrepreneurship: A Conversation," *Artivate* 1, no. 1 (2012). For a more nuanced perspective from the entrepreneurship literature, see Paul Bonin-Rodriguez, *Performing Policy: How Contemporary Politics and Cultural Programs Redefined U.S. Artists for the Twenty-First Century* (London: Palgrave Macmillan Limited, 2014).

13. Baumgardner, *Creative Success Now*.

14. Pierre-Michel Menger, "Artistic Labor Markets and Careers," *Annual Review of*

Sociology 25 (1999); Pierre-Michel Menger, *The Economics of Creativity: Art and Achievement under Uncertainty* (Cambridge, MA: Harvard University Press, 2014); Sophie Hennekam and Dawn Bennett, "Creative Industries Work Across Multiple Contexts: Common Themes and Challenges," *Personnel Review* 46, no. 1 (2017); Andrea Moore, "Neoliberalism and the Musical Entrepreneur," *Journal of the Society for American Music* 10, no. 1 (2016).

15. Baumgardner, *Creative Success Now*, 19.

16. Marisol Sandoval, "From Passionate Labour to Compassionate Work: Cultural Co-ops, Do what You Love and Social Change," *European Journal of Cultural Studies* 21, no. 2 (2018), https://doi.org/10.1177/1367549417719011.

17. Nytch, *The Entrepreneurial Muse*.

18. Nytch, *The Entrepreneurial Muse*, xviii.

19. Richard Crawford, *The American Musical Landscape: The Business of Musicianship from Billings to Gershwin*, Ernest Bloch lectures (Berkeley: University of California Press, 1993); Derek B. Scott, *Sounds of the metropolis: The nineteenth-century popular music revolution in London, New York, Paris, and Vienna* (Oxford; New York: Oxford University Press, 2008); Alexander Stefaniak, *Schumann's Virtuosity: Criticism, Composition, and Performance in Nineteenth-Century Germany* (Bloomington: Indiana University Press, 2016).

20. Pierre Bourdieu, *The Field of Cultural Production*, ed. Randal Johnson, trans. Richard Nice (New York: Columbia University Press, 1993); Pierre Bourdieu, *Distinction: A Social Critique of the Judgement of Taste*, trans. Richard Nice (Cambridge, MA: Harvard University Press, 1984).

21. Mark Rabideau, *Creating the Revolutionary Artist: Entrepreneurship for the 21st-Century Musician* (New York: Rowman & Littlefield, 2018).

22. Rabideau, *Creating the Revolutionary Artist*, 4.

23. Numerous scholars have considered how social forces and historical change informed musical activity and labor, in both professional and pre-professional contexts. See Walter Salmen, Herbert Kaufman, and Barbara Reisner, *The Social Status of the Professional Musician from the Middle Ages to the 19th Century*, trans. Herbert Kaufman and Barbara Reisner (New York: Pendragon Press, 1983); David Hesmondhalgh, *The Cultural Industries*, 2nd ed. (Los Angeles: Sage, 2007); Michael James Roberts, *Tell Tchaikovsky the news: Rock 'n' roll, the labor question, and the musicians' union, 1942–1968* (Durham: Duke University Press, 2014); Timothy Dean Taylor, *Music and Capitalism: A History of the Present* (Chicago: University of Chicago Press, 2016). For an analysis of the ways musical labor has been treated as somehow not work, see Karl Hagstrom Miller, "Working Musicians: Exploring the Rhetorical Ties Between Musical Labour and Leisure," *Leisure Studies* 27, no. 4 (2008); Ana Hofman, "Music (as) Labour: Professional Musicianship, Affective Labour and Gender in Socialist Yugoslavia," *Ethnomusicology Forum* 24, no. 1 (2015), https://doi.org/10.1080/17411912.2015.1009479.

24. Rabideau, *Creating the Revolutionary Artist*, 4.

25. Bruenger, *Making Money, Making Music*.

26   TEACHING DIFFICULT TOPICS

26. William Weber, "The Musician as Entrepreneur and Opportunist, 1700–1914," in *The Musician as Entrepreneur, 1700–1914: Managers, Charlatans, and Idealists*, ed. William Weber (Bloomington: Indiana University Press, 2004).

27. Bruenger, *Making Money, Making Music*, 6.

28. Bruenger, *Making Money, Making Music*, 28.

29. César Graña, *Modernity and its Discontents: French Society and the French Man of Letters in the Nineteenth Century*, Harper Torchbooks, (New York: Harper and Row, 1967); Paul Fussell, *Class: A Guide Through the American Status System* (New York: Summit Books, 1983); Richard L. Florida, *The Rise of the Creative Class and How It's Transforming Work, Leisure, Community and Everyday Life* (New York: Basic Books, 2002). Sara Brouillette has outlined the historical development of the idealization of creative labor, see Sarah Brouillette, *Literature and the Creative Economy* (Stanford, CA: Stanford University Press, 2014).

30. David Harvey, *A Brief History of Neoliberalism* (New York: Oxford University Press, 2005). Beverley Skeggs, *Class, Self, Culture* (New York: Routledge, 2004).

31. David Harvey, *The Limits to Capital*, New and fully updated ed. (New York: Verso, 2006); David Harvey, *The Condition of Postmodernity: An Enquiry into the Origins of Cultural Change* (Cambridge, MA: Blackwell Publishers, 1990); Thomas Piketty, *Capital in the Twenty-First Century*, trans. Arthur Goldhammer (Cambridge, MA: Harvard University Press, 2014).

32. Luc Boltanski and Eve Chiapello, *The New Spirit of Capitalism*, trans. Gregory Elliott, new updated ed. (London: Verso, 2018); Andrew Ross, *Nice Work if You Can Get It: Life and Labor in Precarious Times* (New York: New York University Press, 2009); Angela McRobbie, *Be Creative: Making a Living in the New Culture Industries* (Malden, MA: Polity Press, 2016).

33. Brouillette, *Literature and the Creative Economy*, 53.

34. Miller, "Working Musicians"; Susan McClary, *Feminine Endings: Music, Gender, and Sexuality* (Minneapolis: University of Minnesota Press, 2002); Stefaniak, *Schumann's Virtuosity*. Dominant cultural values have long attempted to devalue manual labor and other types of work. See Kathi Weeks, *The Problem with Work: Feminism, Marxism, Antiwork Politics, and Postwork Imaginaries* (Durham: Duke University Press, 2011).

35. Crawford, *The American Musical Landscape*; Bourdieu, *Distinction*.

36. Rabideau, *Creating the Revolutionary Artist*, 2.

37. David Baskerville, "Career Programs in Higher Education," *Music Educators Journal* 69, no. 2 (1982); Karen Patricia Munnelly, "Understanding Career & Degree Expectations of Undergraduate Music Majors" (Ph.D. Dissertation, The Ohio State University, 2017). Munnelly provides a succinct history of calls for musical higher education to include more focus on professional skills.

38. Linda Essig and Joanna Guevara, *A Landscape of Arts Entrepreneurship in US Higher Education*, ASU Herberger Institute for Design and the Arts (2016), http://dx.doi.org/10.13140/RG.2.2.35204.73606; Scharff, *Gender, Subjectivity, and Cultural*

Work; Brydie-Leigh Bartleet et al., "Preparing for Portfolio Careers in Australian Music: Setting a Research Agenda," *Australian Journal of Music Education*, no. 1 (2012).

39. Hyman Howard Taubman, *Music as a Profession* (New York: Charles Scribner's Sons, 1939); Alan Rich, *Careers and Opportunities in Music* (New York: E. P. Dutton, 1964); Robert Gerardi, *Opportunities in Music Careers* (Lincoln, IL: National Textbook Co., 1984); David Baskerville, *Music Business Handbook & Career Guide*, 3rd ed. (Denver: Sherwood Company, 1982). Baskerville's text has become one of the standard texts of its kind and appears in many editions. Donald S. Passman, *All You Need to Know About the Music Business*, 10th ed. (New York: Simon & Schuster, 2019).

40. Bennett, *Life in the Real World*, 55.

41. Munnelly, "Understanding Career & Degree Expectations of Undergraduate Music Majors"; Hennekam and Bennett, "Creative Industries Work Across Multiple Contexts."

42. Beeching, *Beyond Talent*.

43. Marianna Ritchey makes an extended argument along these lines. See Marianna Ritchey "Resisting Usefulness: Music and the Political Imagination," *Current Musicology* 108 (2021): 26–52.

44. Bruenger, *Making Money, Making Music*, 64–65.

45. Nina Sun Eidsheim, "Marian Anderson and 'Sonic Blackness' in American Opera," *American Quarterly* 63, no. 3 (2011); Ronald Michael Radano, *Lying up a Nation: Race and Black Music* (Chicago: University of Chicago Press, 2003).

46. Eidsheim, "Marian Anderson and 'Sonic Blackness' in American Opera," 652.

47. Jenifer L. Barclay, "Disability, Race, and Gender on the Stage in Antebellum America," in *The Oxford Handbook of Disability History*, ed. Michael Rembis, Catherine Kudlick, and Kim E. Nielsen (Oxford: Oxford University Press, 2018).

48. Eidsheim, "Marian Anderson and 'Sonic Blackness' in American Opera," 653.

49. Edward A. Berlin, "Scott Joplin's *Treemonisha* Years," *American Music* 9, no. 3 (1991), https://doi.org/10.2307/3051431, www.jstor.org/stable/3051431.

50. Ray Argyle, *Scott Joplin and the Age of Ragtime* (Jefferson, NC: McFarland, 2009).

51. Rachel Lumsden, "Uplift, Gender, and Scott Joplin's *Treemonisha*," *Black Music Research Journal* 35, no. 1 (2015), https://doi.org/10.5406/blacmusiresej.35.1.0041.; Janet Hubbard-Brown, *Scott Joplin: Composer* (New York: Chelsea House, 2006).

52. Argyle, *Scott Joplin and the Age of Ragtime*.

53. Lumsden, "Uplift, Gender, and Scott Joplin's *Treemonisha*."

54. Argyle, *Scott Joplin and the Age of Ragtime*.

55. Amy Absher, *The Black Musician and the White City: Race and Music in Chicago, 1900–1967* (Ann Arbor: University of Michigan Press, 2014); Roberts, *Tell Tchaikovsky*; Ingrid T. Monson, *Freedom Sounds: Civil Rights Call Out to Jazz and Africa* (New York: Oxford University Press, 2007).

56. Loren Kajikawa, "The Possessive Investment in Classical Music: Legacies of White Supremacy in U.S. Schools and Departments of Music," in *Seeing Race Again: Countering Colorblindness across the Disciplines*, ed. Kimberlé Williams Crenshaw et al. (Oakland: University of California Press, 2019).

TEACHING DIFFICULT TOPICS

57. Monson, *Freedom Sounds*; Harvey G. Cohen, *Duke Ellington's America* (Chicago: University of Chicago Press, 2010); Paul Steinbeck, *Message to Our Folks: The Art Ensemble of Chicago* (Chicago: University of Chicago Press, 2017); George Lewis, *A Power Stronger than Itself: The AACM and American Experimental Music* (Chicago: University of Chicago Press, 2008).

58. Absher, *The Black Musician and the White City*, 148.

59. Monson, *Freedom Sounds*.

60. Weeks, *The Problem with Work*; Nona Y. Glazer, *Women's Paid and Unpaid Labor: The Work Transfer in Health Care and Retailing* (Philadelphia: Temple University Press, 1993); David Macarov, *Work and Welfare: The Unholy Alliance* (Beverly Hills: Sage Publications, 1980).

Works Cited

Absher, Amy. *The Black Musician and the White City: Race and Music in Chicago, 1900–1967*. Ann Arbor: University of Michigan Press, 2014.

Argyle, Ray. *Scott Joplin and the Age of Ragtime*. Jefferson, NC: McFarland, 2009.

Barclay, Jenifer L. "Disability, Race, and Gender on the Stage in Antebellum America." In *The Oxford Handbook of Disability History*, edited by Michael Rembis, Catherine Kudlick and Kim E. Nielsen, 351–68. Oxford: Oxford University Press, 2018.

Bartleet, Brydie-Leigh, Dawn Bennett, Ruth Bridgstock, Paul Draper, Huib Schippers, and Scott Harrison. "Preparing for Portfolio Careers in Australian Music: Setting a Research Agenda." *Australian Journal of Music Education*, no. 1 (2012): 32–41.

Baskerville, David. "Career Programs in Higher Education." *Music Educators Journal* 69, no. 2 (1982): 33–34.

Baskerville, David. *Music Business Handbook & Career Guide*. 3rd ed. Denver: Sherwood Company, 1982.

Baumgardner, Astrid. *Creative Success Now: How Creatives Can Thrive in the 21st Century*. Oceanside, CA: Indie Books International, 2019.

Beckman, Gary D. "'Adventuring' Arts Entrepreneurship Curricula in Higher Education: An Examination of Present Efforts, Obstacles, and Best Practices." *The Journal of Arts Management, Law, and Society* 37, no. 2 (2007): 87–112. https://doi.org/10.3200/JAML.37.2.87-112.

Beckman, Gary D., ed. *Disciplining the Arts: Teaching Entrepreneurship in Context*. Lanham, MD: Rowman & Littlefield Education, 2011.

Beckman, Gary D., and Linda Essig. "Arts Entrepreneurship: A Conversation." *Artivate* 1, no. 1 (2012): 1–8.

Beeching, Angela Myles. *Beyond Talent: Creating a Successful Career in Music*. 2nd ed. New York: Oxford University Press, 2010.

Bennett, Dawn, ed. *Life in the Real World: How to Make Music Graduates Employable*. Champaign, IL: Common Ground Publishing, 2012.

Bennett, Dawn. *Understanding the Classical Music Profession: The Past, the Present and Strategies for the Future*. Burlington, VT: Ashgate, 2008.

Berlin, Edward A. "Scott Joplin's *Treemonisha* Years." *American Music* 9, no. 3 (1991): 260–76. https://doi.org/10.2307/3051431.

Boltanski, Luc, and Eve Chiapello. *The New Spirit of Capitalism.* Translated by Gregory Elliott. New updated ed. London: Verso, 2018.

Bonin-Rodriguez, Paul. *Performing Policy: How Contemporary Politics and Cultural Programs Redefined U.S. Artists for the Twenty-First Century.* London: Palgrave Macmillan Limited, 2014.

Bourdieu, Pierre. *Distinction: A Social Critique of the Judgement of Taste.* Translated by Richard Nice. Cambridge, MA: Harvard University Press, 1984.

Bourdieu, Pierre. *The Field of Cultural Production.* Translated by Richard Nice. Edited by Randal Johnson. New York: Columbia University Press, 1993.

Brouillette, Sarah. *Literature and the Creative Economy.* Stanford, CA: Stanford University Press, 2014.

Bruenger, David. *Making Money, Making Music: History and Core Concepts.* Oakland: University of California Press, 2016.

Chang, Woong Jo, and Margaret Wyszomirski. "What Is Arts Entrepreneurship? Tracking the Development of Its Definition in Scholarly Journals." *Artivate: A Journal of Entrepreneurship in the Arts* 4, no. 2 (2015): 11–31.

Cohen, Harvey G. *Duke Ellington's America.* Chicago: University of Chicago Press, 2010.

Crawford, Richard. *The American Musical Landscape: The Business of Musicianship from Billings to Gershwin.* Ernest Bloch Lectures. Berkeley: University of California Press, 1993.

Eidsheim, Nina Sun. "Marian Anderson and 'Sonic Blackness' in American Opera." *American Quarterly* 63, no. 3 (2011): 641–71.

Eikhof, Doris Ruth, and Chris Warhurst. "The Promised Land? Why Social Inequalities Are Systemic in the Creative Industries." *Employee Relations* 35, no. 5 (2013): 495–508. https://doi.org/10.1108/ER-08-2012-0061.

Essig, Linda, and Joanna Guevara. *A Landscape of Arts Entrepreneurship in US Higher Education.* ASU Herberger Institute for Design and the Arts (2016). http://dx.doi.org/10.13140/RG.2.2.35204.73606

Florida, Richard L. *The Rise of the Creative Class and How It's Transforming Work, Leisure, Community and Everyday Life.* New York: Basic Books, 2002.

Frank, Thomas. *One Market Under God: Extreme Capitalism, Market Populism, and the End of Economic Democracy.* New York: Random House, 2001.

Fussell, Paul. *Class: A Guide Through the American Status System.* New York: Summit Books, 1983.

Gerardi, Robert. *Opportunities in Music Careers.* Lincoln, IL: National Textbook Co., 1984.

Glazer, Nona Y. *Women's Paid and Unpaid Labor: The Work Transfer in Health Care and Retailing.* Philadelphia: Temple University Press, 1993.

Graña, César. *Modernity and Its Discontents: French Society and the French Man of Letters in the Nineteenth Century.* Harper Torchbooks. New York: Harper and Row, 1967.

30 TEACHING DIFFICULT TOPICS

Harvey, David. *A Brief History of Neoliberalism*. New York: Oxford University Press, 2005.

Harvey, David. *The Condition of Postmodernity: An Enquiry into the Origins of Cultural Change*. Cambridge, MA: Blackwell Publishers, 1990.

Harvey, David. *The Limits to Capital*. New and fully updated ed. New York: Verso, 2006.

Hennekam, Sophie, and Dawn Bennett. "Creative Industries Work across Multiple Contexts: Common Themes and Challenges." *Personnel Review* 46, no. 1 (2017): 68–85.

Hesmondhalgh, David. *The Cultural Industries*. 2nd ed. Los Angeles: Sage, 2007.

Hofman, Ana. "Music (as) Labour: Professional Musicianship, Affective Labour and Gender in Socialist Yugoslavia." *Ethnomusicology Forum* 24, no. 1 (2015): 28–50. https://doi.org/10.1080/17411912.2015.1009479.

Hubbard-Brown, Janet. *Scott Joplin: Composer*. New York: Chelsea House, 2006.

Kajikawa, Loren. "The Possessive Investment in Classical Music: Legacies of White Supremacy in U.S. Schools and Departments of Music." In *Seeing Race Again: Countering Colorblindness across the Disciplines*, edited by Kimberlé Williams Crenshaw, Luke Charles Harris, Daniel Martinez HoSang, and George Lipsitz, 155–74. Oakland: University of California Press, 2019.

Lewis, George. *A Power Stronger Than Itself: The AACM and American Experimental Music*. Chicago: University of Chicago Press, 2008.

Lumsden, Rachel. "Uplift, Gender, and Scott Joplin's *Treemonisha*." *Black Music Research Journal* 35, no. 1 (2015): 41–69. https://doi.org/10.5406/blacmusiresej.35 .1.0041.

Macarov, David. *Work and Welfare: The Unholy Alliance*. Beverly Hills: Sage Publications, 1980.

McClary, Susan. *Feminine Endings: Music, Gender, and Sexuality*. Minneapolis: University of Minnesota Press, 2002.

McRobbie, Angela. *Be Creative: Making a Living in the New Culture Industries*. Malden, MA: Polity Press, 2016.

Menger, Pierre-Michel. "Artistic Labor Markets and Careers." *Annual Review of Sociology* 25 (1999): 541–74.

Menger, Pierre-Michel. *The Economics of Creativity: Art and Achievement under Uncertainty*. Cambridge, MA: Harvard University Press, 2014.

Miller, Karl Hagstrom. "Working Musicians: Exploring the Rhetorical Ties between Musical Labour and Leisure." *Leisure Studies* 27, no. 4 (2008): 427–41.

Monson, Ingrid T. *Freedom Sounds: Civil Rights Call Out to Jazz and Africa*. New York: Oxford University Press, 2007.

Moore, Andrea. "Neoliberalism and the Musical Entrepreneur." *Journal of the Society for American Music* 10, no. 1 (2016): 33–53.

Munnelly, Karen Patricia. "Understanding Career & Degree Expectations of Undergraduate Music Majors." Ph.D. Dissertation, The Ohio State University, 2017.

Nytch, Jeffrey. "The Case of the Pittsburgh New Music Ensemble: An Illustration of Entrepreneurial Theory in an Artistic Setting." *Artivate: A Journal of Entrepreneurship in the Arts* 1, no. 1 (2012): 25–34.

Nytch, Jeffrey. *The Entrepreneurial Muse: Inspiring Your Career in Classical Music.* New York: Oxford University Press, 2018.

Passman, Donald S. *All You Need to Know About the Music Business.* 10th ed. New York: Simon & Schuster, 2019.

Piketty, Thomas. *Capital in the Twenty-First Century.* Translated by Arthur Goldhammer. Cambridge, MA: Harvard University Press, 2014.

Rabideau, Mark. *Creating the Revolutionary Artist: Entrepreneurship for the 21st-Century Musician.* New York: Rowman & Littlefield, 2018.

Radano, Ronald Michael. *Lying up a Nation: Race and Black Music.* Chicago: University of Chicago Press, 2003.

Rich, Alan. *Careers and Opportunities in Music.* New York: E. P. Dutton, 1964.

Ritchey, Marianna. "Resisting Usefulness: Music and the Political Imagination." *Current Musicology* 108 (11/01/2021): 26–52.

Roberts, Michael James. *Tell Tchaikovsky the News: Rock 'n' Roll, the Labor Question, and the Musicians' Union, 1942–1968.* Durham: Duke University Press, 2014.

Ross, Andrew. *Nice Work If You Can Get It: Life and Labor in Precarious Times.* New York: New York University Press, 2009.

Salmen, Walter, Herbert Kaufman, and Barbara Reisner. *The Social Status of the Professional Musician from the Middle Ages to the 19th Century.* Translated by Herbert Kaufman and Barbara Reisner. New York: Pendragon Press, 1983.

Sandoval, Marisol. "From Passionate Labour to Compassionate Work: Cultural Co-Ops, Do What You Love and Social Change." *European Journal of Cultural Studies* 21, no. 2 (2018): 113–29. https://doi.org/10.1177/1367549417719011.

Scharff, Christina. *Gender, Subjectivity, and Cultural Work: The Classical Music Profession.* New York: Routledge, 2018.

Scott, Derek B. *Sounds of the Metropolis: The Nineteenth-Century Popular Music Revolution in London, New York, Paris, and Vienna.* Oxford; New York: Oxford University Press, 2008.

Skeggs, Beverley. *Class, Self, Culture.* New York: Routledge, 2004.

Stefaniak, Alexander. *Schumann's Virtuosity: Criticism, Composition, and Performance in Nineteenth-Century Germany.* Bloomington: Indiana University Press, 2016.

Steinbeck, Paul. *Message to Our Folks: The Art Ensemble of Chicago.* Chicago: University of Chicago Press, 2017.

Taubman, Hyman Howard. *Music as a Profession.* New York: Charles Scribner's Sons, 1939.

Taylor, Timothy Dean. *Music and Capitalism: A History of the Present.* Chicago: University of Chicago Press, 2016.

Wagner, Izabela. *Producing Excellence: The Making of Virtuosos.* Rutgers, NJ: Rutgers University Press, 2015.

Weber, William. "The Musician as Entrepreneur and Opportunist, 1700–1914." In *The Musician as Entrepreneur, 1700–1914: Managers, Charlatans, and Idealists*, edited by William Weber, 3–24. Bloomington: Indiana University Press, 2004.

Weeks, Kathi. *The Problem with Work: Feminism, Marxism, Antiwork Politics, and Postwork Imaginaries*. Durham: Duke University Press, 2011.

Weiss, Hadas. *We Have Never Been Middle Class*. Brooklyn, NY: Verso, 2019.

CHAPTER 2

Teaching Music and the Holocaust

Facilitating Discussions and Trust in an Undergraduate Seminar

Jessica Grimmer

In the fall of 2018, I taught a course entitled Music and the Holocaust at the University of Michigan's Residential College. The Holocaust deeply impacted all areas of modern life, and understanding its effects on musicians, musical life, and musical works is crucial to our interpretation of music in the twentieth century. This subject-specific music history and culture course initially aimed to investigate the intersection of music and the Holocaust. This course grew into a space for students to learn how to effectively contribute thoughts, perspectives, questions, and opinions on sensitive and sometimes personally painful topics. The classroom additionally became a place where contemporary issues could be raised within the boundaries of academic discussion in response to the rise in anti-Semitic, xenophobic, and racist political rhetoric. These skills became of imminent importance in October of that year, when the class used our space to process and respond to the violent anti-Semitic attack on Pittsburgh's Tree of Life Synagogue.

Being honest about historic atrocities without sensationalizing presented itself as a necessary component of the course, and providing a safe space for students to learn without experiencing secondary trauma was one of my central goals. This required sensitivity, nuance, and cooperation from all members of the class. Certainly, the small size of the class, the seminar format, and the assembly of self-motivated emotionally intelligent students who chose to pursue this difficult topic contributed to the overall success of this course. There were also a number of strategies employed to establish clear expectations, empower student agency, and create space and understanding that allowed students to discuss difficult and often uncomfortable topics.

34   TEACHING DIFFICULT TOPICS

COURSE ORGANIZATION AND TOPICS

The Residential College, or, as it is known colloquially, the RC, is a four-year interdisciplinary liberal arts program within the College of Literature, Science, and the Arts, and functions as a living-learning community. The program emphasizes the humanities and social sciences and visual and performing arts and features ample creative and collaborative spaces.[1] The RC also provides the opportunity for graduate students from related disciplines to fully develop small courses on special topics in the humanities for undergraduate students. It typically offers one such musicology course per semester. Though students in the RC program are given preferential registration, all undergraduates are welcome to take the musicology course as an elective.

My class consisted of ten students, a typical size for an elective music course in the RC, which met twice weekly for an hour and twenty minutes. The group of students who elected this course were some of the most academically responsible and emotionally mature I have ever encountered, and much of the credit for the mutual respect built in this course belongs to them.[2] The course was split into six main topics: (1) an Introduction that included background on the Holocaust, a history of anti-Semitism in Europe, and totalitarianism on the continent during the 20th century, (2) the labeling and banning of "degenerate music," (3) music in the ghettos, (4) music in the camps, (5) resistance music, and (6) outside perspectives and works that reflected on the Holocaust. Each of these included selected readings, and, where appropriate, featured accompanying musical works to watch or listen to.[3] While discussion often focused on response to musical works, it rarely ventured into musical analysis, instead focusing on socio-cultural and sometimes political implications.

Given the sensitive and sometimes personally painful nature of our subject matter, several pedagogical methods typical in music courses appeared inappropriate. Traditional exams were one of these elements. Instead, assessment was shifted to class participation in the form of short in-class presentations and regular discussion of assigned readings and musical works. The course concluded with 12–15-page term papers that allowed students to engage in aspects of the course they felt drawn to, and avoid any specific facets that they might find personally painful.

The typical emphasis on attendance was another element that required rethinking. This of course foreshadowed a large-scale reimagination of attendance in college classrooms. At the time, I considered the emotional impact that reading, listening, watching, and discussing historical trauma can inflict, and provided them with mental health resources on campus. In a sharp turn from most undergraduate courses, I also invited them to take a "mental health break" and miss a class if they felt they needed it; I trusted them to not abuse this very liberal policy, and a number of students have cited it in post-course evaluations as a relief when they were feeling stressed or anxious.

During the progression of this course, I expected students would observe the ways the Holocaust intersected with the creation, performance, and reception of music. Beyond the specific subject matter of this course, I intended to empower these students to find means of communicating with one another effectively and respectfully about an extremely sensitive subject. The seminar-style class by its very nature emphasizes student-generated discussion; however, the practice of outlining discussion expectations and engagement in student-led pedagogical practices and techniques created a collaborative space that could extend to different course configurations.

SMALL SEMINAR-STYLE TEACHING

Teaching undergraduates in a seminar-style course that relied heavily on student-generated dialogue did require a good deal of care and the development of a classroom culture that encouraged students to engage in sustained discussion. Large lecture-style classes were the standard in many U.S. colleges and universities as early as 1980.[4] Though there certainly are wonderful large lecture-style courses with engaging professors, as exemplified by Kelsey Klotz and others in this volume, large class sizes rarely present as many opportunities for discussion.[5] These very aspects are the ones that the small seminar-style class highlights, as content engagement and active discussion with peers form the bulk of in-class content. Unfortunately, these types of courses are often reserved for graduate students, and empowering undergraduates to seize their own agency can prove difficult for those used to receiving course content in a lecture format.

The adoption of a seminar-style course for undergraduates emphasizes the interpolation of information into their own understanding, for reflection, and the formulation of critical thought and verbal expression. The ideas, opinions, and reflections of the students and subsequent discussion become the primary content of the course. This can of course frustrate students, especially those undergraduates who are accustomed to the large lecture format. It certainly requires more effort.

To signal our approach from the start, I arranged our chairs in a circle each

36   TEACHING DIFFICULT TOPICS

day. I took to standing for announcements and brief overviews of material or presenting new topics, but joined the seated circle for discussions, using the nonverbal cue to signal the move toward shared discussion. The small class and seminar style promoted discussion both in its form and practice. It allowed for students to build rapport with one another and the instructor. Though students displayed the usual reticence to speak in the first week or two, they adjusted and soon became comfortable sharing their thoughts on the material with their classmates. The familiarity built through small class size is one factor in creating a space for productive discussion and was complemented with clear expectations.

DISCUSSION EXPECTATIONS

The care necessary for undergraduate seminar teaching only increases when teaching music associated with a difficult and emotionally charged event such as the Holocaust. Students were simultaneously tasked with learning to hold a discussion while maintaining the sensitivity necessary when speaking on a subject of such historical gravity. The syllabus, which was made available to students prior to and subsequently reviewed at the first meeting, included a short statement that recognized the historic trauma examined in this course and stated that we would treat the topic with respect. We also engaged in several discussion practices that enabled students to hold appropriate conversations.

One specific method we considered was to discuss ideas, thoughts, and positions, rather than individual classmates. This is a subtle shift many musicians are familiar with. One's musical performance is closely entwined with oneself, but it is not the self. Similarly, thoughts brought up in discussion are malleable and debatable, and not the self. Disagreeing with a thought presented need not equate with dismissing the person, which can lead to distrust within the class. It was helpful when discussing difficult and sensitive topics to make the subject the idea, as in: "I don't think that *idea* considers these factors." This method of discussion allows for further exploration of the idea or opinion rather than pushing a classmate into defensiveness or silence.

Another practice introduced at the outset of the class was the emphasis on education, as not all students approached the class with the same knowledge of the subject matter. Simply put, if a student voiced an idea or opinion that did not reflect our best practices or current understandings, I would gently correct and explain, assuming ignorance of best practices. I gave the example of the term "gypsy," that for many years was used to refer to the Romani or Roma communities persecuted in the Holocaust. Many historians used the term "gypsy" and it still appears in literature currently referenced. However, we now benefit from the voices of the constituent community that inform our current practice. Mere education cannot mitigate the pain felt by the usage of dated or harmful terminology and ideas, and that pain deserves to be acknowledged. In the classroom, missteps can be remedied through education, preventing both perpetuation of outdated or harmful ideas and future pain. This also requires the agreement that within the classroom we did not intend to cause harm, and that corrections or guidance were offered not to chastise but rather to aid all students in a productive and respectful discussion.

Other guidelines of discussions included letting students know I did not expect any of them to be experts on subject matter, and that we could approach new subjects or gaps with scholarly curiosity. I also invited students to share their personal perspectives whenever they felt compelled, while maintaining that it was no student's position to act as spokesperson or share anything they didn't want to. These methods of discussion worked in tandem with the creation of a student-led discussion that put agency and ownership in the hands of students.

STUDENT-LED LEARNING

To best facilitate active participation in discussions, I designed the course to maximize student-led learning. A quick glance at the reading list shows that we wasted no time approaching challenging academic material. I was very much committed to these students tackling canonic and sometimes controversial scholarly positions. The density of readings required some adaptation, and we tackled them in smaller portions, especially in the early weeks of the course. To start conversations on these challenging works, I assigned teams to different portions of the text to facilitate a jigsaw approach.[6] When they arrived in class, each team would meet to talk with one another about their shared portions, coming to agreements about the author's main arguments and their own reactions to them. Each team then had five to ten minutes to teach this to the rest of the class. After each team had presented their material, we would settle into a discussion. The early emphasis on collective student summaries allowed students to gain confidence speaking, particularly during the early weeks of the class.

To facilitate active student participation in subsequent weeks, with shorter readings, I designated a student to introduce and lead each discussion. This consisted of the designated student giving a brief ten-minute introduction to the discussion that included background on the author, a summary of the reading and/or musical work considered, and three to five questions they thought were worthy of discussion. Including background on the author allowed students to see differences between disciplines (historians, philosophers, and musicologists) and also at times led to talks of biases and blind spots, rather than taking readings as infallible. Beginning with a student rather than the instructor also allowed for easier entry of their peers to the conversation. The discussion leader also created copies of a short outline of their presentation with any pertinent citations so that each student built a library of information and resources for further study.

Finally, the 12–15-page final papers were on a topic of the student's choosing, with the approval of the instructor. They examined works influenced by the Holocaust or other twentieth-century political upheavals or investigated lesser-known individual musicians. This provided an opportunity to lean further into their majors or take a step into uncharted territory. Some musicians used this opportunity to research works that they later featured on their degree recitals. One musician researched the genre of the requiem as it intersected with twentieth century political upheavals, including the Holocaust. One psychology major wrote on the self-led music therapy efforts of Holocaust victims. A STEM major created a biography of a female conductor at a concentration camp. Steps to the creation of these papers—a paragraph of intent, an annotated list of ten sources, and a paper outline—were built into the course to allow for incremental input and development. During the last week of the course, the students presented ten-minute presentations of their papers to the group, allowing further sharing of ideas on a breadth of topics. Choosing their area of continued research, and their presentations forming the final topics of the class illustrated the breadth of our subject and increased their ownership of the course.

CHALLENGING CURRENT EVENTS

A course on such an emotionally loaded event as the Holocaust requires a high degree of emotional intelligence and care during any time. I first developed this class prior to the 2016 elections. Painful racism, xenophobia, and anti-Semitic rhetoric endured for generations in America, and the 2016 election cycle reanimated and amplified vitriolic sentiment to mainstream attention. When the course finally ran in 2018, a changed world required renewed efforts to bring understanding to the classroom. This class began a little over a year after the deadly riots in Charlottesville in the wake of the openly white supremacist and neo-Nazi Unite the Right rally in Charlottesville, VA.[7] Rhetoric directly affected students on Michigan's Ann Arbor campus. The fall semester of 2017 brought anti-Latinx and pro-Trump writing on the campus's "Rock," a boulder typically painted in support of school events or Greek life.[8] Likewise, anti-Semitic graffiti was found at a local Ann Arbor skate park.[9] These instances, at both the national and local levels, all informed the care brought to the class from the onset.

On Saturday, October 27, 2018, the country learned of the deeply unnerving shooting at a Pittsburgh synagogue. On that day, a Pennsylvania man with a history of posting anti-Semitic conspiracy theories and vitriol on websites of neo-Nazis, white supremacists, and the alt-right entered the Tree of Life Synagogue in Pittsburgh's Squirrel Hill district, armed with a semi-automatic rifle and three semi-automatic pistols. He fired with intent to kill as many congregants as possible. Three congregations comprising approximately seventy-five people were inside at the time. The attack killed eleven people, and injured six, including four Pittsburgh police officers. The shooting represents the deadliest attack on the Jewish community in the U.S.[10]

I was deeply saddened at the act of violence, and for the Jewish and Pittsburgh communities. My thoughts turned next to my students. We had, for nearly two months, been delving into the deeply upsetting history of the Holocaust. I debated whether and how to bring up the shooting in class when we met. Certainly, they would have seen the non-stop coverage of the event. Would it be best to leave current events at the door, and not re-expose them to violence in class, or to address the fact that the anti-Semitism we discussed daily was still alive and well among us? Would discussing it further in class unnecessarily expose my students to re-traumatization? I decided that ignoring an act of such direct relevance would be unacceptable, and trusted that the maturity that my students demonstrated through the class thus far would extend, and made space to process the shooting as a group.

Not wanting to take any student by surprise, I sent a short email to the class stating that I would hold some time and space for them to acknowledge and comment on the Pittsburgh synagogue shooting and their reactions during the first portion of class. Students understood when entering the classroom at the onset of the course that they would be discussing the cultural reverberations of a traumatic genocide, but it felt necessary to alert

40   TEACHING DIFFICULT TOPICS

them that we would diverge from the syllabus. I noted that participation was not mandatory. One student responded that they would prefer to not be re-exposed to the events and chose not to attend, a perfectly understandable and valid response that demonstrated self-understanding.

I arranged our seats in the usual semi-circle and sat down as they entered. I felt as unsure of myself as I ever have—I am not a psychologist or a therapist. They took their seats. I told them again that given the subject matter of our class, it felt necessary that we acknowledge the violent anti-Semitic attack that had occurred. I repeated some basic facts, and then provided them with credible news sources should they decide to read further, and showed data on the new rise of anti-Semitic hate crimes in the United States. I told them that I didn't have any questions or answers, but if they felt like sharing any of their feelings, they had the floor.

All of the students expressed deep sadness and many of them frustration. Several expressed anger over both the attack and the subsequent media and online commentary and rhetoric that sprung up around it. All expressed frustration that anti-Semitism was allowed to flourish so visibly and was not universally condemned in the twenty-first century. One student referenced their family's Holocaust survivors. Many condemned the lack of condemnation from politicians, including the President, over surrounding anti-Semitic and xenophobic events, including the Charlottesville rally. Some became visibly upset. Through our half-hour space, students never required moderating, and instead respectfully responded and added to one another's comments and observations. Much of this is to the credit of the specific individuals' intelligence and character. This student-led discussion was also possible in a classroom culture where students had built trust with one another where the practice and expectations of discussion had been practiced at all meetings and where they understood their agency and contributions were important and valued.

STUDENT REFLECTIONS AND SUBSEQUENT WORK

Throughout this course, I was impressed by the students' level of academic commitment, thoughtful consideration, and emotional intelligence. Certainly, there were moments of tension that arose during the discussion, but the students maintained respect for one another throughout, the fact of which I am immensely proud. In the wake of the 2016 election, many students felt newly invested in politics, and they were quick to make connections between historic and current xenophobic and exclusionary language. While

Teaching Music and the Holocaust 41

the course didn't venture into overt political divisions along party lines, at times tension arose around current events and identity politics.

Critiques in student feedback can point toward ways we can improve our handling of sensitive and difficult topics, and something all educators should be open to, especially from constituent communities. One student who identified as Jewish reflected that they observed their peers engaging in misplaced empathy when they attempted to "put themselves in the shoes of" the suffering. This appears as a common pitfall when speaking of persecuted groups, and while students grapple with understanding, it is important to reinforce that they should not attempt to speak on behalf of those communities.

Most student feedback was positive, especially toward the opportunity to go deeper into a subject than typically allowed in courses that must cover many topics over the course of the semester. Some voiced that though the material was academically challenging, they appreciated reading Arendt and Adorno as opposed to a textbook. Others were surprised at the impact that the Holocaust and the totalitarian uprising of the 20th century had on music and musicians, and how long that impact has lasted. Some students were eager for the opportunity to discuss current resonances and experiences. One student expressed relief at being able to talk about current events, especially as they had felt silenced in discussing the Black Lives Matter movement in other classes. This points to an increasing desire for spaces for students to respond to the world outside academia; certainly a class built around respectful discussion is one way we can fulfill that need.

Teaching music and culture in relation to historically traumatic events requires special care. In teaching an undergraduate course of the far-reaching impact of the Holocaust on music, musicians, and musical life, I shaped the course around the ability to hold a small seminar-style course for undergraduates, set clear expectations for student discussions, spoke frankly about the emotionally charged subject matter, and shifted assessments to a discussion-based format and projects. This created a space in which students were able to speak clearly and with a high degree of sensitivity to one another about the challenging subject matter of hate, anti-Semitism, and violence inherent in any examination of the Holocaust. The foundation that these students created allowed them to subsequently grieve and reflect on renewed violence as a group.

It is my hope that our willingness to lead students toward uncomfortable conversations with respect and sensitivity will form lasting skills both within and outside our musical disciplines, and that some of the tenets I developed within the context of this course can be applied in other classes. Explicitly naming mental health as health within course materials and allow-

42   TEACHING DIFFICULT TOPICS

ing students to take "sick days" whenever they determine they need space treats students like the young adults they are and as capable of making decisions for themselves. The discussion among the small seminar of students was particularly engaging; in larger format classes, this can be replicated by creating small discussion groups that meet regularly throughout the course, and can develop a rapport with one another. Spending time establishing the boundaries and rules of discussion within a course can feel like valuable time spent away from the topics of a course. However, it turned out to be time well-invested as the students felt comfortable speaking with each other within the structured environment I built and sustained. Developing student-led activities, including jigsaw-style approaches to academically challenging material allows students to expand their abilities and take ownership of a course's subject matter. Finally, holding space for students to comment when current events intersect with the class can be a meaningful way to bring ongoing issues to the fore and allow students a safe space to express their feelings. Implementing these tools provides students further opportunities to meaningfully engage with materials both within courses and as it relates to their lives outside academia.

APPENDIX 2.1: COURSE CONTENT

Week 1   **Introduction**
         Read: D. Bergen, *War and Genocide: A Concise History of the Holocaust*
Week 2   **Introduction: Anti-Semitism & Totalitarian Systems,**
         Read: Hannah Arendt, *The Origins of Totalitarianism:*
         Part Three: Totalitarianism, pages 305–482
         Group A: 305–388 Group B: 389–460
Week 3   **"Degenerate" Music**
         Read: Albrecht Dümling, "The target of racial purity: The 'Degenerate Music' exhibition in Düsseldorf, 1938," in *Art, Culture, and Media Under the Third Reich*, pages 43–72.
         David Snowball, "Controlling Degenerate Music: Jazz in the Third Reich," in *Jazz and the Germans: Essays on the Influence of 'Hot' American Idioms on the 20th-century German Music*, pages 149–66.
Week 4   **Music in the Ghettos**
         Read: Joe Pearce, "*Brundibár* at Theresienstadt," *The Opera Quarterly* (Summer 1994): 39–50.
         View: PBS Documentary: *Brundibár* and the Children of Terezín
         Hans Krása, *Brundibár*
Week 5   **Music in the Ghettos, cont.**
         Read: Linda Hutcheon, "'Death, Where Is Thy Sting?' *The Emperor of Atlantis*," *The Opera Quarterly* 16, no. 2 (Spring 2000): 224–39.
         View: Viktor Ullmann, *The Emperor of Atlantis, or, Death Abdicates*

Teaching Music and the Holocaust   43

Week 6	**Music in the Camps**
	Read: Katarzyna Naliwajek-Mazurek, "Music and Torture in Nazi Sites of Persecution and Genocide in Occupied Poland, 1939–1945," *The World of Music* (2013).
	L. Czackis, "Tangele: The History of Yiddish Tango," *The Jewish Quarterly* (2003): 45–52.
	Listen: *Der Tango fun Oshvientshim* (Slave Tango)
Week 7	**Music in the Camps, cont.**
	Read: Guido Fackler, "'We all feel this music is infernal . . .': Music on Command in Auschwitz," in *The Last Expression: Art and Auschwitz*, 114–25.
	Daniel K., "Singing the Ode 'To Joy' in Auschwitz: A Ten-year-old's Story," *The Beethoven Journal* (Spring 1995): 2–5.
Week 8	**Music in the Camps, cont.**
	Read: Yaakov Strumzah, *Violinist in Auschwitz: From Salonica to Jerusalem, 1913–1967*
Week 9	**Resistance Music**
	Read: Pierre Bourdieu, *Language and Symbolic Power*,
	GROUP A: Part II: pages 105–62
	GROUP B: Part III (first portion): pages 163–202
	GROUP C: Part III (second portion): pages 203–51
Week 10	**Resistance Music, cont.**
	Read: Patrick Henry, *Jewish Resistance Against the Nazis* (2014),
	Introduction, pages xiii–xxxvii
	Part 1: Myths and Facts, pages 1–70
	Listen: Jewish Partisan Songs (Yiddish)
	Tsayt-lid (Song of the Times)
	Tsum Besern Morgn (Toward a Better Tomorrow)
	Shtil, Di Nakht Iz Oysgeshternt (The Silent Night was Filled with Stars)
	Dort Baym Breg Fun Veldl (There, By the Edge of the Forest)
	Partizaner-Marsh (March of the Partisans)
	Shtey Oyf Tsum Kamf (Rise Up and Fight)
	Tsum Roytarmayer (To the Red Army Soldiers)
	Yid, Du Partizaner (The Jewish Partisan)
Week 11	**Outside Perspectives**
	Read: Anne Marshman, "Music as Dialogue: Bakhtin's model applied to Tippett's *A Child of Our Time*." Available on Canvas.
	Listen: Michael Tippet *A Child of Our Time*
Week 12	**Outside Perspectives, cont.**
	Read: Adorno, Chapter 3 from *Notes to Literature*
	Listen: Arnold Schoenberg *A Survivor From Warsaw*
Week 13	**Outside Perspectives, cont.**
	Read: Steve Reich, "Different Trains" in *Writings on Music*, 151–55.
	Naomi Cumming, "The Horrors of Identification: Reich's *Different Trains*," in *Perspectives of New Music* (Winter 1997): 129–52.
	Listen: Steve Reich, *Different Trains*
Week 14	**FINAL PRESENTATIONS IN CLASS**
Week 15	**Conclusions and Roundtable Discussion**
	Possible topics: Playing Wagner in Israel, student ideas.

Notes

1. LSA Residential College, University of Michigan, "About Us," https://lsa.umich.edu/rc/about-us.html

2. To preserve the privacy of students, I will refer to all with the non-gendered singular "they." About half the students identified as musicians or music majors, but all had musical experience. Just under half the class identified as Jewish. Over three-quarters of the class were female.

3. Appendix 2.1 contains a list of readings and works considered in this course.

4. W. J. McKeachie, "Class Size, Large Classes, and Multiple Sections," *Academe* 66, no. 1 (1980): 24–27.

5. Catherine Mulryan-Kyne, "Teaching Large Classes at College and University Level: Challenges and Opportunities," *Teaching in Higher Education* 15, no. 2 (April 2010): 177.

6. To facilitate your own jigsaw approach, see the University of Michigan's "Jigsaw Collaborative Discussion Method," https://sites.lsa.umich.edu/inclusive-teaching/jigsaw-collaborative-discussion-method/

7. Joe Heim, "Recounting a day of rage, hate, violence and death," *Washington Post*, 14 August 2017.

8. Riyah Basha and Alexa St. John, "Anti-Latinx, pro-Trump writing found on University Rock," *Michigan Daily*, 2 September 2017.

9. Jennifer Meer and Nisa Khan, "Racist, anti-Semitic graffiti found in skate park," *Michigan Daily*, 18 August 2017.

10. Kris Mamula, Andrew Goldstein, Paula Reed Ward, Liz Navratil, and Shelly Bradbury, "Eleven dead, six wounded in massacre at Squirrel Hill synagogue," *Pittsburgh Post-Gazette*, 27 October 2018.

Works Cited

Basha, Riyah, and Alexa St. John. "Anti-Latinx, pro-Trump writing found on University Rock," *Michigan Daily* (Ann Arbor) September 2, 2017.

Heim, Joe. "Recounting a day of rage, hate, violence and death." *Washington Post* (Washington, D.C.), August 14, 2017.

Mamula, Kris, Andrew Goldstein, Paula Reed Ward, Liz Navratil, and Shelly Bradbury. "Eleven dead, six wounded in massacre at Squirrel Hill synagogue." *Pittsburgh Post-Gazette* (Pittsburgh, PA), October 27, 2018.

McKeachie, W. J. "Class Size, Large Classes, and Multiple Sections." *Academe* 66, no. 1 (1980): 24–27.

Meer, Jennifer, and Nisa Khan, "Racist, anti-Semitic graffiti found in skate park." *Michigan Daily* (Ann Arbor, MI), August 18, 2017.

Mulryan-Kyne, Catherine, "Teaching Large Classes at College and University Level: Challenges and Opportunities," *Teaching in Higher Education* 15, no. 2 (April 2010): 177.

CHAPTER 3

Teaching Difficult Topics in Large Enrollment Classes

Kelsey Klotz

In Spring 2019, I had just started a class session on music and privilege when a student stormed out of class.[1] I had completed the requisite reminders (finish this online discussion, remember this quiz), and had begun a short video meant to remind students that race is a social construct rather than a biological reality. Shortly after the video's narrator had made that point (and within the first roughly seven minutes of class), I heard the unmistakable sound of a student vigorously shoving one of the metal doors to the classroom open; I looked up to see one student of the over 100 in the classroom—they appeared to be a white man—leave the room.

I have no idea who they were or if they ever returned to class.

What is the ideal music classroom in which to teach difficult topics? Difficult topics, however defined, seem to inherently require an intimate setting, offering opportunities to check in with students individually, and providing space for their voices to be heard. A crucial part of teaching challenging subject matter is reading the room, and identifying the bend/break point within each classroom environment and for each student: where can you, as the instructor, challenge students, where do they need space, and how will the course continue to be most effective? This point is different at each institution, in each semester, and with each class and modality. While it can be difficult to assess this environment in small enrollment classes, large enrollment classes offer additional challenges. How can instructors assess student knowledge and understanding, as well as student subjectivity, when they do not know students' names? How can students demonstrate agency and engage in the material as they uncomfortably sit elbow to elbow in a stuffy lecture hall, or when hundreds of students you may never meet sit at their computers?

While some colleges and universities are showing increased interest in the "diversity" aspects of a liberal arts curriculum, there is a tension between their desire to offer such courses and their decreased budgets (and, increasingly, the ideological pursuits of state legislatures and politically appointed Boards of Trustees). One solution in general education curricula is to offer such "diversity" courses in large-enrollment formats, often taught by contingent faculty—a solution that reflects a general lack of institutional investment in "diversity" initiatives and interdisciplinary programs.[2] Such systemic imbalances, while beyond the scope of this particular essay, nevertheless operate as a key frame as I and other contingent faculty like me attempt to mitigate these challenges on an individual level.

In my role as a lecturer at the University of North Carolina at Charlotte (2018–2023), I typically taught between 400–500 students each semester in a general education Arts and Society course (currently LBST 1103—the course designation is Liberal Studies). In-person course enrollment caps are set at 124 students per section; online enrollment caps were initially set at 100 students per section, but they have in recent semesters been adjusted to 124. The assigned course objectives underscore that this is a bit of an undercover diversity course, including language like, "Students will demonstrate awareness of how individuals or groups in a society may create or respond to art in different ways shaped by their own particular perspectives and position in that society."[3]

This essay focuses on my experiences with and approaches to teaching "diversity topics" in large enrollment, general education music classes. It does so semi-chronologically: The first part of this essay offers reflections and suggestions based on my experiences in my first year of teaching LBST 1103 (AY 2018–2019), while the second part primarily considers my second year teaching the class (AY 2019–2020), offering space to acknowledge the challenges brought by the teaching of difficult topics, particularly for the contingent/non-tenure track faculty assigned to teach them (positions which tend to be occupied by identities facing additional modes of precarity, whether as women and/or as people of color).[4] In particular, the latter part of this essay is less an optimistic reflection on what one teaching center consultant described to me as the "opportunities" of large-scale teaching than it is an ambivalent and realistic reaction to and acknowledgment of the added stress of teaching difficult topics in large and largely anonymous settings. Instead, the experiences shared in the second part opens up space for increased nuance around student agency and safe/brave spaces.

YEAR 1 (AY 2018–2019): BEFORE

In my first year (AY 2018–2019), I approached LBST 1103 a bit as a laboratory experiment—furnished by my research in and commitment to social justice,

Teaching Difficult Topics in Large Enrollment Classes 47

I experimented with readings, videos, and assignments, trying to master the alchemy of a large-scale course that prioritized "difficult topics." With the exception of the course objectives, I was given nearly total control over the course design. To increase student engagement and interest, I organized the course around a guiding provocation; as a scholar of American music, I chose, "What does it mean to sound American?" In the first year of class, not wanting to hide what I interpret to be the clear orientation around inclusion and identity in LBST 1000-level courses, I created three units that clearly demonstrated the course's commitment to diversity, equity, and inclusion: 1) Race/Ethnicity; 2) Gender/Sexuality; 3) American Sounds and the Nation (in which we applied the knowledge from the first two units to a variety of musical genres).[5] While the core question of the course implicitly oriented chosen genres and artists around western music, I attempted to include a wide variety of source materials, not only introducing students to western classical, present-day pop, jazz, and country, but global hip hop, K-pop, and Lumbee Indian music.

I incorporated a wide variety of genres to aid in creating a community of inclusion, and I extended that inclusion through my chosen resources: for example, out of concern that students might be unable to afford the high prices of a required textbook (and ultimately not purchase one), I often do not require a textbook for my students. Instead, I combine accessible essays and articles relevant to the topics I have chosen (these range from NPR and Vox articles to *Switched on Pop* podcast episodes to short essays from edited volumes and journals accessed through library services). In some semesters, I have required the *Switched on Pop* text by Nate Sloan and Charlie Harding, a low cost option that the library has available digitally for students for free. In selecting the readings, as with the musicians and artists in listening examples (provided on YouTube), I incorporate a diverse field of authors and, where possible, show videos of the author speaking; for example, when we discuss intersectionality (which I do in connection with Nina Simone or Janelle Monáe), I show a video of Kimberlé Crenshaw speaking about and explaining the concept.[6] We begin the class discussing how to define music by juxtaposing Ralph Ellison and Amiri Baraka's approaches toward understanding the blues.[7] I also include a day called "Listening for Silences," in which we discuss why it is hard to find women in music history books (noting the structural issues they face in particular).[8] The second part of class focuses on the additional challenges faced by women of color in the documentary *20 Feet from Stardom*.[9]

Recognizing that many of my students would feel too intimidated to contribute to class discussions in such a large class, and that I would easily lose

48 TEACHING DIFFICULT TOPICS

track of many of my students, I separated each section into three groups at two points in the semester. Each group was required to come to class on one out of three class days; on the other two days, they were required to complete online Canvas modules. Because the class was smaller during the small group units, I was able to get to know some of my students better, and students who normally would not raise their hands in the big class contributed extensively to our smaller class discussions. While I did give up some student engagement in the Canvas modules (students anonymously reported spending anywhere between 10 minutes and 2 hours on these modules), the results in participation and engagement in the smaller class days were well worth it, and past student responses reflected that these smaller days were some of their more enjoyable class days, even when they do not enjoy the content. Students also explain that being able to spread out physically made it easier to work in small groups on active learning assignments, and having a reduced class size made them pay attention more to what was going on. By periodically splitting the class up, I was able to give more students the attention they need to feel heard.[10]

I encourage students to engage in community-building exercises from the beginning of the course. In the first few days of the semester, using Poll Everywhere, I ask students three questions: 1) What do they need to do to succeed this semester?; 2) What do they need their classmates to know to succeed this semester?; 3) How can I help them succeed this semester? With the last two questions, I compile their responses into PowerPoint slides to show overlapping answers so that students understand both what they need from each other (usually things like a quiet and non-distracting space, empathy and understanding, and notes or a study buddy), and that I listen when they tell me what they need.[11] Showing these responses also demonstrates that in almost every case, every student shared an answer with a handful of others—in other words, they need what many others need. This list becomes a sort of code of conduct for our class, and I remind students of this list throughout the semester (particularly on discussion-heavy days).

Early in the semester, I sensed that I needed to balance content that focused heavily on diversity and inclusion with days in which issues of race, gender, or sexuality were still present, but not highlighted. To that end, I centered musical analysis during class sessions on K-pop, the Beatles, and country music. I also deployed significant musical analysis on some days that focused on more sensitive material, for three primary reasons: 1) to subtly and carefully re-assert my authority in a class where I rarely assert it (I often tell my students that there will be genres—hip hop and country, for example—in which they know more than me and some of their fellow classmates); 2) to provide some breathing room away from challenging social content; and 3) to demonstrate how music is intricately implicated in the social concepts we discuss. For example, when I pair intersectionality with Janelle Monáe's "Make Me Feel," I include Nate Sloan and Charlie Harding's detailed musical analysis and interpretation of gender bending from their podcast *Switched on Pop*. In a discussion of lynching and Billie Holiday's "Strange Fruit," we take time to compare and contrast Holiday's 1939 and 1959 recordings, connecting the musical differences to the heightened visibility of lynchings in the 1950s, demonstrated through the story of Emmett Till. This approach unfolds in class through a mixture of lecture and active-learning strategies, including small group work centered around a particular question or primary source document, listening activities, and Poll Everywhere feedback from students. Based on course evaluations and polling, this approach has seemed to essentially justify the cultural/historical work the course does to students who might otherwise complain about learning about Emmett Till in a course about music (such as in my first semester evaluations).

YEAR TWO (AY 2019–2020): AFTER

On April 30, 2019, the last day of classes of my first year at UNC Charlotte, a gunman opened fire in a classroom not too many buildings away from mine, half an hour after I had dismissed my last class for the semester. The shooter—who had initially been enrolled at UNC Charlotte in the Spring 2019 semester, but had withdrawn early into the semester—targeted a 2000-level LBST course with a 100-person enrollment. Because the shooting had happened on the last day of classes and the university subsequently made all final exams optional, I didn't see most of my students afterward, and was not in a full classroom again until the first day of the following fall '19 semester. I spent the summer in the relative isolation of many academics, teaching an online class, working on a book chapter, and revising the syllabus for my fall LBST course.

It took me most of the Fall 2019 semester to understand the full impact the shooting had on me and, by extension, on my teaching. Some changes were more noticeable than others: I moved the desk in my office so that I would have easier access to the exit, and I began to explicitly inform my students where each of the doors in the classroom led.[12] Others impacted my effectiveness in teaching difficult topics. For example, over the summer, I revised my syllabus, making changes that I convinced myself would enhance and strengthen the musical analytical portion of my course, but that I also knew deep down were simultaneously limiting the extent to which I led students through difficult topics. Instead of organizing the course around themes like Race/Ethnicity, Gender/Sexuality, and the Nation, as I had previously, I began the course with a "Musical Bootcamp," to teach terms and listening strategies, before moving onto a selection of broad histories of American music and "diverse perspectives" in music (to use the language of the assigned course objectives). Much of the content of these portions of the course remained the same, but stripped of transparency through titles and overt framing, my Fall 2019 students seemed less able to make connections between different stories of identity, power, and representation in different case studies across the semester (as evidenced in their assignments and responses).

In the classroom, I became more anxious before each class—particularly before sessions that might challenge some world views more than others, like the day on "Janelle Monáe, Intersectionality, and Queerness" or "Listening for Silences." In part because I had received such positive feedback about those days from students excited to see queer musicians discussed at all, I refused to compromise on those lessons. But I found each day physically exhausting, as if I had to prepare myself for battle with the students who complained that Monáe's "Make Me Feel" was inappropriately sexually explicit (the same complaint was not made on a day that focused on the "Blurred Lines" copyright case).

One day, mid-way into the Fall 2019 semester, a white male student walked into class 15 minutes late with something dark in his hand; heart pounding, I stared at his hand while continuing to lecture until I realized he was holding an iPhone. As I reflected on that moment after class and realized how close I had come to dashing behind my podium because of a cell phone, I began to understand some of the toll teaching difficult topics in a largely anonymous setting had had on me on my campus in the aftermath of the shooting. I do not always know who my students are or if the person in my classroom is supposed to be there. And without teaching assistants, I have no other conceivable check on who is in my classroom and what they are doing in it.[13] The inherent anonymity of classes with 124+ students, and of teaching multiple large sections, intersects with the subject matter of my course, creating challenges beyond simply "large class size" and "difficult subject matter." Because I do not know who my students are, I do not always have an adequate understanding of how much farther I can push them, when I need to back off, or who they should work with on a given group assignment. Compared to my

Teaching Difficult Topics in Large Enrollment Classes 51

prior small-class teaching experiences, which delved deeply into race and racism, teaching difficult topics in classes of this size can be like teaching with blinders on.[14]

SAFE SPACES, BRAVE SPACES, AND BIG SPACES

We talk a lot about safe spaces in higher education: we debate their potential for students' intellectual rigor, the legitimacy of them, the equity in their distribution to all students, and the varying degrees of safety our students should feel depending on the context. Indeed, feminist pedagogy challenges the notion that a safe space is safe for all; as the writers of *A Guide to Feminist Pedagogy* explain, "'Safety' is a mutable concept that will mean disparate things to people positioned differently, so the question becomes: when we say we are committed to creating safe spaces, whose safety are we concerned with?"[15] Other diversity scholars in higher education suggest "brave spaces," which foregrounds the idea of bravery to create more genuine dialogue and prepare students to participate in challenging conversations.[16] However, for some of our students, and ourselves, simply being in a room with 124 other people—and especially speaking in that room—automatically requires bravery, before we even approach concepts like "dialogue" and "difficult topics," and before we had to contend with a global pandemic that made such spaces an actual physical threat.

Further, for instructors like myself, who believe in the usefulness of the concept of safe spaces in the inherently intimidating context of 124 students or more in a classroom, we do not tend to talk about what a safe or brave space means for ourselves. When we are dealing with "difficult topics," our facts and our histories—which we, as "expert" instructors, are supposed to marshal to intellectually assert ourselves and our authority—are not always safe, and authority, however strongly or gently wielded, is challenged. As a young woman, I have always known that my authority in my classroom is not a given;[17] in fact, the relative anonymity of my classroom has resulted in some male students openly flirting with me, to the point where other students have asked them to stop on my behalf.[18] One anonymous instance of sexual harassment, in response to my opening community-building question of "what do you need your classmates to know," resulted in my having to explain to a classroom of 124 students how the comment constituted sexual harassment—without knowing which of them had targeted me.[19]

Some ways I make my classroom safe(r) include: 1) telling my students

52   TEACHING DIFFICULT TOPICS

what I needed to feel safe (for instance, I ask them to let me know when they need to be late or leave early so I am not surprised by their entrances/ exits); 2) employing strategic agency by carefully crafting small group discussion questions to encourage students to focus primarily on what a particular person (such as Janelle Monáe or Merle Haggard) might say or do, rather than on students' opinions; 3) asking for specific facts or quotes from primary sources or studies, rather than lecturing on such data (such as the USC Annenberg Inclusion Initiative on Inequality in the Recording Studio);[20] 4) offering moments of "safe" self-expression and agency, such as journaling to a more opinion-oriented question or assigning them short writing prompts on music or concerts of their choice; 5) offering opportunities for students to reflect to me on assignments (through prompts that recognize the emotional labor they have done in, for example, learning about blackface minstrelsy, and ask if they would like to reflect on what they have learned); and (perhaps most importantly), 6) telling students they can come to me with issues and concerns, and being able to reflect both calmness and empathy toward those concerns, putting aside any defensiveness of pedagogical choices to deliver what that student needs. I operate under the assumption that offering students places to feel heard and acknowledged will yield some of the same for myself.

Engaging student buy-in is another key way I try to make my classroom safe(r). Student input and agency are important to my teaching philosophy; I want my students to be able to apply what they learn in class to the music they listen to and participate in, and I aim to offer them spaces in which they can practice those personal connections. Furthermore, there is a vast body of research linking student agency and motivation to student success, and I see firsthand how leveraging my students' experiences and values enhances their learning.[21] But knowing when and how to encourage student agency is crucial in my context. For example, I incorporate student feedback throughout the semester, and make those moments of incorporation visible to students. In one semester's course evaluations, a student suggested a student choice day; not only did I incorporate that idea, but I also tell my students every semester that this idea came from a course evaluation suggestion. Another example comes from early in the pandemic, when I asked students if there was anything their other instructors were doing that might be useful for this course; based on their response, I began to incorporate video recaps at the end of each week.

Among student-centered teaching approaches, student agency is often celebrated as a standard ideal, and it is certainly one I strive toward; however, large-enrollment classes require a more nuanced approach to agency—what I might call strategic agency. Given some of the material we cover, combined with the fact that I am virtually unable to monitor all individual student responses in real-time on discussion boards, I carefully structure assignments and questions, creating strategic limitations in prompts in order to avoid students from, say, taking the opportunity on an assignment about blackface minstrelsy to deny that racism exists (it's happened more than once). For example, my course day on blackface minstrelsy is highly structured: I preface the content with a statement warning students that this will be a particularly challenging day, that if they need to leave the room or look away from the screen they should feel free to do so, and that if they would like to speak privately with me about what they have seen, we can do so; this not only indicates my willingness to hear their concerns, but it sets the stage for students who might not take the class as seriously as they perhaps should. I move into a more lecture-based class than I usually would, supported by images, a video from CBS, images from sheet music, and performances by Rhiannon Giddens. Following the lecture, I build in time for students to engage with primary source documents: their assignment is to view skits, images of Bert Williams, sheet music covers, and lyrics to identify the recurring stereotypes they observe and the political power they had. In this way, they are given individual time to digest the material on their own and offered a structured space to respond and reflect. However, because this is an assignment, they are graded on their ability to use the sources to answer a specific question that does not require or request their personal reflections.[22]

For especially challenging assignments, I have found limiting responses to a specified prompt to be particularly useful. However, I do not want my students to feel unheard; therefore, I offer other places in the class for them to exert some agency.[23] For example, on a unit that focuses on intersectionality, they might choose between Aretha Franklin, Dolly Parton, or Selena Quintanilla-Pérez to focus their analysis. At the end of the semester, I give students four different prompts to choose from for their final essay exam on protest music (1. What is protest music? 2. Create a protest playlist for an activist. 3. Write a protest song. 4. What other protest movements should be included in this unit?).

Another primary space for agency is Student Choice Day, where students are able to vote on the content for that day. Sometimes, this means I choose four different topics, and students vote via Poll Everywhere.[24] Other times, students suggest genres and artists they feel are missing from the course and over a few weeks, we slowly narrow down the list through a combination of rank choice voting and popular vote (this has often resulted in a class day on the music of rapper and North Carolina native J. Cole). When I ask my students at the end of the semester what their favorite days were, student choice days usually receive the top vote. These votes also tell me what genres students feel are missing from the class; so while 1970s rock rarely wins over hip hop and rap in a student choice day vote, the numbers are consistently high, and I have created a new day on that genre for future semesters to try to represent the students wanting to learn more about that music. The result of this constant balance between student input, agency, and strategic limitations is to create a safe(r) space for students within the context of a very big classroom.

But even with the positive changes I have made to my pedagogy in order to prioritize both my own and my students' safety, I have stumbled, finding myself teaching out of fear and anxiety. Because of that fear, I made changes to my course between my first and second years that I believe neutered the full potential impact of the stories about power, inequality, and injustice I had intended to tell, which ultimately reflects a fundamental misalignment between how I taught in Fall 2019 and the goals of my teaching philosophy. I have struggled to rebuild that confidence in in-person classes.

In the pandemic AY 2020–2021 (my third year), I taught eight sections of the course online asynchronously (a total of 800 students passed through my online course that year). Teaching online, while challenging in its own right, freed me from my concerns of physical safety, and allowed me to curate a kind of online persona that felt more individualized to some of my students (because I had more time to provide individual feedback and flexibility, and recorded short, informal, reflective videos in various spaces in my home). Returning to the classroom in Fall '21 in the midst of the Delta variant's spread across the United States only exacerbated the threat my classroom space had become to me—a threat I had only just identified and begun to unpack a few short weeks before the abrupt shift online in Spring '20.

CONCLUSION

To me, this is an incomplete, unsatisfying story—one that offers experience-based suggestions and some triumphs, but also represents setbacks in my teaching effectiveness. When combined with the onset of a global pandemic and a political landscape increasingly hostile to teaching difficult topics, both of which created multiple sets of other classroom anxieties, I sometimes wonder if my in-person teaching effectiveness has yet to truly recover. Nevertheless, it may be a story that many need to hear. It is easy to think someone else has the answers, and that those answers came easily for them. It can be easy to assume that if teaching these topics—in any setting—is hard for us, that we are doing something wrong, or that we are missing an easy fix. It is hard to acknowledge that there is rarely a steady progression forward as we try to find the best way to talk about blackface minstrelsy in a way that is relevant but not traumatic, or to talk about pansexuality that highlights its importance in Janelle Monáe's stated experience of writing the album *Dirty Computer* (2018), but does not suggest that there is a single sound of queerness, or that that is the only reason Monáe is worth studying.

I struggle with knowing whether any of these pedagogical and course organizational decisions "worked"—whether they sparked some sense of added knowledge, whether the stories got through. I could share quotes from course evaluations from students writing that they liked the "social focus" of the course or that they felt seen by the content for the first time, or emails from students after the course ended saying that even though they were a music major or had years of musical experience they nevertheless learned how to think about music differently, but I fear that would simply be cherry-picking the words of kind students for whom the course worked. It would ignore those students who write in accusatory tones that I am too liberal, and who bristle at the notion that a course titled "The Arts in Society: Music" would position music within a societal context—but they are my students, too. For them, I do what I can to offer those moments of musical analysis that they desire, and I avoid words that trigger them, like "feminism." I offer them moments of strategic agency—agency that I hope encourages their engagements, interests, and minds, and an agency that I hope will maintain a sense of community (what one might call a "safe space") for students who carry diverse traumas into the classroom.

But mostly, with 400–500 students per semester, I have to get used to not witnessing my students' moments of revelation, and not being able to respond to each student individually the way I believe they deserve. It means letting the student storm out of the room, and not knowing when or if that reaction will happen again, or if it will escalate. As one dean told me, "You are planting seeds that will bear fruit perhaps years from now." In other words, if there are successes or breakthroughs, I will likely never see them. As they leave my classroom, and however they leave my classroom, I can simply hope that those unseen breakthroughs will come.

Notes

1. Much gratitude is due to Elizabeth Dister, for her critical feedback and crucial guidance regarding the scholarship of teaching and learning; Daniel Fister, for his keen editing eye and suggestions; and Anna Nekola, Laura Moore Pruett, and Olivia Lucas for their insightful edits and revisions. Note: I began this essay in late 2019. Given the fundamental teaching changes that occurred as a result of the COVID-19 pandemic, I provide "pandemic updates" throughout the essay; many of these are in the footnotes. I am completing a final edit in April 2023, in the aftermath of political assaults on higher education in North Carolina, as with other states around the United States. The idea of teaching difficult topics—and the maneuvers I have to make to continue doing so in my current context—has changed more quickly than I can edit this essay. Thus, this essay is inevitably but one snapshot, as I attempted to grapple with my large enrollment classrooms between 2018–2022.

2. For more on the lack of investment of resources, including tenure-track lines, for general education and "diversity" courses, see Ryan A. Miller and Laura E. Struve, "'Heavy Lifters of the University': Non-Tenure Track Faculty Teaching Required Diversity Courses," *Innovative Higher Education* 45 (2020), 437–55.

3. The general education requirement is currently undergoing a revision that would more clearly forefront identity and equity in some classes, and that would maintain current course enrollments.

4. Colleen Flaherty, "More Faculty Diversity, Not on Tenure Track," *Inside Higher Ed*, 21 August 2016: https://www.insidehighered.com/news/2016/08/22/study-finds -gains-faculty-diversity-not-tenure-track; Kelly J. Baker, "Contingency and Gender," *ChronicleVitae*, 24 April 2015: https://chroniclevitae.com/news/984-contingency-and -gender; "Contingent Appointments and the Academic Profession," *American Association of University Professors*, 2014 [2003]: https://www.aaup.org/report/contingent-ap pointments-and-academic-profession

5. Transparency in teaching has been shown to enhance student success, particularly for underrepresented students. See Mary-Ann Winkelmes, Matthew Bernacki, Jeffrey Butler, Michelle Zochowski, Jennifer Golanics, et al., "A Teaching Intervention that Increases Underserved College Students' Success," *Peer Review* 18, no. 1/2 (Winter/Spring 2016): 31–36.

6. Kimberlé Crenshaw, "The Urgency of Intersectionality," *TEDWomen 2016*, October 2016: https://www.ted.com/talks/kimberle_crenshaw_the_urgency_of_intersect ionality?language=en

7. Ralph Ellison, "Blues People," *Shadow and Act* (New York: The Modern Library, 1995 [1963]), 247–58; Amiri Baraka [LeRoi Jones], excerpt from *Blues People* (New York: William Morrow and Company, 1963). While Baraka defines the genre primarily through the history of struggle faced by black Americans, Ellison sought to define the blues through musical terminology, demonstrating its potential as art.

8. Kelsey Klotz, "*The Absent Women of Jazz*," *The Common Reader*, 9 Jan. 2017:

Teaching Difficult Topics in Large Enrollment Classes 57

https://commonreader.wustl.edu/c/absent-women-jazz/; Ingrid Monson, "Fitting the Part," in *Big Ears: Listening for Gender in Jazz Studies*, ed. Nichole T. Rustin and Sherrie Tucker (Chapel Hill, NC: Duke University Press, 2008), 267–90; Sherrie Tucker, "It Don't Mean a Thing If It Ain't in the History Books," in *Swing Shift: "All-Girl" Bands of the 1940s* (Chapel Hill, NC: Duke University Press, 2000), 1–32. Pandemic update: In the online version of the course, I offer students a myriad of articles from mainstream news sources focusing on the experiences of women in genres such as country, heavy metal, bluegrass, hip hop, jazz, and EDM. Students choose which to focus on for a written response.

9. Merry Clayton and Lisa Fischer, *20 Feet From Stardom*, dir. by Morgan Neville (New York: RADiUS-TWC, 2013).

10. Pandemic update: During the first academic year of the pandemic (Fall 2020 and Spring 2021), I taught all sections of LBST 1103 online asynchronously. In Fall 2021 and Spring 2022, I taught two sections of the class in-person (the other two were offered online asynchronously). In an effort to de-densify my classroom due to the ongoing COVID-19 pandemic, I created a hyflex option for students, in which on any given day students could choose to either come to the classroom for in-person learning or complete their work online (their work mirrored the asynchronous online work being done in my online sections). Creating this option naturally created smaller class sizes, allowing me to engage in more active learning assignments later in the semester. As of Spring 2022, students have seemed to appreciate the flexibility that online content affords in a general education class (especially amid pandemic-related isolation and other increasingly common stressors), while also engaging in smaller group work when they attend in-person. As student engagement decreased, I began to require attendance in Spring 2023, though I still allowed students to miss up to 8 class days, and continued to provide online make up content.

11. Research in "compassionate pedagogy" shows that students benefit (in terms of confidence, motivation, and even retention) from faculty-student interaction in which the student perceives the faculty member as being approachable and respectful. For more, see Ashley Grantham, Emily Erin Robinson, and Diane Chapman, "'That Truly Meant a Lot to Me': A Qualitative Examination of Meaningful Faculty-Student Interactions," *College Teaching* 63, no. 3 (2015): 125–32.

12. Pandemic update: I have since moved my desk back to its original position to create more distance between my space and the space for people who stop by my office.

13. Pandemic update: Before the pandemic, the university provided funds for undergraduate teaching assistants (we call them preceptors) in large classes for non-majors like mine. Already overwhelmed by students and fearing the extra workload in managing and advising a team of four preceptors, I had always declined. During the pandemic, however, they became instrumental in my ability to create active online assignments for my 400–500 students, and I have continued to employ them as I've moved back to the classroom (and I have been fortunate to work with some truly ex-

58   TEACHING DIFFICULT TOPICS

cellent undergraduates). However, I do not require my preceptors to attend class, and most complete their work online.

14. Past small enrollment courses I have created and taught included "Hearing Race in 1950s American Musical Culture" and "Music and Black Political Protest," taught at Washington University in St. Louis and Emory University, respectively.

15. Raquelle Bostow, Sherry Brewer, Nancy Chick, Ben Galina, Allison McGrath, Kirsten Mendoza, Kristen Navarro, and Lis Valle-Ruiz, "Habits of Hand: Learning Environment," *A Guide to Feminist Pedagogy*, Vanderbilt University Center for Teaching (March 2015): https://my.vanderbilt.edu/femped/habits-of-hand/learning-environment/

16. Brian Arao and Kristi Clemens, "From Safe Spaces to Brave Spaces: A New Way to Frame Dialogue Around Diversity and Social Justice," in *The Art of Effective Facilitation: Reflections From Social Justice Educators*, ed. Lisa M. Landreman (Sterling, VA: Stylus, 2013), 135–50.

17. However, as a white woman, I benefit from the assumed authority of my whiteness. Black scholars and scholars of color, and women of color in particular, have long written about their experiences dealing with the cultural assumptions within academia that authority looks white and is male. For more, see Juanita Johnson-Bailey and Ming-Yeh Lee, "Women of Color in the Academy: Where's Our Authority in the Classroom?" *Feminist Teacher* 15, no. 2 (2005): 111–22.

18. I do not think it is a coincidence that incidents like these became less frequent after my partner and I purchased and I began wearing a more prominent wedding ring and band.

19. Less than one month after that incident, the Trump administration's Department of Education, led by Secretary Betsy DeVos, announced proposed changes to Title IX policies that disqualified the comment as sexual harassment. Erica L. Green, "Proposed Rules Would Reduce Sexual Misconduct Inquiries, Education Dept. Estimates," *New York Times* 10 Sept. 2018: https://www.nytimes.com/2018/09/10/us/politics/campus-sexual-misconduct-rules.html

20. Stacy L. Smith, "Inclusion in the Recording Studio?" USC Annenberg Inclusion Initiative (Feb. 2019): http://assets.uscannenberg.org/docs/aii-inclusion-recording-studio-2019.pdf

21. For a summary of the literature on engaged and transformational learning, see George M. Slavich and Philip G. Zimbardo, "Transformational Teaching: Theoretical Underpinnings, Basic Principles, and Core Methods," *Educational Psychology Review* 24, no. 4 (2012): 569–608. For strategies and approaches to use in the classroom, see Margery B. Ginsberg and Raymond J. Wlodkowski, *Diversity and Motivation: Culturally Responsive Teaching in College*, 2nd ed. (San Francisco: Jossey-Bass, 2009).

22. Pandemic update: in moving this assignment online, I added an optional reflection space to the assignment (we do not use a discussion board in this unit), providing students with some questions to get them started, but also instructing them that if they would prefer to reflect on their own, they should simply write that. 2022 update:

Given the increased stress and mental health concerns reported by students (and especially Black students), I have temporarily paused the blackface minstrelsy unit. I plan to re-incorporate this unit in the future, based on how I understand my students to be able to handle the content without being additionally traumatized.

23. For more literature on creating student agency within the college classroom, see Suzanne S. Hudd, "Syllabus Under Construction: Involving Students in the Creation of Class Assignments," *Teaching Sociology* 31, no. 2 (Apr. 2003): 195–202.

24. Pandemic update: In the online version of this course, I created online modules for three musicians who were particularly popular in previous semesters of the course (J Cole, Merle Haggard, and Janelle Monáe) and one of my own favorites (Kishi Bashi). Students register which artist they'd like to focus on through a quick poll. I then assign them into the corresponding artist group in Canvas.

Works Cited

Arao, Brian, and Kristi Clemens. "From Safe Spaces to Brave Spaces: A New Way to Frame Dialogue Around Diversity and Social Justice." In *The Art of Effective Facilitation: Reflections From Social Justice Educators*, edited by Lisa M. Landreman. Sterling, VA: Stylus, 2013: 135–50.

Baker, Kelly J. "Contingency and Gender." *ChronicleVitae*, April 24 2015. https://chroniclevitae.com/news/984-contingency-and-gender

Baraka, Amiri [LeRoi Jones]. *Blues People*. New York: William Morrow and Company, 1963.

Bostow, Raquelle, Sherry Brewer, Nancy Chick, Ben Galina, Allison McGrath, Kirsten Mendoza, Kristen Navarro, and Lis Valle-Ruiz. "Habits of Hand: Learning Environment." *A Guide to Feminist Pedagogy*. Vanderbilt University Center for Teaching (March 2015): https://my.vanderbilt.edu/femped/habits-of-hand/learning-environment/

Clayton, Merry, and Lisa Fischer. *20 Feet From Stardom*. Directed by Morgan Neville. New York: RADiUS-TWC, 2013.

"Contingent Appointments and the Academic Profession." *American Association of University Professors* 2014 [2003]: https://www.aaup.org/report/contingent-appointments-and-academic-profession

Crenshaw, Kimberlé. "The Urgency of Intersectionality." *TEDWomen 2016*. October 2016: https://www.ted.com/talks/kimberle_crenshaw_the_urgency_of_intersectionality?language=en

Ellison, Ralph. "Blues People." *Shadow and Act*. New York: The Modern Library, 1995 [1963]: 247–58.

Flaherty, Colleen. "*More Faculty Diversity, Not on Tenure Track.*" *Inside Higher Ed.* (21 August 2016): https://www.insidehighered.com/news/2016/08/22/study-finds-gains-faculty-diversity-not-tenure-track

Ginsberg, Margery B., and Raymond J. Wlodkowski. *Diversity and Motivation: Culturally Responsive Teaching in College*, 2nd ed. San Francisco: Jossey-Bass, 2009.

60   TEACHING DIFFICULT TOPICS

Grantham, Ashley, Emily Erin Robinson, and Diane Chapman. "'That Truly Meant a Lot to Me': A Qualitative Examination of Meaningful Faculty-Student Interactions." *College Teaching* 63, no. 3 (2015): 125–32.

Hudd, Suzanne S. "Syllabus Under Construction: Involving Students in the Creation of Class Assignments." *Teaching Sociology* 31, no. 2 (Apr. 2003): 195–202.

Klotz, Kelsey. "The Absent Women of Jazz." *The Common Reader* (9 Jan. 2017): https://commonreader.wustl.edu/c/absent-women-jazz/

Johnson-Bailey, Juanita, and Ming-Yeh Lee. "Women of Color in the Academy: Where's Our Authority in the Classroom?" *Feminist Teacher* 15, no. 2 (2005): 111–22.

Miller, Ryan A., and Laura E. Struve. "'Heavy Lifters of the University': Non-Tenure Track Faculty Teaching Required Diversity Courses." *Innovative Higher Education* 45 (2020): 437–55.

Monson, Ingrid. "Fitting the Part." In *Big Ears: Listening for Gender in Jazz Studies,* edited by Nichole T. Rustin and Sherrie Tucker, 267–90. Chapel Hill, NC: Duke University Press, 2008.

Slavich, George M., and Philip G. Zimbardo. "Transformational Teaching: Theoretical Underpinnings, Basic Principles, and Core Methods." *Educational Psychology Review* 24, no. 4 (2012): 569–608.

Smith, Stacy L. "Inclusion in the Recording Studio?" USC Annenberg Inclusion Initiative (Feb. 2019): http://assets.uscannenberg.org/docs/aii-inclusion-recording-studio-2019.pdf

Tucker, Sherrie. *Swing Shift: "All-Girl" Bands of the 1940s.* Chapel Hill, NC: Duke University Press, 2000.

Winkelmes, Mary-Ann, Matthew Bernacki, Jeffrey Butler, Michelle Zochowski, Jennifer Golanics, et al. "A Teaching Intervention that Increases Underserved College Students' Success." *Peer Review* 18, no. 1/2 (Winter/Spring 2016): 31–36.

CHAPTER 4

Decentering Whiteness in the Music Appreciation Classroom

An Anti-Racist Approach

Everette Scott Smith

> "Stop pushing a liberal agenda for your class. I took this class to learn the history of Music, not to learn about how one race was being taken advantage over another. The sad reality is that you try and push this liberal agenda, but once I do my actual research, it's obvious that there are two sides to the story and narrative that you are trying to push, which you conveniently leave out."

Though initially begun in 2018 as a project to revive my Music Appreciation course into something more than a throwaway course that students hate, it was ultimately student reactions and feedback that led me to a larger project of not only decentering whiteness via diversity and inclusion but also one of antiracist teaching and learning.[1] I compiled diverse and inclusive content before asking the students about it, and then when I asked them about it later they overwhelmingly affirmed the positive impact. The majority of music appreciation (as with music history) curricula and textbooks center whiteness, with greatness being measured by how close or far away from that whiteness someone/something is. In response to the calls for more diversity and inclusion, some textbooks have added a few token women and people of color, but all have been situated within the same patriarchal Eurocentric framework, thereby continuing (even when included) to be measured against whiteness. Despite likely good intentions, this method retains the impact of what Robin DiAngelo calls "unconscious racism."[2] In restructuring the course into a thematic organization while diversifying content, I attempted to remove the hegemony of the Western European classical canon by presenting those musics in a way where they were situated alongside music of non-European cultures, women, people of color, and diverse expressions of gender and sexuality. In doing so this also helped us go beyond the "black-white binary" framework.[3] The course content does not merely include diversity among the participants of the story but situates itself among and examines diverse perspectives and celebrates the achievements and greatness of diverse groups of people.

62   TEACHING DIFFICULT TOPICS

Further, the conservatory-style system of music schools and departments in which many of us teach supports and upholds white racial bonding; the white supremacist culture of "professionalism";[4] and what Joe Feagin refers to as "backstage racism."[5] Citing the work of Feagin and his colleague Leslie Houts Picca in examining the journals of white students, George Yancy created a similar "Race Journal" assignment for his students to document observed incidents of "backstage racism."[6] Though currently outside the scope of student assignments for my introductory-level music appreciation course, I began chronicling encounters with people, policies, and course content within my music department and those of colleagues, often through a lens I saw as a possible addition to Bruno Nettl's fieldwork study "Society of Musicians," in *Heartland Excursions*.[7] As with Yancy's students I found my collected observations far outnumbered those expected, even as a white-presenting male who does not see America as a post-racial environment. Keeping my own journal of "backstage racism" as it pertained to my courses and department helped inform me as a pedagogue in a way that shaped and re-shaped how (not merely 'that') I included diverse perspectives and accomplishments in my course content, and how I situated my teaching in a way that became purposefully antiracist. Student resistance to these changes (solely among white students as of the date of this publication), highlights Loren Kajikawa's assertions that music is an investment in white supremacy.[8] They come for the possessive investment, but possessive investment is what helps us understand the pushback while student responses/reactions back up Kajikawa's claims.[9] In the sense that "teaching and learning are not discrete movements [but rather] are linked gestures," the teaching of difficult topics is "teaching the segregated and suppressed, the banned and the exiled."[10] Because difficult and uncomfortable topics often lead to more student engagement, productive discomfort has been shown to work as an effective learning tool, echoing the words of Frederick Douglass in the "West India Emancipation" speech: "If there is no struggle, there is no progress." Particularly in discussions of difficult topics like race (though I have found the same in those of gender and sexuality), Pamela Barnett advocates for strategically "Negotiating Content" rather than avoiding or eliminating it.[11] We must honor pushback, which occurs often for those of us doing interdisciplinary work, but also must help students navigate that pushback.

While issues surrounding religion, systems of privilege and oppression, race, gender and LGBTQ+ communities, etc. are not new to music history and appreciation classrooms, I find myself, like many of my colleagues, in a difficult place (geographically and departmentally), to introduce those topics and methodological approaches. Teaching at a regional university of about 15,000 students, I am confronted with the realities of trying to introduce intersectional approaches dealing with topics not popular in a politically conservative environment. Moreover, my University is in a parish in Louisiana which still has current, active branches of the Ku Klux Klan, making student pushback, especially with topics involving race, one of my biggest challenges. Adding to this difficulty is that the Music Appreciation textbook used not only centers whiteness in its content but is also a department-wide dictate for which individual instructors have no input.

Citing the AAC&U's list of the "Top Ten Things Employees Look For in New College Graduates," I began to restructure the outdated historical-timeline-survey model of my music appreciation course in the summer of 2018.[12] Shifting the focus from content to skills-via-content, I began to examine ways in which students could find relevance in this course (often a dreaded fine arts requirement of non-majors). In the course's introductory lecture, I discussed the AAC&U list and specific, tangentially related skills that students could gain through our study of music. In an anonymous survey following this lecture, students were asked to identify two skills, of several listed, that they hoped to gain from this course. Woven among teamwork, writing, and listening skills was an option for learning about experiences and cultures outside of their own. In the most recent eleven iterations of this course, the overwhelming majority of students indicated they wanted to increase their knowledge and understanding of cultures and lived experiences that were not their own. This data seemed promising given my class demographics were majority white and considering these results in the context of recent research among college students regarding discussions of race. A 2016 Pew Research Center poll showed that black students identified discussing commonalities and differences between races as equally important while the majority of white students thought it was only important to discuss commonalities.[13] Because the research indicated students of color have more experience discussing race than their white colleagues, I felt it important to note the class demographics as it relates to both desire to learn about other cultures and pushback from that learning and the discussion of difficult topics (particularly those of race). In an online welcome assignment, the students identifying as BIPOC were consistently around twenty to thirty percent of the class over multiple semesters and multiple years. This aligns with the University's published demographics of 36.36% BIPOC students.[14]

Inspired by the topic-based organization of Steven Cornelius and Mary Natvig's text *Music: A Social Experience* (which is not our department-adopted text),[15] and initiatives of the American Alliance of Museums and The Inclusive Museum Project to utilize theme-based curation,[16] I created a theme-based music course in which various intersectional and sometimes "difficult" topics are interwoven into the traditional music appreciation course content.[17] The diversifying of content, especially, led me to also incorporate aspects of anti-racist teaching. By removing the temporal organization of content from the traditional, historical or six-period timeline and instead inserting that same content into thematic sections, I was able to create a learning experience that didn't Other difficult topics as outlying asides separate from Western Eurocentric Music, but rather treated these topics as co-equal content within the course curriculum. Because I reorganized the content from the department-sanctioned text into themes, it then allowed me to artfully insert non-Western and popular musics into our study while showing their direct relation to the topics at hand. In addition to diversifying the content, this also paved the way for me to more broadly utilize different methodological approaches from critical and comparative theories, thereby adding another layer of both extramusical content and extramusical skills.

The first two weeks of the course comprise an introductory unit of foundational material to both music and the interdisciplinary approaches we encounter. Some of the subsequent organizational themes include: Music, Gender, and Sexuality; Music and Dance; and Music and Social Movements. Situating the course content of the required text within these broad themes allows me to integrate content from outside the text (and the Western art music narrative). Removing the organization based on historical timeline balances breadth and depth, while emphasizing relationships across different cultures paves the way to address both commonalities and differences. For example, in the unit on Music and Dance we learn canon standards from European Renaissance and Baroque genres as well as the various goings on at the Ballets Russes, but do so alongside dance traditions from the Americas and Africa. I worked to make this section especially relevant to my students when viewed with localized Louisianian perspectives. We begin our non-European examples by examining Ann Powers's assertion that American music IS dance music by looking at the archival correspondence of Thomas C. Nicholls, whose reminiscences of early 19th-century New Orleans serve as a firsthand account of daily life.[18] Almost a hundred years before Jazz, Powers notes Nicholls's observations that "New Orleans was dance-mad" and further that "music became the medium through which dancers absorbed the city's myriad subcultures—even ones that law and propriety might have kept them from openly embracing."[19] Discussing the roots, style, and execution of traditional Angolan Capoeira from African/Brazilian cultures allows us to pivot into examining music cultures at the Louisiana State Penitentiary, also known as "Angola." Watching clips from Benjamin Harbert's 2012 documentary *Follow Me Down: Portraits of Louisiana Prison Musicians* allows us to use local music-making to study the racialized past and present of Angola Prison, and as a platform for critiquing the Louisiana prison system and the storied political history therein.[20] Examining socio-political elements of prisons through a musical lens also allows us to look at the anti-black systemic racism that pervades almost every element of United States History.[21] In discussions such as these we answer Ijeoma Oluo's calls to "include the school-to-prison pipeline in . . . broader discussions of racial inequality and oppression" and to "challenge the legitimacy of white-centered education."[22]

Our course section on dance also included a section on Ghanaian "Baamaaya," which Cornelius and Natvig describe as "a colorful, traditional dance of the Dagbamba, an ethnic group residing in Ghana's Northern Region."[23] In this stylized dance, men utilize twists and extensive hip and lower body movements; in addition, it is often distinguished in that the men dress in what is traditionally considered women's clothing as parody. Baamaaya is examined in a side-by-side comparison with New Orleans Bounce music. Using Big Freedia's "Azz Everywhere" as an example, students observe striking similarities in both the movements and dress of the performers (people assigned male at birth wearing feminine-gendered clothing). This gives us the framework to discuss creole, black, and queer identities in New Orleans Bounce music and its shift from the hypermasculinity of Rap subgenres to its controversial popularization by Queer and Transgender individuals, as many popular Bounce performers present some visible element of queer or trans identity. Doing so also serves as a space to scaffold in some of the critical tools we learned and utilized in the earlier course section on gender and sexuality to discuss queer spaces and methodologies, to critique clothing as gender markers, the queerness of not following those rules, and what it means across different countries, societies, and sub-groups within societies. Reiterating these examples as part of the dance unit, I also find it important to maintain the framework of the unit so that as we continue to add breadth and depth, especially with intersectionality, students are at all times able to see how music remains at the core.

At my institution, race seems to be one of the more difficult topics to bring into the music classroom. I am careful to avoid launching into what Ijeoma Oluo describes as "racial dialogues filled with assumptions, stereotypes, and microaggressions that [I] am completely unaware of."[24] Even the inclu-

66   TEACHING DIFFICULT TOPICS

sion of blackface minstrelsy content early in the semester caused anger in some white students that they were being "forced" to acknowledge its mere existence, let alone discuss race and power structures relevant to the genre.

Having used the dance unit as an introduction to our discussions of race, I continue to scaffold more in-depth study in a subsequent unit on nationalism and protest music by comparing the United States National Anthem as sung by The Chicks (formerly The Dixie Chicks) with instrumental versions played by The President's Own military band and Jimi Hendrix's 1969 live Woodstock performance. Not only does this activity have students engage in critical analysis and use music terminology they have learned, but it also lets us consider similarities and relevance to the current social and political climate in the United States. Once students have a framework for these issues presented through the country and patriotic genres they seem to find more palatable, we can pivot to the unit on Music and Social Movements.[25] Two things are done to help mitigate unproductive student resistance or classroom disruptions in what seems to be the toughest unit to navigate pedagogically: a mini-workshop on observer objectivity and a *fishbowl* discussion. When dealing with topics like race, police brutality, and artistic reactions to both, I have found success in using the *fishbowl* classroom setup, which Adriana Estill notes "can provide some intimacy for a difficult topic while also inviting all to participate. A small group of four to six students sit at the center and begins the conversation. The remaining students sit in a larger circle around them, listening. Students 'tap out' participants in order to join the inner circle."[26] This lowers the occurrence of disruptive outbursts, and the time taken by the tap out gives students more time to think about constructive responses rather than to immediately react. Successful pedagogy may come from what we don't do or say but rather creating and holding safe, tolerant, spaces for students to communicate among themselves. Leonard Moore recollected his Black Power class in November 2014 following the decision of the St. Louis district attorney to not indict Darren Wilson for Michael Brown's murder. Rather than make a verbal statement he made a statement which held more power, having the class talk to each other.[27] Especially when dealing with difficult topics in the classroom, I have often found the most success in simply getting "offstage" and letting the students learn from each other. It is incumbent upon us to create environments for our students to have these conversations as "students often avoid the 'contentious and difficult.'"[28]

Our social movements unit is also prefaced by an avatar-based discussion and activity where students list avatars of different hypothetical, historically situated, persons (broadly defined) and discuss viewpoints, beliefs, and posi-

Decentering Whiteness in the Music Appreciation Classroom   67

tions of those people in the context of our course material.[29] This allows them to step back and take a viewpoint more as an objective cultural anthropologist than allowing their personal views to adulterate their observations and critique. This activity teaches students how to observe and critique through an objective, academic lens, in which they learn to not let biases interfere with their study. After this setup and our in-class discussions, students are given a low-stakes writing assignment which asks them to do a comparative analysis of the text, music, and music video images between Lauryn Hill's "Black Rage" and G-Unit's "Ahhh Shit." Because "Black Rage" uses the familiar melody of "My Favorite Things" from Rodgers and Hammerstein's 1959 musical *The Sound of Music*, it appeals to a broader audience and the text acts as much as a tool of education and empathy as a call to action. "Ahhh Shit" on the other hand is an artistic expression of anger channeled through music as felt by the black community following the deaths of Michael Brown, Eric Gardner, and Trayvon Martin. This music was created as an outlet, not as an outreach.[30] Many of the white students first point out the strong and even violent anti-police language. This assignment and subsequent class discussion also provides a good example of student pushback. When discussing these two pieces in terms of audience, reception, and for whom, specifically, these works were written, many of the white students are surprised when I ask them to consider that they need not tolerate the language and anti-police sentiment, nor need they even understand the piece because it was not written for them.[31] More than the language and anti-police themes, the student reactions to exclusion and being told this music was not written for them elicits the same responses described by DiAngelo in *White Fragility*: "emotions such as anger, fear, and guilt and behaviors such as argumentation, silence, and withdrawal from the stress-inducing situation. These responses work to reinstate white equilibrium as they repel the challenge, return our racial comfort, and maintain our dominance with the racial hierarchy."[32] For many white students this may have been the first time in their education learning about black perspectives and experiences and, having never been confronted with information outside or in relation to the white racial frame, they do not have the requisite skills to navigate this information or the types of critiques we discuss.[33]

Through data collected over the course of eleven semesters, student impact has shown to be overall positive, despite some anticipated pushback. Student pushback has been almost entirely centered around discussions relating to systems of privilege and oppression, and by students identifying with the oppressor group, whether that be straight, cisgender, white, male,

Christian, etc. Here my data includes the qualitative, documented statements students have made in response to various prompts, assessments, and evaluations of the course, which clearly show the impact this inclusive and divergent course organization has had on students of various races, ethnicities, genders, religions, and political ideologies. Despite most students indicating a desire or willingness to learn about cultures and experiences of other people in the introductory survey, one of the most difficult experiences I have had to navigate is egocentrism and intense student pushback. Following a discussion of blackface minstrelsy and modern instances of blackface in theater or at Halloween, one white student responded that they did not believe that this should be offensive, arguing that just like any other performance it was art and music.[34] When discussing race, pushback has thus far been entirely from white students. The opening epigraph to this essay is an anonymous student response from end-of-semester teaching evaluations during the second semester of teaching this newly designed course. Regarding an assignment examining some of the musical reactions to police brutality and the events surrounding the protests of 2020 one student refused to complete the assignment. "I watched the videos pertaining to this assignment and it goes against my personal beliefs and morals. I refuse to complete the assignment. Having grown up in a first responder family this upsets me immensely. I signed up for a music class and not a class about politics. I understand that music will overlap with the times and current social happenings. I do not feel that it is okay to force students to listen to music like that and feel as though an agenda is being forced upon them."[35] While I actively encourage free discussion, dissent, and debate in class, students thus far have not voiced pushback publicly but rather via email and in end-of-semester evaluations. Having said that, one of my classroom ground rules is that in any of our discussions and work we do not give a platform for harmfully violent views that further dehumanize minoritized students and identities. What we are discussing is their experiences learning about equity, but there is no safe space for their violence. Adding to the pedagogical difficulties inherent in teaching this material are anecdotes such as that of Minneapolis Community and Technical College tenured professor Shannon Gibney's reprimand of conduct when two white male students became angry she was discussing institutionalized racism in a communications class.[36] Some of the student feedback and evaluations I've received feel uncomfortably familiar to the complaints against professor Gibney. Some students find uncomfortable the way this material invites them to confront some of their biases, and examining music within these contexts often interrupts white comfort. The anger and pushback evidenced in this student feedback serves as an example of white fragility, a term originally coined by Robin DiAngelo describing how "the smallest amount of racial stress is intolerable—the mere suggestion that being white has meaning often triggers a range of defensive responses."[37] However, the email from the student with the "first responder family" brings two important points to bear that seem to occur around these discussions of difficult topics in music: 1) why are we learning about this non-music content or seemingly unrelated issues in a music class, and 2) what authority or expertise do I, as a music professor, have to teach topics involving race, gender studies, politics, etc. Cyndi Kernahan discusses the importance of making explicit our individual expertise and affirming the expertise of the students.[38] She goes on to talk about affirmation theory and how affirming a student's expertise allows us to also claim ownership of our own experiences and expertise.[39] As a white-presenting cisgender male I think it is important to discuss these issues in the context of my lived experience and lifelong learning. Having lived and worked in New Orleans and, working to know about place (given the highly political nature of spaces), I openly talk about my work in the Historic New Orleans Collection archives, my research and participant-observation in New Orleans Bounce clubs, and my passion for politics and civic engagement—all of these deeply rooted in my scholarly journey.

As this course continues to morph each semester, the constant difficulty I experience is the facilitation of content that causes students to confront biases (both personal and systemic). Adding to this difficulty are current national news events which have caused many students to double down on certain tribalisms and become more averse to learning some of this content and thinking about things in different ways. From the outset I make explicit the learning goals of this course include, but also go beyond, gaining factual knowledge of music content as well as gaining or strengthening objective and critical thinking skills and broader understandings of the many ways music functions in various similar and differing cultures. For those finding difficulty I think the first step is to remove the structures which center and privilege whiteness so that all diversity and inclusion measures you incorporate are presented alongside and as equal to traditional music appreciation course content. This is especially important for colleagues in situations like mine where they use a department-adopted text. Once students are presented with this type of structure as the norm, it becomes easier to incorporate other disciplinary elements which hopefully seem less radical and less removed from the opening epigraph's demands for a class on: "the history of music."

The larger significance of this course design is that, despite some push-

70   TEACHING DIFFICULT TOPICS

back, inclusive curriculum improves student success.[40] This is embedded in the larger national movement toward inclusive curricula and practices of teaching and learning as the research shows this improves student success, retention, and persistence to graduation. A truly inclusive curriculum is one where various student identities and lived experiences are represented in the course content, and where the learning process invites them to connect their identity and lived experience to what they are learning. Equitable teaching processes, in-class activities, and assignments, invite students to connect their lived experiences to what they are learning and to have those be valued equally. Additionally, students are able to actively see their identities represented in inclusive curricula. In an equitable curriculum, students can see their identity as one of many, rather than some students still seeing their identity as minoritized in a primarily white context which further marginalizes.[41] Even so, "Psychological and instructional interventions are only a modest step forward and are far from sufficient to deal with past and present impacts of racial oppression inflicted on African Americans and other Americans of color" and there needs to be advocacy for macro-level changes.[42]

In the future, further adaptation will be required given pushback legislated by civil servants. As we see a polarized national discussion in which legislators want to restrict equitable content and processes, the work that remains for the future is a better understanding of how to maneuver through and find better teaching resources for this constantly changing landscape. We must and will find new ways to explain the value of diversity, equity, and inclusion as part of the content and skills that we teach.

Notes

1. Ibram Kendi, *How To Be An Antiracist* (New York: One World, 2019).

2. Robin DiAngelo, *Nice Racism: How Progressive White People Perpetuate Racial Harm* (Boston: Beacon Press, 2021).

3. Richard Delgado and Jean Stefancic, *Critical Race Theory: An Introduction*, 2nd edition (New York: New York University Press, 2012), 75–98.

4. See Tema Okun, *White Supremacy Culture*, https://www.whitesupremacyculture .info/, accessed June 30, 2023. This is a recent update of the 1999 article: Tema Okun, "White Supremacy Culture," *Dismantling Racism Works*, https://www.dismantlingraci sm.org/uploads/4/3/5/7/43579015/okun_-_white_sup_culture.pdf

5. Feagan writes, ". . . my colleagues and I have found that much blatantly racist thought, commentary, and performance has become concentrated in the social backstage where only whites are present. Much less is performed in the social frontstage settings where there are strangers or people from diverse racial groups present. This

Decentering Whiteness in the Music Appreciation Classroom 71

is because of pressures to be socially correct (colorblind) in frontstage areas such as workplaces and public accommodations." Joe R. Feagin, *The White Racial Frame: Centuries of Racial Framing and Counter-Framing*, 2nd ed. (New York: Routledge, 2013), 123. See also: Loren Kajikawa, "The Possessive Investment in Classical Music: Confronting Legacies of White Supremacy in U.S. Schools and Departments of Music," in *Seeing Race Again: Countering Colorblindness across the Disciplines*, ed. Kimberlé Williams Crenshaw, Luke Charles Harris, Daniel Martinez HoSang, and George Lipsitz (Berkeley: University of California Press, 2019), 155–74.

6. Yancy writes, "At the beginning of my courses on race, I assign my white students the task of keeping a journal or diary of their everyday encounters with white racism, many of which they would normally simply overlook or interpret as of no significant meaning for themselves or their white friends and family members whom they are required to record." George Yancy, "Guidelines for Whites Teaching About Whiteness," in Stephen D. Brookfield and Associates, *Teaching Race: How to Help Students Unmask and Challenge Racism* (San Francisco: Jossey-Bass, 2019), 33.

7. Bruno Nettl, "Society of Musicians," in *Heartland Excursions: Ethnomusicological Reflections on Schools of Music* (Urbana and Chicago: University of Illinois Press, 1995).

8. Kajikawa, "The Possessive Investment in Classical Music."

9. Kajikawa examines music as cultural currency of whiteness through the lens of George Lipsitz's assertions that whiteness is a social construct and "fictive identity." Lipsitz argues that various structural and systemic advantages maintain the comforts and benefits of whiteness and those who benefit "possessively" cling to these structures at all costs to maintain hierarchies they enjoy. George Lipsitz, "The Possessive Investment in Whiteness: Racialized Social Democracy and the 'White' Problem in American Studies," *American Quarterly* 47, no. 3 (Sep., 1995): 369–87. George Lipsitz, *The Possessive Investment in Whiteness: How White People Profit from Identity Politics* (Philadelphia: Temple University Press, 1998; 2018).

10. Rick Ayers and William Ayers, *Teaching the Taboo: Courage and Imagination in the Classroom*, second edition (New York: Teachers College Press, 2014), 97.

11. Pamela E. Barnett, "Building Trust and Negotiating Content When Teaching Race," in *Stephen D. Brookfield and Associates, Teaching Race: How to Help Students Unmask and Challenge Racism* (San Francisco: Jossey-Bass, 2019), 121–28.

12. "How Should Colleges Prepare Students to Succeed in Today's Global Economy?" Based on Surveys Among Employers and Recent College Graduates, Conducted on Behalf of The Association of American Colleges and Universities (Washington, DC: Peter D. Hart Research Associates, December 28, 2006), http://www.sg.inter.edu /wp-content/uploads/Documentos/asuntos_academicos/PEG/How_Should_Colle ges_Prepare_Students_To_Succeed_in_Todays_Global_Economy_AACU_2006.pdf; see also Hart Research Associates, "Fulfilling the American Dream: Liberal Education and the Future of Work," July 2018, https://www.aacu.org/sites/default/files/files /LEAP/2018EmployerResearchReport.pdf; Hart Research Associates, "It Takes More Than a Major," *Liberal Education* 99, no. 2 (Spring 2013), https://www.aacu.org/publ

72   TEACHING DIFFICULT TOPICS

ications-research/periodicals/it-takes-more-major-employer-priorities-college-learn ing-and

13. "On Views of Race and Inequality, Blacks and Whites Are Worlds Apart," Pew Research Center, June 27, 2016. Accessed June, 15, 2020, https://www.pewsocialtrends.org /2016/06/27/on-views-of-race-and-inequality-blacks-and-whites-are-worlds-apart/

14. Southeastern Louisiana University, "Fast Facts [Demographic Highlights]" https://www.southeastern.edu/about/general/index.html; Numerical breakdown published as: Southeastern Louisiana University "2022 University Race/Ethnicity Distribution: [Chart] Enrollment by Race/Ethnicity." https://www.univstats.com/colleg es/southeastern-louisiana-university/student-population/#:~:text=There%20are%20 13%2C456%20students%20including,male%20and%208%2C586%20female%20stud ents

15. Steven Cornelius and Mary Natvig, *Music: A Social Experience*, second edition (New York: Routledge, 2019).

16. IMP is a Project of The Inclusive Museum Research Network, a group founded in 2008 whose goal is to bring inclusivity to museums and whose mission is organized by the three themes of Visitors, Collections, and Representations, each with various aims and considerations.

17. Since the original writing of this essay, Esther Morgan-Ellis has released a similar theme-based Music Appreciation text which is available as a free open educational resource (OER). Esther Morgan-Ellis, ed., *Resonances: Engaging Music in Its Cultural Context* (Dahlonega: University of North Georgia Press, 2020). https://open.umn.edu /opentextbooks/textbooks/891

18. Housed in the Special Collections of Hill Memorial Library at Louisiana State University are the Col. W.W. Pugh family papers and a record book written by Thomas C. Nicholls. These reminiscences authored by Nicholls, dating from 1840–1842, document the move of the Nicholls family from Baltimore, MD to New Orleans in 1805 while Thomas was a 17-year-old military school student.

19. Ann Powers, *Good Booty: Love and Sex, Black and White, Body and Soul in American Music* (New York: HarperCollins Publishers, 2017), 8.

20. Benjamin J. Harbert, dir., *Follow Me Down: Portraits of Louisiana Prison Musicians*, (Films for the Humanities & Sciences: 2012).

21. Ibram X. Kendi, *Stamped from the Beginning: The Definitive History of Racist Ideas in America* (New York: Bold Type Books, 2016).

22. Ijeoma Oluo, *So You Want to Talk About Race* (New York: Hachette Book Group, 2018), 129/132.

23. Steven Cornelius and Mary Natvig, *Music: A Social Experience*, second edition (New York: Routledge, 2019), 254.

24. Oluo, *So You Want to Talk About Race*, 39.

25. This section of the course is informed by my reading of Rob Rosenthal and Richard Flacks, *Playing for Change: Music and Musicians in the Service of Social Movements* (Boulder, CO: Paradigm Publishers, 2012).

26. Adriana Estill, "Feeling Our Way to Knowing: Decolonizing the American Studies Classroom," in *Difficult Subjects: Insights and Strategies for Teaching About Race, Sexuality, and Gender*, eds. Badia Ahad-Legardy and OiYan A. Poon (Sterling, VA: Stylus Publishing, 2018), 121.

27. Leonard N. Moore, *Teaching Black History to White People* (Austin: University of Texas Press, 2021).

28. Novella Z. Keith, "Getting Beyond Anaemic Love: From the Pedagogy of Cordial Relations to a Pedagogy for Difference," *Journal of Curriculum Studies* 42 (4): 539–72; also cited in Pamela E. Barnett, "Building Trust and Negotiating Conflict When Teaching Race," in Stephen Brookfield & Associates, *Teaching Race: How to Help Students Unmask and Challenge Racism* (San Francisco: Jossey-Bass, 2019), 111.

29. For more on the pedagogical use of avatars, see Washington Collado et al., "Why Scenarios as an Educational Tool?," in *Beyond Conversations About Race: A Guide for Discussions with Students, Teachers, and Communities* (Bloomington, IN: Solution Tree Press, 2021), 29–32.

30. See Loren Kajikawa, *Sounding Race in Rap Songs* (Oakland: University of California Press, 2015).

31. See Jennifer Lynn Stoever, *The Sonic Color Line: Race and the Cultural Politics of Listening* (New York: New York University Press, 2016).

32. Robin DiAngelo. *White Fragility: Why It's So Hard for White People to Talk About Racism* (Boston: Beacon Press, 2018), 2.

33. Moore, *Teaching Black History to White People.*

34. Fall 2021 student response. Here I use "egocentric" not as a pejorative but merely to be descriptive of the responses. The argument for student inability to understand another perspective is strengthened in this case when the same student was outraged in a later discussion of music and text that spoke about hearing Orlando di Lasso's "Matona mia cara" was performed in a church Christmas concert.

35. Anonymized student email, 2021. Via Louisiana Public Records RS 44:1, §1.A.(2) (a).

36. Colleen Flaherty, "Taboo Subject?" in *Inside Higher Ed*, December 2, 2013. Flaherty goes on to point out that after this particular incident "Gibney engaged a national audience in her struggles with an article on Gawker, called 'Teaching while Black and Blue.' It reveals this semester's complaint is the third time she's been investigated by the college for talking about race." https://www.insidehighered.com/news /2013/12/03/black-professors-essay-raises-questions-why-she-was-investigated-aft er-offending

37. DiAngelo. *White Fragility: Why It's So Hard for White People to Talk About Racism*, 2. DiAngelo originally coined the term in her 2011 article "White Fragility" in the *International Journal of Critical Pedagogy*.

38. Cyndi Kernahan, *Teaching About Race and Racism in the College Classroom: Notes from a White Professor* (Morgantown: West Virginia University Press, 2019), 37.

39. Kernahan, *Teaching about Race and Racism*, 38–41.

74   TEACHING DIFFICULT TOPICS

40. See Tia Brown McNair, Susan Albertine, Michelle Asha Cooper, Nicole McDonald, Thomas Major, Jr., *Becoming A Student-Ready College: A New Culture of Leadership for Student Success* (San Francisco: Jossey-Bass, 2016); Cia Verschelden, *Bandwidth Recovery: Helping Students Reclaim Cognitive Resources Lost to Poverty, Racism, and Social Marginalization* (Sterling, VA: Stylus Publishing, 2017).

41. Frank Tuitt, Chayla Haynes, and Saran Stewart, eds., *Race, Equity, and the Learning Environment: The Global Relevance of Critical and Inclusive Pedagogies in Higher Education* (Sterling, VA: Stylus Publishing, 2016).

42. Joe R. Feagin, *The White Racial Frame: Centuries of Racial Framing and Counter-Framing*, 2nd ed. (New York: Routledge, 2013), 218.

Works Cited

Ahad-Legardy, Badia, and OiYan A. Poon, eds. *Difficult Subjects: Insights and Strategies for Teaching About Race, Sexuality, and Gender.* Sterling, VA: Stylus Publishing, 2018.

Ayers, Rick, and William Ayers. *Teaching the Taboo: Courage and Imagination in the Classroom*, second edition. New York: Teachers College Press, 2014.

Brookfield, Stephen D., & Associates. *Teaching Race: How to Help Students Unmask and Challenge Racism.* San Francisco: Jossey-Bass, 2019.

Collado, Washington, et al. "Why Scenarios as an Educational Tool?," in *Beyond Conversations About Race: A Guide for Discussions with Students, Teachers, and Communities.* Bloomington, IN: Solution Tree Press, 2021.

Cornelius, Steven, and Mary Natvig. *Music: A Social Experience*, second edition. New York: Routledge, 2019.

Delgado, Richard, and Jean Stefancic. *Critical Race Theory: An Introduction*, 2nd edition. New York: New York University Press, 2012.

DiAngelo, Robin. *Nice Racism: How Progressive White People Perpetuate Racial Harm.* Boston: Beacon Press, 2021.

DiAngelo, Robin. *White Fragility: Why It's So Hard for White People to Talk about Racism.* Boston: Beacon Press, 2018.

Feagin, Joe R. *The White Racial Frame: Centuries of Racial Framing and Counter-Framing*, 2nd ed. New York: Routledge, 2013.

Flaherty, Colleen. "Taboo Subject?" in *Inside Higher Ed*, December 2, 2013. https://www.insidehighered.com/news/2013/12/03/black-professors-essay-raises-questions-why-she-was-investigated-after-offending

Harbert, Benjamin J., dir. *Follow Me Down: Portraits of Louisiana Prison Musicians.* Films for the Humanities & Sciences: 2012.

Hart Research Associates. "Fulfilling the American Dream: Liberal Education and the Future of Work." July 2018. https://www.aacu.org/sites/default/files/files/LEAP/2018EmployerResearchReport.pdf

Hart Research Associates. "It Takes More Than a Major." *Liberal Education* 99, no. 2 (Spring 2013). https://www.aacu.org/publications-research/periodicals/it-takes-more-major-employer-priorities-college-learning-and

Hart Research Associates. "How Should Colleges Prepare Students to Succeed in Today's Global Economy?" Based on Surveys Among Employers and Recent College Graduates, Conducted on Behalf of The Association of American Colleges and Universities (Washington, DC: Peter D. Hart Research Associates, December 28, 2006), http://www.sg.inter.edu/wp-content/uploads/Documentos/asuntos_academicos /PEG/How_Should_Colleges_Prepare_Students_To_Succeed_in_Todays_Global _Economy_AACU_2006.pdf

Kajikawa, Loren. "The Possessive Investment in Classical Music: Confronting Legacies of White Supremacy in U.S. Schools and Departments of Music." In *Seeing Race Again: Countering Colorblindness across the Disciplines*, ed. by Kimberlé Williams Crenshaw, Luke Charles Harris, Daniel Martinez HoSang, and George Lipsitz, 155–74. Berkeley: University of California Press, 2019.

Kajikawa, Loren. *Sounding Race in Rap Songs*. Oakland: University of California Press, 2015.

Keith, Novella Z. "Getting Beyond Anaemic Love: From the Pedagogy of Cordial Relations to a Pedagogy for Difference." *Journal of Curriculum Studies* 42 (4): 539–72.

Kendi, Ibram X. *How To Be An Antiracist*. New York: One World, 2019.

Kendi, Ibram X. *Stamped from the Beginning: The Definitive History of Racist Ideas in America*. New York: Bold Type Books, 2016.

Kernahan, Cyndi. *Teaching about Race and Racism in the College Classroom: Notes from a White Professor*. Morgantown: University of West Virginia Press, 2019.

Lipsitz, George. "The Possessive Investment in Whiteness: Racialized Social Democracy and the 'White' Problem in American Studies." *American Quarterly* 47, no. 3 (Sep., 1995): 369–87.

Lipsitz, George. *The Possessive Investment in Whiteness: How White People Profit from Identity Politics*. Philadelphia: Temple University Press, 1998; 2018.

McNair, Tia Brown, Susan Albertine, Michelle Asha Cooper, Nicole McDonald, Thomas Major, Jr. *Becoming A Student-Ready College: A New Culture of Leadership for Student Success*. San Francisco: Jossey-Bass, 2016.

Moore, Leonard N. *Teaching Black History to White People*. Austin: University of Texas Press, 2021.

Morgan-Ellis, Esther, ed. *Resonances: Engaging Music in Its Cultural Context* (Dahlonega: University of North Georgia Press, 2020). https://open.umn.edu/opentextbooks /textbooks/891

Nettl, Bruno. *Heartland Excursions: Ethnomusicological Reflections on Schools of Music*. Urbana and Chicago: University of Illinois Press, 1995.

Oluo, Ijeoma. *So You Want to Talk About Race*. New York: Hachette Book Group, 2018.

Pew Research Center. "On Views of Race and Inequality, Blacks and Whites Are Worlds Apart." June 27, 2016. https://www.pewsocialtrends.org/2016/06/27/on-views-of-ra ce-and-inequality-blacks-and-whites-are-worlds-apart/

Powers, Ann. *Good Booty: Love and Sex, Black and White, Body and Soul in American Music*. New York: HarperCollins Publishers, 2017.

Rosenthal, Rob, and Richard Flacks. *Playing for Change: Music and Musicians in the Service of Social Movements*. Boulder, CO: Paradigm Publishers, 2012.

Stoever, Jennifer Lynn. *The Sonic Color Line: Race and the Cultural Politics of Listening*. New York: New York University Press, 2016.

Tuitt, Frank, Chayla Haynes, and Saran Stewart, eds. *Race, Equity, and the Learning Environment: The Global Relevance of Critical and Inclusive Pedagogies in Higher Education*. Sterling, VA: Stylus Publishing, 2016.

Verschelden, Cia. *Bandwidth Recovery: Helping Students Reclaim Cognitive Resources Lost to Poverty, Racism, and Social Marginalization*. Sterling, VA: Stylus Publishing, 2017.

CHAPTER 5

Opera and Masculinity

Sean M. Parr

"What does it mean to be a *real* man?"
"What does it mean to *sound* masculine?"
"How does one *sing* like a man?"

Pause for awkward silence—only rarely does a student venture a response. Posing such questions can put students (and readers) on the defensive, confronting them with masculinity's contingent, fraught status. By beginning my opera and gender class with rhetorical questions like these I can challenge students to think carefully about their assumptions about masculinity and to question their and our society's construction of gender. Our era is one of complicated perspectives on sex and gender, and while we are likely in the midst of a paradigm shift, traditional gender roles continue to exert a strong influence. And for most of the undergraduate students at our small liberal arts school, this course is the first and possibly only time they have a sustained, critical engagement with gender. Naturally, because the topic is something that crucially informs their identities but is viewed as perhaps too personal or too controversial, the construction of gender—masculinity in particular—is a difficult topic for many students to discuss.

My opera and gender course covers both masculinity and femininity—with units that explore opera as the "undoing" and "empowering" of women, while also interrogating opera's presentation of men.[1] But even (or perhaps especially) as a cisgender male professor, I have noticed that discussing masculinity can be more intimidating to students than discussing femininity.[2] Thus, though I engage students in exploring female voices more than male voices in the course, I have chosen to focus on masculinity in this chapter because of the way discussions of the male operatic voice can challenge students.

In a way, with its wild, dramatic, and almost unbelievable performances of gender, opera offers enough distance from the intimate reality of the pres-

77

78   TEACHING DIFFICULT TOPICS

ent for students to become more comfortable discussing the topic. Although opera conforms in certain ways to gender norms, it also offers striking, even shocking, examples that defy society's conventions of gender and voice. In fact, opera has long featured women dressed like men and men singing like women. Examples of such gender crossing and ambiguity make opera the perfect vehicle for teaching students about how gender and bodies can be constructed and read.

Of course, while the outrageousness of gender presented on the operatic stage can embolden students to discuss the construction of gender more easily, the historical veracity of such examples can also be difficult for students to accept; in our seminar class of 12–18 students (only a few of whom are music majors or minors), opera, as well as gender, are academic topics new to them. In this essay, I examine how two historicized operatic case studies help students in the seminar interrogate traditional ideas of masculinity: operatic castrati and the tenor hero. The cases introduce students to historical constructions of gender and to current ways of thinking and writing about issues of gender and sexuality, facilitating their development of an informed, self-aware position in relation to recent scholarship and challenging them to rethink notions of looking and sounding "masculine." I hope that readers gain ideas that might offer models for approaching opera and gender in their own classes, ones that will help students listen differently to the gendering of voice.

On our first day in class, I draw students' attention to gender conventions first by posing the rhetorical questions of this chapter's epigraph, and then by asking students to articulate their ideas about stereotypical masculinity. In response, they call out many adjectives describing the look of masculinity (facial and body hair, a v-shaped torso, chiseled features, a muscular frame), as well as character traits (powerful, strong, brave, dominant, risk-taking, unemotional, consumed by thinking about sex). Occasionally, students will mention the masculinity of a low, deep voice, but they are generally unaccustomed to discussing gendered sound and voice. Nor are students apt to consider how masculinity is contingent, something that can only be achieved, something that must be continually demonstrated, even proven.

Finally, I tell them that over the course of the semester, we will see that gender is *performed* both on and off stage—that it is not natural or innate—and that ambiguous gender can provoke cognitive dissonance as audiences try to massage a character's identity into one that aligns with their preconceived notions of gender. Since students begin the semester less accustomed to viewing gender as a topic for critical analysis, this hopefully primes students to think critically about gender, both on the operatic stage and off. What is at stake for students is nothing less than a radical re-thinking of how we understand gender, challenging their assumptions about the way we read and hear gender. As a course that also serves as part of my institution's core aesthetic engagement requirement, students learn to respond to artistic expression with increasing sophistication and engage in the various debates about the character and purposes of aesthetic forms as expressions of meaning, as sources of beauty, and as objects of critical inquiry. As they learn to understand how opera reflects particular historical and cultural contexts, students also recognize, at the same time, a wide spectrum of human creativity and gender expression. In doing so, they begin to undo their assumptions about gender and reconstruct and refine their understanding of what it means to sound masculine (and feminine).

Before I assign theoretical and historical readings, we watch a video of philosopher and gender theorist Judith Butler explaining the performativity of gender.[3] This excellent three-minute video explains the concept of performativity (as "producing a series of effects," thus differentiating it from performance) and presents a starting point for our discussion about how gender is created, how it is continually being produced, and how it is the consolidation of behaviors. I unpack several of Butler's claims and explanations with the class as we deconstruct conventional ideas of gender. For example, Butler states: "We act and walk and speak and talk in ways that consolidate an impression of being a man or being a woman." This sentence by itself prompts an often-spirited discussion of gendered behaviors, and can lead students to share their own stories of being bullied or constrained by pressure to conform to a certain stereotypically gendered behavior. Butler later relates the performativity of gender to everyday life by mentioning how non-conforming gender presentation can occasion name-calling ("sissy" and "tomboy" are their examples) and threats of violence. This raises the stakes of gender construction for students and helps them understand how much of our lives and identities—and even our physical safety—depend on certain assumptions about gender. With these high stakes in mind, the class can then turn to the case of the castrato in opera.

INCOMPLETE MEN

Beginning with castrati—the loved and hated idols of Baroque opera—spurs on our discussion of both opera and gender. Castrati on the one hand offer

80 TEACHING DIFFICULT TOPICS

students a direct case study of the vocal virtuosity of the operatic voice. On the other hand, the idea of castrati as professional adult artists who began their careers as boys whose bodies were surgically mutilated before puberty confronts students with an idea that confounds the prevailing conception of gender and sex as a binary system. A provocative example of what we might today consider a non-binary gender, the figure of the castrato shocks most students.[4] That the Catholic Church allowed the practice of castrating pre-pubescent boys for over 300 years in order to preserve the high male voice into adulthood is a historical fact difficult to face from our twenty-first-century vantage point. (It is perhaps even more disturbing for my students because I teach at a Catholic institution. Although not all castrations were carried out by the Church, castrati as professional singers [*musici*] first populated church choirs in the sixteenth century before they became celebrated stars on the operatic stage beginning in the seventeenth century.) I admit that when I introduce the topic, I emphasize and increase the shock by showing students images of the historical castratori, the tools used to perform the deed (and still used today in a modern form for animal husbandry). Students, of course, are quick to ask why this was done and the answers lead us to explore the construction of gender during the early modern period and then to consider the gendered voice.

One of the first things I explain to students during a quick overview of the subject is that our understanding of men and women as following a two-sex model of gender and anatomical difference was not firmly codified until the late eighteenth and early nineteenth centuries. Before then, as Thomas Laqueur has demonstrated, a one-sex model held sway, which imputes a hierarchy of gender, with the adult male at the top, followed by the pre-pubescent boy (an emerging male), and then the adult woman (an imperfect male).[5] Further, in the early modern Church, women were banned from choirs, and in the Papal States they were banned from the stage, leaving only men and boys allowed to perform in public. Castrati were the solution to the problem the ban created, and students are usually surprised to learn that certain castrati became hugely successful and popular singers. That the boys chosen usually came from poorer families and only a very small portion of the thousands castrated become successful opera singers helps us to discuss socioeconomic disparities and the historical commodification of children. History highlights the "rock star" castrati instead of those who didn't make it, belying the perniciousness of the practice, as does the fact that the practice continued well into the nineteenth century.

But the question of the castrato's position in the one-sex model hierarchy also allows me to encourage students to broaden their perspective on gender and sexuality. For castrati were incomplete men, and as men, they held a higher position than women, occupying a middle ground of sorts. It is at this point that I typically finish our first session and ask the class to read Roger Freitas's seminal article on the eroticism of emasculation for homework.[6] When we return, the students are eager to discuss the reading, stunned by the rigor with which Freitas demonstrates evidence that both boys and castrati were viewed as erotic objects in the early modern period. They are quick to discuss physicality, the castrato's body—sounding like a boy, but with the torso of a man, and the idea that castrati were sexually desirable. Of course, they often express disbelief, even revulsion, and it is this discomfort that provides the opportunity for us to hypothesize about the sound of the castrato's voice, the otherworldly singing that now seems mythical. We first look at images of the castrato, then read from primary sources that run the gamut from deeming the castrato voice strange to brilliant and strong (see **Appendix 5.1**).

Finally, we make the hypothetical exercise both more literal and more fun: I tell the students they will be taking a listening quiz, one that tests their ability to hear gender in the recorded operatic singing voice. The stakes are low—it's an ungraded quiz, merely a thought exercise to challenge students' assumptions about gender and voice. I preface the quiz by asking students: If many Baroque operas originally employed castrati in leading roles, how do we cast these roles today? After we discuss ideas for a bit—female sopranos and mezzos taking on the roles, tenors singing them transposed down the octave—some brave student usually asks about falsetto, leading us to consider the countertenor, a voice unknown to these liberal arts students (mostly non-music majors). The idea that men can and do cultivate their falsettos to sing operatically floors the students, and it makes them instantly curious about the sound, providing a perfect segue into the listening quiz.

The quiz compels students to think about how they align timbre and singing with notions of femininity and masculinity, and to wonder about the voice itself as identity, as gendered, and even to question the voice as something fixed, authentic, or natural. I vary the singers included on the quiz, but there are always a few favorites, such as Cecilia Bartoli, Anne Sofie von Otter, Frederica von Stade, Brigitte Fassbaender, Marilyn Horne, Michael Chance, Michael Maniaci, Philippe Jaroussky, Aris Christofellis, and of course, Alessandro Moreschi, "the last castrato." Students are prompted to write down two things as they listen to the examples: a guess at the gender of the singer, and their reasoning for the choice, i.e., why does the voice sound of a man or woman? Inevitably, students are surprised both when the answers are equally

82   TEACHING DIFFICULT TOPICS

split and when answers that are unanimous end up being completely wrong. Over time, I have noticed that students often hear Jaroussky in particular as female, and, even more interestingly, Horne as male. The survey is decidedly unscientific, but the results always cause the students frustration and wonder, lightening the mood while simultaneously allowing us to open up the conversation about sounding "powerful" and how a singer like Marilyn Horne can be heard as masculine. (Horne's use of chest voice in the "Liber scriptus" of the Verdi *Requiem* is indeed quite striking.) We pivot from issues of vocal register (chest vs. head voice) to timbre (the "hollow" sound of falsetto) to recordings and style (the otherworldly and historically removed sound of Moreschi). The chance for us to ask the paradoxical question of what constitutes a "masculine" sound in the treble vocal range allows the class to explore issues of vocal power, authority, and authenticity, while also keeping students engaged and curious. (See a sample quiz here: https://www.youtube.com/playlist?list=PL3SYrb4Nq6ej6aN88tLmlm6S5AVCcDjQ_.)

Castrati sang in a manner that their contemporaries recognized as noble and even heroic. But their numbers declined over the eighteenth century as the practice of castrating young boys for the purpose of preserving their high singing voices was increasingly questioned. As Martha Feldman has argued, it was Enlightenment morality that anchored the practice's decline.[7] The French had always held in disdain the Italian practice of castrating young boys, and when Napoléon's empire stretched into Italy, the Emperor banished the practice. He forbade castrated boys from entering the schools and conservatories, and in so doing strengthened the rights of prepubescent males in Europe. When our seminar returns later in the semester (around the seventh week) to the topic of the heroic male singer, students hear what our more familiar construction of a masculine voice sounds like on the operatic stage.

REAL MEN

By the early nineteenth century, opera needed a new heroic voice. After a brief experiment with female contralto heroes *en travestie*, the tenor reigned as Romantic hero united in love with the (female) soprano. Tenors in the nineteenth century had to learn a new vocal technique for achieving loud, trumpet-like high notes in order to gain this status, and this technique aimed to achieve the brilliant, noble, heroic, *masculine* sound formerly epitomized by the castrato voice. Tenors, beginning with Giovanni David (1790–1864) and Domenico Donzelli (1790–1873), and later Gilbert-Louis Duprez (1806–1896), began using a fuller tone to sing high notes up to high C (C5). Carrying the chest voice into the upper register was the exception rather than the rule for tenors until the 1830s and 1840s, when performers such as Duprez began to use an almost shout-like technique as a trademark of their singing. Gregory Bloch has argued persuasively that though Duprez, the tenor, composer, and pedagogue, may not have been the first to sing a loud, chested high C (the so-called *ut de poitrine* or *do di petto*), he was clearly an innovative vocal technician.[8] Employing what is commonly referred to today as "covering," "hooking," "turning," or *aggiustamento* (vowel modification or darkening), Duprez's singing often featured a veiled or darker tone than audiences were used to hearing from a tenor. Duprez lowered his larynx to achieve this sound, and this new technique was a revolution in the fundamental mode of singing. In the early nineteenth century, such a move was thought artificial and forced.

Today, this technique is a fundamental facet of everyday classical vocal training, so much so that it is more commonly described as "maintaining a low laryngeal position."[9] The resulting sound is perceived as darker, rounder, fuller, and sometimes more veiled, particularly in the middle high register, the notorious *passaggio*. When the technique is used to sing higher tones, the veiled aspect fades and the resultant sound is loud and trumpet-like.

Operatic singing became louder in general over the course of the nineteenth century. So did orchestras and instruments, responding in part to technological developments, larger theaters (and audiences), and increasing compositional demands. In response, the techniques pioneered by Duprez to increase vocal amplitude in the high range became the new standard for tenor trumpeting. Wagnerian heft further cemented this shift in the history of singing.[10]

As I detail this watershed moment in the history of singing to my students, I often demonstrate the sound of the low larynx and its effect on timbre in the upper range especially. Just as effective is a comparison of a pop star tenor (e.g., Adam Levine, Justin Timberlake) singing in the high range with an elevated larynx, with an operatic tenor singing high notes using a lower laryngeal position. Presenting the students with a sound from pop music allows them a reference point more familiar to them, heightening the contrast between high and low larynx more starkly than I can do alone. To emphasize the difference, I often play what I feel is the quintessential heroic tenor sound: Franco Corelli singing "Di quella pira" from Verdi's *Il trovatore*. I keep the volume turned up a little higher than I usually set it, in order to heighten the students' experience of visceral tenor singing, with the famously difficult and thrilling interpolated high C at the end of the cabaletta. Corelli's

84   TEACHING DIFFICULT TOPICS

singing gives students the perfect sound to correlate to our familiar notion of masculinity: loud, strong, aggressive, angry, even militaristic. In addition to discussing this straightforward gender labeling of male operatic sound, I ask students to consider how the new tenor's sound demonstrates that the nineteenth-century operatic hero is a "real man."

My hope with this discussion is twofold: first, to remind students that masculinity in this case is still fraught, still contingent, still subject to failure—the omnipresent fear that the tenor's voice will crack on a high note, for instance; and second, to point out the irony of associating the familiar with the natural. Certainly an example of human vulnerability, vocal cracks on high notes can also signify a failure of masculinity to an audience in the sense that the performance seems unstable, unreliable, while the crack also uncovers the higher falsetto register, a sign of vocal weakness revealing the smaller, lighter sound that, in the nineteenth century, was associated with the feminine. Even if we do not always associate vocal cracking with a failure of masculinity today, the event still points to the construction of an operatic vocal ideal. In the case of castrati, the voice was created via surgery, and then idealized; with tenors, the natural, ideal sound still had to be created, this time with a different kind of technology—vocal technique, an artificially lowered larynx. So definitively did this new vocalism define male singers' masculinity, that when a few brave tenors dared to sing softly in the upper range later in the nineteenth century, their sweet *voix mixte* sounds were received as enigmatic and feminine, intensely vulnerable, precious, or even erotic.

In my historical research, I have argued that in our era of trumpeting tenors, we might try to encourage a revival of this soft singing performance practice.[11] We have few recorded examples that approach *voix mixte*, but Nicolai Gedda's beautiful rendition of "Je crois entendre encore" from Bizet's *Les pêcheurs de perles* is perhaps the best approximation. The soft-grained *voix mixte* exceptions to loud tenor high notes prove the rule of what it takes to sound masculine in the mid-late nineteenth century, an ideal that in many ways still holds sway today.

A NEW MAN?

Finally, in order to demonstrate the relevance and importance of opera's gender and body constructions today, I present a current example at the conclusion of the semester: a recent *New York Times* article on how transgender opera singers are further complicating and enriching the conversation about gender, performance, and the body on stage.[12] In the twenty-first century, we

Opera and Masculinity 85

seem poised at the brink, or even in the midst, of a paradigm shift in our conception of gender. Gender fluidity seems more accepted and more "in the air" than ever before. Students, I think, are aware of this, and simultaneously want and are afraid to talk about it. I ask them to read this short article that describes the lives of three up-and-coming singers who have each dealt with their trans identity in different ways, all the while honing their singing craft: a tenor, originally trained as a mezzo-soprano before transitioning and undergoing testosterone hormone therapy; a trans woman who continues to sing as a dramatic baritone in mostly male roles onstage, since estrogen therapy does not raise the voice in the same way that testosterone lowers it; and a trans man who continues to sing as a mezzo-soprano, not electing to undergo the hormone therapy, in case it might be detrimental to his singing. In small group discussions, students explore how these singers broaden our discussion of gender and how they perform masculinity onstage versus living their personal identities offstage. We listen to recordings of these singers and talk about the effects of hormone therapy on the voice. By the end of the conversation, we begin to doubt whether we can even talk about a gendered voice type anymore. As a way to wrap-up the course, I then remind students of where we started—in much more familiar gender territory, and with a much less refined understanding of the complexity of how we construct personhood and gender both visually and sonically.

The case of castrati shocked the students into thinking more radically about the construction of gender and voices. Nineteenth-century tenor singing exposed the problems and limitations of our familiar gender binary system. And finally, the contemporary examples of transgender singers and operatic gender fluidity helped students to become aware of current and new constructions of gender, as well as the high stakes involved in our conception of gender, as the prevailing paradigm shifts. These examples of masculinity constructed by operatic voices help students understand the many, varied, and vital ways that opera teaches us about gender, the body, and ourselves.

APPENDIX 5.1: SELECTED PRIMARY SOURCE EXCERPTS ON THE VOICES OF CASTRATI

Jean-Jacques Rousseau defining the castrato:

"CASTRATO. A musician, who in his infancy had been deprived of the organs of generation, for the sake of preserving a shrill voice, who sings that part called sophrano [sic]. However small the connection may appear between

86   TEACHING DIFFICULT TOPICS

two such different organs, it is a certain fact that the mutilation of the one prevents and hinders in the other that change which is perceptible in mankind, near the advance of manhood, and which, on a sudden, lowers their voice an eighth. There exist in Italy, some inhuman fathers, who sacrificing nature to fortune, give up their children to this operation, for the amusement of voluptuous and cruel persons, who have the barbarity to require the exertion of voice which the unhappy wretches possess."[13]

Castrato-writer Filippo Balatri on the gender of castrati:

"He started by asking me whether I was male or female, and where from; whether such people are born (or rain down) with a voice and ability to sing. I was all confused about how to answer. If 'male,' I'm practically lying, if 'female,' still less do I say what I am, and if 'neuter,' I would blush. But, screwing up my courage, I finally answer that I'm a man, Tuscan, and that cocks are found in my region who lay eggs, from which sopranos come into the world; that these cocks are called *norcini*, who go on brooding for many days among our people; and that once the capon is made, the eggs are festooned with flattery, caresses, and money."[14]

Charles Burney on the castrati who fail to succeed on the operatic stage:

"[I]t is my opinion that the cruel operation is but too frequently performed without trial, or at least without sufficient proofs of an improvable voice; otherwise such numbers could never be found in every great town throughout Italy, without any voice at all, or at least without one sufficient to compensate such a loss. Indeed all the *musici* in the churches at present are made up of the refuse of the opera houses, and it is very rare to meet with a tolerable voice upon the establishment in any church throughout Italy."[15]

Burney on the famed castrato, Farinelli:

"In the famous air *Son qual Nave*, which was composed by his brother, the first note he sung was taken with such delicacy, swelled by minute degrees to such an amazing volume, and afterwards diminished in the same manner to a mere point, that it was applauded for full five minutes. After this he set off with such brilliancy and rapidity of execution, that it was difficult for the violins of those days to keep pace with him. In short, he was to all other singers as superior as the famous horse Childers was to all other running-horses; but it was not only in speed that he excelled, for he had now every excellence of every great singer united. In his voice, strength, sweetness, and compass; and in his style, the tender, the graceful, and the rapid. Indeed he possessed such powers as never met before, or since, in any one human being; powers that were irresistible, and which must have subdued every hearer; the learned and the ignorant, the friend and the foe."[16]

Susan Burney (Charles's daughter) on soprano castrato, Gaspare Pacchierotti:

"Such a Murmur spread, especially from that corner of the Pitt where My Father sat, of whispered bravos as I scarce ever heard—& the moment, nay even *before* the song was quite done there was a burst of vehement applause, which affected me in a *new* way—indeed I felt sensations very exquisitely delightful."[17]

Johann Joachim Quantz on contralto castrato, Gaetano Orsini:

"Gaetano Orsini, one of the greatest singers that ever was, had a beautiful, even, and stirring contralto voice of no small compass; a pure intonation, beautiful trill, [and] an uncommonly charming delivery. In Allegros he articulated passaggi, especially triplets, very beautifully with his chest; and in Adagios, masterfully artful, the direct, moving qualities were so touching that he went right through the heart of the listener, whom he overcame in the highest degree."[18]

François Raguenet on castrati:

"[T]hese voices, sweet as nightingales, are enchanting in the mouths of actors playing the part of lover. Nothing is more touching than the expression of their pains uttered with that timbre of voice, tender and impassioned. And the Italians have in this a great advantage over the lovers in our [French] theaters whose voices, heavy and virile, are consistently much less suitable to the sweet words that they address to their mistresses."[19]

Raguenet on castrati sounding like female voices and the Italian preference for treble voices:

"Besides, the blending of the basses with the upper parts forms an agreeable contrast, and makes us perceive the beauties of the one from the opposition they meet with from the other, a pleasure to which the Italians are perfect strangers, the voices of their singers, who are, for the most part, castrati, being perfectly like those of their women."[20]

Title character of Honoré de Balzac's **Sarrasine** *reacting to the effect of a castrato's singing, misidentified as that of a female singer:*

"When La Zambinella sang, the effect was delirium. The artist felt cold; then he felt a heat which suddenly began to prickle in the innermost depth of his being, in what we call the heart, for lack of any other word! He did not applaud, he said nothing, he experienced an impulse of madness, a kind of frenzy which overcomes us only when we are at the age when desire has something frightening and infernal about it. . . . Last, this agile voice, fresh and silvery in timbre, supple as a thread shaped by the slightest breath of air, rolling and unrolling, cascading and scattering, this voice attacked his soul so vividly that several times he gave vent to involuntary cries torn from him by convulsive feelings of pleasure which are all too rarely vouchsafed by human passions."[21]

Gioachino Rossini on the castrato's voice:

"I have never forgotten them. The purity, the miraculous flexibility of those voices and, above all, their profoundly penetrating accent—all that moved and fascinated me more than I can tell you."[22]

Casanova on the gender ambiguity of castrati:

"In comes a pretty-faced abate. His hips and thighs make me think him a girl in disguise. . . . He gives me a bold look and says that if I will spend the night with him he will serve me as a boy or a girl, whichever I choose."[23]

Goethe on castrati:

"I reflected on the reasons why these singers pleased me so greatly, and I think I have found it. In their representations, the concept of imitation and of art was invariably more strongly felt, and through their able performance a sort of conscious illusion was produced. Thus a double pleasure is given, in that these persons are not women, but only represent women. The young men have studied the properties of the female sex in its being and behavior; they know them thoroughly and reproduce them like an artist; they represent not themselves, but a nature absolutely foreign to them."[24]

Notes

1. In this, I of course rely on the seminal feminist musicological approaches pioneered by Catherine Clément and Carolyn Abbate, respectively.

2. I have often wondered if my identity as a man and as an opera singer has facilitated or hindered these conversations. I try to be as forthright as I can with my students, being sure also to self-identify as a feminist to my classes to model a sense of how identity informs our approach to the topic. In so doing, I also attempt to impart an awareness of positionality, that even though we might try to remain neutral and objective in our discussions, true objectivity is impossible as our identities are always bound up in the ways we discuss issues in class.

3. Judith Butler, "Your Behavior Creates Your Gender" (Big Think, https://www.you tube.com/watch?v=Bo7o2LYATDc)

4. While Martha Feldman does not call the castrato "non-binary," she does observe the danger of castrati as threatening to a "binary sexual regime." See Martha Feldman, *The Castrato: Reflections on Natures and Kinds*, (Oakland: University of California Press, 2015), 303.

5. Thomas Laqueur, *Making Sex: Body and Gender from the Greeks to Freud* (Cambridge, MA: Harvard University Press, 1990).

6. Roger Freitas, "The Eroticism of Emasculation: Confronting the Baroque Body of the Castrato," *Journal of Musicology* 20, no. 2 (2003): 196–249.

7. See Feldman, *The Castrato*.

8. Gregory W. Bloch, "The Pathological Voice of Gilbert-Louis Duprez," *Cambridge Opera Journal* 19, no. 1 (2007): 11–31.

9. The classic text is Richard Miller, *The Structure of Singing: System and Art in Vocal Technique* (New York: Schirmer, 1986).

10. Indeed the heroic sound of the Wagnerian tenor and the strength of the Wagnerian voice more generally is the apex of operatic vocal power. See for example, Sean M. Parr, "Wagnerian Singing and the Limits of Vocal Pedagogy," *Current Musicology* 105 (Fall 2019): 56–74, and Jens Malte Fischer, "Sprechgesang or Bel Canto: Toward a History of Singing Wagner," in *Wagner Handbook*, edited by Ulrich Müller and Peter Wapnewski, translation edited by John Deathridge, 524–46 (Cambridge, MA: Harvard University Press, 1992).

11. Sean M. Parr, "Vocal Vulnerability: Tenors, *Voix Mixte*, and Late Nineteenth-Century French Opera," *Cambridge Opera Journal* 30, 2–3 (November 2018): 138–64.

12. Michael Cooper, "Transgender Opera Singers Find Their Voices," *New York Times* (July 11, 2019, https://www.nytimes.com/2019/07/11/arts/music/transgender-opera -singers.html).

13. Jean-Jacques Rousseau, *A Complete Dictionary of Music* (London, 1779), 56.

14. Filippo Balatri "Frutti del mondo esperimentati da F.B. nativo dell'Alfea, in Toscana," 2 vols., Munich, Bayerische Staatsbibliothek, cod. It. 39, vol. 1, fols. 35v–36. Quoted and translated in Martha Feldman, *The Castrato: Reflections on Natures and Kinds*, (Oakland: University of California Press, 2015), 18.

90   TEACHING DIFFICULT TOPICS

15. Percy A. Scholes, ed., *Dr. Burney's Musical Tours in Europe*, (London: Oxford University Press, 1959), I, 248. Quoted in Piero Weiss and Richard Taruskin, eds. *Music in the Western World: A History in Documents* (Belmont, CA: Thomson Higher Education, 2008), 191.

16. Scholes, *Dr. Burney's*, I, 153–55, quoted in Weiss and Taruskin, *Music in the Western World*, 193.

17. Susan Burney, *The Journals and Letters of Susan Burney: Music and Society in Late Eighteenth-Century England*, edited by Philip Olleson (Farnham, Surrey, England: Ashgate, 2012), 121–22. Quoted in Feldman, *The Castrato*, 196.

18. Willi Kahl, "Herrn Johann Joachim Quantzens Lebenslauf, von ihm selbst entworfen," in Friedrich Wilhelm Marpurg, *Historisch-kritische Beyträge zur Aufnahme der Musik*, vol. 1, st. 5. Berlin: Schütz, 1755. Quoted and translated in Feldman, *The Castrato*, 95.

19. François Raguenet, *Paralele des italiens et des François, en ce qui regarde la musique et les opéra* (Paris, 1702). Quoted and translated in Roger Freitas, "The Eroticism of Emasculation: Confronting the Baroque Body of the Castrato," *Journal of Musicology* 20, no. 2 (2003), 238–39.

20. Raguenet, *Paralele des italiens et des François*, (Paris, 1702); English translation drawn from *A Comparison Between the French and Italian Musick and Opera's* (London, 1709). Quoted in Margaret Murata, ed. *Strunk's Source Readings in Music History, Volume 4* (New York: W. W. Norton, 1998), 165.

21. Honoré de Balzac, *Sarrasine* (Paris, 1830). Quoted in Roland Barthes, *S/Z*, translated by Richard Miller (New York: Hill and Wang, 1974), 238–39.

22. Rossini in conversation with Richard Wagner, as transcribed in Edmond Michotte, *Richard Wagner's Visit to Rossini (Paris 1860) and An Evening at Rossini's in Beau-Sejour (Passy) 1858*, translated from the French and annotated with an introduction and appendix by Herbert Weinstock (Chicago: University of Chicago Press, 1968). Quoted in Naomi André, *Voicing Gender: Castrati, Travesti, and the Second Woman in Early-Nineteenth-Century Italian Opera* (Bloomington and Indianapolis: Indiana University Press, 2006), 26.

23. Giacomo Casanova and Chevalier de Seingalt, *Histoire de ma vie* (Paris, 1822), translated and edited in Willard R. Trask, *History of My Life* (Baltimore: Johns Hopkins University Press, 1997). Quoted in Dorothy Keyser, "Cross-Sexual Casting in Baroque Opera: Musical and Theatrical Convention," *Opera Quarterly* 5, no. 4 (1987), 50.

24. Johann Wolfgang von Goethe, "Auszüge aus einem Reise-Journal," in *Der Teutsche Merkur* 4, (1788). Translation quoted in Angus Heriot, *The Castrati in Opera* (London: Secker & Warburg, 1956), 26.

Works Cited

Abbate, Carolyn. "Opera; or, the Envoicing of Women," in *Musicology and Difference: Gender and Sexuality in Music Scholarship*, ed. Ruth A. Solie, 225–58. Berkeley: University of California Press, 1993.

Bloch, Gregory W. "The Pathological Voice of Gilbert-Louis Duprez." *Cambridge Opera Journal* 19 (2007): 11–31.

Clément, Catherine. *Opera, or The Undoing of Women.* Translated by Betsy Wing. Minneapolis: University of Minnesota Press, 1988.

Cooper, Michael. "Transgender Opera Singers Find Their Voices." *The New York Times,* July 11, 2019. https://www.nytimes.com/2019/07/11/arts/music/transgender-opera-singers.html

Feldman, Martha. *The Castrato: Reflections on Natures and Kinds.* Oakland, CA: University of California Press, 2015.

Fischer, Jens Malte. "Sprechgesang or Bel Canto: Toward a History of Singing Wagner." In *Wagner Handbook,* edited by Ulrich Müller and Peter Wapnewski, translation edited by John Deathridge, 524–46. Cambridge, MA: Harvard University Press, 1992.

Freitas, Roger. "The Eroticism of Emasculation: Confronting the Baroque Body of the Castrato." *Journal of Musicology* 20 (2003): 196–249.

Laqueur, Thomas. *Making Sex: Body and Gender from the Greeks to Freud.* Cambridge, MA: Harvard University Press, 1990.

Miller, Richard. *The Structure of Singing: System and Art in Vocal Technique.* New York: Schirmer, 1986.

Parr, Sean M. "Vocal Vulnerability: Tenors, *Voix Mixte* and Late Nineteenth-Century French Opera." *Cambridge Opera Journal* 30 (November 2018): 138–64.

Parr, Sean M. "Wagnerian Singing and the Limits of Vocal Pedagogy." *Current Musicology* 105 (Fall 2019): 56–74.

PART II

Social Justice, Activism and Decolonization, and Building Resilience

CHAPTER 6

Beyond the Canon

Using Contemporary Works to Address Sexual Violence in the Music Drama

Annalise Smith

I first saw *Thumbprint* in a production by Opera Ithaca in 2016. Composed by Kamala Sankaram to a libretto by Susan Yankowitz in 2014, the opera tells the story of Mukhtar Mai, the first Pakistani woman to seek justice after being gang raped "in the name of honor." Moved by this powerful story, I made *Thumbprint* the culminating work in my undergraduate class on opera and society at Cornell University in 2017, with the intent of using Mukhtar's story to exemplify "opera as activism." That semester, however, saw the rise of the #MeToo movement. As the world finally listened to women's stories—and men finally began to face consequences—the sexual violence in *Thumbprint* was thrust into the foreground. While I had always planned to address the prevalence of sexual violence in opera, the #MeToo movement made it imperative that we tackle it directly. Classes became uncomfortable as we reflected on how the lived experiences of victims today were reflected in the casual depiction of sexual violence contained in so many canonical operas. If there had been a tendency in the classroom to skirt around the issue of rape, the collision between *Thumbprint* and the #MeToo movement made any side-stepping an impossibility.

Scholarship has begun to reckon with the legacy of sexual violence in opera, particularly in regard to how we teach such works in the classroom.[1] Kassandra Hartford's article "Beyond the Trigger Warning: Teaching Operas that depict Sexual Violence" outlines four such techniques: acknowledging sexual violence; allowing time for student processing; carefully choosing examples of staged productions; and creating opportunities for campus-wide dialogue.[2] While managing the classroom environment is critical, as instructors we can encourage deeper engagement by teaching contemporary works like *Thumbprint* that challenge the norms of rape culture, a system of social beliefs that views gendered violence—including "slut shaming and victim blame, female

95

96   TEACHING DIFFICULT TOPICS

sexualization and objectification, 'naturally' aggressive (cishetero) masculinity, and victims who are 'damaged goods'"—as an inevitable and potentially beneficial outcome of normative gender roles and relationships.[3] This essay presents *Thumbprint* as a model for how our repertoire choices influence our students' recognition of and response to depictions of sexual violence. This work has four pedagogical advantages. First, the sexual violence is explicit, and cannot be obfuscated by staging choices. Second, the plot focuses on the experiences of the victim which are central to the plot. Third, the contemporary storyline makes it less likely that students will dismiss the violence as the product of a different era. Lastly, *Thumbprint* provides an opportunity for students to discuss what they expect violence to sound like and how beautiful music can often cloud our judgment of a work's dramatic content. I close with a brief learning guide that introduces methods I have found effective when teaching *Thumbprint* in my undergraduate classes.

THE SEXUAL VIOLENCE IS EXPLICIT

Opera often hides its sexual violence behind euphemistic text that only alludes to rape and violation. Gilda never actually tells her father Rigoletto that she was raped by the duke, but both he and the audience know what has happened. As Coppélia Kahn notes, women in works of fiction rarely articulate experiences of sexual violence, for "to be raped and to speak about it are . . . similarly indecorous, alluding to matters about which a woman ought to be silent."[4] Such propriety leaves room for stage directors to obscure sexual violence, or even worse, reinterpret it through a romantic lens, even when the libretto gives clear indications of what has happened. In "The Sexual Politics of Teaching Mozart's *Don Giovanni*," Liane Curtis details how directors often stage the Don's relationship with Donna Anna as a love affair gone wrong, despite Donna Anna clearly stating that she has no interest in a sexual tryst with the nighttime invader.[5]

Thumbprint has no such ambiguity. Even if the audience did not know Mukhtar's story in advance, Yankowitz's libretto makes the sexual violence explicit.[6] Mukhtar's ordeal begins when her twelve-year-old brother Shakoor is accused of rape by the powerful Mastoi tribe and thrown in jail. Mukhtar goes to the Mastoi to beg forgiveness, believing her apology will win her brother's freedom. Instead, the Mastoi rape her in retaliation for her brother's supposed crimes. The gang rape takes place on stage, in full view of the audience. The music, which up to this point has been continuous, stops. Timed in conjunction with breathy gasps and exhalations, Mukhtar and the other two women go through a series of jerky stylized poses. At the end of each, a male actor splits open bags of rice at the rear of the stage with a large knife, the grains pooling on the floor and remaining there for the remainder of the performance. Yankowitz carefully uses euphemistic language to reflect commonly held societal beliefs and show how Mukhtar and her family process the rape. When Mukhtar's mother asks what has happened, her father can only respond "they have done the worst," reflecting the difficulty rape victims and their families often have in talking about sexual assault.[7] Similarly, the villagers' taunts that Mukhtar has committed an "act of lewdness" reflect the victim blaming pervasive in rape culture. While Mukhtar initially believes she has brought dishonor to her family, she gradually finds the courage to label her assault for what it is. When the leader of the Mastoi, Faiz, tells her "You are the fate all girls hope to escape: dishonor, shame!" she responds, "Dishonor? Shame? That fate is rape." From that point on, Mukhtar's sexual assault is referred to as rape, assuring that there can be no confusion as to what has taken place.

THE EXPERIENCES OF THE VICTIM ARE CENTRAL TO THE PLOT

For all that they suffer sexual violence, operatic women are remarkably silent about their experiences. Resistance is possible—in *The Abduction from the Seraglio*, Konstanze quashes the Pasha's sexual advances with her virtuosic declaration that she will endure torture rather than submit.[8] But upon her rescue, Konstanze immediately forgets she was the victim of any such violence. Operatic women generally aren't given the space to process their trauma because sexual violence in opera functions primarily to motivate a male character who sees it as his duty to protect or avenge the victimized woman. This is a common trope in Western media. In Issue #54 of DC Comic's *Green Lantern*, the eponymous hero returns home to find his girlfriend has been killed and shoved in the fridge. Borrowing the imagery of this infamous example, Gail Simone invented the concept of "fridging," the moment when a female character is injured, killed, depowered, or deflowered to advance a male character's plot.[9] If less centered on gruesome deaths, operatic fridging still occurs—Konstanze's captivity motivates her fiancé Belmonte's rescue attempt. While such rescue plots frequently have happy ends, their celebratory quality has the effect of minimizing the sexual violence shown on stage—if everything turned out all right, surely a little rape is nothing to worry about?[10]

While in another opera Mukhtar's rape may have been a motivating force

98   TEACHING DIFFICULT TOPICS

for a lover or father, *Thumbprint*'s dramatic and emotional arc follows her quest for healing and justice. Even the depiction of the rape centers her experiences, moving quickly from a presentation of the explicit physical act to an exploration of Mukhtar's emotional reaction. As the music slowly restarts, Mukhtar narrates her out-of-body experience.

> They take, they take, they take me
> from darkness into darkness
> from night into another night
> They take, they take
> This petrified body, these collapsing legs
> Is this me? I fall away from myself
> Is this me? This is not me.

While this provides a respite from the visceral depiction of sexual violence, more importantly, it allows Mukhtar's voice to become the lens through which the audience interprets what is happening. Joined by the other two actresses, who at this moment represent not her mother and sister but a universal expression of female personhood, Mukhtar's words force the audience to reflect on the ubiquity of sexual violence against women—and women's fear of such violence happening to them.

> A man can come and break into your body, take you into darkness.
> Day and night, night and day, every girl fears this fate.

In the aftermath of her rape, Mukhtar contemplates suicide, believing it will restore her family's honor. With support from her mother, she instead decides to take her attackers to court. The men who raped Mukhtar are sentenced to death, and she uses compensation provided by the Pakistani government to open a school where girls can learn how to read and write, revealing the inspiration behind the opera's name—prior to the trial Mukhtar was illiterate and had to sign her court documents with her thumbprint.[11] Emphasizing Mukhtar's experiences, *Thumbprint* negates any normalization or justification of the rape. As Suzanne Cusick notes,

> There is no slut shaming here, no blaming or objectifying of the woman raped, no denial of the damage done to her by sexual violence. There is, in short, no representation consonant with the norms of rape culture.[12]

Beyond the Canon 99

THE STORYLINE IS CONTEMPORARY AND LESS LIKELY TO BE DISMISSED

In recent years, the frequent and often casual depiction of sexual violence in opera has yielded increased criticism. A recurring justification of such operas is that we should view them as representative of the time in which they were created.[13] Such interpretations encourage us to view the Count's pursuit of Susanna in *The Marriage of Figaro* through the fictional lens of the *droit du seigneur*, rather than an all-too-realistic tale of a man who repeatedly tries to coerce a woman into sleeping with him.[14] But we cannot interpret *Thumbprint* as the product of a less-civilized, fictionalized past. While students today will not have experienced Mukhtar's quest for justice as a contemporary news event, she is still alive. Students can look up her charity, find interviews she has given on the internet, and hear first-hand accounts of her experiences. *Thumbprint*'s focus on justice, rather than rescue, also grounds the opera in the modern age. Mukhtar's story is not a romantic adventure, but a righteous quest to rectify a wrong that echoes the true crime TV shows and podcasts common in our digital landscape.

While students cannot distance themselves from *Thumbprint* temporally, they often use its geographic and cultural setting as an opportunity to create space between themselves and the events of the opera. One student recounted how her roommate, upon hearing Mukhtar's story, made the comment that honor rapes were a thing that happened "over there," implicitly referencing both the Middle East and the Muslim faith. Another student suggested that Mukhtar volunteered knowing what would happen to her, since honor rape was common in Pakistan. As Fawzia Afzal-Khan points out, if *Thumbprint* is the only experience the audience has with Pakistan or the Muslim faith, the story could potentially entrench cultural biases about how women are treated in the Middle East, diminishing the important work being done to create more just societies in this region and reinforcing ideas that it needs to be "saved" by the Western world.[15] When teaching works like *Thumbprint*, we must combat any perceptions that stigmatize Middle Eastern cultures or the Islamic faith. I have found it effective to explore how the feelings expressed by characters in the opera parallel those in Western society; I provide several examples in the final section of this chapter.

100 TEACHING DIFFICULT TOPICS

THE OPERA CHALLENGES OUR PRIORITIZATION OF MUSICAL BEAUTY OVER DRAMATIC CONTENT

Across institutions, I have found that opera classes attract students who are fascinated by the music—perhaps even more so when the students are not music majors themselves. Opera sells itself on the beauty of its music, even outside the opera house. "Vesti la giubba," Canio's lament from Leoncavallo's *Pagliacci*, has appeared in movies, advertisements, and even *The Simpsons*, where the beauty of Sideshow Bob's performance inspires Homer to temporarily forget that the clown is trying to kill him. Homer's dismissal of potential violence parallels audiences' reactions to the actual opera where the musical beauty of Canio's aria compels the listener to sympathize with him even as he stands over the body of his murdered wife. *Pagliacci* is hardly the only opera in which musical beauty trumps moral ugliness. In a promotional video for the 2015 Glyndebourne production of Britten's *The Rape of Lucretia*, the rape was framed as an "erotic" and "sexy" encounter based largely on the beauty of Tarquinius's aria. Neither the cast nor the director describe the titular event as rape, nor mention that Lucretia repeatedly says no to Tarquinius, nor that she ends up killing herself afterwards in shame.[16]

Thumbprint provides no musical panacea to the violence taking place on stage. Instead, the music stops. From the opening of the opera up to the rape scene, the music of *Thumbprint* is continuous, combining Pakistani and Indian musical idioms with a minimalistic compositional style. As the Mastoi reject Mukhtar's apology, the rhythmically active accompaniment grinds to a halt, replaced by a tense, discordant drone in the strings. The drone underpins Faiz's declaration of Mukhtar's fate, dropping out as he intones "Do what you want with her." Sankaram scored the rape as a series of pitched inhales and exhales for the 6 singers, punctuated by shrill, whistling sounds on the flute (See Figure 6.1). These 30 seconds present a deeply embodied experience. Absent words, the moment does not tell us what is happening to Mukhtar but shows us—her pain and grief conveyed through bodily sound and action. On both occasions where I saw the opera, the audience was entirely still, watching this intake and expression of breath while we held our own. This sonic shift marks the moment of rape as a moment of rupture within the opera. By removing conventional music, Sankaram prevents the audience from ignoring the dramatic reality of what is happening. Rape is not to be celebrated as a moment of beauty but recognized as a moment of brokenness, one that has fundamentally altered the shape of Mukhtar's life.

When teaching opera, I ask students to submit daily questions to assess engagement and identify potential concerns. One student questioned the effectiveness of graphic rape scenes, asking if they could do more than make an audience uncomfortable. In the case of *Thumbprint*, the answer is yes. Showing Mukhtar's rape forces us to grapple with society's acceptance of sexual violence and underscores the traumatic impact it has on victims. At the same time, it allows us to celebrate Mukhtar's courage and her determination to make a difference. Our willingness to deal with an authentic representation of rape—the moment it occurs, as well as its aftermath—makes such moments not only effective art, but a necessary expression of human life. While a music classroom may seem a less-than-ideal spot to have such discussions, the pleasure we derive from music as a sonic phenomenon makes it necessary to approach representations of sexual violence directly. If we encourage our students to embrace the beauty and drama of opera while refusing to acknowledge the sexual violence they contain, we implicitly tell our students that opera can justify any number of social immoralities, no matter how damaging.[17] As Bonnie Gordon notes, it is imperative that we "think about the power of sound to make listeners and dancers enter an ecstatic rhythmic space that obliterates the words they know are wrong."[18] We can continue to enjoy such pieces, but we must consider their moral and social implications when we teach them in the classroom. These works, which our profession values and we often personally profess to admire, are teaching our students lessons about the world we live in, and we must have an active role in shaping and challenging those messages.

TEACHING *THUMBPRINT*

I have taught *Thumbprint* in elective opera courses for both undergraduate music majors and music minors. It could easily fit into courses that focus on contemporary music, as well as courses that address the intersection of music and society. This learning guide outlines some techniques I use to encourage students to think critically about the depiction of sexual violence in opera. We must be sensitive to the fact that students in the class may have been victims of sexual violence or, like Mukhtar, had suicidal thoughts. Others may have seen such traumas among their family and friends. While we should not shy away from these important discussions, we must also create a space where students feel comfortable processing their reactions.[19]

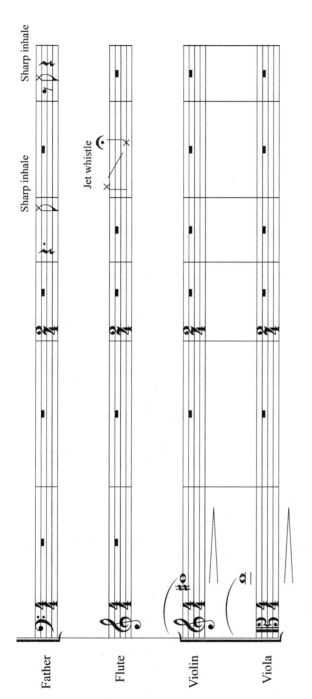

Figure 6.1: Musical depiction of the rape in *Thumbprint*

104   TEACHING DIFFICULT TOPICS

Introducing Thumbprint

I normally schedule *Thumbprint* late in the semester. Students will have already discussed several operas with sexual violence; nevertheless, the explicit nature of the rape in *Thumbprint* demands an upfront disclosure of the storyline. This is an opportune moment to discuss consent. When discussing operas that have more ambiguous depictions of sexual violence, students have disagreed about what "counted" as rape. Studies have shown that undergraduate students often lack a clear understanding of what sexual consent means.[20] The explicit non-consent in *Thumbprint* provides an opportunity to solidify class understanding on this crucial topic.

Prior to listening to *Thumbprint*, I have found it useful to discuss the prevalence of sexual violence in the media my students consume outside of class. Some initial questions I ask include:

- In the media you consume, where have you seen violence, sexual or otherwise, against women?
- Can you think of any media that focuses on the experiences of the women who face sexual violence?

In general, students easily recall examples of violence against women, and when introduced to the concept of fridging readily provide examples of the "damsel in distress" trope.[21] Examples of media that focus on a woman's understanding of her own experiences are rarer.[22] This questioning primes students to question why media contains so much violence against women, and allows them to better understand the important work *Thumbprint* does in providing a space for a woman to process her trauma.

Addressing the Rape

While the amount of *Thumbprint* I play in class varies based on the structure of a given course, I always listen to the rape scene and its surrounding music. Before listening, I share with my students the dramatic context, a brief description of the music, and how it was staged in the original Beth Morrison production. This moment allows us to address two crucial topics: what should rape look like on stage, and what should rape sound like in the music? In my discussions, I generally start by asking questions about the visual aspect of the scene.

Beyond the Canon   105

- How do you feel about the creators' choice to have the rape take place in full view of the audience? Why do you think they made this choice? Would the scene have the same effect if it took place off stage?
- How does this compare to the sexual violence we've seen in other operas?
- If you were staging this opera, how would you handle this scene?

Students are generally very uncomfortable with having a rape portrayed so explicitly; some have expressed that they would hesitate to attend *Thumbprint* knowing that it contained such a scene. Recognize that some students will find this moment deeply disturbing and create space for these reactions. Acknowledging this discomfort has often prompted my students to explore why they didn't have similar reactions to works that depicted sexual violence more ambiguously.

When addressing the music of *Thumbprint*, keep in mind that in an introductory class a significant portion of students will have listened to—but never seen—opera. Consuming opera primarily as a musical experience obscures moments of sexual violence. There are some operas where the music is suggestive of a physical act, but in most cases, the music that accompanies sexual violence does not sound particularly different from the rest of the opera.[23] Students listening to an opera may have read a basic plot synopsis, but they don't have the language skills or visual cues that would allow them to identify moments of sexual violence and think critically about the music they hear when it occurs. *Thumbprint*'s sonic treatment of rape opens a door to asking questions about how rape sounds in opera. Reflecting on both this work and other operas discussed in class, I ask my students,

- Does this music match what is happening on stage? Why or why not?
- If you were scoring this scene, how would you want it to sound?

Contextualizing Thumbprint

As a white woman teaching at a North American institution where most students are also white, I am consciously aware that *Thumbprint*'s depiction of Pakistan and Muslim culture strikes many students as uncomfortably foreign. Without proper framing, *Thumbprint* may, as Afzal-Khan warned, serve to reinforce negative Western stereotypes about South Asian cultures and religious practices. Plan to provide your students with a brief history of Pakistan, emphasizing the colonial forces that shaped the country's creation and the

106   TEACHING DIFFICULT TOPICS

political instability that followed the Partition of India in 1947. The regressive sexual politics seen in *Thumbprint* should be framed not as an expression of the Muslim faith, but an attempt by Pakistan's leaders—especially the military dictatorship of General Zia-ul-Haq (1978–88)—to control the populace and impose a patriarchal social system. Zia-ul-Haq used—and misinterpreted—the Quran to justify the repression of women, including their ability to seek legal recourse in the case of rape. These laws were finally reformed in 2006, four years after the rape of Mukhtar. Stress to your students that while the international attention generated by Mukhtar's case did put pressure on Pakistan to reform its laws, women in Pakistan had been opposed to and actively campaigning against these laws since their inception, and that the fight for women's rights in South Asia and Muslim communities can be traced to the nineteenth century.[24]

To ensure that students do not view *Thumbprint* as a story representative only of Pakistan or Islamic cultures, I draw connections between the cultural values espoused in the opera and those found in Western society. For example, Mukhtar's sister initially believes that she has lost her value because of the rape, singing "a woman is like a shawl. Stained, she is ruined, ruined forever." This idea mirrors Western purity culture which prioritizes female virginity. Rape survivor Elizabeth Smart questioned her self-worth following her traumatic experiences as her abstinence-only education had taught that having sex made her the equivalent of "a chewed-up piece of gum."[25] *Thumbprint* also mirrors Western society's difficulty in seeing the damage rape causes to its victims unless there is a personal connection. Mukhtar's father admits at the trial, "I did not see the crime, until the daughter was mine," echoing a rape campaign of the early twenty-first century that asked men to imagine rape victims as their mother, sister, daughter or wife to engender an emotional reaction. Similarly, during the #MeToo movement, many men began their statements with the phrase "as the father of daughters."[26] The sense of powerlessness that Mukhtar's family feels when they sing "truth dies in the mouth of power" is also echoed in Western culture where elected officials espouse the idea that "when you're a star ... you can do anything."

In its final chorus, *Thumbprint* celebrates the first steps that lead to broader social change, with Mukhtar singing:

In the dry season, someone must be the first drop of rain.
Let it be me. Let it begin with me.

As educators, the repertoire we present to our students and the tools we use to investigate it are, in their own way, a beginning for our students. The courses they take as undergraduate students will shape how they approach music and understand the role it plays in the world. The prevalence of sexual violence in canonical music dramas presents a challenge to many students who, seeing the pervasiveness of such injustice in the modern world, have little desire to engage with a genre that frequently appears as outdated, if not actively harmful in its presentation of rape culture. By including contemporary works like *Thumbprint* that reject such outdated perspectives, we can demonstrate to our students that opera, and music more broadly, can reflect the values of a more just society.

Notes

1. The 2016 annual meeting of the American Musicological Society included a panel discussion entitled "Sexual Violence on Stage," later published as a colloquy in the *Journal of the American Musicological Society* 71, no. 1 (2018): 213–53. Operas discussed included Mozart's *Don Giovanni*, Floyd's *Susannah*, Monteverdi's *L'Arianna*, Britten's *The Rape of Lucretia*, Mazzoli's *Breaking the Waves*, and Sankaram's *Thumbprint*.

2. Kassandra L. Hartford, "Beyond the Trigger Warning: Teaching Operas that Depict Sexual Violence," *Journal of Music History Pedagogy* 7, no. 1 (2016): 21–22.

3. Caroline Blyth, Emily Colgan, and Katie B. Edwards, introduction to *Rape Culture, Gender Violence, and Religion: Interdisciplinary Perspectives*, ed. Caroline Blyth, Emily Colgan, and Katie B. Edwards (Cham, Switzerland: Palgrave Macmillan, 2018), 3.

4. Coppélia Kahn, "*Lucrece*: The Sexual Politics of Subjectivity," in *Rape and Representation*, ed. Lynn A. Higgins and Brenda R. Silver (New York: Columbia University Press, 1991), 142.

5. Liane Curtis, "The Sexual Politics of Teaching Mozart's *Don Giovanni*," *NWSA Journal* 12, no. 1 (2000): 128–31.

6. Commissioned by Beth Morrison Projects and HERE, *Thumbprint* premiered at the Prototype Festival at Baruch College, NY in 2014. The same production was given at LA Opera in June 2017, featuring a discussion with Mukhtar Mai following the opening night performance.

7. Sarah E. Ullman, *Talking About Sexual Assault: Society's Response to Survivors* (Washington, D.C.: American Psychological Association, 2010), 83. Victims who report rape face a variety of negative reactions, including victim blaming and stigmatization, even from members of their family. As Shonna Trinch determined in her study of sexual violence in the Latina community, the use of euphemism allows victims to disclose incidents of sexual violence while "maintaining a level of delicacy that does not violate cultural constraints on their speech." "Managing Euphemism and Transcending Taboos: Negotiating the Meaning of Sexual Assault in Latinas' Narratives of Domestic

108   TEACHING DIFFICULT TOPICS

Violence," *Text: An Interdisciplinary Journal for the Study of Discourse* 21, no. 4 (2001): 575.

8. Gretchen A. Wheelock, "Konstanze Performs Constancy," in *Siren Songs: Representations of Gender and Sexuality in Opera*, ed. Mary Ann Smart (Princeon: Princeton University Press, 2000), 52–53. While Wheelock notes that Konstanze's "Marten aller Arten" stands—somewhat problematically—as "a demonstration of the strength of Western feminine virtue under siege by sinister forces of Islamic culture," she also emphasizes that Konstanze's ability to resist is predicated on her association with Belmonte, her plea not so much to avoid torture but the freedom to remain faithful to her fiancé.

9. http://www.lby3.com/wir/. Simone's website contains numerous examples of fridging in comics, as well as commentary on the trope from fans and creators.

10. This is to say nothing of the many operas that show acts of sexual violence against minor or even anonymous characters to create a dramatic atmosphere or further the characterization of a main character. The 2015 production of Rossini's *Guillaume Tell* at the Royal Opera House in London received sharp critiques when the director Kasper Holten inserted a scene of sexual violence into one of the opera's ballets to "convey the horrible reality of warfare" (Micaela Baranello, "When Cries of Rape are Heard in Opera Halls," *New York Times* [July 16, 2015]).

11. Tina Karkera, "The Gang-Rape of Mukhtar Mai and Pakistan's Opportunity to Regain its Lost Honor," *Journal of Gender, Social Policy & the Law* 14, no. 1 (2006): 166–70. As Mukhtar's case began to draw national and international attention, it was assigned to an anti-terrorism court to ensure a speedy trial. The trial convicted six men—four rapists and two members of the tribal council who approved the rape—and sentenced them to death, but the men would successfully appeal this conviction, with the case eventually moving to the Pakistan Supreme Court.

12. Suzanne Cusick, "Women in Impossible Situations: Missy Mazzoli and Kamala Sankaram on Sexual Violence in Opera," *Journal of the American Musicological Society* 71, no. 1 (2018): 247.

13. Calls to stop elevating problematic people and works have increasingly faced criticism and accusations of "cancel culture," primarily from the right-leaning press. For example, Louis Sarkozy's article in the *Washington Examiner* (July 2, 2018) argues for a separation between art and artist, with individual considerations for how historical figures and works reflected their own time period.

14. Alain Boureau, *The Lord's First Night: The Myth of the Droit de Cuissage*, trans. Lydia G. Cochrane (Chicago: University of Chicago Press, 1998), 4–5. In tracing the historical fiction of the *droit de seigneur*—more commonly known as the *droit de cuissage* in France—Boureau argues that both the "otherness" of the custom as well as its reinforcement of the barbarity of the medieval era have contributed to its durability as a cultural myth.

15. Fawzia Afzal-Khan, "The politics of pity and the individual heroine syndrome: Mukhtaran Mai and Malala Yousafzai of Pakistan," *Performing Islam* 4, no. 2 (2015): 155–56.

Beyond the Canon   109

16. Glyndebourne, "The Rape of Lucretia—Directed by Fiona Shaw," YouTube video, 4:06, June 29, 2015, https://www.youtube.com/watch?v=BbeVV8jPcek

17. The response to allegations of sexual exploitation against James Levine, the long-serving music director of the Metropolitan Opera, exemplifies how artistic accomplishment can be seen as a justification for abhorrent behavior. When the news broke, many on social media argued that Levine's skills as a conductor and director justified his continued leadership at the Met. Following Levine's death, the controversial classical music blog *Slipped Disc* continued to uphold the value of Levine's musical activities, stating "His achievements will outweigh this seedy episode." Norman Lebrecht, "James Levine is Dead," *Slipped Disc*, March 17, 2021. https://slippedisc.com/20 21/03/james-levine-is-dead/

18. Bonnie Gordon, "Why We Matter," *Women and Music: A Journal of Gender and Culture* 19 (2015): 124.

19. Katelin B. Double and Jenny H. Pak, "Campus Sexual Violence: The Impact of Disclosure on Mental Health," *Journal of Psychology and Christianity* 38, no. 4 (2019): 249. Double and Pak suggest that colleges should include disclosure training that focuses on "empowering the victim/survivor and assisting the survivor to reclaim their voice," recognizing that a negative reaction to a disclosure, even if unintentional, can lead to heightened distress and a reluctance to seek justice through formal systems.

20. Renae Franiuk, "Discussing and Defining Sexual Assault: A Classroom Activity," *College Teaching* 55, no. 3 (2007): 105–6. As Franiuk states, "Consent is the key issue in cases of sexual assault, and research shows that many people do not fully understand this term in the context of sexual situations."

21. For students who are interested, the video series *Feminist Frequency*, created by Anita Sarkeesian, has several videos that address the representation of women in video games, including three on the trope of the damsel in distress.

22. A small subset of media allows women to seek revenge, rather than giving that dramatic role to a romantic or paternal figure. Rape-revenge films such as *I Spit on Your Grave* (1977) have often been viewed as a sub-genre of horror films due to their violence and gore. However, as Jacinda Read points out, most films in which a woman seeks revenge can be found in a wide variety of genres and are best thought of as a narrative structure. *The New Avengers: Feminism, Femininity and the Rape-Revenge Cycle* (Manchester: Manchester University Press, 2000), 25.

23. Sheila Fitzpatrick, *The Cultural Front: Power and Culture in Revolutionary Russia* (Ithaca: Cornell University Press, 1992), 187–88. *Lady Macbeth of Mtsensk* was denounced in *Pravda*, the official newspaper of the communist party, following Stalin's attendance at a performance of the opera in January 1936. The rape scene between Sergei and Katerina received special attention in the editorial, which stated, "The music shouts, quacks, explodes, pants, and sighs, so as to convey the love scenes in the most naturalistic manner. And 'love' is smeared all over the opera in the most vulgar form."

24. Ayesha Khan, "Introduction: Midnight's Daughters," in *The Women's Movement in Pakistan: Activism, Islam and Democracy* (London: I. B. Tauris, 2018), 1–18. Khan's

110   TEACHING DIFFICULT TOPICS

introduction provides an accessible history of both the Islamization of Pakistan under General Zia-ul-Haq and the women's rights movement that sought to undo its impacts.

25. Kristen Howerton, "The Damaging Effects of Shame-Based Sex Education: Lessons from Elizabeth Smart," *Huffington Post*, July 5, 2013. "I thought, 'I'm that chewed-up piece of gum.' Nobody re-chews a piece of gum. You throw it away. And that's how easy it is to feel you no longer have worth. Your life no longer has value."

26. Jessica Contrera, "As 'the fathers of daughters' they were offended by harassment. But what did that really mean?" *Washington Post* (October 13, 2017).

Works Cited

Afzal-Khan, Fawzia. "The Politics of Pity and the Individual Heroine Syndrome: Mukhtaran Mai and Malala Yousafzai of Pakistan." *Performing Islam* 4, no. 2 (2015): 151–71.

Baranello, Micaela. "When Cries of Rape are Heard in Opera Halls." *New York Times*, July 16, 2015.

Blyth, Caroline, Emily Colgan, and Katie B. Edwards. *Introduction to Rape Culture, Gender Violence, and Religion: Interdisciplinary Perspectives*. Edited by Caroline Blyth, Emily Colgan, and Katie B. Edwards, 1–8. Cham, Switzerland: Palgrave Macmillan, 2018.

Boureau, Alain. *The Lord's First Night: The Myth of the Droit de Cuissage*. Translated by Lydia G. Cochrane. Chicago: University of Chicago Press, 1998.

Contrera, Jessica. "As 'the fathers of daughters' they were offended by harassment. But what did that really mean?" *Washington Post*, October 13, 2017.

Curtis, Liane. "The Sexual Politics of Teaching Mozart's *Don Giovanni*." *NWSA Journal* 12, no. 1 (2000): 119–42.

Cusick, Suzanne. "Women in Impossible Situations: Missy Mazzoli and Kamala Sankaram on Sexual Violence in Opera." *Journal of the American Musicological Society* 71, no. 1 (2018): 243–48.

Cusick, Suzanne G., and Monica A. Hershberger. "Sexual Violence in Opera: Scholarship, Pedagogy, and Production as Resistance." *Journal of the American Musicological Society* 71, no. 1 (2018): 213–53.

Double, Katelin B., and Jenny H. Pak. "Campus Sexual Violence: The Impact of Disclosure on Mental Health." *Journal of Psychology and Christianity* 38, no. 4 (2019): 237–52.

Fitzpatrick, Sheila. *The Cultural Front: Power and Culture in Revolutionary Russia*. Ithaca: Cornell University Press, 1992.

Franiuk, Renae. "Discussing and Defining Sexual Assault: A Classroom Activity." *College Teaching* 55, no. 3 (2007): 104–8.

Glyndebourne. "The Rape of Lucretia—Directed by Fiona Shaw." June 29, 2015. Video, 4:05. https://www.youtube.com/watch?v=BbeVV8jPcek

Gordon, Bonnie. "Why We Matter." *Women and Music: A Journal of Gender and Culture* 19, no. 1 (2015): 116–24.

Hartford, Kassandra L. "Beyond the Trigger Warning: Teaching Operas that Depict Sexual Violence." *Journal of Music History Pedagogy* 7, no. 1 (2016): 19–34.

Howerton, Kristen. "The Damaging Effects of Shame-Based Sex Education: Lessons from Elizabeth Smart." *Huffington Post*, July 5, 2013.

Kahn, Coppélia. "*Lucrece*: The Sexual Politics of Subjectivity." In *Rape and Representation*, edited by Lynn A. Higgins and Brenda R. Silver, 141–59. New York: Columbia University Press, 1991.

Karkera, Tina. "The Gang-Rape of Mukhtar Mai and Pakistan's Opportunity to Regain its Lost Honor." *Journal of Gender, Social Policy & the Law* 14, no. 1 (2006): 166–70.

Khan, Ayesha. "Introduction: Midnight's Daughters." In *The Women's Movement in Pakistan: Activism, Islam and Democracy, 1–18*. London: I. B. Tauris, 2018.

Lebrecht, Norman. "James Levine is Dead." *Slipped Disc.* March 17, 2021. https://slippe disc.com/2021/03/james-levine-is-dead/

Read, Jacinda. *The New Avengers: Feminism, Femininity and the Rape-Revenge Cycle.* Manchester: Manchester University Press, 2000.

Sarkozy, Louis. "Don't Judge Works of the Past by Today's Moral Standards." *Washington Examiner,* July 2, 2018.

Simone, Gail. *Women in Refrigerators.* Accessed April 3, 2019. http://www.lby3.com/wir/

Trinch, Shonna L. "Managing Euphemism and Transcending Taboos: Negotiating the Meaning of Sexual Assault in Latinas' Narratives of Domestic Violence." *Text. An Interdisciplinary Journal for the Study of Discourse* 21, no. 4 (2001): 567–610.

Ullman, Sarah E. *Talking about Sexual Assault: Society's Response to Survivors.* Washington, D.C.: American Psychological Association, 2010.

Wheelock, Gretchen A. "Konstanze Performs Constancy." In *Siren Songs: Representations of Gender and Sexuality in Opera*, edited by Mary Ann Smart, 50–57. Princeton: Princeton University Press, 2000.

CHAPTER 7

Asking Non-Majors to Music in Reclamation and Remix Projects

Challenging Topics, Collaborative Learning, and Creative Assignments

April L. Prince

The general education, music history non-major classroom is filled with students who have ranges of musical experiences. Through confusing terminology, content historically dedicated to the Western art music canon, and a cultural system that has "[gradually shifted] in thinking of music making as a social activity to music as an object," today's non-majors are ever-alienated from participatory musical experiences.[1] While traditional Music Appreciation and Music and Society classes remain popular ways to satisfy general education requirements, changing demographics and evolving pedagogical possibilities ask music historians to reconsider course content, modes of student engagement, and methodological approaches.[2] With increasingly diverse classrooms and ever-increasing access to higher education, calls to "decolonize" the music history classroom grow increasingly urgent; creative, team-based assignments can play a powerful role in this vital endeavor.[3] Asking non-majors to compose, revise, and curate—"to music"—in cooperative settings provides students opportunities to engage with challenging topics in deeply personalized and inclusive ways.[4] Additionally, "students who work collaboratively have more opportunities to articulate and thus to own their individual learning."[5] Relying on discussions of collaborative learning techniques, this chapter focuses on practical ways to construct non-major, participatory assignments. These assignments ask general education students to wrestle with difficult topics like anti-Black racism, gender oppression, economic inequality, and environmental disparity in both historical and contemporary settings. The Reclamation Project examines blackface minstrelsy and guides students on analyzing, deconstructing, and revising songs

Asking Non-Majors to Music in Reclamation and Remix Projects   113

from this tradition. The Remix Project asks students to choose an issue and explore it creatively through musical borrowing, sampling, and remixing.[6] In carefully structured activities, students synthesize class materials, while reflecting more broadly on aspects of resiliency and activism. Most fundamentally, however, these creative assignments can become deeply personal, thereby centering the import of empathetic and contemplative learning.[7]

Creative assignments encourage students to grapple with the challenging concepts of social power and historical narrative, and, ultimately, to interrogate the entrenched power structures of the world around them.[8] These questions, of course, must extend into our higher education classrooms; these spaces should embrace active lectures, open and fair discussions, and diverse assessments.[9] By its very nature, collaborative learning resists the hierarchical classroom environment and encourages students to assume more responsibility over their learning processes. As Elizabeth Barkley, Claire Howell Major, and K. Patricia Cross argue,

> Instructional methods such as lecturing tend to constrain students as passive observers, which may result in surface learning that is easily forgotten. Well-crafted collaborative learning activities challenge students to be active participants in the acquiring and organizing of knowledge that results in reformatted neuronal networks, thereby promoting deeper learning[10]

Collaborative learning asks students to build on their pre-existing knowledge and, in focused social interactions, develop and refine their comprehension.[11] A crucial component of collaborative learning, therefore, relies on the instructor's ability to provide students with the strategic resources they need to be able to develop knowledge. As such, cooperative learning easily complements discussion-based lectures and individual active-learning activities, while also meeting different kinds of learning intelligences and differentiations. Creative assignments encourage students to develop new skills: to create more nuanced and empathetic understandings of course materials.[12]

Because these projects center creative expression, they require a kind of embodied, physical knowledge. Non-major populations, however, most often define themselves as "consumers" of music. They frequently express a general alienation from musical practice and music's idiomatic vocabulary. Through democratized music-making, however, students create arguments in new ways and, ultimately, work to embrace the deeply humanistic goals of music. As Thomas Turino argues,

114   TEACHING DIFFICULT TOPICS

> music is not a unitary art form, but rather . . . this term refers to fundamentally distinct types of activities that fulfill different needs and ways of being human. . . . musical participation and experience are valuable for the processes of personal and social integration that make us whole.[13]

The fundamental, human experience of music-making, therefore, is perhaps even more important than content mastery. While much of my career has focused on teaching non-major populations, shifting students' perspectives to "musicking"—thinking of music as a social process that they actively participate in—evolved out of my limited experiences working with music majors.[14] When teaching the music history survey, I was inspired by Eleonora Beck's discussion of creative assignments. From re-compositions to concept music to a class opera, Beck argues that creative assignments, like collaborative learning, "encourage freedom of thought [and] have the potential to delight a student like no other college endeavor."[15] More pointedly, she writes that "asking students to perform in class as much as possible, so that they actually create and feel what they are learning, is more effective than passively listening."[16] This focus on learned empathy, on creating and feeling through musicking, rests at the core of these creative, interdisciplinary assignments.[17]

In my position at the University of North Texas, I teach non-major courses that range in size from 75 to 350.[18] UNT is a minority-majority university and designated Hispanic Serving Institution. The university is also currently undergoing a comprehensive review to assess the inclusivity of our curricula and instructional practices. Aligned with the university's initiative, all my classes incorporate collaborative, creative projects, which are modified depending on content and course learning objectives. As a white, middle-aged, cisgender, heterosexual woman who speaks with an obvious southern accent, I am continuously examining my positionality, inherent biases, and closeness to (and distance from) my students' positionalities and lived experiences.[19] Just as the Reclamation and Remix projects give us the space to come to terms with challenging histories and contemporary social injustices, these projects also provide opportunities to discuss our own identities in relationship to the narratives we examine in class.

The Reclamation assignment guides students on deconstructing and revising a nineteenth-century minstrel tune. This project intersects with the work of Rhiannon Giddens, John Sims, and other performing artists who have grappled with this inherently complex, anti-Black racist tradition through revision. René Marie describes her transformation of "Dixie"—wherein she combines it with Billie Holiday's "Strange Fruit"—thusly,

"Why should I let someone's misuse of a song determine whether I like it? I want to reclaim it as my mine—I'm from the South, too," she says. "But instead of singing it in this happy, up-tempo way it's usually played, I'm going to put some grit in there and some dirt, and sing it from the perspective of my people"[20]

Following an in-depth discussion of historical context, blackface minstrelsy, cultural appropriation, and African American music, students choose a popular tune, rewrite the lyrics, revise basic elements of the song, and record their versions. Students can also argue that these songs cannot and should not be reclaimed; in those cases, teams choose another popular song from the nineteenth century and revise its contents in accordance with the assignment guidelines. While the Reclamation project is very fixed in its parameters and requirements, the Remix assignment provides students more freedom in their creative focuses and musical choices. For this project, students create an audio remix and accompanying album artwork that communicate an issue of social concern. Student projects have been incredibly wide-ranging, focusing on the Black Lives Matter movement, the implications of #MeToo, as well as issues such as immigration, environmentalism, feminism and gender representation, and even aspects of mental health. This Remix assignment complements course materials that examine how music engages political issues and cultural ideas. Both musical processes conclude with conscientiously structured written and oral reflections. The following guides provide the practical scaffolding steps for both assignments, with the Reclamation project being much more detailed in its guidelines, given the nature of the assignment, the anxiety it can create, and the possible pitfalls.[21]

Along those lines, it is crucially important to scaffold, oversee, and provide detailed feedback on each phase of these assignments. Not only can students become overwhelmed with the creative aspects, but projects have the potential to become problematic. (It is sometimes challenging for students to grapple directly with aspects of dialect, entrenched stereotypes, and dynamic issues.) When I have encountered projects that I worry will invalidate the social justice work at the core of these assignments, I provide constructive feedback, suggest a reframing in terms of perspectives, ask students to reconsider classroom materials, and brainstorm with the team on ways to move forward. This kind of close guidance re-emphasizes the importance of the collaborative process, empowers students, and supports teams through each phase of the process. This oversight also ensures that learning continues throughout the construction of the project itself.

116   TEACHING DIFFICULT TOPICS

Creative, collaborative assignments ask students to reflect on music's historical and cultural role, and to embody their inherent musicality. And, because both projects can satisfy a range of learning objectives, learning differentiations, and curricular goals, these assignments can be adapted across core curriculums more broadly. For instance, inside music history classrooms, the Reclamation project could be adjusted to challenge representation of women in country music, to reflect on the appropriation of the blues in rock 'n' roll, or to call for a radical alteration of exoticism in opera. Depending on student bodies and curricular focus, these projects could also work outside of music history classrooms and easily complement curriculums in English, language arts, visual art, theater, American history, political science, and media studies. Because of its inherent interdisciplinarity, music can stimulate powerful affinities across non-major electives. When students are given opportunities to work within a more synthesized general education curriculum, one which repeatedly asks them to develop empathetic and personal connections to their course materials, they can better understand the incredible value of these electives. As Steven Mintz argues,

> Let's not juvenilize our college students. Let's give them options that do precisely what gen ed is supposed to do: promote student development along multiple vectors—cognitive, emotional, interpersonal and ethical—expose them to a variety of methodologies and interpretive strategies; and teach them to look, listen, read, think, speak and write critically and analytically.[22]

The value of general curriculum rests in not content coverage, but in guiding students to think and engage with content that challenges them in meaningful and dynamic ways.

APPENDIX 7.1: RECLAMATION PROJECT

Explaining and Interpreting

Assignment Prework

The prework for the Reclamation Project is extensive and requires a series of additional assignments from sheet music analysis to a reflection on representations of African American music and history in recent media.

Resources

There are so many accessible and powerful resources on blackface minstrelsy that work well for non-major populations. Below is a small sampling that can be easily amended and complemented, depending on student population or curricular goals.

Primary Sources

- *African American Sheet Music Project.* Brown University Library Center for Digital Scholarship. https://library.brown.edu/cds/sheetmusic/afam/ (accessed May 28, 2020).
- *Documenting the American South.* University of North Carolina, Chapel Hill. https://docsouth.unc.edu/browse/collections.html (accessed May 28, 2020).

Secondary Sources

- Cockrell, Dale. "Nineteenth-Century Popular Music" in *The Cambridge History of American Music*, edited by David Nicholls, 165–75. Cambridge: Cambridge University Press, 1998.
- Cruz, Jon. *Culture on the Margins: The Black Spiritual and the Rise of American Cultural Interpretation.* Princeton: Princeton University Press, 1999.
- Gay, Roxane. "Where Are the Serious Movies About Non-Suffering Black People?" *New York Magazine: Vulture.* https://www.vulture.com/2013/11/12-years-a-slave-black-oscar-bait-essay.html (accessed May 28, 2020).
- Kaskowitz, Sheryl. "Before It Goes Away" *The Avid Listener.* https://www.theavidlistener.com/2017/07/before-it-goes-away-performance-and-reclamation-of-songs-from-blackface-minstrelsy.html (accessed May 28, 2020).
- Morris, Wesley. "For centuries, black music, forged in bondage, has been the sound of complete artistic freedom. No wonder everybody is always stealing it." *The New York Times Magazine 1619 Project.* https://www.nytimes.com/interactive/2019/08/14/magazine/music-black-culture-appropriation.html (accessed May 28, 2020).
- Morris, Wesley. "The Song of Solomon: The Cultural Crater of *12 Years a Slave.*" *Grantland.* https://grantland.com/features/the-cultural-crater-12-years-slave/ (accessed May 28, 2020).
- Powers, Ann. "*12 Years a Slave* Is This Year's Best Film About Music."

118   TEACHING DIFFICULT TOPICS

National Public Radio: The Record. https://www.npr.org/sections/there-cord/2013/11/12/244851884/12-years-a-slave-is-this-years-best-film-about-music (accessed May 28, 2020).
- Qureshi, Bilal. "The Anthemic Allure of 'Dixie,' an Enduring Confederate Monument." *National Public Radio.* https://www.npr.org/2018/09/20/649954248/the-anthemic-allure-of-dixie-an-enduring-confederate-monument (accessed May 28, 2020).
- Southern, Eileen. *The Music of Black Americans: A History*, 3rd Edition. New York: W. W. Norton & Company, 1997.

Media

- *Blackface Minstrelsy.* University of Virginia. http://utc.iath.virginia.edu/minstrel/mihp.html (accessed May 28, 2020).
- *Jim Crow Museum of Racist Imagery.* Ferris State University. https://www.ferris.edu/jimcrow/ (accessed May 28, 2020).
- *12 Years a Slave*, DVD. Directed by Steve McQueen. Century City, CA: Fox Searchlight Pictures, 2013.
- *Minstrel Songs.* Library of Congress. https://www.loc.gov/collections/songs-of-america/articles-and-essays/musical-styles/popular-songs-of-the-day/minstrel-songs (accessed May 28, 2020).

Application, Interpretation, Perspective, and Empathy

Assignment Guidelines

General Information

For your final collaborative project, you will "reclaim" a popular tune from nineteenth-century American history. You will analyze, deconstruct, and recompose the lyrics. You will then change at least two fundamental aspects of the original musical structure (tempo, dynamics, form, texture, etc.).

This project was inspired by performing artists like Rhiannon Giddens, René Marie, Cécile McLorin Salvant, and John Sims who have confronted this tradition through reclamation.[23] This assignment also builds on recent discussions related to this music, and how we grapple with its presence in popular and institutional structures. Essentially, this project asks you and your team to transform the song from one of degradation to one of protest or empowerment. Your team can also argue that these songs *cannot* and *should not* be reclaimed or altered in any musical form. In this instance, you can choose another kind of nineteenth-century song to transform.

As Sheryl Kaskowitz describes in "Before It Goes Away: Performance and Reclamation of Songs from Blackface Minstrelsy,"

> In "Better Get Yer Learnin," Giddens has turned the disconnect that she experiences in minstrel songs—a great tune queasily paired with degrading lyrics—and transformed it into a protest song. With a chorus that repeats the title phrase and an added warning ("Better get yer learning, before it goes away"), the verses give poignant voice to the lived experiences of African Americans during Reconstruction: "The year was 1863, the paper said that I was free / But no one read it to my ears, and so I slaved for two more years"; and "I heard about a school was free, way out east in Tennessee / before I got to go to town, the damned old Rebs had burned it down."

The song's power is multilayered: the contrast between the poignant, serious lyrics and their jaunty musical messenger makes the song's protest message unexpected and thus forceful. The song illuminates multiple levels of transformation as an African-American performer—herself transformed when she came to understand the song's history—replaced offensive lyrics with those that uncover, rather than denigrate, the experience of African Americans. This process of transformation provides a counter-narrative that challenges the minstrel tradition's power of definition.[24]

You could choose one of the songs we discussed in class:

- "Oh! Susanna"
- "Camptown Races"
- "Shoo Fly, Don't Bother Me"
- "Turkey in the Straw"
- "Old Folks at Home"
- "Dixie"
- "I've Been Working on the Railroad"
- "Carry Me Back to Old Virginia"
- "Old Dan Tucker"
- "My Old Kentucky Home"

You might also consider a song from Gumbo Chaff's book, one of the earliest publications of minstrel tunes, or songs that you know well (but you might have been unaware of their origins).[25] You can also search around on the Web or even work with the songs from your sheet music analyses.

The project contains several components: in-class workdays, a song revision (MP3), a short essay, and a final team assessment. We will also take the last day of class to preview your revisions and reflect on the assignment more broadly.

Song Revision

Your song revision should be submitted as an MP3. You can alter or remix your song by using SoundTrap (available on soundtrap.com), an easy-to-use, free audio tool. You must sing or recite your song.

Short Essay

This essay should explain why your team selected the song, the changes your team has made to the song, the rationale behind those changes, and what you want your audience to "take away" from your revision. You must incorporate classroom and outside sources to support your creative choices.

Team Assessment

This assessment will outline your contributions and those of your team members and reflect on the process of teamwork more broadly.

Scaffolding the Assignment

These steps are completed during in-person and online sessions so that students can receive extensive feedback and guidance from the instructor.

Step 1: Brainstorming

- Brainstorm at least two songs you could use as the scaffolding for your revision.
- Brainstorm what main themes, perspectives, or issues you want to emphasize in your reclamation.

Asking Non-Majors to Music in Reclamation and Remix Projects   121

Step 2: Deciding

- Decide on your song and thematic focus.
- Find source materials that align with your thematic focus.
  - You can search *Documenting the American South* to find additional primary sources.
    - Harriet Ann Jacobs
    - Harriet Tubman
    - Bethany Veney
    - Nat Turner
    - Solomon Northup
    - Frederick Douglass
  - You can ground your work in the nineteenth, twentieth, or twenty-first centuries. Some possible points of focus:
    - Perspectives of the enslaved
    - Perspectives of abolitionists
    - Discrimination in Criminal Justice
    - Voices of the Segregated South
    - Voices of the Civil Rights Era
    - The Black Lives Matter Movement

Step 3: Transcribing and Revising

- Transcribe one verse of the original lyrics.
- Discuss the original tune and at least one musical way you could disrupt the musical structure effectively.
- Draft at least one "verse" of lyrics. (You will eventually need to have a total of four verses.)

Step 4: Drafting

- Finish up your song draft. You should have at least four verses, depending on the song length and structure.
- Decide what two musical elements you will change.
- Outline your short, accompanying essay.

122 TEACHING DIFFICULT TOPICS

Step 5: Finalizing

- Work on outlining and drafting your short essay.
- Finish up touches on song.
- Record and edit song.

Application, Interpretation, Perspective, and Empathy

Post-Assignment Reflections

Following completion of the assignment, teams preview their reclamations and reflect on the creative process.

- How do creative assignments ask you to engage with historical and musical source materials in new ways?
- What does it mean to "embody" and perform these revised songs? How does it make you feel?
- What are the problems in performing even revised versions of these songs? What is the value?
- What challenges did your team encounter throughout the process?
- How is your revision relevant in today's American society?
- In what ways is this process related to you personally and your major interests?

APPENDIX 7.2: REMIX PROJECT

Explaining and Interpreting

Assignment Prework

The prework for the Remix Project can be determined by the instructor's preference.

If a course is organized by topic, the instructor can approach an idea from a variety of non-chronological and diverse perspectives. Within these categories, instructors can incorporate all kinds of historical and contemporary music and a variety of source materials. This more flexible structure gives students the chance to explore and discuss music that intersects with a range of ideas and perspectives.

Some ideas for topic-based approaches are listed below, but the possibilities are endless!

- music and spirituality
- music and technology
- music and gender
- music and identity
- music and social class
- music and politics
- music and drama
- music and race
- music and identity
- music and experimentation

Application, Interpretation, Perspective, and Empathy

Assignment Guidelines

General Information

For your final project, you and your team members are part of a new music DJ collective and are tasked with creating a powerful, socially conscious new remix. The goal of this final project is to use music to "communicate" creatively about an issue or idea.

The project has several main components: in-class workdays, a composition (MP3), a one-page overview of samples and composition, album artwork, and a final team assessment.

Composition

Your composition ("remix") should engage with issues and ideas that are relevant in today's world. Your composition can have musical samples, lyrics, sounds, speeches, and other musical materials that resonate with your overarching "socially conscious" concept and main goals. Your team members can also sing, read spoken word, play music, and/or contribute homemade or self-recorded sounds of your choice. You should also feel free to explore CreativeCommons.org or YouTube's Audio Library for a variety of open-sourced images and samples.[26] Your remix should run around 3–5 minutes long. Here is a handy guide on how to get started.[27]

124 TEACHING DIFFICULT TOPICS

It is best if your remix comes from open-access sources. If you do decide to remix an original tune, your remix must be fundamentally and significantly different than the original. Please keep samples of popular tunes to less than 30 seconds.

One-Page Overview

This overview should explain how your team approached this project, how you decided to organize your remix, the rationale behind these choices, and what you want your audience to "take away" from your remix. You should incorporate classroom and outside sources to support your creative choices.

Album Artwork

Your accompanying artwork should synthesize the goals of your remix and express those visually.

Team Assessment

This assessment will outline your contributions and those of your team members and reflect on the process of teamwork more broadly.

Scaffolding the Assignment

These steps are completed during in class and online sessions. Students receive detailed feedback at every step.

Step 1: Collaborative Soundtrap Board

- Create a free account in soundtrap.com and review the required tutorials.
- Set up your collaborative remix board, making sure each team member has access and is connected to this board.
- Make some sounds—create a series of small loops that could potentially serve as the underscore for your remix.

Step 2: Brainstorming

- Brainstorm political and social issues you are passionate about and why. What issues matter to you and your team?

Asking Non-Majors to Music in Reclamation and Remix Projects 125

- Brainstorm possible samples, speeches, and sounds you would like your composition to include.

Step 3: Deciding and Sampling

- Decide on your issue.
- Collate at least five unique remixing materials from both historical and contemporary sound source material.
- Consider classroom and outside source material that will help you examine your theme.

Step 4: One-Page Overview and Album Artwork Ideas

- Craft a rough draft of your one-page overview and provide rationale for the import of your remix. Please include outside sources to help substantiate your remixing goals.
- Discuss at least one idea regarding the album artwork. (Your album artwork reflects the goals of your remix. It can be drawn or it can be a collage: be creative!)

Step 5: Organizing and Finalizing

- Assemble all accumulated sounds, lyrics, etc., for final project in Soundtrap.
- Decide on final loops and create a working "draft" of the composition.
- Craft a plan to finalize all components of the project.

Application, Interpretation, Perspective, and Empathy

Post-Assignment Reflections

Following completion of the assignment, teams preview their remixes and reflect on the creative process.

- How do creative assignments ask you to engage with historical and musical source materials in new ways?
- What is the goal of your remix, and what creative and artistic choices did you make? Why did you make these choices?
- What challenges did your team encounter throughout the process?

126   TEACHING DIFFICULT TOPICS

- In what ways is this process relevant to you personally and your major interests? Can you draw connections across your major and non-major electives?

Notes

1. Thomas Turino, *Music as Social Life: The Politics of Participation* (Chicago: University of Chicago Press, 2008), 24.

2. As student bodies become increasingly diverse, university general education curriculums must come to reflect their student bodies. See Nathan D. Grawe, *Demographics and the Demand for Higher Education* (Baltimore: Johns Hopkins University Press, 2018). For a quick overview of these issues, see Nathan D. Grawe, "How Demographic Change is Transforming the Higher Ed Landscape," *Higher Ed Jobs*, February 18, 2019 https://www.higheredjobs.com/blog/postDisplay.cfm?blog=25&post=1843 (accessed April 21, 2020). See also Margaret E. Walker, "Towards a Decolonized Music History Curriculum," *Journal of Music History Pedagogy* 10, no. 1 (2020): 1–19.

3. As Margaret E. Walker argues, taking "steps toward decolonizing university music history curricula can lead to a more intellectually responsible and rigorous approach to historical study for both our students and ourselves. It is the teleological narrative, the European supremacist narrative, that binds us, rather than the musics we choose, and it is here we must start." Walker, "Towards a Decolonized Music History Curriculum," 19. See also Travis D. Stimeling and Kayla Tokar, "Narratives of Musical Resilience and the Perpetuation of Whiteness in the Music History Classroom," *Journal of Music History Pedagogy* 10, no. 1 (2020): 20.

4. I borrow the term "musicking" from Christopher Small and rely on his argument for inherent musicality. This sentiment is an important one for student populations who deny their own musicianship. As Small writes, "The fundamental nature and meaning of music lie not in objects, not in musical works at all, but in action, in what people do. It is only by understanding what people do as they take part in a musical act that we can hope to understand its nature and the function it fulfills in human life. Whatever that function may be, I am certain, first, that to take part in a music act is of central importance to our very humanness, as important as taking part in the act of speech, which it so resembles (but from which it also differs in important ways), and second, that everyone . . . is birthed with the gift of music no less than with the gift of speech. . . . It means that our powers of making music for ourselves have been hijacked and the majority of people robbed of the musicality that is theirs by right of birth." Christopher Small, *Musicking: The Meanings of Performing and Listening* (Middletown, CT: Wesleyan University Press, 1998), 8.

5. Elizabeth F. Barkley, Claire Howell Major, and K. Patricia Cross, *Collaborative Learning Techniques: A Handbook for College Faculty* 2nd ed. (San Francisco: Jossey-Bass, 2014), 17. Emphasis mine.

6. Both assignments have the potential for modification, depending on course content and learning objectives. I designed the Reclamation project for *19th-century*

Asking Non-Majors to Music in Reclamation and Remix Projects   127

Music, which is an upper-level general education course at the University of North Texas. I have used slightly modified versions of the Remix Project in a variety of courses: *Music as Communication, Music Appreciation, Music as Politics,* and *Music, Gender, Sexuality.*

7. See Laura I. Rendón, *Sentipensante (Sensing/Thinking) Pedagogy: Educating for Wholeness, Social Justice, and Liberation* (Sterling, VA: Stylus Publishing, 2009).

8. Alongside these curriculum adjustments, the opportunities for new kinds of music history electives are vast, and large state universities are approving new kinds of general education courses with ease. For example, while all general education classes must go before the Texas Higher Education Coordinating Board (THECB), a state entity for approval, the University of North Texas has had no pushback from the THECB on dramatically altering the music history courses inside the UNT-Core Curriculum. Within the past several years, we have added *Gender, Music, Sexuality; Music as Politics;* and *Sounds and Cinema* to our more "traditional" general education offerings: *Music Appreciation, Music as Communication, 19th-Century Music,* and *20th-Century Music.*

9. See James D. Kirylo, ed., *Reinventing Pedagogy of the Oppressed: Contemporary Critical Perspectives* (New York: Bloomsbury Academic, 2020).

10. Barkley, Major, and Cross, *Collaborative Learning Techniques,* 16.

11. "Social constructivists believe that groups construct knowledge, collaboratively creating a culture of shared meanings. Rather than knowledge being held by individuals, it is socially held and is a socially based phenomenon." Barkley, Major, and Cross, *Collaborative Learning Techniques,* 17.

12. *Barkley,* Major, and Cross, 18.

13. Turino, *Music as Social Life,* 1.

14. Beginning in 2008, I spent several years adjuncting at Oklahoma City Community College (OCCC) and the small liberal arts college, Oklahoma City University (OCU). While at OCCC and OCU I worked in traditional, fast-track, online, and dual-enrollment programs, engaging with incredibly diverse student bodies. Following these appointments, I moved to Loyola University New Orleans, wherein I was tasked with teaching and developing non-major curriculum for a more "traditional," yet highly diverse student body. I am now a Principal Lecturer at the University of North Texas, and again, I focus on designing and teaching non-major music history courses. I have incorporated creative projects in nearly all of these higher education environments, in class sizes ranging from 20–320 students.

15. Eleonora M. Beck, "Assignments and Homework," in *The Music History Classroom,* ed. James A. Davis (New York: Routledge, 2016), 61.

16. Beck, "Assignments and Homework," in *The Music History Classroom,* 62.

17. "Musicologists, have, in the last twenty years, reached out to the fertile ground of interdisciplinary study, and are becoming well versed in speaking about art and philosophy as well as music." Beck, "Assignments and Homework," in *The Music History Classroom,* 82.

18. You can find more resources about UNT's student body here "Designated a

Hispanic-Serving Institution, UNT Can Amplify Resources for Growing and Better Serving Hispanic Student Population," *University of North Texas,* May 15, 2020, https://news.unt.edu/news-releases/designated-hispanic-serving-institution-unt-can-amplify-resources-growing-and-better?unttoday=052720 (accessed June 1, 2020). In light of these facts, in fall 2021 the provost called for a re-examination of curriculum and instructional practices. "Inclusive Curricula and Pedagogy Review Process," *University of North Texas,* September 24, 2021, https://vpaa.unt.edu/InclusiveReviewProce (accessed October 5, 2021).

19. I mention my accent given the plethora of stereotypes of white southerners and this group's long associations with racist views and behavior.

20. Bilal Qureshi, "The Anthemic Allure of 'Dixie,' an Enduring Confederate Monument," National Public Radio, https://www.npr.org/2018/09/20/649954248/the-anthemic-allure-of-dixie-an-enduring-confederate-monument (accessed May 28, 2020).

21. Taking the time to scaffold activities is crucial when implementing creative projects. Because non-majors often have anxiety around "musicking," they must receive feedback at every stage. The nature of feedback will depend on the classroom (in-person or virtual), but without consistent criticism and guidance, these projects are not nearly as fulfilling or successful. Indeed, in the case of the Reclamation project, they would have the potential to become problematic. See Barkley, Major, and Cross, "The Case for Collaborative Learning," in *Collaborative Learning Techniques,* 14–33. The following guides align with the "Six Facets of Understanding": Explaining, Interpreting, Applying, Demonstrating Perspectives, Empathizing, Demonstrating Self-Knowledge. Grant Wiggins and Jay McTighe, *Understanding by Design* 2nd Edition (Alexandria, VA: Association for Supervision and Curriculum Development, 2005).

22. Steven Mintz, "The General Education Curriculum We Need," *Inside Higher Ed* June 22, 2020 https://www.insidehighered.com/blogs/higher-ed-gamma/general-education-curriculum-we-need (accessed October 21, 2021).

23. For a sampling of performance artists who have revised and reclaimed these songs, see: Craft in America, "Rhiannon Giddens Sings 'Better Git Yer Learning' and Tells Why She Wrote It," YouTube Video, 2.37, October 30, 2015, https://www.youtube.com/watch?v=VlhuZIZAAGQ; WNYC, "Cecile McLorin Salvant: 'Nobody,' Live on Soundcheck," YouTube Video, 3.42, July 24, 2013, https://www.youtube.com/watch?v=8kxDdkphgwQ; Smoddeka, "Rene Marie—Strange Fruit," YouTube, 7.99, October 22, 2011, https://www.youtube.com/watch?v=DjCJAs-56nI; John Sims, "AfroDixie: The Rain Mix," YouTube Video, October 23, 2015, https://www.youtube.com/watch?v=Dh2TFQo8MaQ.

24. Sheryl Kaskowitz, "Before It Goes Away," The Avid Listener, https://www.theavidlistener.com/2017/07/before-it-goes-away-performance-and-reclamation-of-songs-from-blackface-minstrelsy.html (accessed May 28, 2020).

25. Gumbo Chaff, The Ethiopian Glee Book: A Collection of Popular Negro Melodies Arranged for Quartett [sic] Clubs by Gumbo Chaff, A.M.A., First Banjo Player to the King of Congo, (Boston: Elias Howe, 1848).

26. YouTube has an extensive audio library of open-access music and sound effects. YouTube Audio Library, https://support.google.com/youtube/answer/3376882?hl=en -GB (accessed October 21, 2021).

27. Tyler Connaghan, "How to Remix a Song: The Ultimate Beginner's Guide," Mastered Blog, https://emastered.com/blog/how-to-remix-a-song (accessed October 28, 2021).

Works Cited

Barkley, Elizabeth F., Claire Howell Major, and K. Patricia Cross. *Collaborative Learning Techniques: A Handbook for College Faculty* 2nd ed. San Francisco: Jossey-Bass, 2014.

Beck, Eleonora M. "Assignments and Homework." In *The Music History Classroom*, edited by James A. Davis. New York: Routledge, 2016.

Chaff, Gumbo. *The Ethiopian Glee Book: A Collection of Popular Negro Melodies Arranged for Quartett [sic] Clubs by Gumbo Chaff, A.M.A., First Banjo Player to the King of Congo.* Boston: Elias Howe, 1848.

Connaghan, Tyler. "How to Remix a Song: The Ultimate Beginner's Guide." *Mastered Blog.* https://emastered.com/blog/how-to-remix-a-song. Accessed October 28, 2021.

Craft in America. "Rhiannon Giddens Sings 'Better Git Yer Learning' and Tells Why She Wrote It." YouTube Video, 2.37. October 30, 2015. https://www.youtube.com/watch?v=V1huZIZAAGQ

Grawe, Nathan D. *Demographics and the Demand for Higher Education.* Baltimore: Johns Hopkins University Press, 2018.

Grawe, Nathan D. "How Demographic Change is Transforming the Higher Ed Landscape," *Higher Ed Jobs*, February 18, 2019. https://www.higheredjobs.com/blog/postDisplay.cfm?blog=25&post=1843. Accessed April 21, 2020.

Kaskowitz, Sheryl. "Before It Goes Away." *The Avid Listener.* https://theavidlistenerblogcom.wordpress.com/2020/07/28/before-it-goes-away-performance-and-reclamation-of-songs-from-blackface-minstrelsy/. Accessed May 28, 2020.

Kirylo, James D., ed. *Reinventing Pedagogy of the Oppressed: Contemporary Critical Perspectives.* New York: Bloomsbury Academic, 2020.

Mintz, Steven. "The General Education Curriculum We Need." *Inside Higher Ed*, June 22, 2020. https://www.insidehighered.com/blogs/higher-ed-gamma/general-education-curriculum-we-need. Accessed October 21, 2021.

Qureshi, Bilal. "The Anthemic Allure of 'Dixie,' an Enduring Confederate Monument." *National Public Radio.* https://www.npr.org/2018/09/20/649954248/the-anthemic-allure-of-dixie-an-enduring-confederate-monument. Accessed May 28, 2020.

Rendón, Laura I. *Sentipensante (Sensing/Thinking) Pedagogy: Educating for Wholeness, Social Justice, and Liberation.* Sterling, VA: Stylus Publishing, 2009.

Sims, John. "AfroDixie: The Rain Mix," YouTube Video, 8.22. October 23, 2015. https://www.youtube.com/watch?v=Dh2TFQo8MaQ

Small, Christopher. *Musicking: The Meanings of Performing and Listening*. Middletown, CT: Wesleyan University Press, 1998.

René Marie - Topic. "Dixie/Strange Fruit." YouTube, 7.00. January 26, 2016. https://www.youtube.com/watch?v=dGQ_6dgIClE&ab_channel=Ren%C3%A9Marie-Topic

Stimeling, Travis D., and Kayla Tokar, "Narratives of Musical Resilience and the Perpetuation of Whiteness in the Music History Classroom." *Journal of Music History Pedagogy* 10, no. 1 (2020): 20–38.

Turino, Thomas. *Music as Social Life: The Politics of Participation*. Chicago: University of Chicago Press, 2008.

Walker, Margaret E. "Towards a Decolonized Music History Curriculum." *Journal of Music History Pedagogy* 10, no. 1 (2020): 1–19.

Wiggins, Grant, and Jay McTighe, *Understanding by Design*, 2nd Edition. Alexandria, VA: Association for Supervision and Curriculum Development, 2005.

WNYC. "Cecile McLorin Salvant: 'Nobody,' Live on Soundcheck." YouTube Video, 3.42. July 24, 2013. https://www.youtube.com/watch?v=8kxDdkphgwQ

CHAPTER 8

"Decolonizing" the Music in Canada Course[1]

Colette Simonot-Maiello

On the first day of the fall semester, I begin the first-year Western art music history survey class by advising the students to get into the practice of asking, "What music are we *not* studying . . . and why?" This question, along with "Why *this* music?", becomes a refrain in my subsequent classes and hopefully, provides the students with a foundation on which to build a robust critical apparatus. These simple questions effectively foreground historiographical issues that musicology has been addressing in a number of ways over the past few decades, especially pertaining to diversifying and even dismantling the canon. Musicology's trajectory of diversification has courted critiques not just of the accepted canon but also of theoretical frameworks and methodologies applied to that repertoire. Subsequently, music scholars' engagement with cultural theories and critical frameworks, and their intersection with academic studies that address areas such as gender, sexuality, and disabilities, has transformed the research landscape. Despite all of these developments, cutting-edge research is rarely reflected in curricula with any immediacy, leaving some of us who teach in this field, especially those of us at institutions with more traditional programs, to daily leap the massive gulf between the latest research (to which we ourselves might even be contributing) and our classroom curricula. To be sure, incremental changes are slowly transforming textbooks for traditional general survey and period history courses, which now feature at least a few more people from underrepresented groups, like women, BIPOC individuals, and people from the LGBTQIA+ communities. Some of these texts also present a wider view of music culture with a focus funnelled away from genius composers and masterworks and toward performers, critics, patrons, audiences, instrument makers, and others. Amateur music occasionally garners a mention, and often jazz, popular music, and a few traditional or non-Western examples are woven into the narrative as well.[2] Incremental changes have added up to a significant shift in musicology in the past thirty years, but is it enough?

More insistent calls for change—specifically, to *decolonize*—have come from senior scholars such as Margaret Walker and Tamara Levitz. In her 2020 article, "Towards a Decolonized Music History Curriculum," Walker reminds us that academic decolonization is an aspiration in many parts of the world beyond North America, including Africa (where a 2015 incident at the University of Cape Town instigated the Rhodes Must Fall movement), as well as Europe and South America. In Levitz's 2017 speech for the Society of American Music (later published as "Decolonizing the Society for American Music" in that society's bulletin), she suggested that diversity cannot be championed without a parallel critical examination of white and Eurocentric structures of not only the society itself, but also of music programs and pedagogies, lest the legacy of settler colonialism simply be reinforced.[3] Levitz encouraged SAM members to interrogate vigorously the term American—in the context of American music or in the names of societies like the SAM or the AMS (American Musicological Society), and also to take a closer look at American settler colonialism and ongoing coloniality.[4] In their seminal 2012 article, "Decolonization Is Not a Metaphor," Eve Tuck and K. Wayne Yang critique academia's casual adoption of the term "decolonization," arguing, "Decolonization brings about the repatriation of Indigenous lands and life; it is not a metaphor for other things we want to do to improve our societies and schools."[5] While I admit that the decolonization I will discuss in this essay is metaphorical in that it repatriates space in a Music in Canada class from white settlers like myself to Indigenous peoples, this choice was not a random one. Decolonization inherently implies attention to the land, to place, so deliberately choosing to begin decolonizing curriculum with this class, one that includes music from the land that includes Treaty 1, where I currently live and teach, is a meaningful act. In Canada, calls for decolonization in the academic context are connected directly to Indigenous peoples' rights and the Truth and Reconciliation Commission, which took place between 2008 and 2015. Examining the purpose, process, and results of the Commission and details of the enactment of colonialism in Canada has provided me with greater insights about music and musicology's role in colonialism and how I can lay that bare in the classroom. The strategies I have developed to decolonize the Music in Canada course can then be adapted to other courses in the curriculum.

THE CANADIAN CONTEXT FOR DECOLONIZATION: THE TRUTH AND RECONCILIATION COMMISSION

The Truth and Reconciliation Commission (TRC) of Canada was undertaken between 2008 and 2015, following the Indian Residential Schools Settlement

Agreement between the Government of Canada and over 80,000 Indigenous peoples who had been enrolled in Canada's Indian residential school system. Residential, or boarding, schools were just one of the strategies used to try to assimilate Indigenous peoples into Canada's Eurocentric colonial society. The residential school system was put in place in the 1800s and was not completely dismantled until 1996. This school system ripped families apart, worked to wipe out cultural traditions including traditional language acquisition, and was, for many children, a place of physical and sexual abuse. Residential school survivors pursued a class-action lawsuit against the Canadian government and, in 2005, a compensation package for survivors was announced. On June 1, 2008, Canada's Truth and Reconciliation Commission was established in order to document the impacts of the Indian residential school systems on not only those who had been students but also on their families and subsequent generations. The Commission hosted meetings across the country and gave thousands of witnesses an opportunity to share their experiences, either in public or in private. The TRC's priority was to give survivors a voice and to educate Canadians about the damaging history and legacy of Canada's assimilationist residential school system.[6]

The Truth and Reconciliation Commission on the Indian residential school system marked neither the beginning nor the end of truth telling for Indigenous peoples in Canada. The TRC was preceded by the Qikiqtani Truth Commission (2004–2010), which was meant to give voice to the Inuit experience, primarily focusing on the colonial period between 1950 and 1975. This commission, and the subsequent report, shed light on damaging colonial practices that aimed to end traditional hunting practices, such as forced relocation to permanent settlements and sled dog killings, as well as family separations due to lack of medical services in the North.[7] The TRC was followed by the National Inquiry into Missing and Murdered Indigenous Women and Girls (2015–19), aimed at detailing the human rights violations that are the cause of the high rate of violence against this group of people. The resulting report, *Reclaiming Power and Place*, contains details from survivors and their families and "Calls for Justice," akin to the TRC's "Calls to Action."[8]

The TRC's multi-volume final report, released in 2015, concluded that the residential school system amounted to cultural genocide. This report and all testimonies and other documentation from the meetings held across Canada were collected and are now housed in the archives of the National Centre for Truth and Reconciliation on the University of Manitoba campus in Winnipeg, Manitoba, Canada. Further evidence of the conditions at Indian residential schools continues to come to light. While unmarked gravesites have been identified near the former locations of Indian residential schools since the

1990s, more intentional investigations were launched after the publication of the TRC's final report. By 2021, hundreds of graves had been discovered across the country and many investigations are currently being undertaken.

The TRC also released a document outlining "94 Calls to Action" that can help further reconciliation between settlers and Indigenous peoples. These calls to action address several areas, such as child welfare, education, language and culture, health, justice, professional development and training for public servants, museums and archives, media, sports, business, youth programs, and others.[9] The TRC's recommendations for changes in education directly impact Canada's educational systems at all levels, including universities. In order to help students of all ages develop intercultural understanding and mutual respect, they call for age-appropriate curricula that addresses residential schools, treaties, and Indigenous peoples' contributions to Canada, both historical and contemporary. The TRC also recommends that Indigenous knowledge and teaching methods be integrated into classrooms from the earliest grades to post-secondary programs, that senior level government positions dedicated to higher education be established with the goal of advancing reconciliation through education, and that a national research program with multi-year funding be put in place to advance understanding of reconciliation. Since the TRC's final report and calls to action were published in 2015, universities have been encouraged to address reconciliation. According to my own observations as a faculty member at two different universities in Manitoba, the administration, faculty, and staff have been challenged, more specifically, to decolonize and Indigenize in a number of ways, including the following: a) reconsider hiring policies and practices so that more Indigenous candidates are hired in administration, faculty, and staff positions; b) develop student recruitment strategies to draw more Indigenous students to the university and establish programs to encourage their success; c) increase awareness of the land we inhabit through land acknowledgement practices; d) critically examine our curricula and courses and subsequently decolonize and Indigenize[10] them; and e) reflect on our teaching practices and incorporate Indigenous models.[11]

As a settler academic working in Canada faced with this enormous challenge, my first instinct was to consider what Indigenous content could be added to my courses, and to which courses that content could be added, rather than to examine the structure of the courses and curricula themselves. This approach is not unlike earlier diversification strategies in musicology which aimed to bring music of underrepresented groups into the curriculum, and this was likely the knee-jerk reaction of many people working in Canadian universities across various disciplines. Adding Indigenous content was also the implicit approach of one of the workshops on Indigenizing curriculum that I attended in 2019, and my frustration by the end of that workshop was a good reminder that content alone does not constitute discourse.

Bringing Indigenous content into a discourse is a limited strategy if the discourse has a colonial structure; articulated another way, Indigenization is an empty gesture when not accompanied by decolonization. While adding Indigenous content into classes, inviting an Indigenous guest lecturer into a class, adding Indigenous content to the curriculum, and hiring an Indigenous faculty member are all positive steps, they do not absolve faculty from decolonizing the structure of their discipline. Similarly, in the specific context of music programs, leaving the decolonizing and Indigenizing to the ethnomusicologist on faculty, or hiring an ethnomusicologist to do this work, does not mean all of the other music faculty members can abdicate their responsibility in this process. Adding Indigenous content to a course whose structure is not decolonized, or adding a course on Indigenous musics into a program with a structure that is not decolonized, is akin to creating a metaphorical reservation system in the curriculum. Indigenous content is there, but it is limited to one case study in one or two courses, or one or two courses in a curriculum, or one faculty member in a department. It is bounded by certain strictures and cordoned off from the rest of the class, curriculum, or faculty. It has a separate status and probably is not seen as equal to the rest of the course or curriculum content. This is tokenism.[12] Decolonizing curriculum cannot move beyond tokenism without parallel efforts to deconstruct the current curriculum by experts with an intrinsic knowledge of their discipline's intellectual history and structure.

DECOLONIZATION IN PRACTICE: THE MUSIC IN CANADA COURSE

Given that the Truth and Reconciliation Commission, the subsequent "Calls to Action," and Canadian universities' adoption of decolonization and Indigenization policies are specific to the Canadian context, a Music in Canada course is an obvious place to start putting these policies into practice in a music program. It may appear at first glance that the Music in Canada class is in need of decolonization more than other courses in the curriculum because of the specificity of place inherent to this course and its subsequent connec-

136   TEACHING DIFFICULT TOPICS

tion to a particular colonial context. However, in practice, the strategies I used to structure this discourse have inspired similar structural changes to several other courses in the curriculum.[13]

I have taught a Music in Canada course several times over the past twenty years and have made it a practice to use a combination of resources from musicology and ethnomusicology; however, since the TRC, I have reflected more deeply on this course's structure and subsequently foregrounded it, making the structure itself the content of the course. My initial goals for this class were to address a varied repertoire of musics in Canada and put them in dialogue with each other in order to provide a fuller picture of music culture in this country—including Western and non-Western classical traditions, popular musics, and traditional musics of Indigenous peoples and cultural groups who initially colonized this land as well as that of more recent settlers—and I employed the discourse of historical musicology when discussing Western art music and the discourse of ethnomusicology when discussing all other repertoires. More recent iterations of this course, especially since the TRC's 2015 final report and "Calls to Action," have featured an increasingly transparent pedagogy that foregrounds historiography, rather than the music itself. Highlighting the competing narratives that music researchers have constructed about music in Canada lays bare the role that music can play and has played in colonization and, hopefully, points a way toward decolonization by encouraging the students to think about who is creating these narratives or telling these stories, who are the people represented in the stories, and how the stories are being told.

The boundaries of historical musicology and ethnomusicology are constantly in flux, but scholarship on music in Canada historically has been divided into two ideological approaches: a) an historical musicological approach that focuses on the development of the Western European art music tradition in Canada and b) an ethnomusicological approach that considers music cultures active in Canada apart from the art music tradition. For some scholars, including myself, the boundaries between historical musicological and ethnomusicological research in Canadian music are becoming increasingly hazy, but my discussion of these two approaches in the context of the Music in Canada class (and in this essay) is somewhat simplified in order to contrast the structural differences between these two approaches more starkly.

Decades ago, historical musicologists began to develop a grand narrative of music history in Canada, shaped at least in part through publications meant to be used as textbooks.[14] This narrative normally begins as a social

"Decolonizing" the Music in Canada Course 137

history, outlining early amateur musical activity and the establishment of a colonial musical infrastructure, before moving definitively in the twentieth century to a more traditional musicological discourse—a discussion of the evolution of a professional compositional style in Canada. This narrative usually begins with the music of early missionaries and subsequently moves to a discussion of amateur music making by early settlers. The slow development of the colonial musical infrastructure is then outlined, as church musicians, music teachers, and musical instrument makers (especially piano and organ builders) joined the colonies and provided music for the communities. In the nineteenth century, amateur choirs, bands, and orchestras were established in larger urban centers, conservatories opened in some cities, and touring musicians provided audiences with professional performances. Young men (and the occasional woman) with musical ambition typically travelled overseas to study with European composers.

In the twentieth century, this narrative becomes a story about professional composition of European-style art music in Canada, always articulated as two streams—the English and the French, normally centered in Toronto and Montreal. The colonial national identity most popular before the 1960s can easily be mapped onto this narrative. At the same time, more rigorous musical training programs were established in conservatories and later, universities, and professional performing ensembles became a standard feature of large urban centers. Once a professional Western art music infrastructure had been established, the narrative normally shifts to the challenge of creating and articulating a characteristically Canadian compositional style and, typically, the discussion focuses on composers who have incorporated French or English folk song, or possibly Indigenous themes of some kind, into their compositions. The land itself is sometimes a characteristic feature (Claude Champagne's *Altitude* is a popular example), or more commonly, the cold. Some texts on Canadian music include a chapter on Indigenous musics, awkwardly placed either at the beginning or the end of the book, acting as a kind of introductory flashback, or a clumsy epilogue. Indigenous musics are often portrayed in this grand narrative as part of a culture frozen in time that has since been collected, archived, and stored in museums, but in the present has been lost to assimilation. Indigenous themes or rhythms were often used by English or French Canadian composers as raw materials or inspiration for their compositions, perhaps in an attempt to reanimate some lost culture to create a quintessential Canadian sound. In short, the Indigenous musics chapter is not fundamentally part of the narrative.

The grand narrative I have recounted above reflects musicological values

138   TEACHING DIFFICULT TOPICS

from decades ago, and I am certain it will sound colonial to many twenty-first century readers. Some of the more recent musicological research on the Western art music tradition in Canada sensitively addresses broader issues of identity in composition, for example, or attempts to revise the narrative vis-à-vis Indigenous topics. But this grand narrative persists, at least in the shadows.[15] In the 1990s, Beverley Diamond's deconstruction of the historiography of Canadian music textbooks significantly contributed to the development of an ethnomusicological model for the study of music in Canada.[16] One of the markers of ethnomusicological research in Canadian music since then, especially in the work by Diamond and her students, is a disruption of this grand narrative with microhistories, counternarratives, and other alternatives that explore not only tensions and interactions, but also power relationships between communities. Ethnomusicology examines issues of identity in individuals, communities, and regions within Canada and the overlaps and tensions between them. It addresses transnationalism, assimilation, and the effects of hybridity and syncretism on culture and tradition. This field also investigates iterations of national identities, and while it may seem that ethnomusicology fits especially well with Canada's multiculturalism policies, researchers cast a critical eye toward multicultural nationalism, as well as Eurocentric colonial nationalism, and also consider how the inherent power relationship in the settler-colonial construct is both enacted and reflected in musical culture. In 2006, Diamond stated, "Canadian history is marked by a lack of consensus about the desirability or even the possibility of studying Canada as a nation," and ethnomusicological research in Canada has reflected that statement by countering the musicological narrative with so many conflicting and contrasting voices that it is no longer possible, or desirable, to talk about Canadian music with any consensus on style or any other unifying elements at all.[17]

Not surprisingly, many ethnomusicological publications on Canadian music are similarly multivocal, providing an indirect historiographical critique that effectively disrupts the narrative of music history in Canada in a way that I try to replicate in the classroom. Monographs are not typically used as textbooks when teaching about music in Canada from an ethnomusicological viewpoint, but a number of essay collections have been published that could function as a text for a Music in Canada course. The earliest is Beverley Diamond and Robert Witmer's 1994 edited collection, *Canadian Music: Issues of Hegemony and Identity*, but there have since been a number of excellent collections that represent ethnomusicological research on Canadian music, including Anna Hoefnagels and Beverley Diamond's *Aboriginal Music in Contemporary Canada* and the recently-published *Contemporary Musical Expressions in Canada*, edited by Anna Hoefnagels, Judith Klassen, and Sherry Johnson.[18] These collections typically include essays by a wide array of authors who investigate music cultures from specific communities, but also address ethnographic issues and issues of genre, among other critical issues that I outlined above. Rather than conveying an overarching grand narrative, these collections show the student that multiple stories about music cultures coexist in Canada. The most comprehensive survey of music cultures in Canada is the Canada section of the United States and Canada volume of the *Garland Encyclopedia of World Music*, edited by Ellen Koskoff. This ten-volume encyclopedia pushes against structural norms by organizing information and ideas geographically, instead of alphabetically. While it makes no claim to be completely comprehensive, it includes a number of short articles on various music cultures, with other articles that provide a theoretical framework of issues and policies.[19]

Critical historiography yields many pedagogical benefits: by making the structures, rather than the content, of musicological and ethnomusicological texts paramount, the students are better able to develop higher order questions about what musics we study and what questions we ask about those musics, thus uncovering the implicit value systems of those discourses. Instead of foregrounding content or skills acquisition, in the Music in Canada course I encourage students to interrogate competing narratives of the history of music in Canada, putting historical musicology's narrative structure in a dialogic relationship with the structure of ethnomusicology, which privileges multiple voices and microhistories. The students also learn that musics can be addressed from a variety of viewpoints and in different contexts. Because context is crucial for meaning-making, context can also be a key to recognizing colonizing practices and taking part in decolonization.

Consider, for example, how Indigenous musics are treated in the historical musicologists' grand narrative as existing outside that narrative, included as something of an add-on, or viewed as a culture "frozen in time," without a history. These cultural artifacts are considered a resource—a culture of the past that has been collected, archived, and is now stored in museums—from which raw materials can be mined by (usually non-Indigenous) composers in the Western art music tradition. According to this narrative of a frozen past, all of the people who practiced these traditions must either be long gone or assimilated into settler culture. By disrupting that narrative we can open up space to study Indigenous musical cultures in different ways. For example, creating a counternarrative in which Indigenous musics *have a history*

140   TEACHING DIFFICULT TOPICS

provides space to discuss specific cultural and musical practices that were outlawed due to colonial policies and how Indigenous peoples revived old traditions or created new musical practices.

Furthermore, within a structure comprised of multiple conflicting and complementary stories, including those of both individuals and communities, students can see contemporary Indigenous peoples as active musicians in a variety of contexts: they participate in traditional ceremony—sometimes as culture-bearers—which normally involves music, but they are also musicians, composers, and listeners in popular music and art music traditions, as professionals or amateurs. Some of their music might speak directly to their Indigenous identities and some may be connected to other aspects of their identities or other communities of which they are a part. When all of these competing narratives, counternarratives, and microhistories are presented in the classroom, students can more easily identify colonialist structures at work. They start to identify instances of cultural subjugation, music's role in diplomacy, and how music might be used to maintain colonial power. Students also witness music's role in processes of decolonization. There are countless examples of Indigenous peoples and other groups using music for sociocultural adaptation or to resist colonial powers. Music can also play a role in the mediation of privilege and power and contribute to nationalist movements.

My Music in Canada class case study clearly uses a narrative structure from historical musicology that is inherently colonial in that it tells the story of how Europeans colonized Indigenous peoples and established Western art music as the dominant music culture in North America, and a marker of cultural superiority. This colonial narrative is then disrupted by an ethnomusicological structure that gives voice to a wide variety of people who, for the most part, are not represented in the grand narrative. While I contend that this is an effective strategy to teach about colonizing structures and decolonizing practices in the context of a Music in Canada class, I am not suggesting that historical musicology is essentially colonial and ethnomusicology is not—far from it. While ethnomusicology gives voice and space to musics other than Western art music in research and teaching, as a discipline dominated by white scholars who primarily study musics of people of color via a power-laden methodology, ethnomusicology has its own colonial practices to contend with. In the classroom, I problematize this overly-simplified view of historical musicology as colonial and ethnomusicology as decolonized by discussing more recent musicological research that, for example, addresses Indigenous musics in a respectful light with a view to reparation, prioritizing research by Indigenous scholars, and at the same time, questioning whose voices we are really hearing in the multi-vocal ethnomusicological structure by discussing their methodology in depth.

CONCLUSIONS

A two-pronged approach that focuses on the *structures* of musicological discourse, as demonstrated by this case study, can productively contribute to a broader practice of decolonization, beyond the implications of the TRC in Canada and even further afield. On the one hand, scholars' continued vigorous application of critical historiography will be effective in uncovering problematic value systems that keep musicology connected to colonialism; on the other hand, as Tamara Levitz and Margaret Walker suggest, creating new structures for our discourse should be prioritized.

As I noted in the opening to this chapter, critical historiography can be embedded in our courses from the first day of the first-year class onward, and subsequently, we can work to develop strategies for every course that we teach. Historiographical critique can counter the view of European exceptionalism in curricula in a number of ways. For example, while the chronological narrative might not need to be dismissed entirely, we do need to convey to students the problem of the all-too-easy assumption of evolutionary aesthetic progress that structure encourages. Avoiding the "composer as genius" rhetoric allows some space for a discussion of other participants in this music culture, including listeners, performers, patrons, and others, creating a fuller picture by including amateur music making in the discussion. Making a habit of fully contextualizing works in the historical, political, social, and cultural contexts from which they emerged encourages students to see these works as part of an active music culture, rather than as stand-alone aesthetic objects that somehow transcend their own cultural context, and in so doing, represent the superiority of Western European culture. Pointing out Western art music's interaction with and influences from other musics not only lays bare this art form's blatant practice of mining other cultures for raw musical materials, but also demonstrates how it participates in an inter-cultural dialogue. Keeping categories of music separate in the classroom is another way that musicology and ethnomusicology uphold colonial structures. While topics courses offer a potential space in which to intermingle these musics and break down these structures, they are more often used to focus on critical issues like gender or race in music or topics such as war and politics, rather

142   TEACHING DIFFICULT TOPICS

than incubating new structural models. These are just a few examples of elements of musicological discourse that can be targeted with historiographical critique.

In my experience, foregrounding historiography is an important step in teaching students to critically recognize the colonial structure of musicology, but it rarely goes far enough to teach them how to recognize, and even create, a decolonized musicology. I see great potential in the new subfield of global music history to offer a model of the decolonized structure I am suggesting here. As Walker points out,

> The first step, therefore, must be to contextualize Western art music's history and historiography firmly within a larger framework of critically and globally situated histories of music . . . the recent surge of interest in global music history is perhaps laying a foundation for this type of pedagogical change.[20]

In a similar way to the ethnomusicological model in my Music in Canada class, global music history essentially defines music history as the result of multiple voices and stories interacting with one another, creating a dialogical, dialectical model. Global music history, along with historical ethnomusicology, a parallel subfield, can act as a bridge between musicology and ethnomusicology by addressing different categories of music together and demonstrating how the Western tradition is in a dialogical relationship with other musics. This approach also considers socio-political and historical circumstances that have affected music in different parts of the world, and represents both cultural practices' transmission across time and movement throughout geographic space. Global music history brings diverse views together and addresses historical practices of music in different parts of the world, thus reflecting and problematizing the East-West imagination, and hopefully, providing a decolonized structural model for musicology in the future.[21]

Notes

1. "Decolonize" is a contested term, especially in a settler-colonial state like Canada. (See Eve Tuck and K. Wayne Yang, "Decolonization is Not a Metaphor," *Decolonization: Indigeneity, Education & Society* 1, no. 1 [2012]: 1–40.) I use "decolonize" here to parallel the terminology of "decolonization" and "Indigenization" that is now widely used by Canadian academic institutions to indicate the types of changes they aspire to make in response to the Truth and Reconciliation Commission (2015) and the subsequent "Calls to Action." In this context, "decolonization" generally refers to the remov-

"Decolonizing" the Music in Canada Course   143

al or dismantling of colonial structures, ideologies, processes, and other elements, while "Indigenization" refers to the inclusion of Indigenous knowledges, values, processes, and structures.

2. Several music history textbooks with long publication histories provide evidence of these changes. One of the best examples might be W. W. Norton's *A History of Western Music*, first published in 1960 and currently in its tenth edition. The most recent edition is J. Peter Burkholder, Donald Jay Grout, and Claude V. Palisca, *A History of Western Music* (New York: W. W. Norton, 2019). W. W. Norton's newest period history series, "Western Music in Context," edited by Walter Frisch, is a good example of a radically revisioned period music history textbook series which aims to shift the focus away from the "great works" canonic model and toward a richer context, although it essentially maintains the chronological format.

3. See Margaret Walker, "Towards a Decolonized Music History Curriculum," *Journal of Music History Pedagogy* 10, no. 1 (2020): 1–19 and Tamara Levitz, "Decolonizing the Society for American Music," *The Bulletin of the Society of American Music* XLIII, no. 3 (2017): 1–13, https://cdn.ymaws.com/www.american-music.org/resource/resmgr /docs/bulletin/vol433.pdf. Also see "Decolonizing Music Pedagogies," a special issue guest-edited by Robin Attas and Margaret E. Walker, of *Intersections* 39, no. 1 (2019).

4. Margaret Walker distinguishes between "colonialism" and "coloniality" with reference to scholars such as Nelson Maldonado-Torres, who defines "coloniality" as "long-standing patterns of power that emerged as a result of colonialism, but that define culture, labor, intersubjective relations, and knowledge production well beyond the strict limits of colonial administrations" in "On the Coloniality of Being: Contributions to the Development of a Concept," *Cultural Studies* 21, nos. 2–3 (March-May 2007): 243. As referenced in Walker, "Towards a Decolonized Music History Curriculum," 6 (fn 16).

5. See Tuck and Yang, "Decolonization is Not a Metaphor," 1.

6. See The Truth and Reconciliation Commission of Canada's page on the Government of Canada's website at https://www.rcaanc-cirnac.gc.ca/eng/1450124405592/15 29106060525

7. The website for the Qikiqtani Truth Commission, including the final report and other resources is at https://www.qtcommission.ca/index.php/en

8. The website for the National Inquiry into Missing and Murdered Indigenous Women and Girls, including the final report and other documents is at https://www .mmiwg-ffada.ca/final-report/

9. The *Truth and Reconciliation Commission: Calls to Action* (2015) public-domain document is available at https://publications.gc.ca/collections/collection_2015/trc/ IR4-8-2015-eng.pdf.

10. The ubiquitous use of "decolonize" and "Indigenize" did not originate with the TRC or the 94 Calls to Action. Those terms are rarely used in the hundreds of pages of TRC documentation. According to Tuck and Yang, "the language of decolonization has been superficially adopted into education and other social sciences, supplanting

144   TEACHING DIFFICULT TOPICS

prior ways of talking about social justice, critical methodologies, or approaches which decenter settler perspectives" (Tuck and Yang, "Decolonization is Not a Metaphor," 2). In Canadian educational institutions, however, these terms normally connect back to the TRC process.

11. While not the focus of this essay, it is important to acknowledge that education around cultural understanding and sensitivity is the bedrock of this work. Non-Indigenous administration, faculty, and staff members used to working within a settler paradigm are faced with significant challenges in moving forward with decolonization and Indigenization. Settlers should follow Indigenous leadership in undertaking this work, especially as pertains to protocols of respectful working relationships and engaging with Indigenous culture, material or otherwise. Sensitivity toward issues of authority, authenticity, and appropriation needs to be prioritized.

12. Similarly, separating different types of music is not new to faculties of music, or to musicology in particular, where discrete discourses have developed for different types of musics. Western European art music is generally kept separate from popular musics, which are in turn segregated from traditional and non-Western musics.

13. For example, in an Introduction to Ethnomusicology course I taught recently, the theories, histories, and methodologies of ethnomusicology constituted the discourse, as filtered through the consideration of how that discourse might be colonial, decolonial, or how it could be decolonized. A number of case studies were used to exemplify these concepts. In choosing the case studies, I deliberately avoided the "tourist model" of world music courses that so commonly focuses on the traditional musics of different countries, or even continents, around the globe by instead choosing a mix of classical, popular, and traditional musics. I highlighted the problem of tying music cultures to a geographical location and instead, highlighted the movement and interactions of musics across the globe. I also included music of communities constituted in ways other than by geography. Finally, I purposely chose some historical case studies in order to push against the assumption of ahistoricity that plagues this discipline. (On the "tourist model," see Juliet Hess, "Decolonizing Music Education: Moving Beyond Tokenism," *International Journal of Music Education* 33, no. 3 (2015): 336–47.)

14. While this narrative has been shaped by countless publications, two were most influential in shaping my early thinking about the narrative of music history in Canada: Clifford Ford's *Canada's Music: An Historical Survey* (Agincourt, ON: GLC Publishers, 1982) and Timothy McGee's text, *The Music of Canada* (New York: W. W. Norton, 1985).

15. For example, Elaine Keillor's *Music in Canada: Capturing Landscape and Diversity* (Montreal & Kingston: McGill-Queen's University Press, 2006) was groundbreaking in the sense that Keillor covered a variety of musics, including those typically addressed by both musicological and ethnomusicological researchers; however, the book essentially maintains the grand narrative structure, and fits the ethnomusicology topics into this chronological structure.

16. A literature review of Canadian music research is beyond the scope of this essay; however, Diamond's critique provides an excellent summary of three major Canadian

"Decolonizing" the Music in Canada Course   145

music textbooks written with this grand narrative model: Helmut Kallmann, *A History of Music in Canada, 1534–1914* (Toronto, ON: University of Toronto Press, 1987 is 2nd edition of 1960); Ford, *Canada's Music: An Historical Survey*; and Mcgee, *The Music of Canada.* For her critique, see Beverley Diamond, "Narratives in Canadian Music History," in *Canadian Music: Issues of Hegemony and Identity*, eds. Beverley Diamond and Robert Witmer (Toronto, ON: Canadian Scholars' Press, 1994), 139–71. Reprinted in *Taking a Stand: Essays in Honour of John Beckwith*, ed. Timothy McGee (Toronto, ON: University of Toronto Press, 1995), 273–305.

17. Beverley Diamond, "Canadian Reflections on Palindromes, Inversions, and other Challenges to Ethnomusicology's Coherence," *Ethnomusicology* 50, no. 2 (2006): 328.

18. Diamond and Witmer, eds., *Canadian Music: Issues of Hegemony and Identity*; Anna Hoefnagels and Beverley Diamond, eds., *Aboriginal Music in Contemporary Canada: Echoes and Exchanges* (Montreal & Kingston: McGill-Queen's University Press, 2012); Anna Hoefnagels, Judith Klassen, and Sherry Johnson, eds., *Contemporary Musical Expressions in Canada* (Montreal & Kingston: McGill-Queen's University Press, 2019).

19. Ellen Koskoff, ed., *The Garland Encyclopedia of World Music*, Vol. 3, *The United States and Canada* (New York: Routledge Publishers, 2001). For a recent literature review and comprehensive bibliography on ethnomusicological research on Canadian music, see Hoefnagels, Klassen, and Johnson, "Ch. 1 The Study of Music in Canada: Ethnomusicological Sources and Institutional Priorities," in *Contemporary Musical Expressions in Canada*, eds. Hoefnagels, Klassen, and Johnson, 13–38.

20. Walker, "Towards a Decolonized Music History Curriculum," 15. Please note that a parallel subfield, historical ethnomusicology, has similar aims and methodologies to global music history. These two subfields essentially bridge musicology and ethnomusicology. See Jonathan McCollum and David G. Hebert, eds., *Theory and Method in Historical Ethnomusicology* (New York: Lexington Books, 2014).

21. For more resources, see Mark Hijleh, *Towards a Global Music History: Intercultural Convergence, Fusion, and Transformation in the Human Musical Story* (London and New York: Routledge, 2019); Reinhard Strohm, ed., *Studies on a Global History of Music: A Balzan Musicology Project* (New York: Routledge, 2018); and Reinhard Strohm, ed., *The Music Road: Coherence and Diversity in Music from the Mediterranean to India* (Oxford: Oxford University Press, 2019).

Works Cited

Attas, Robin, and Margaret E. Walker, eds. "Decolonizing Music Pedagogies." *Intersections* 39, no. 1 (2019).

Burkholder, J. Peter, Donald Jay Grout, and Claude V. Palisca. *A History of Western Music.* New York: W. W. Norton, 2019.

Diamond, Beverley, and Robert Witmer, eds., *Canadian Music: Issues of Hegemony and Identity.* Toronto, ON: Canadian Scholars' Press, 1994.

Diamond, Beverley. "Narratives in Canadian Music History." In *Canadian Music: Issues of Hegemony and Identity*, eds. Beverley Diamond and Robert Witmer, 139–71. Toronto, ON: Canadian Scholars' Press, 1994.

Diamond, Beverley. "Canadian Reflections on Palindromes, Inversions, and other Challenges to Ethnomusicology's Coherence." *Ethnomusicology* 50, no. 2 (2006): 324–36.

Ford, Clifford. *Canada's Music: An Historical Survey*. Agincourt, ON: GLC Publishers, 1982.

Hess, Juliet. "Decolonizing Music Education: Moving Beyond Tokenism." *International Journal of Music Education* 33, no. 3 (2015): 336–47.

Hijleh, Mark. *Towards a Global Music History: Intercultural Convergence, Fusion, and Transformation in the Human Musical Story*. London and New York: Routledge, 2019.

Hoefnagels, Anna, and Beverley Diamond, eds. *Aboriginal Music in Contemporary Canada: Echoes and Exchanges*. Montreal & Kingston: McGill-Queen's University Press, 2012.

Hoefnagels, Anna, Judith Klassen, and Sherry Johnson, eds. *Contemporary Musical Expressions in Canada*. Montreal & Kingston: McGill-Queen's University Press, 2019.

Hoefnagels, Anna, Judith Klassen, and Sherry Johnson. "Ch. 1 The Study of Music in Canada: Ethnomusicological Sources and Institutional Priorities." In *Contemporary Musical Expressions in Canada*, edited by Anna Hoefnagels, Judith Klassen, and Sherry Johnson, 13–38. Montreal & Kingston: McGill-Queen's University Press, 2019.

Kallmann, Helmut. *A History of Music in Canada, 1534–1914*. Toronto, ON: University of Toronto Press, 1987 [1960].

Keillor, Elaine. *Music in Canada: Capturing Landscape and Diversity*. Montreal & Kingston: McGill-Queen's University Press, 2006.

Koskoff, Ellen, ed. *The Garland Encyclopedia of World Music*, Vol. 3, *The United States and Canada*. New York: Routledge Publishers, 2001.

Levitz, Tamara. "Decolonizing the Society for American Music." *The Bulletin of the Society of American Music* XLIII, no. 3 (2017): 1–13, https://cdn.ymaws.com/www.american-music.org/resource/resmgr/docs/bulletin/vol433.pdf

Maldonado-Torres, Nelson. "On the Coloniality of Being: Contributions to the Development of a Concept." *Cultural Studies* 21, nos. 2–3 (March–May 2007): 240–70.

McCollum, Jonathan, and David G. Hebert, eds. *Theory and Method in Historical Ethnomusicology*. New York: Lexington Books, 2014.

McGee, Timothy. *The Music of Canada*. New York: W. W. Norton, 1985.

McGee, Timothy, ed. *Taking a Stand: Essays in Honour of John Beckwith*. Toronto, ON: University of Toronto Press, 1995.

Qikiqtani Inuit Association. "Qikiqtani Truth Commission." https://www.qtcommission.ca/index.php/en

"Reclaiming Power and Place: The Final Report of the National Inquiry into Missing and Murdered Indigenous Women and Girls." National Inquiry into Missing and Murdered Indigenous Women and Girls. Accessed August 3, 2023. https://www.mmiwg-ffada.ca/final-report/

Strohm, Reinhard, ed. *Studies on a Global History of Music: A Balzan Musicology Project.* New York: Routledge, 2018.

Strohm, Reinhard, ed. *The Music Road: Coherence and Diversity in Music from the Mediterranean to India.* Oxford: Oxford University Press, 2019.

Truth and Reconciliation Commission of Canada. Government of Canada. Modified September 29, 2022. https://www.rcaanc-cirnac.gc.ca/eng/1450124405592/152910 6060525

Truth and Reconciliation Commission of Canada. *Truth and Reconciliation Commission of Canada: Calls to Action.* Government of Canada, 2015. https://publications.gc .ca/collections/collection_2015/trc/IR4-8-2015-eng.pdf

Tuck, Eve, and K. Wayne Yang. "Decolonization is Not a Metaphor." *Decolonization: Indigeneity, Education & Society* 1, no. 1 (2012): 1–40.

Walker, Margaret. "Towards a Decolonized Music History Curriculum." *Journal of Music History Pedagogy* 10, no. 1 (2020): 1–19.

CHAPTER 9

Reimagining Indigenous Existence in Period Performance Practice in the Academic Classroom

Breana H. McCullough

INTRODUCTION

"kúna vúra kúkuum ôok tá ni'uum, pananífyiivshas nimúsarukti, kári vúra pakáruk váhi ni'aapúnmiikti."—William Bright, Speech to Karuk Tribal Council, 2004

The quote opening this chapter means "and so I slowly learn the Indian Language, the Indian customs, the Indian stories." This is a reflection of how myself, as well as many other Native peoples, acknowledge the process of reconnecting with our peoples, customs, histories, and the land. This speech was given in Karuk to the Tribal Council by William Bright who was 74 years old when it was delivered and worked closely with the language and members of the Karuk Tribe. Our Elders recognize that the process of learning is continuous and prioritize the humble approach to knowledge acquisition; these methods have been passed down for generations. This has always been the way. Indigenous peoples are often labeled as resilient, which is correct, but we have also always been able to adapt while holding on to our knowledge systems, perspectives, and worldview despite experiencing an apocalypse. Knowledge and learning are conceptualized through community rather than as individualized, owned, or collected; this differs from practices within Western societies. Author Shawn Wilson outlines this idea in his book *Research is Ceremony: Indigenous Research Methods* through the recognition that a "lifelong analysis is extremely important in an Indigenous way of being and within an Indigenous paradigm."[1] He further expands on the importance of relationships and the "methods available to us that will allow us to ful-

148

Reimagining Indigenous Existence in Period Performance Practice 149

fill our obligations or relationship to the community."[2] We gather knowledge, learn and develop our worldview, creating a toolbox with certain perspectives that help us understand the world we interact with from diverse angles. Colonization, genocide, and racism have impacted how Indigenous peoples move through this world and the ways in which we relate to knowledge. An important element in engaging with Indigenous peoples and our knowledge systems is recognizing and respecting that not all knowledge, perspectives, ceremonies, or conversations, exist for everyone to experience. To the non-Indigenous readers, there is knowledge that is not to be accessed, shared, or created by you. Western society prioritizes individuality and the acquisition of property and frames knowledge as a collectible. The act of taking this knowledge when it is not gifted to you is an act of consumption, extractivism, exploitation, and assault, further perpetuating the violence of colonization and continuing its deadly cycle.

The contents of this chapter should be engaged with and understood as a living entity to be added to and developed on. Claiming space and writing from a place of openness allows me to enact practices of sovereignty and continue traditional forms of knowledge gathering and sharing. Just like William Bright working with our Elders, it is important to acknowledge that I am still learning, developing, and challenging myself to employ these concepts and further enact Indigenization within the colonial institutions that often disallow for Indigenous peoples to live out our epistemologies and ontologies. Of course, the act of writing and publishing creates a certain permanence to these concepts that are alive and developing. I choose to recognize the written word as a process rather than a destination. Indigenous peoples are present, contributing and enacting sovereignty every day. Our epistemologies and ontologies are not conceptually stuck in history but continue to flourish and develop. Indigenous peoples are often framed in the past along with our knowledge systems. It is important to understand that we, as a people, are alive, present, and hold contemporary space in this world. With this in mind, it is important to consider that the experience of music and song is not an isolated event but rather a complex expression of our worldviews, ceremonies, transmissions systems, and our histories. We consider songs relatives and strive to recognize our responsibilities to this kinship by allowing them to exist, live, and expand within their respective rights. These responsibilities have much larger implications. They call for the practices and enactment of Indigenous sovereignty and challenging the way in which history and current interaction with the world are framed. We challenge through the revitalization of our epistemological perspectives, the Indigenizing of sound and space,

150   TEACHING DIFFICULT TOPICS

building relations through kinship, and the call to recognize the past in ways that honor contemporary Indigenous peoples and our respective histories.

The realm of Early Music is lacking in the ability to recognize and consider the development of cross-cultural perspectives, especially in relation to works written for and about Indigenous peoples. Within the field, we are contemporary artists looking to engage the past through understanding rather than re-enacting through misguided assumptions. To be an accountable performer and to stay true to the goal of performance practice, the recognition of complex epistemologies, musical practice, and cultural understandings allow the development of perspective and further the ability to accomplish the intended goal. Historically informed performance practice, conceptually, is understood as the faithfulness of performing a work with the consideration of the cultural, intellectual, and social factors in mind while performing the work in a manner or style of the era it originated from. As an Indigenous person participating in the realm of period performance practice, I have been challenged in the ethical engagement and execution of these works. I am a trained violist in both modern and period styles and have made a significant portion of my living as a performer both in early music and contemporary orchestras. It was while working in early music that the realities of racism, discrimination, inequity, and injustice became the forefront of my experience as a Karuk woman. It became so difficult to function and exist in this realm that I had to remove myself from performance and scholarship in order to continue the work I had originally intended on pursuing. I uprooted my career due to the racial slurs, objectification, and abuse I experienced within the institution I was a part of as well as the broader community at large. I was isolated as a scholar and musician and forced to put my work on hold until I was able to find a different environment that proved supportive of my work and existence in the field. Since then, I was able to move to a place that has extended support, allowing me to rebuild my relationship with my instrument, music, scholarship, and my community. Although my work is not considered performance-focused, my performing and scholarship career is in a space encouraging of growth and recognition. While participating in this field, it not only became a question regarding the oppressive structures and systems that we interact with every day but also a question of how the music I have a passion for was furthermore enforcing the colonial agenda. I started to ask myself: how do I engage with this music in a Good Way and create an environment where all people are welcome and able to learn? The concept of doing things "in a Good Way" is understood by many Indigenous peoples to promote intentional action and reflection that centers the betterment of one's community, spirit, land and all of their relations. Doing things "in a Good Way" challenges me to establish relationships, mend trauma, dismantle hierarchy, and fulfill my responsibilities to future generations, Elders, and the land. This led to my pursuit of the elevation of Indigenous histories, epistemologies, and perspectives in the process of engaging with western art music and encouraging those I engage with to be intentional with the music and peoples they engage with.

Within the music history classroom, the works shared with students always encapsulate rich histories that are rarely recognized. For example, the creation of works like *Les Sauvages*, an entrée act in Jean-Philippe Rameau's opera *Les Indes Galantes* and one of the most recognized works in the current canon, was inspired by a group of Indigenous peoples from the Mitchigamea Tribal Nation who visited Paris in 1735. The accounts of the visit are often only referenced through a Eurocentric lens, without the consideration of the types of sounds that inspired Rameau and his work. This is where challenging and learning ways to engage with this music from an alternative perspective is valuable to the enactment of performance practice. Historical performance cannot be successful if the only histories interacted with are one-sided. Those who created the original design that inspires the creation of these recognized works ought to be acknowledged for their contributions. Without an understanding of those inspirations and the peoples behind them, one cannot fully understand its complexities and therefore its intended affect.

Affect is a concept that is often referenced in the sphere of Early Music. The affect is defined as the distinct emotional states that can be inspired through music and rhetoric. Many French and Italian treatises reflect on the impact of affect and its potential if used correctly. For example, René Descartes, a French philosopher reflects on musical affect when he writes, "the basis of music is sound; its aim is to please and arouse the various emotions in us" in *Compendium Musicae* in 1618 (Dissmore, 3). Understanding the affect can only be accomplished through the diligent practice of interpretation and put into practice through execution. I propose that this interpretation cannot be fully realized unless one is to consider the complex aspects of history, story, song, and perspectives of its original creators while acknowledging that the understanding of sound might be radically different within these inspirational communities.

TERMINOLOGY

> "That language came out of surviving there, whether you come from there or not. By somebody learning that Indigenous language of the land that you are on, you learn a little bit more about what is around there, about where that language comes from."
>
> —Phil Albers reflecting on the Karuk Language,
> Karuk: Language of a River, 2019

Terminology is of utmost importance to clarify in order to understand some of the concepts and methodologies discussed later in this chapter. Words and language hold power, positionality, and help us conceptualize the world we live in. The richness of language in various cultures helps the way in which we interact with and relate to the land. This quote by Phil Albers recognizes that language can be born of survival. The terminology that I use throughout this chapter was developed by BIPOC and LGBTQIA+ theorists, scholars and peoples as a means of survival. It was created to articulate the inequalities and violence inflicted on them while existing within these structures of oppression. Therefore, I have decided to take space and expand on some of the terms I use and how they are employed in my work so that my understanding is clearly conveyed.

I often employ the word "Indigenous" as a term that can refer to a collection of peoples who are from a specific place. I also use this term to define an identity of that which is linked to the land, specific epistemological and ontological differences, and is experiencing colonization. Furthermore, "Indigenous" is a term that I apply to encapsulate a broader global context. On the other hand, American Indian is a term that will be used to specify Native peoples who have been specifically impacted by the settler colonial forces that have created the United States. Systemically, heteropatriarchy is at the forefront of the institutions and is based on the oppression of BIPOC and LGBTQIA+ peoples. Heteropatriarchy enforces heterosexuality as the norm and patriarchy as the epitome of power and structure. Heteropaternalism is enacted through the enforcement of gender roles, a hierarchy of masculine over feminine, eurocentrism, and the continuation of colonialism. Concepts that disengage heteropaternalism, colonization, and racism and inspire action toward the deconstruction of these systems include, but are not limited to, Indigenization, decolonization, and intersectionality. Indigenization is the enactment of Indigenous ways of interacting and engaging with the world. It includes the process of reintroducing Indigenous epistemologies and ontologies and challenges the colonial methods, perspectives, and concepts as universals or the objective. Decolonization is a term that is actively being moved away from due to the centering of the act of colonization and its overuse by non-Native scholars in academic spheres. Decolonization can be recognized as the enactment of sovereignty and resilience against colonization and the structures it enforces. The term intersectionality was coined by Kimberlé Crenshaw in 1989 as an "analytical framework through which feminist scholars in various fields talk about the structural identities of race, class, gender and sexuality" in relation to each other rather than as individual experiences.[3] This concept, although not completely fluid with Indigenous ways of existence, allows for the applicable understanding of societal constructs and oppressions to be recognized as opposed to isolated static experiences. This is especially important seeing that many Native peoples are confronting colonialism through the challenging of gender constructs that are not considered traditional, reclamation of sexuality, and the restoration of equitable social structures. It is important to recognize the diversity that arises when Indigenous people take these concepts and relate them to the land, their individual journeys, and their community stories. Although many of these are experiences under heteropaternalism, through various acts of decolonization, the re-Matriation of cultural perspectives, and revitalization of ceremony create opportunities for Indigenous people and concepts to flourish and restore balance. Overall, the concepts outlined under the various terminology I have listed are all ways in which I understand and participate in the challenging of settler colonization and the oppressive structures it has implemented within society.

These terms have been developed by a collective of various scholars and are reflective of the ways in which Indigenous and feminist scholars are currently engaging in dialogue around these topics. I have taken space to frame the way in which I conceptualize these articulations in my work in order to create reference. Reflecting back to the way Phil Albers speaks about the Karuk language, I remember that language is created through survival, and these are ways in which we articulate ourselves while surviving these systems and working toward the restoration and reclamation of our languages, histories, and world ways. We as Karuk people have always understood who we are as World Renewal people, creating time to reflect on the ways in which we can balance the world in our everyday lives. As a Karuk person, I encourage those around me to find ways in which they are able to contribute and better the world in a "Good Way." My understanding of what it means to do things in a "Good Way" as a Karuk person is the empowerment of Indigenous peoples through the enaction of reciprocity, relationship, and kinship.

154   TEACHING DIFFICULT TOPICS

ALTER-NATIVE HISTORIES

"The Karuk did not know 'the pipe of peace,' but they knew the pipe of friendship. When men or doctor women met together on the trail or elsewhere, it was the regular custom to offer each other their pipes, each himself smoking the first in true Indian style."

—John P. Harrington on the Peace Pipe in *Tobacco among the Karuk Indians of California*

There are various collections of works in early music that engage in the depiction of Indigenous peoples from the Americas including suites, operas, and maskes. One of the most recognized works of this time is Jean-Philippe Rameau's *Les Indes Galantes*. The fourth act of this work is titled *Les Sauvages* and was originally written as a work for harpsichord but was then developed as a part of the opéra-ballet presented privately for French European courts as a part of a tradition known as a courtly pastoral.[4] These courtly performances often depict various peoples that were found to be exotic and often would reference the engagement of French peoples meeting with various depicted cultures. In many ways, a courtly pastoral could be thought of as an ethnographic account of an encounter between the French entity and cultures they deemed exotic. The depictions of these cultures often reflect the social and political structures of the time in France but also give some hints in the way French courts engaged in cross-cultural exchange. The music that was written about these peoples is performed and written in the French Baroque style, but there are hints in the music of cultural practice that one can identify, especially if familiar with the performance practice of the depicted culture.

Jean-Philippe Rameau witnessed a performance given in 1725 by Agapit Chicagou and other members of the Mitchigamea Tribal Nation. These performances were held in royal French theaters; the attendees would have been French aristocrats under the reign of King Louis the XV. Rameau witnessed these performances and was inspired to create a work in the style of Jean-Baptiste Lully. Although they are in the French musical style, there are still reflections of Indigenous performance within the piece itself. Tara Browner identified the style of the call and response used as the basic framework in the theme of the work as seen in Figure 9.1.[5] The performance that Rameau and others witnessed were articulated as three separate dances: peace, war, and victory. Rameau likely heard the structure of call and response and associated it with the French Rondeau and therefore wrote his work in this style in order to depict what he witnessed. The first two measures outline the theme, then

Figure 9.1: *Les Sauvages* as seen in the manuscript of *Nouvelles Suites de Pieces de Clavecin*

it is repeated in the following two measures, likely to mimic the response of the song he heard. This is then followed by a conclusion to the phrase which would have been similar to the dances heard in this performance. The notes on the page would have likely been heard in the French style with notes inégales[6] which is stylistically part of French performance practice.

Rameau likely also read about Indigenous peoples of the Americas and was familiar with the depiction of Native peoples that were created by French explorers and missionaries. The interaction that was written about in the *Mercure de France* depicted in great detail the use of a pipe and the complexities of these peoples, of course with significant mention of their allegiance to the crown. These depictions of Native peoples became a significant part in the development of tropes that we still see enacted in entertainment today. For example, the peace pipe was an item that was assigned to many depictions of Native peoples from illustrations to the characters in the courtly pastorales. Figure 9.2 is a depiction of Inoca War Chief by French Jesuit Father Louis Nicolas in 1701. This illustration is the earliest known image of the Inoca and allows for a glimpse into French portrayal of Native peoples. The peace pipe

Figure 9.2: *Inoca War Chief in 1701*, Gilcrease Museum

in this illustration is a significant part of the image as it is being held in the style of a cornetto or trumpet, signifying nobility and importance. The trope of the peace pipe and its association with nobility can also be seen in *Les Indes Galantes* in "Forêts Paisibles" when the character Zima, the daughter of the chief, expresses the need for peace, fortune, and favors. The peace pipe was a cultural and physical representation of differing political practices of Native peoples compared to French courts. The edition of *Mercure de France* published in December of 1725 writes an elaborate depiction of the Indigenous peoples and their attire along with objects they had while visiting the king. The mention of the peace pipe and use of it in political gestures is seen throughout the essay and further emphasizes the hierarchy and importance of the one who holds the pipe:

"Ils avoient à la main des arcs & des fléches, & celui qui marchoit le premier portoit une longue pipe qu'ils appellent Calumet, d'où pendoit un ornement de plumes de differentes couleurs, dans la même forme que les banderolles des Trompettes. Ce même Sauvage étoit chargé de porter la parole pour tous."

"They had bows and arrows in their hands, and he who walked first carried a long pipe which they call Calumet, from which hung an ornament of feathers of different colors, in the same form as the banners of the Trumpets. This same savage was charged to speak for all." (Translation by author)

The peace pipe is one example of a trope that can be found as early as the 17th century but is still witnessed in media and culture today. The peace pipe is a comprehensive example that can be presented to students for practice in recognizing how tropes and stereotypes have developed and evolved. The impact of this trope can further be seen in the political accounts such as in the *Mercure de France*, illustrations in the journals of French missionaries, and within the depiction of peace in Rameau's *Les Indes Galantes*.

Overall, these depictions of Indigenous peoples shape how we understand and conceptualize Native peoples today. The imagery used of the peace pipe is an example of how certain cultural elements were used to define and create certain caricatures and perspectives of American Indian peoples within Europe. Tropes like these can be seen in all aspects of culture including in courtly pastoral such as *Les Indes Galantes* and within political accounts such as the example from *Mercure de France*.

INDIGENOUS EXISTENCE: PAST, PRESENT AND FUTURE

"Xás vúra uumkun hitíhaan pakaan kunivyiihmutihanik peekxaréeyav, váa kumá'ii pakun'úuhyanaihanik, hûut áta pakunkupítiheesh, yaas'ára."
—Yaas telling the story of how Grizzly got his Ears Burnt Off, Oral Narrative from Ararahih'urípih, 1930

Since time immemorial, Karuk peoples have developed relationships with the land on the Klamath and Salmon rivers in what is known now as Northern California and Oregon. From what I understand, our creation story expands on the generosity of the Spirit Peoples. They were preparing, learning lessons, and placing the salmon so that when Áraar (the people) arrived, the world would be ready for us. This took place at Katimîin, the center of our world.

158   TEACHING DIFFICULT TOPICS

Ákatimîin made the salmon for us and watched over them until they were large enough to be sent into the river. They went to the ocean and once they returned, they were caught in a dip net. This is how the Karuk people learned to fish. The Spirit People ensured that they learned and shared these teachings in order for us to survive and to remind us to give thanks to the salmon and plants that feed our people. The quote beginning this section reflects on the Spirit People gathering together to discuss well-being and what the humans would do in the world.

I share a small telling of the Karuk creation story because it is an example of a history that we as a people carry. It is important to recognize that the Spirit People were thinking about and preparing for us before we even existed. They were learning ways to work with, create and contribute to the world and their surroundings in the most respectful way. These practices were passed to us when we were brought into this world and are reflected in our life ways and ceremonies. We too, do things in a "Good Way" for the past, present, and future generations. The recognition of diversity in relation to the cyclical ways in which some Native peoples' concept of time, thought, and existence is an important aspect of differentiation from western society. These concepts also tend to include a set of outlined responsibilities we have for the land and all of its relations. Robin Wall Kimmerer acknowledges these responsibilities in her book *Braiding Sweetgrass* when she writes "give your gifts and meet your responsibilities."[7] She further expands on these responsibilities by relating the land to the Ancestors as well as future kin and taking care of it as if "our lives and the lives of all our relatives depend on it." This is an example of the cyclical thought process and engagement with the world that Indigenous peoples hold. It is expressive of the responsibilities we hold to the past, present, and future.

There are many theories on why colonization, violence, and exploitation were tools used by European powers. Extractivism and the practice of demanding natural resources in order to build wealth and power are intertwined with the history of colonialism. European conquest sought to obtain natural, cultural, and economic capital by removing resources and exporting them back to Europe in order to build wealth and power within its capitalistic structures.[8] The need to capitalize on lands outside of Europe fulfilled demands for trade goods. The combination of demand, generation of wealth in exchange for resources, and the goal of land acquisition inspired the use of violence on cultures that did not participate in these practices. Throughout dominant history, Indigenous peoples have been considered "underdeveloped" or "primitive" because they did not have the weapons or tools to defend

Reimagining Indigenous Existence in Period Performance Practice 159

themselves when colonists arrived. The reality is reflective of how Indigenous people, especially American Indians, collectively differ from colonial powers. That difference is the recognition of life and respecting each life as sacred. Therefore, the ways in which many Native peoples move through the world are vastly different from the ways of outside cultures. This said, there was not a need to develop the tools to enact force and violence on other peoples in order to collect resources. If there was any process of killing that happened among certain Tribal Nations, there was a recognition that a life had been taken and therefore replaced for those who lost a relative.

This recognition for life translated to the respect and political equity that women experienced in various Tribal Nations across the Americas. This was so prominent and noticeable to colonists that women became the target of assimilation. For example, the coming-of-age ceremonies that were practiced by Karuk peoples were ceased because European colonizers targeted women due to "their ability to reproduce" and because they "represented a threat to the culture and organization" that colonizer societies were attempting to implement.[9] In Karuk society, women were recognized for their contributions and it was acknowledged that their power and understanding of the world was essential to the success and balance of the world. The prominence of this cultural practice was so strong that it was often included as a cultural spotlight in the depictions of Native women, similar to the "noble savage" depiction for men. The noble savage trope is a character that embodies the concept of the untamed wilderness and the wholehearted commitment to his people, even if this commitment results in his death. He essentially becomes a representation of the culture dying or going extinct but in a noble way.[10] These tropes have always been present within the sphere of depiction of Native peoples from a Eurocentric lens.

In Rameau's *Les Sauvages*, the female character, Zima, is recognized for her independence, vocal participation in conversation, and her right to choose. She has various scenes in which she is the cultural center and is the deliverer of knowledge to the audience and other characters. Her character as the central part of the opera is what I believe is a reflection of Indigenous ontology witnessed by the French and Rameau. Women as the center of decision making was a common practice among many Indigenous peoples. Zima has a central part in the opera in which she is tasked with choosing a suitor. This frames her as a "princess" and can be seen as a projection of French ways onto a culture they are trying to understand in a digestible manner. She must choose between marrying within the tribe or to liaise with suitors from France and Spain, depicting a choice between assimilation or continuing her life of

160   TEACHING DIFFICULT TOPICS

freedom. She is warned by the character Damon, the French suitor, when he expresses "Belle Zima, craignez un si triste esclavage!" meaning she should fear such slavery, meanwhile continuing to express his love to her. Although it is a duel to win the heart of Zima, it still portrays the choice of assimilating to a different life or staying with her people and living the life she currently holds. The expression of slavery is a blatant example of the rights and power she holds with her people as opposed to if she were to choose a European life. These rights would be lost if she were to give up her life and spend it with a suitor in Europe. This example can be interpreted as a reflection of the cultural differences and an example of the freedom women in Indigenous societies experienced as perceived by French composer Jean-Philippe Rameau.

The character Zima and the tropes assigned to her are examples of the ways in which the French saw and interacted with Native peoples. While looking at these historical works that were written about Native peoples, one should always consider the histories, stories, and traditions that inspired the creation of these works. There are many examples of inaccurate representations of Indigenous peoples in these works but by getting to know the histories and alternative perspectives, one can identify these inaccuracies and replace them with more accurate representations. I have outlined the creation story of my people to share some reasons why we interact with the world the way we do, and to draw an example of a culture that developed in vastly different ways. European powers attempted to understand these differences and created tropes within their depictions of Indigenous peoples that we still see today. Rameau wasn't any different and within *Les Sauvages* we see these characters enacting these tropes. Overall, while engaging with these works, it is important to recognize the history and learn the complex ways in which Indigenous people existed in order to understand the work and what it is attempting to portray. This will ultimately allow for one to get closer in achieving the goal of accurate performance practice, opportunity to elevate Indigenous histories, and create a comprehensive understanding around this work.

Storytelling, whether through opera or creation stories, can be a way in which perspectives and history are shared and culturally captured. Within the classroom, we should feel empowered to engage in different ways of transmission when it comes to the knowledge we are sharing with students. When sharing these works that often disengage Indigenous peoples and narratives, we hold a responsibility to share these works in a way that is constructive in the creation of space and opportunity for Indigenous peoples. So often in the music classroom an Indigenous person is either not present or not very

Reimagining Indigenous Existence in Period Performance Practice 161

excited to learn about these works, not because they don't want to be, but because we participate in a system that doesn't allow for us to fully cultivate or exist within our passions, tokenizes us, or obstructs our worldview. These systems can be challenged by engaging in critique and encouraging students to develop ways that they see fit in moving forward while dismantling these barriers of exclusion. Situating the music within its context, whether historical or contemporary, can be helpful in starting the conversation. The production created by William Christie and Les Arts Florissants is often used to introduce this piece in a classroom. This production is often referenced for reasoning in the drastic measures to completely erase this piece from being used or contextualized at all within classrooms due to the many offensive and insensitive elements throughout. Another production that is radical in thought is the Clément Cogitore production that centers the dance style of Krump, which was a style developed in Los Angeles in response to police brutality and the beating of Rodney King. This production is admirable in its ability to start conversation around diversity, representation, and political empowerment. Both productions, even in comparison with each other, can be a rich opportunity for dialogue. It is important to note that both productions did not include or incorporate Indigenous peoples or narrative into their creation. They are examples of Indigenous erasure, especially in the lack of recognition of the Mitchigamea peoples who inspired the original production of this work and the lack of inclusion of contemporary Indigenous peoples and their insights. Whether intentional or not, the act of not engaging Indigenous peoples and their direct relationship with this work fulfills tropes and promotes the perspective of a vanishing race and contributes to the violence and erasure of Native peoples. When contextualizing these productions within the classroom, there is often a focus on the blatant erasure, objectification, and dehumanization of Native peoples. Although those elements of focus should be recognized, the goals within the classroom should aspire to inspire students to envision what amazing opportunities there are in the celebration and recognition of Indigenous brilliance, artistry, and sovereignty.

GRAPPLING WITH THE PAST/CONCLUSION

Throughout this chapter, I have outlined ways in which Indigenous peoples exist within a settler colonial society and how they have contributed to the influence on one of the most recognized works in the early music canon. In addition, I have given examples of Indigenous epistemology and ontology

162   TEACHING DIFFICULT TOPICS

directly from various parts of Karuk culture and how recognizing these differences can allow us to engage these works in a more expansive way. Although I outline my understandings and worldview as a Karuk person, I hold a certain positionality as I reconnect and identify with a specific Tribal Nation, and it is important to consider these intersections while engaging with these works. There are vast perspectives and diverse practices that ought to be recognized when engaging with Indigenous peoples and Nations. I consider aspects of Rameau's *Les Indes Galantes* as an opportunity to investigate elements and how this can be used as a tool to see into the ways in which Indigenous people interacted and engaged with the French in the 18th century. There are various ways that knowledge transmission within Indigenous cultures can provide living histories and help scholars and artists engage with these musical works. Indigenous perspectives offer an alternative lens into the interactions between Native peoples and the French and can allow us as artists to interpret and understand these works in a more expansive and ethical way. The example of the peace pipe was a trope that can be assessed and perhaps challenged in its use in order to recognize its status as a stereotype. I often think about when this work will be performed again and how to accurately represent and forge space for Indigenous epistemology to be included in this musical work. By allowing Indigenous peoples to exist and be a part of the contemporary field of performance practice, we can challenge ourselves in the acquisition of histories that will enrich and inspire these works. Considering the goal of period performance practice, it is of utmost importance that all cultures, peoples, and practices are being respected and recognized while engaging with these works and histories, whether it be in a concert hall or music classroom.

To teach *Les Indes Galantes* and other similar works within the classroom setting demands that students and teachers learn to engage critically in the ways they experience and interact with music. The challenge is making sure that one is aware and understanding of Indigenous epistemologies and pedagogies without appropriating them. Many of my suggestions relate in the creation and opportunity to practice the understanding of kinship and not isolating music from its domain. Some of the ways in which this can be enacted are through the engagement of texts that don't isolate music as a subject but recognize its broader application as song in the lives and communities of Indigenous peoples. One comes to realize that much of the rhetoric that happens within Indigenous communities centers one living entity: the land. It is required to spend time within the classroom redefining the ways that students engage with Indigenous texts and peoples that encourage the centering of kinship and relationship to land and its caretakers. Drawing those connections requires the engagement with texts that talk about kinship in diverse ways through various lenses that reflect a handful of different Tribal Nations. By incorporating perspectives that range from ethnobotany, Indigenous feminisms, Indigenous futurisms, and even decolonial theory, students have the opportunity to start humanizing and developing a comprehension of the complexity of Indigenous peoples. In many situations, the understanding of Native peoples is often in an objectifying, dehumanizing or dismissive way and within classrooms it is important to challenge these perspectives by elevating Indigenous histories through their own contemporary voices.

In conclusion, I have shared various depictions, stories, and forms of knowledge in order to convey the importance of creating space while engaging the works that are written about Indigenous peoples. By participating in performance and scholarship of these works, or any other works depicting another culture, it is essential to consider the cultural complexities that peoples hold and how it may be inaccurately portrayed in these musical pieces and contribute to the creation of stereotypes. The challenge to understand, learn, and internalize the ways in which other cultures differ allows us to start the process to ethically engage with the pieces we enjoy. It becomes an ethical question when we work with these pieces of music and use them to generate revenue, fulfill the desire to exotify or "Other" a group of people, or use it to further the colonial agenda. Performing and studying these works demands the space and time taken to deconstruct the normalized ways we create the concert stage, classroom, or written word in relation to these musical works.

The question I am asked the most is always whether it is worthwhile to engage and perform works like Rameau's *Les Indes Galantes*. I always respond to those who ask that question, "because I love this music!" I acknowledge myself and the many other Indigenous artists who hold love and passion for the realm of Western art music. I ask those who hold this question in them to humanize us by allowing us to tell the stories that inspired these works and to respect our eagerness to engage. The assumption that these works are not worth the engagement is a disservice to those who are delving into ways that reimagine these works through practices of kinship, reciprocity, and community. The truth is, I love this music and there are many other Indigenous peoples, past, present, and future, who deserve to be celebrated through the reimagining of these works and their historical context. Currently, productions that do not incorporate or elevate Indigenous voices dehumanize us and our existence. So when asked the question of whether this music is worthwhile, I say respond with a resounding "yes!" and ask those who also are

164   TEACHING DIFFICULT TOPICS

interested in it to create space that humanizes and elevates the brilliance of Indigenous peoples and musicians. This means building long term relations with the Indigenous communities in the area, creating opportunities for Native peoples to tell our own stories, and being open to the ways we enact sovereignty as individuals, families, and Tribal Nations. A majority of the negative interactions I have had with students, scholars, performers, audiences, and teachers were not based out of malicious intent but rather a lack of understanding about the complexities of Indigenous peoples. We cannot re-rite, re-write, re-right our stories if we are not there to teach and engage and express ourselves. Non-Native peoples have a responsibility, like me, to recount and confront the histories of these works while engaging with them. Teaching within the realm of history demands that we reflect on the journeys of those in the past. Why can't we include the incorporation of alter-Native histories when sharing our work with students, colleagues, or audiences? We can, and if we do not, we are contributing to the enaction of white supremacy and the assimilation of people and sound within the realm of "performance." We have always been here and are always present, this is our land. Many of us are present and trying to enjoy the music we love. We want to be collaborators, friends, and build community by celebrating our histories and being humanized through our enaction of sound sovereignty. We are already singing the songs; tíi naa kúna kan'árihishrih nanunipákurih (let me sing our song now).

Notes

1. Shawn Wilson, *Research Is Ceremony: Indigenous Research Methods* (Manitoba, Canada: Fernwood Publishers, 2008), 120.

2. Wilson, 111.

3. Brittney Cooper, "Intersectionality," in *The Oxford Handbook of Feminist Theory*, edited by Lisa Disch and Mary Hawkesworth (Oxford Handbooks, 2016), 385–406; online edition, Oxford Academic (6 January 2015), https://doi.org/10.1093/oxfordhb/978 0199328581.013.20, accessed 15 Aug. 2023.

4. Reinhard Strohm, "*Les Sauvages*, Music in Utopia, and the Decline of the Courtly Pastoral," in *Il Saggiatore Musicale* 11, no. 1: 23.

5. Personal conversations with Tara Browner alluded to the beginnings of research she had conducted including musical insights of the structure and format Rameau used in *Les Sauvages* to reflect performance practice of Woodland Indian Peoples, including the Mitchigamea Tribal Nation.

6. *Notes inégales* is a style of performance practice that was observed in France primarily in the 17th and 18th century. This style employs the swung or unequal dura-

Reimagining Indigenous Existence in Period Performance Practice   165

tion of notes creating stylistic freedom within the beat. See François Couperin, *L'art de toucher le clavecin* (Paris: Chés l'Auteur, le Sieur Foucaut, 1716) https://imslp.org/wiki/Special:ReverseLookup/302585, 39.

7. Robin Wall Kimmerer, *Braiding Sweetgrass: Indigenous Wisdom, Scientific Knowledge, and the Teachings of Plants* (Minneapolis: Milkweed Editions, 2013), 242.

8. Daniel Nettle and Suzanne Romaine, *Vanishing Voices: The Extinction of the World's Languages* (Oxford: Oxford University Press, 2000), 101.

9. Cutcha Risling Baldy, *We Are Dancing for You: Native Feminisms and the Revitalization of Women's Coming-of-Age Ceremonies* (Seattle: University of Washington Press, 2018), 13.

10. Jacquelyn Kilpatrick, *Celluloid Indians: Native Americans and Film* (Lincoln: University of Nebraska Press, 1999), 5.

Works Cited

Baldy, Cutcha Risling. *We Are Dancing for You: Native Feminisms and the Revitalization of Women's Coming-of-Age Ceremonies*. Seattle: University of Washington Press, 2018.

Bloechl, Olivia A. *Native American Song at the Frontiers of Early Modern Music*. Cambridge: Cambridge University Press, 2020.

Bright, William. *The Karuk Language*. Anaheim, Legal Books Distributing: 2003.

Cooper, Brittney. "Intersectionality." In *The Oxford Handbook of Feminist Theory*, edited by Lisa Disch and Mary Hawkesworth. Oxford Handbooks, 2016, 385–406; online edition, Oxford Academic, 6 January 2015. https://doi.org/10.1093/oxfordhb/9780199328581.013.20

Couperin, François. *L'art de toucher le clavecin*. Paris: Chés l'Auteur, le Sieur Foucaut, 1716. https://imslp.org/wiki/Special:ReverseLookup/302585

Descartes, René, Charles Kent, and Walter Robert. *Compendium of Music*. Rome: American Institute of Musicology, 1961.

Dissmore, Joshua L. "Baroque Music and the Doctrine of Affections: Putting the Affections into Effect." *The Research and Scholarship Symposium*, 18. Cedarville University. https://digitalcommons.cedarville.edu/cgi/viewcontent.cgi?article=1384&context=research_scholarship_symposium. Accessed December 1, 2021.

Harrington, John P. *Tobacco Among the Karuk Indians of California*. United States Government Printing Office. *Bureau of American Ethnology Bulletin*, 94: 1–284. Washington: Smithsonian Institution, 1932.

"Inoca War Chief in 1701." In the *Codex Canadensis. 4726.7*. Gilcrease Foundation. Tulsa: Gilcrease Museum, 2017. https://collections.gilcrease.org/object/47267

Kilpatrick, Jacquelyn. *Celluloid Indians: Native Americans and Film*. Lincoln: University of Nebraska Press, 1999.

Kimmerer, Robin Wall. *Braiding Sweetgrass: Indigenous Wisdom, Scientific Knowledge, and the Teachings of Plants*. Minneapolis: Milkweed Editions, 2013.

Lang, Julian. *Ararapíkva: Creation Stories of the People: Traditional Karuk Indian Literature from Northwestern California*. Berkeley, CA: Heyday Books, 1994.

166   TEACHING DIFFICULT TOPICS

Stelle, Lenville J. *Inoca (Ilimouec, Illinois, Illini, Peoria) Ethnohistory Project: Eye Witness Descriptions of the Contact Generation, 1673–1700*. Center For Social Research, Parkland College. http://virtual.parkland.edu/lstelle1/len/center_for_social_research /inoca_ethnohistory_project/inoca_ethnohistory.htm. Accessed 15 August 2023.

Mercure de France. Genève: Slatkine Reprints, 1968.

Nettle, Daniel, and Suzanne Romaine. *Vanishing Voices: The Extinction of the World's Languages.* Oxford: Oxford University Press, 2000.

Rameau, Jean-Philippe. *Les Indes galantes.* http://opera.stanford.edu/iu/libretti/indes gal.htm. Accessed December 1, 2021.

Rameau, Jean-Philippe. *Les Indes Galantes.* 1735.

Robinson, Dylan. *Hungry Listening: Resonant Theory for Indigenous Sound Studies.* Minneapolis: University of Minnesota Press, 2020.

Strohm, Reinhard. "*Les Sauvages*, Music in Utopia, and the Decline of the Courtly Pastoral." *Il Saggiatore Musicale* 11, no. 1: 21–50. January 1, 2004.

Wilson, Shawn. *Research Is Ceremony: Indigenous Research Methods.* Manitoba, Canada: Fernwood Publishers, 2008.

CHAPTER 10

Less Is More

Opportunity for Deeper Dialogue through the Jesuit Examen[1]

Trudi Wright

SLOWING THE MUSIC CLASSROOM

In 2010, scholar and 30th Superior General of the Society of Jesus (the Jesuits) Adolofo Nicolás, S.J., challenged educators to reimagine higher education. In his speech to conference attendees in Mexico City, he identified a disturbing by-product of globalization that he saw affecting 21st-century academic culture, which he named the "globalization of superficiality."[2] The thematic question of his words resonates as loudly today as it did in 2010: At a time in history when humans have the greatest access to knowledge and the highest potential for connectivity, why do we feel lonely and incapable of the deep thinking necessary to solve our culture's social injustices?

In delivering this address, it was as if Nicolás could see into 2020's Coronavirus pandemic that put the world on pause. He admits his appreciation of the connection and communication possibilities afforded by the internet and its applications. Our higher education communities have experienced these technological benefits as we continued teaching our college courses (for better or worse) during an isolating pandemic, and maybe most importantly maintained our connections with students. Without technology, traditional university learning and teaching would have ceased the moment we were asked to leave our campuses to shelter at home. The speed and accessibility of this tool, however, comes with a price.

Because our students can "access information so quickly and painlessly" and can "publish one's reaction to anything so immediately and unthinkingly . . . then the laborious, painstaking work of serious, critical thinking often gets short-circuited."[3] Our culture is currently seeing the effects of this mass movement of information and people's reliance on sound bites instead of well-researched information as we experienced the unfolding of a pan-

168   TEACHING DIFFICULT TOPICS

demic. On the one hand, scientists shared important, up-to-date information almost instantaneously to keep people safe, and on the other, propaganda and misinformation permeated newsfeeds and social media sites creating fear, rage, and polemic feelings among large segments of our population. This is, in part, because people are not taking the necessary amount of time to read and digest the information provided.

At a basic level, are we giving our music students, especially those in the performing arts who will be navigating the physical, emotional, and mental care of students and audiences affected by catastrophes like the COVID pandemic, the tools needed to critically assess sources of information to discern for accuracy? Can they confidently rely on their reasoning skills to feel deeply informed, just as choral instructors did throughout the pandemic, to judge the safety of rehearsal spaces and performance opportunities?[4] At a deeper level, this evaluation of safety (and the mere time it takes to process information in a meaningful way) was of utmost importance to singers who required the connection of group performance and the audience members who needed to be moved by the musical arts in community with one another to cope.

At a time in our history when so many are in need—physically, mentally, economically, emotionally and dare I say spiritually—it is the University music program's job to nurture students into citizens who can creatively and critically think and act for the good of the community. Now, more than ever, we need our students to flourish into people thinking about how they can serve through their work at home, professionally, and voluntarily. Although a course in music history might not seem like the epicenter of cultural or personal change, it is my fierce belief that we all have a small but significant role to play in the large-scale changes we dream of fulfilling. I am doing this in my classroom by teaching a personal reflection technique, which allows my students to practice slowing down to engage in deeper levels of thinking while also creating community through group sharing.

Recent conversations have emerged rallying for ways to allow college faculty the mental space for discourse, writing, community building, and especially reflection as they grapple with the difficulties of our cultural experiences.[5] Leading the charge in support of "slow," and against the globalization of superficiality for professors of the academy, are Maggie Berg and Barbara K. Seeber.[6] The authors describe the stress produced by the corporatization of universities and the Western world's cultural celebration of untenable workloads. How do we minimize this stress for our colleagues, students, and selves? If at all possible (and of course, the ability to which faculty members

Less Is More   169

have the ability to enact change, due to the unfairly varying states of precarity in the academy and beyond can dictate the extent to which change can occur), *we must slow down.*

Through research done on capturing timelessness or "flow" (the experience of transcending time and one's self by becoming immersed in a captivating present-moment activity or event) to cultivate creativity (a skill/way of being desperately needed to help solve societal problems), Berg and Seeber suggest ways for scholars to reclaim their headspace in order to do their best work.[7] Music scholars have also joined the discussion.

Thomas Turino also engages with Mihaly Csikszentmihalyi's idea of "cognitive flow" and how it can be obtained through music, thus allowing individuals to reach "fuller integration of the self through involvement with artistic processes."[8] If scholars need to transition into timelessness to do their best work, so too do students, especially when they are in the act of learning. As their mentors, it is our job to teach and model this behavior, which is where the classroom examen comes in. In this chapter, I will offer concrete examples of examen reflections to slow students down in order to transition them into a time of flow for more thoughtful conversations about how they communicate with one another as they grapple with difficult subjects, such as social injustices introduced in the music of NWA.

THE EXAMEN AS REFLECTIVE PRACTICE BASED IN PRAYER TRADITION

Although originally intended as a strictly religious practice, the examen allows practitioners the opportunity to transition into a time of focus, in the short term and, if practiced regularly, has the potential to lessen their anxiety about the future by keeping them grounded in the present, while centering their actions toward the common good.[9] I fully understand that this meditation, with its deep roots in a Catholic Order, may not feel appropriate or comfortable in all college settings or for all faculty members. Although the Jesuits hold magnanimous ideals, they, like many religious orders, were involved in violent settler colonialism, the Catholic Church's sexual abuse scandal, a position against birth control, and of course, not allowing women to join their order.[10] These difficult truths, however, make the examen an interesting topic for students wrestling through critical thinking. By introducing the examen and its problematic history, the instructor is allowed the chance to guide students through the complications of accepting an effective medita-

170   TEACHING DIFFICULT TOPICS

tion reflection practice while simultaneously condemning other practices of the order from which it comes.[11]

James Martin (a Jesuit, author, and minister to the LGBTQIA+ community), introduces the *examen* in its most traditional form: as a daily conversation with God. He writes,

> [The examen] is a prayer designed to enable believers to find God in their lives. (Actually, it's more accurate to say that he popularized the prayer, since versions of it had been around for some time.) [Ignatius of Loyola] called it the 'examination of conscience.' And he used to say that it was so important that even if Jesuits neglected all other forms of prayer in their day, they should never neglect this one.[12]

The importance placed on this prayer by the founder of the Jesuits explains its ubiquitous place on Jesuit college campuses. In my experiences at Regis University, the examen (pronounced either "ex-ae-men," or like the English word "examine") is practiced in obviously religious settings like a Maundy Thursday Mass, but also in traditionally secular settings, like teaching retreats (to help educators discern their experiences throughout the day), and even as a way for Jesuit institutions to reflect on and improve their shared educational mission.[13] Modern Jesuit campuses welcome students from all belief and non-belief systems and although the examen is a Christian prayer practice, the Jesuits encourage its use by everyone, no matter their background. In order to make the examen more welcoming, I will substitute or add "The Good" wherever "God" is used or implied throughout this chapter, except in places where "God" is part of a direct quotation. You are welcome to do the same if you choose to use the examen in your classroom or meeting and can feel free to substitute any term that feels right.[14] The point is to acknowledge that you are communing with a power or force that is bigger than humanity.

According to Jesuit historian John W. O'Malley, the founder of the Jesuit order, Ignatius of Loyola, was a proponent of adaptability when it came to cultivating personal spirituality. James Martin explains, "... Ignatius wanted as many people as possible to enjoy the [Spiritual] Exercises (from which the examen comes), so he included several notes, or annotations, in his text for the sake of flexibility. Some people might not be ready for the whole Exercises, he wrote, so they could complete them only in part. Others might profit from having insights of the Exercises taught to them."[15] O'Malley writes, "Ignatius's most fundamental teaching was that individuals had to find the way that suited them best."[16] Although all the steps of the Spiritual Exercises (Ignatius's manual for a four-week period of meditation of the life of Jesus) were methodically explained, the final instruction was always, "if this method doesn't work, try something else."[17] Because of the Jesuit's amenity to adaptability, it comes as little surprise that my colleagues at Regis University, one of the 27 Jesuit Universities in the U.S., encourage the adaptation of the examen practice for classroom use.[18]

THE STRUCTURE AND PRACTICE OF THE EXAMEN

The traditional examen has five steps, as seen in Appendix 10.1, although in my classroom example I have included the transition into and out of the examen as steps of the process.[19] When practicing the examen in private, it is typically done in silence, but when experienced in a group, it is common for a leader to guide the exercise by introducing each step followed by silence for reflection. It is only after the examen is finished that the leader might ask those in the room to share their reflections with one another. This is when the practice can do double duty as a reflective meditation and community builder.

After one has transitioned into the examen space, the reflection begins with a time of gratitude. Ignatius discussed this as a time for being thankful for any "benefits."[20] In your class you can guide your students to think about obvious things like landing a role in the musical or finishing a research paper after many weeks of hard work, but the time of gratitude should also be used to reflect on "the little things." These moments might include the sun on their face as they walk through the quad or the sound of their best friend practicing her aria in the next-door practice room. All of the moments, big and small, are "occasions for gratitude." These are the times that, when recalled, should be "relished" or "savored."[21] According to Martin,

> Savoring is an antidote to our increasingly rushed lives. We live in a busy world, with an emphasis on speed, efficiency, and productivity, and we often find ourselves hurriedly moving on to the next task at hand ... Savoring slows us down. In the examen we don't recall an important experience simply to add it to a list of things that we've seen or done; rather we savor it as if it were a satisfying meal. We pause to enjoy what has happened.[22]

The intentional act of relishing a memory allows students and faculty alike the opportunity to work against a culture that promotes "faster" as a way of

172   TEACHING DIFFICULT TOPICS

life. The examen's emphasis on slowing down is why I think this activity is a crucial one for the college classroom, especially when taking on difficult conversations. In Appendix 10.2, you will see that the transition into an examen and the first step of gratitude mimic the traditional examen. The next steps in this example I use before difficult class discussions, however, are modified to focus on specific lessons or pedagogical themes for the class period.

In the traditional examen, the next steps focus on reviewing the past twenty-four hours and allow time to think about, as Martin puts it, "where you have turned away from the deepest part of yourself, the part that calls you to [The Good]. Where did you act contrary to your better judgment or to [The Good] inside you, to the divine spark within?"[23] After reviewing the day, practitioners are then asked to acknowledge the times where they fell short and to then make amends, if necessary. These traditional questions, as well as the more pedagogically themed questions in the "Review events" step (Appendix 10.2, #3) are great to use in the classroom because they give students the space and the time to reflect on their day or on a specific pedagogical skill, like verbal communication or their writing practice. Reflecting on one's experience in order to take action is a celebrated part of the Ignatian Pedagogical Paradigm. The paradigm (found in Figure 10.1), in its simplest form, keeps experience, reflection, and action in conversation as a student learns.[24]

For example, when a student moves into "Deeper reflection" (Appendix 10.2, #4) and remembers a conversation from the previous day where they did not truly listen to a friend who was talking, but instead were formulating a witty (but turned out to be hurtful) comment, may likely listen more carefully and speak more thoughtfully in the class discussion about Ice Cube's lyrics, for example. This occurs because students are given the opportunity to think about their discourse in the past day, mimic what they liked about it and adjust their actions where necessary. The act of slowing down is crucial. Students can learn to be more mindful of the power of their words and the way they can show care through thoughtful listening. According to the creators of The Teaching Commons at Georgetown University, "The students who have been through [the Ignatian Pedagogical Paradigm] will have had old ideas unsettled in the service of developing a fuller understanding of self and the world, and in service of helping that world."[25] By taking the time to reflect on past actions, either school related or not, students have the opportunity to grow into life-long learners and change-makers.

Far too often as college music professors, we focus on what is wrong with a paper, a performance, a presentation, etc., and do not let students know

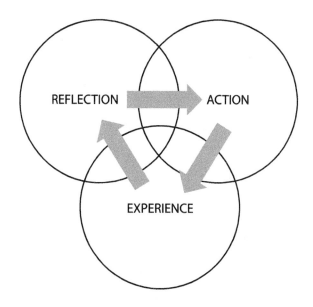

The Ignatian Pedagogical Paradigm:
a constant interplay of *experience – reflection – action*

Figure 10.1: The Ignatian Pedagogical Paradigm

when they have done something well. Group discussion after the examen is an excellent time to hear about successes and celebrate them as a community. Although I am in full support of the traditional examen's instructions to reflect on instances where the best choices were not made by students (this could be interrupting someone in conversation, for example) and ask them to reflect on how they can make better choices going forward, I am also a firm believer of reflecting on actions that are worth repeating and encouraging more of those behaviors.

To learn about what your students are reflecting on internally, taking a few minutes after the examen to discuss what came up for the class is beneficial (see Appendix 10.2, #7, "Follow up to the examen"). Be sure that after students have made their "Personal commitments," (see Appendix 10.2, #5) time is given to transition out of the reflection space (see Appendix 10.2, #6). This practice mimics the start of the examen by offering gratitude for the time in "The Good" space and then bringing their focus back to the classroom for time to share. Some students may not be comfortable sharing information about more personal examens, which is perfectly acceptable, but I have found that most stu-

174   TEACHING DIFFICULT TOPICS

dents want to share about their communication skills and writing practices. I call on students (a practice I start on the first day of class to learn their names) to share their reflections, but the rule in my class is that you can say "pass" any time you are called on with no questions asked. I find students feel supported when they learn others are having similar struggles with writing, for example, and they are inspired by the good work of their classmates.

COULD THE EXAMEN WORK IN YOUR CLASSROOM?

In a foundational article on the purpose of the examen, George Aschenbrenner, stresses the importance of the notion that "The Good" is in all things and this becomes easier and easier for the practitioner to understand the longer they practice the examen. A continued practice then allows for more and more of "The Good" to influence their choices and their actions. It is important to point this out because Aschenbrenner warns against the examen working in superficial ways. He states,

> The dangers of an empty self-reflection or an unhealthy self-centered introspection are very real. On the other hand, a lack of effort at examen and the approach of living according to what comes naturally keeps us quite superficial and insensitive to the subtle and profound ways of God deep in our hearts.[26]

Aschenbrenner's words point to a challenge with the classroom examen.

Although it is easy to make time for an examen every few weeks within a class at my Jesuit institution and to experience the more civil conversations conducted after the examen in my classroom and meeting spaces, I reiterate my understanding of this meditation's complicated position in Catholic history. A music teacher using the examen must also consider whether or not they are ready to let go of some of their content in order to make room for these practices. For an examen to be done well with time for group reflection afterwards, a teacher must dedicate ten to twenty minutes of class time each day the examen is performed. I also acknowledge it will take more rigorous questioning through entrance and exit surveys to more deeply understand students' perception of whether or not they are tapping into "The Good" to make their life decisions, both short and long term, to better understand the examen's efficacy.

My next step is to conduct more formal research in the classroom to

Less Is More   175

include student surveys in order to learn more about how they experience the examen as an agent of personal change. For now, however, I am content with introducing them to a tool they can use to center themselves in the classroom or choose to use the rest of their lives for personal reflection. The examen may or may not be influential at the moment they experience it, but I invite and encourage them to use or return to the practice whenever and if ever they are ready.

I have found that the act of focused reflection is an excellent tool to enter into difficult conversations surrounding the scholarly discipline of Music, in order to cultivate more meaningful dialogue and scholarly skills. I believe this act of "slow" is an important step toward deeper thinking around issues of social change and a way to fight off the globalization of superficiality in our students and ourselves. But, do I have all the answers about the examen's efficacy? Not yet.

Is silent reflection before a class discussion something that is commonly practiced in college music classrooms? Not yet. Do you feel prepared to lead these meditations? Maybe not yet. That, however, is the beauty of life-long learning, according to Amy Collier, Jen Ross, and Kevin M. Gannon, that we want to instill in our students, and I would argue, ourselves.[27] In what they call "not-yetness," Gannon explains that our job is to get our students (and ourselves) closer to "yet." If we are being encouraged, as Gannon contends, "to encounter students as people in process, not as fixed and insurmountable deficits," then can the same not be true of us?[28] Let's challenge ourselves and our colleagues to find practices that allow our students time to think and reflect beyond the first article they find in a search on Google Scholar. Let's use the suggestions of the scholars within this book to resist the injustices of our culture by broadening our pedagogical palettes. By making room to reflect on our actions in the music classroom, just as our students do in the examen, we begin to be the change we want to see in the world.[29]

APPENDIX 10.1: THE EXAMEN IN FIVE STEPS FROM JAMES
MARTIN'S *THE JESUIT GUIDE TO (ALMOST) EVERYTHING*

1. **Gratitude:** Recall anything from the day for which you are especially grateful and give thanks.
2. **Review:** Recall the events of the day, from start to finish, noticing where you felt [The Good's] presence, and where you accepted or turned away from any invitations to grow in love.

176   TEACHING DIFFICULT TOPICS

3. **Sorrow**: Recall any actions for which you are sorry.
4. **Forgiveness**: Ask for . . . forgiveness. Decide whether you want to reconcile with anyone you have hurt.
5. **Grace**: Ask . . . for the grace you need for the next day and an ability to see [The Good's] presence more clearly.

APPENDIX 10.2: *EXAMEN* TO PREPARE FOR A DIFFICULT
CONVERSATION/CLASS DISCUSSION

1. **Physical transition**
   a. Ask the students to get comfortable in their chairs.
   b. Give them time to feel the floor under their feet and where the chair is touching their body.
   c. Ask students to close their eyes, or if that is not comfortable, to softly focus on something in the middle distance about 2–3 feet in front of them.
2. **Gratitude**
   a. Ask the students what they are grateful for today as college students.
   b. Encourage them to think about who or what supported their journey today and the moments that brought them joy.
3. **Review events**: specifically conversations you had throughout the past 24-hours
   a. "When were you facing toward the light?"
      i. "When did you feel good about the content you were offering in conversation?"
      ii. "When were you truly listening—not simply waiting to make a comeback, but actually listening to what others had to say?"
   b. "When were you facing away from the light?"
      i. "When did you say something thoughtless or hurtful?"
      ii. "When were you hearing the other person speak, but not truly listening to what they had to say?"
4. **Deeper reflection**
   a. "Choose a few significant moments that continue to surface as you reflect."
   b. "What's going on there?"
5. **Personal commitments**
   a. "What do you want to do differently today?"
   b. "What things do you want to repeat because they were fruitful?"

Less Is More   177

6. **Transition back into the space**
   a. "When you feel ready, offer a sentence of gratitude to God/The Good/The Universe/The Light for the time to reflect."
   b. "Then, slowly open your eyes if they were closed, and shift back into the present moment in this classroom."
7. **Follow up to the *examen*:** To finish this exercise, take a few minutes to reflect out loud as a group for community building.
   a. Ask the students about their strongest moments of conversation and let them tell you what was going on. Also ask for their opportunities for growth. "Where can they improve their speaking and listening today and into the week?"
   b. Congratulate them and ask them to mimic the habits that worked for them and also encourage them to try again with the moments that didn't go as well as they had hoped. **This is the point of the *examen*.** Through reflection and awareness of our behaviors and choices, we can learn to be better in the world.

Notes

1. I want to thank Christopher Pramuk, Anna Nekola, Laura Moore Pruett, Olivia Lucas, and the anonymous reviewers of this collection for helping me develop the ideas found within this chapter. Generous colleagues are great gifts.

2. Adolfo Nicolás, S.J., "Depth, Universality, and Learned Ministry: Challenges to Jesuit Higher Education Today," Remarks for "Networking Jesuit Higher Education: Shaping the Future for a Humane, Just, Sustainable Globe," Mexico City, April 23, 2010. http://www.sjweb.info/documents/ansj/100423_Mexico%20City_Higher%20Educati on%20Today_ENG.pdf, accessed July 27, 2020.

3. Nicolás, "Depth, Universality, and Learned Ministry," 2.

4. For examples from choral communities navigating the COVID-19 pandemic see, American Choral Director's Association, "Resources for Choral Professionals During the Pandemic," https://acda.org/resources-for-choral-professionals-during-a-pand emic, accessed December 16, 2021; Boston's Gay Men's Chorus, "COVID 19 & BGMC," https://www.bgmc.org/covid-19-bgmc/, accessed December 16, 2021; Barbershop Harmony Society, "Covid-19 Interim Guidance for BHS Ensembles and Singing Communities," https://acda-communications.s3.us-east-2.amazonaws.com/COVID-19-In terim-Guidance-for-BHS-Ensembles-and-Singing-Communities-v1.5.pdf, accessed December 16, 2021.

5. See for example: Margaret A. L. Blackie, Jennifer M. Case, and Jeff Jawitz, "Student-centredness: The Link Between Transforming Students and Transforming Ourselves," *Teaching in Higher Education* 15, no. 6 (2010): 637–46; Robert Boice, *Advice for New Faculty Members: Nihil Nimus* (Boston: Allyn and Bacon, 2000); Daniel

178   TEACHING DIFFICULT TOPICS

Kahneman, *Thinking, Fast and Slow* (Toronto: Anchor Canada, 2013); Susan Robison, *The Peak Performing Professor: A Practical Guide to Productivity and Happiness* (San Francisco: John Wiley and Sons, Jossey-Bass), 2013; Sarah L. Wright, "Organizational Climate, Social Support and Loneliness in the Workplace: The Effect of Affect in Organizational Settings," *Research on Emotion in Organizations* 1 (2005): 123–42.

6. Maggie Berg and Barbara K. Seeber, *The Slow Professor: Challenging the Culture of Speed in the Academy* (Toronto: University of Toronto Press, 2016), see specifically their preface and "Chapter 1: Time Management and Timelessness." "The Slow Movement—originating in Slow Food—challenges the frantic pace and standardization of contemporary culture. While slowness has been celebrated in architecture, urban life, and personal relations, it has not yet found its way into education. Yet, if there is one sector of society which should be cultivating deep thought, it is academic teaching . . . Time for reflection and open-ended inquiry is not a luxury but is crucial to what we do" (Berg, Seeber, ix–-x). *The Slow Professor* is but one book in the now growing academic conversation on Slow Pedagogy in higher education. Other early articles include: Alison Mountz, Anne Bonds, Becky Mansfield, Jenna Loyd, Jennifer Hyndman, Margaret Walton-Roberts, Ranu Basu, Risa Whitson, Roberta Hawkins, Trina Hamilton and Winifred Curran, "For Slow Scholarship: A Feminist Politics of Resistance through Collective Action in the Neoliberal University," *ACME* 14, no. 4 (2015): 1235–59; and Yvonne Hartman and Sandy Darab, "A Call for Slow Scholarship: A Case Study on the Intensification of Academic Life and Its Implications for Pedagogy," *Review of Education, Pedagogy, and Cultural Studies* 34, nos. 1-2 (2012): 49–60.

7. In Berg and Seeber, *The Slow Professor*, 27. (See their discussion of timelessness on pp. 25–32). Quote from Charalampos Mainemelis, "When the Muse Takes It All: A Model for the Experience of Timelessness in Organizations," *Academy of Management Review* 26, no. 4 (2001): 548.

8. Thomas Turino, *Music as Social Life: The Politics of Participation* (Chicago: University of Chicago Press, 2008), 4; Mihaly Csikszentmihalyi, *Flow: The Psychology of Optimal Experience* (New York: Harper & Row, 1990).

9. There are a variety of published books and articles on the examen including Timothy M. Gallagher, O.M.V, *The Examen Prayer: Ignatian Wisdom for Our Lives Today* (New York: The Crossroad Publishing Company, 2006); James Martin, S.J., The Jesuit Guide to (Almost) Everything: A Spirituality for Real Life (New York: HarperCollins Publishers, 2012); Louis M. Savary, *The New Spiritual Exercises: In the Spirit of Pierre Teilhard de Chardin* (New York: Paulist Press, 2010); Herbert Alphonso, *The Personal Vocation: Transformation in Depth Through the Spiritual Exercises, Seventh Edition* (Rome: LitoPomel, 1996); Joan L. Roccasalvo, C.S.J., *Prayer for Finding God in All Things: The Daily Examen of St. Ignatius of Loyola* (Saint Louis: The Institute of Jesuit Sources, 2005); Jim Manney, *A Simple Life-Changing Prayer: Discovering the Power of St. Ignatius Loyola's Examen* (Chicago: Loyola Press, 2011); George Aschenbrenner, S.J., "Consciousness Examen," *Review for Religious* 31 (1972): 14–21; Kenneth S. Sagendorf, Susan A. Scherer, James D. Nash, et al., "Are We Fulfilling the Promise of a Jesuit Education?:

A Group of Educators' Reflective Examen," *Jesuit Higher Education* 5, no. 2 (2016): 62–75; Joel Boehner, "Praying for Change: The Ignatian Examen in the 'Remedial' Classroom," *Journal of Education and Christian Belief* 16, no. 2 (2012): 215–27. The examen can also be experienced electronically. I recommend the app, Reimagining the Examen (Loyola Press "Reimagining the Examen," 1.22 (2018), https://apps.apple.com/us/app /reimagining-the-examen/id1065042173, accessed July 28, 2020, or the podcast "The Examen with Fr. James Martin, S.J.," https://podcasts.apple.com/us/podcast/the-exa men-with-fr-james-martin-sj/id1346804716, accessed July 28, 2020.

10. To read about examples of the Jesuit's painful history see, for example: Micah True, *Masters and Students: Jesuit Mission Ethnography in Seventeenth-Century New France* (Montreal: McGill University Press, 2015); Bronwen McShea, *Apostles of Empire: The Jesuits and New France* (Lincoln: University of Nebraska Press, 2019); Jesse Paul and Jennifer Brown, "52 Catholic Priests in Colorado, Including Iconic Father Woody, Abused 212 Victims, Further Investigation Finds," *Colorado Sun*, December 1, 2020, https://coloradosun.com/2020/12/01/colorado-catholic-church-priest-abuse-father -woody/, accessed December 16, 2021.

11. As a white, female, United Methodist, musicologist tenured at a Jesuit University, there are many parts of the examen practice that are natural fits with my pedagogy, and, of course, parts of Jesuit history that are certainly not.

12. Martin, *The Jesuit Guide to (Almost) Everything,* 87. Ignatius's *Examen* can be found in Ignatius, *Spiritual Exercises of St. Ignatius*, 2nd ed., trans. Anthony Mottola (New York: Double Day, 1989), 53. (The original work was written in 1522.)

13. See Tom Reynolds, "The AJCU Institutional Examen: A Shared Ignatian Experience," *Jesuit Higher Education: A Journal* 5, no. 1 (May 2016): 102–4.

14. Other terms I have heard used in my experiences with the examen are "The Light," "The Universe," "Yahweh," "Abba," and "Goddess Mother." Again, please feel free to use what is comfortable and inviting for you and your students.

15. Martin, *The Jesuit Guide to (Almost) Everything,* 19–20.

16. John W. O'Malley, *The First Jesuits* (Boston: Harvard University Press, 2015), 12.

17. I am grateful to Kari Kloos, Assistant Vice President of Missions at Regis University, for her thoughtful teachings on the Spiritual Exercises. I have been learning from Kari since my arrival at Regis and admire her open and giving way of teaching Ignatian thought and pedagogy.

18. It is also being used in college classrooms of non-Jesuit institutions. See, Boehner, "Praying for Change," 215–27.

19. Gallagher, *The Examen Prayer*, 25. Gallagher lists his steps as "Transition," "Step 1," "Step 2," etc., and then ends with "Transition" essentially making the Examen a seven-step process. Martin also suggests a transition but offers it as an introduction before the beginning of the examen. He writes, "Before you begin, as in all prayer, remind yourself that you're in God's presence, and ask God to help you with your prayer." (Martin, *The Jesuit Guide to (Almost Everything)*, 97.)

20. Martin, *The Jesuit Guide to (Almost) Everything*, 88.

180 TEACHING DIFFICULT TOPICS

21. Martin, *The Jesuit Guide to (Almost) Everything*, 88.

22. Martin, *The Jesuit Guide to (Almost) Everything*, 88.

23. Martin, *The Jesuit Guide to (Almost) Everything*, 89.

24. Jesuit Institute, "Ignatian Pedagogy: A Practical Approach," https://jesuitinstitu te.org, accessed June 19, 2024.

25. Georgetown University, "Ignatian Pedagogy," https://cndls.georgetown.edu/reso urces/ignatian-pedagogy/, accessed June 19, 2024.

26. Aschenbrenner, "Consciousness Examen," 15.

27. I originally read about "Not-yetness" in Kevin Gannon, *Radical Hope: A Teaching Manifesto* (Morgantown: University of West Virginia Press, 2020), 25, but the term and concept come from Amy Collier and Jen Ross, "For Whom, and For What? Not-yetness and Thinking Beyond Open Content," *Open Praxis* 9, no. 1 (2017), http://dx.doi.org/10 .5944/openpraxis.9.1.406, accessed July 29, 2020.

28. Gannon, *Radical Hope*, 25.

29. This final sentence is based on the quote typically attributed to Mahatma Gandhi, "Be the change you want to see in the world." What Gandhi actually said was, "We but mirror the world. All the tendencies present in the outer world are to be found in the world of our body. If we could change ourselves, the tendencies in the world would also change. As a [person] changes [their] own nature, so does the attitude of the world change towards [them]. This is the divine mystery supreme. A wonderful thing it is and the source of our happiness. We need not wait to see what others do." See Brian Morton, "Falser Words Were Never Spoken," *New York Times* (August 29, 2011) https://www.nytimes.com/2011/08/30/opinion/falser-words-were-never-spok en.html, accessed July 28, 2020.

Works Cited

Alphonso, Herbert. *The Personal Vocation: Transformation in Depth Through the Spiritual Exercises*, 7th ed. Rome: LitoPomel, 1996.

American Choral Directors Association. "Resources for Choral Professionals During the Pandemic." Accessed December 16, 2021. https://acda.org/resources-for-choral -professionals-during-a-pandemic

Aschenbrenner, George, S.J. "Consciousness Examen." *Review for Religious* 31 (1972): 14–21.

Barbershop Harmony Society. "Covid-19 Interim Guidance for BHS Ensembles and Singing Communities." Accessed December 16, 2021. https://acda-communications .s3.us-east-2.amazonaws.com/COVID-19-Interim-Guidance-for-BHS-Ensembles -and-Singing-Communities-v1.5.pdf

Berg, Maggie, and Barbara K. Seeber. *The Slow Professor: Challenging the Culture of Speed in the Academy*. Toronto: University of Toronto Press, 2016.

Blackie, Margaret A. L., Jennifer M. Case, and Jeff Jawitz. "Student-centredness: The Link Between Transforming Students and Transforming Ourselves." *Teaching in Higher Education* 15, no. 6 (2010): 637–46.

Boehner, Joel. "Praying for Change: The Ignatian Examen in the 'Remedial' Classroom." *Journal of Education and Christian Belief* 16, no. 2 (2012): 215–27.

Boice, Robert. *Advice for New Faculty Members: Nihil Nimus*. Boston: Allyn and Bacon, 2000.

Boston's Gay Men's Chorus. "COVID 19 & BGMC." Accessed December 16, 2021. https://www.bgmc.org/covid-19-bgmc/

Collier, Amy, and Jen Ross. "For Whom, and For What? Not-yetness and Thinking Beyond Open Content." *Open Praxis* 9, no. 1 (2017). Accessed July 29, 2020. http://dx.doi.org/10.5944/openpraxis.9.1.406

Csikszentmihalyi, Mihaly. *Flow: The Psychology of Optimal Experience*. New York: Harper & Row, 1990.

Gallagher, Timothy M., O.M.V. *The Examen Prayer: Ignatian Wisdom for Our Lives Today*. New York: The Crossroad Publishing Company, 2006.

Gannon, Kevin M. *Radical Hope: A Teaching Manifesto*. Morgantown: University of West Virginia Press, 2020.

Georgetown University. "Ignatian Pedagogy." Center for New Designs in Teaching and Scholarship. Accessed June 19, 2024. https://cndls.georgetown.edu/resources/ignatian-pedagogy/.

Hartman, Yvonne, and Sandy Darab. "A Call for Slow Scholarship: A Case Study on the Intensification of Academic Life and Its Implications for Pedagogy." *Review of Education, Pedagogy, and Cultural Studies* 34, nos. 1–2 (2012): 49–60.

Ignatius. *Spiritual Exercises of St. Ignatius*, 2nd ed. Translated by Anthony Mottola. New York: Double Day, 1989.

Kahneman, Daniel. *Thinking, Fast and Slow*. Toronto: Anchor Canada, 2013.

Jesuit Institute. "Ignatian Pedagogy: A Practical Approach." Accessed June 19, 2024. https://jesuitinstitute.org/.

Loyola Press. "Reimagining the Examen." 1.22, (2018). Accessed July, 28, 2020. https://apps.apple.com/us/app/reimagining-the-examen/id1065042173

Mainemelis, Charalampos. "When the Muse Takes It All: A Model for the Experience of Timelessness in Organizations." *Academy of Management Review* 26, no. 4 (2001): 548–65.

Manney, Jim. *A Simple Life-Changing Prayer: Discovering the Power of St. Ignatius Loyola's Examen*. Chicago: Loyola Press, 2011.

Martin, James. "The Examen with Fr. James Martin, S.J." Accessed July 28, 2020. https://podcasts.apple.com/us/podcast/the-examen-with-fr-james-martin-sj/id134680 4716

Martin, James. *The Jesuit Guide to (Almost) Everything: A Spirituality for Real Life*. New York: HarperCollins Publishers, 2010.

McShea, Bronwen. *Apostles of Empire: The Jesuits and New France*. Lincoln: University of Nebraska Press, 2019.

Mountz, Alison, Anne Bonds, Becky Mansfield, et al. "For Slow Scholarship: A Feminist Politics of Resistance through Collective Action in the Neoliberal University." *ACME* 14, no. 4 (2015): 1235–59.

Nicolás, Adolfo, S.J. "Depth, Universality, and Learned Ministry: Challenges to Jesuit Higher Education Today." Remarks for "Networking Jesuit Higher Education: Shaping the Future for a Humane, Just, Sustainable Globe," Mexico City, April 23, 2010. Accessed July 27, 2020. http://www.sjweb.info/documents/ansj/100423_Mexico%20City_Higher%20Education%20Today_ENG.pdf

O'Malley, John W. *The First Jesuits*. Boston: Harvard University Press, 2015.

Paul, Jesse, and Jennifer Brown. "52 Catholic Priests in Colorado, Including Iconic Father Woody, Abused 212 Victims, Further Investigation Finds." *Colorado Sun*. December 1, 2020, https://coloradosun.com/2020/12/01/colorado-catholic-church-priest-abuse-father-woody/, accessed December 16, 2021.

Reynolds, Tom. "The AJCU Institutional Examen: A Shared Ignatian Experience." *Jesuit Higher Education: A Journal* 5, no. 1 (May 2016): 102–4.

Robison, Susan. *The Peak Performing Professor: A Practical Guide to Productivity and Happiness*. San Francisco: John Wiley and Sons, Jossey-Bass, 2013.

Roccasalvo, Joan L., C.S.J. *Prayer for Finding God in All Things: The Daily Examen of St. Ignatius of Loyola*. Saint Louis: The Institute of Jesuit Sources, 2005.

Sagendorf, Kenneth S., Susan A. Scherer, James D. Nash, et al., "Are We Fulfilling the Promise of a Jesuit Education?: A Group of Educators' Reflective Examen." *Jesuit Higher Education* 5, no. 2 (2016): 62–75.

Savary, Louis M. *The New Spiritual Exercises: In the Spirit of Pierre Teilhard de Chardin*. New York: Paulist Press, 2010.

True, Micah. *Masters and Students: Jesuit Mission Ethnography in Seventeenth-Century New France*. Montreal: McGill University Press, 2015.

Turino, Thomas. *Music as Social Life: The Politics of Participation*. Chicago: University of Chicago Press, 2008.

Wright, Sarah L. "Organizational Climate, Social Support and Loneliness in the Workplace: The Effect of Affect in Organizational Settings." *Research on Emotion in Organizations* 1 (2005): 123–42.

PART III

Critical Race Studies

CHAPTER 11

Transdisciplinary Antiracism Research and Teaching as a Foundation for Revising Music Coursework

John Spilker-Beed

INTRODUCTION

Transdisciplinary teaching and research on racial justice provide content and processes to identify and decenter whiteness along with other intersecting dominant ideologies in all aspects of my courses.[1] This includes examining content, assignments, grading, and approaches to teaching, all of which are rooted in my thinking about teaching and students. My work has led to the creation of racial justice courses for the Interdisciplinary Studies program at Nebraska Wesleyan University, a predominantly white institution that draws at least half of its enrollment from small towns across the state. These courses form the foundation for "Music History 2: Antiracist Liberation," a topic-based approach to the second-semester music history course required for music majors.[2] Within the higher education landscape, my work is inspired by the Truth, Racial Healing and Transformation initiative of the American Association of Colleges and Universities along with other forms of scholarship of teaching and learning that address equity.[3] It also represents one possibility for classroom applications of Bryan Stevenson's call for the United States to reckon with our history of genocide, slavery, racial terrorism, and economic and educational inequity.[4] As the founding executive director of the Equal Justice Initiative (EJI), Stevenson invests in the powerful connections between music and culture.[5] In May 2021, he partnered with Wynton Marsalis and the Jazz at Lincoln Center Orchestra for the "Freedom, Justice, and Hope" concert.[6] Two years later, I was among the invited guests for a collaborative gathering of classical musicians at the Equal Justice Initiative hosted by Anthony McGill (New York Philharmonic) and Bryan Stevenson.[7] This chapter explores the transdisciplinary research and interdisciplinary teaching I used to create and teach "Music History 2: Antiracist Liberation."

185

TRANSDISCIPLINARY RESEARCH AND TEACHING

I designed and taught two racial justice topics for the First-Year "Archway Seminar" in NWU's Interdisciplinary Studies Program, including mass incarceration (fall 2019) and racial terror lynching (fall 2020). These topics are drawn from the four pillars of the Equal Justice Initiative's Legacy Museum in Montgomery, Alabama.[8] The United States has continuously preserved a narrative of racial difference and inequity through slavery, racial terror lynchings, segregation, and mass incarceration. In the face of backlash against our nation's 2020 racial reckoning, now more than ever we need courses that highlight the scholarship of racial justice. I want to help my students ask, "What are histories? Who creates them? How are they transmitted? How are they hidden? What are the consequences for us and our communities?" Or as Lin-Manuel Miranda asks in *Hamilton: An American Musical*, "Who Lives? Who Dies? Who Tells Your Story?"[9] Speaking at the Malcolm X and Dr. Betty Shabazz Memorial and Educational Center, Nikole Hannah-Jones asserted, "history is not simply what happened on what day and who did it, but what powerful people want us to remember about what happened. And so, what we commonly call history is actually memory. And that memory in the United States has been shaped too often by white men in power who want us to remember the history of a country that never existed."[10] Black, brown, and Indigenous lives and perspectives have always been excluded from informal and formal means of education in white society, from segregated local newspapers to school textbooks that perpetuate white supremacy. These remain the tools and means of white silence, which is reinforced by legal means and our local, state, and national government.

While studying racial justice, music appeared in striking ways that helped me see more clearly the need and opportunities for reparative work inside our discipline. These examples presented vital "a-ha" moments, inviting me to rethink the music discipline, and therefore, to conceptualize, create, teach, and revise "Music History 2: Antiracist Liberation." They also reaffirm the value of a transdisciplinary approach, which admittedly lies outside the norm for music faculty, and is uncomfortably pointed out in pejorative ways by music colleagues and students at my liberal arts institution. I wondered, "Why have I never learned about this information during my education? How could musicians bring repair into our discipline by integrating this historically excluded information into how we teach music history and performance? What would our disciplinary conversations, processes, and environments look like if more equitable histories undergirded our musical work?"

In 1900, as they worked for the vaudeville industry in New York City, lyricist and future NAACP leader James Weldon Johnson, together with his brother and musical collaborator J. Rosamond Johnson, witnessed racialized violence perpetrated by a white mob that included police.[11] In 1911, white Kentuckians used the stage of the Livermore opera house to lynch Will Potter, and they sold tiered tickets to participate in the murder. People sang hymns at public executions and "spectacle lynchings," which were publicized in local newspapers and drew crowds ranging from 2,000 to 15,000 people, some of whom brought picnics.[12] Paul Robeson faced racialized violence in 1949 at his Peekskill concerts, likely due to his antilynching activism, which propelled him to an international stage at the United Nations in 1951.[13] The Mississippi State Penitentiary, which continued the slavery practices of Parchman Farm during Jim Crow and beyond, housed many blues musicians, drawing the research of folklorist scholars.[14] Finally, in *The Souls of Black Folk*, W. E. B. Du Bois connects each chapter with a "sorrow song," which are discussed more fully in the chapter, "Of the Sorrow Songs."[15] In the preceding chapter, he tells a story of escaping the rural south through education, only to experience racialized violence at a classical music concert in the north.[16]

Any of these examples could serve as a touchstone to reshape how we think about, research, perform, and teach music. But, do we see music programs as a place of interaction with and accountability toward advancing equity or addressing legacies of racial difference reinforced by violence? And what changes need to occur if we do? More specifically, as musicians continue debates about upholding racist traditions of repertoire and performance practices—such as blackface in opera, preserving dialect in historically white choirs, and using minstrelsy songs to teach music fundamentals in the K–12 classroom—the above documented historical experiences open opportunities for truth telling and reconciliation as we reconsider teaching and performing music more equitably.[17]

"MUSIC HISTORY 2: ANTIRACIST LIBERATION"

Rather than beginning with disciplinary research on African American music, my transdisciplinary research and teaching lay the foundation to create "Music History 2: Antiracist Liberation."[18] This course uses a topic-based approach and *Project-Based Learning in the First Year* to transform the second semester of music history required for music majors.[19] Our collaborative work in Music History 2 is anchored in the Equal Justice Initiative's reparative

188   TEACHING DIFFICULT TOPICS

vision. Racial healing and transformation in the U.S. can be accomplished through learning about the history of black experiences and perspectives that remain intentionally excluded in most schools, and how those past experiences and perspectives along with the intentional concealing of them in our curriculum impacts all of us, right now. The research project connects the EJI's mission of reckoning with narratives and legacies of racial difference and violence to student research on music and culture. Students design a concert plan to educate a Nebraska audience about the EJI.[20] Using music and spoken word, they create multiple concert segments focused on the EJI's reports on slavery, reconstruction, lynching, and segregation.[21] A cursory search illuminates the dire relevance of the EJI's work for Nebraskans. In 2019, the EJI supported a local Omaha coalition's community soil collection to remember the racial terror lynching of Will Brown and George Smith.[22] Further reconciling work remains in Otoe and Cherry counties, where Nebraskans lynched Henry Martin and Henry Jackson in 1878 and Jerry White in 1877, respectively.[23] Nebraskans voted to reinstate the death penalty in 2016, only one year after the state legislature repealed it.[24] In 2020, thirty-two percent of Nebraskans voted to keep slavery in the state constitution.[25] Thus, the music history classroom presents an opportunity for students to explore the relationships between music and racial justice education that addresses local legacies of injustice.

Using the methods and processes of *Project-Based Learning in the First Year*, research comprises the first ten weeks of the semester and project work guides the remaining five weeks. Students develop information literacy skills and a foundational knowledge about racial justice with readings that explore how white supremacy undergirds institutions and ideologies.[26] As we navigate the content using discourse instruction, students also develop skills in social emotional learning,[27] including empathy for BIPOC people and their diverse experiences, perspective taking, careful listening to understand, and inviting multiple perspectives and questions to remain at the table.[28] I am currently researching and integrating nonviolent communication skills into my discourse instructive model.[29] Following this work, six class sessions examine "The Story We Tell," a brief overview of art music from the Classic Period, Nineteenth Century, and Twentieth Century, including social and cultural context, key genres, and styles. The podcast episode on American music in Nikole Hannah-Jones's *1619 Project* explains "What Is Missing in the Story We Tell."[30] Then, we examine "Why Is It Missing?" using Loren Kajikawa's article about the possessive investment in white supremacy in the structure and practices of U.S. music departments.[31] Finally, to engage in "Repair by Teaching the Story Not Taught," we study Henry Louis Gates Jr.'s research on the inculcation of white supremacy during the nineteenth and twentieth centuries through the arts and mass media in order to culturally reinforce Jim Crow legal suppression of Reconstruction racial equity.[32]

Students guide their research with a handout of time periods that chronicle an honest appraisal of black experiences in the U.S., including antebellum, emancipation, reconstruction, redemption, Jim Crow, the New South, the New Negro, great migration, civil rights, black power, colorblind, and postracial. Drawn from a range of transdisciplinary research sources, these terms signify periods of time with porous and overlapping boundaries. Additionally, students bring to each class session one piece of music from African American experiences, using Burnim and Maultsby's *African American Music* as a suggested resource.[33]

The pressure of white supremacy in music departments often manifests in students' and colleagues' pushback to difference. Though they may not realize it consciously, many students entering the music major expect to be immersed in the department's "possessive investment" in whiteness. Kajikawa defines this throughout his chapter in *Seeing Race Again*, but the possessive investment plays out via exclusionary practices and resistance to change, in order to uphold the primacy of classical music as bearing the only content and practices to achieve success.[34] Of course, whiteness along with our white racialized group identity are never named, because the first rule of white club remains, "don't talk about white club." Our nation's history documents how white backlash controls and suppresses black lives and gains made toward equity.[35] During summer 2020, Sen. Tom Cotton mounted political pushback to Nikole Hannah-Jones's *1619 Project*, which led to President Trump's "1776 commission."[36] This fomented ongoing political policy-making that opposes teaching U.S. history that honestly embraces and appraises black experiences, which necessarily includes the ways in which institutions and ideologies suppress black experiences while simultaneously upholding those of white people.[37] Furthermore, given the hegemony of aesthetic autonomy, pointed out by William Cheng in *Just Vibrations*, students understandably question why any non-music-making information, let alone racial justice, begins a music course, or is part of a music course.[38] Although musicology brings together history, sociology, music, critical theory, and humanities, our subdiscipline still resonates with the divisive, harmful imperative that privileges making music and only talking about the music itself.

190   TEACHING DIFFICULT TOPICS

HOW WE WORK TOGETHER: THEORY

Content about racial justice and antiracism should result in processes that expose and dismantle modes of domination. In fact, black studies scholars have provided a robust foundation for care pedagogy.[39] Dominant ideologies associated with the "imperialist white-supremacist capitalist patriarchy" remain the norm in music teaching, research, creative activity, conference presentations, and committee work.[40] These ways of being are so pervasive in music that William Cheng wrote two books to name these problems and invite us to learn. *Just Vibrations* applies scholarship from critical race theory, queer theory, disability studies, and care ethics to ask us to be more humane in our work. He provides resources for music faculty to consider the impact of our ways of thinking, being, and musicking (i.e., "business as usual" or "the way things work in the profession") on individuals from minoritized groups.[41] *Loving Music Till It Hurts* explores the often ignored negative impacts of our music culture through these vital questions, "Is it possible for our love and protection of music to go too far? Can such devotion ever do more harm than good? Can our intense allegiances to music distract, release, or hinder us from attending to matters of social justice?"[42]

Rooted in the work of critical and inclusive pedagogies, Dorinda Carter Andrews and Bernadette Castillo's humanizing pedagogy speaks to process.[43] They write, "In order to build trusting and caring relationships with [all] students as a way to further their willingness to take learning risks in the classroom, we must disrupt dominant group ideologies and practices."[44] In fact, they assert, "The project of humaniz[ing pedagogy] involves simultaneously highlighting the voices of those who have been historically oppressed *and* humanizing sociocultural knowledge."[45] Finally, they argue that faculty must "consider our positionality as individuals who benefit from the oppressive racial power structure and perpetuate its features (unknowingly and knowingly) in how we cover course material."[46] These are compelling guidelines for me to observe my courses and make important changes to support intersectional antiracist equity.

Lee Ann Bell's definitions of social justice, justice, and social justice education along with their interlocking relationship provide further guidance to reconsider the processes associated with teaching and learning, such as course design, assignments, grading, and use of class time. She asserts,

> The *goal* of social justice is full and equitable participation of people from all social identity groups in a society that is mutually shaped to meet their needs.

The *process* for attaining the goal of social justice should also be democratic and participatory, respectful of human diversity and group differences, and inclusive and affirming of human agency and capacity for working collaboratively with others to create change. . . . Our *vision* for social justice is a world in which the distribution of resources is equitably and ecologically sustainable, and all members are physically and psychologically safe and secure, recognized, and treated with respect. Domination cannot be ended through coercive tactics that recreate domination in new forms. Thus, a 'power with' vs. 'power over' paradigm is necessary for enacting social justice. Forming coalitions and working collaboratively with diverse others is an essential part of social justice.[47]

Bell defines justice through resources and recognition and advocates for "fair and equitable *distribution of resources* . . . with the imperative to address those who are least advantaged. . . . [and] the importance of fair and equitable *social processes*, including recognition and respect for marginalized or subjugated cultures and groups."[48] Finally, social justice education "includes both an interdisciplinary conceptual framework for analyzing multiple forms of oppression and their intersections, as well as *a set of interactive, experiential pedagogical principles and methods/practices. . . .* we use the term 'oppression' rather than discrimination, bias, prejudice, or bigotry to emphasize the per vasive nature of social inequality that is woven throughout social institutions as well as embedded within individual consciousness."[49]

One way that I have begun to apply this scholarship includes asking: How can I continually interrogate my courses and learning environments, now that I'm aware that they have been shaped by dominant white ideologies? How can I explore ways to invite "full and equitable participation of people from all social identity groups in a [course] that is mutually shaped to meet their needs?" First, I have to be honest about the ways I benefit when my courses and learning environments maintain the "imperialist white-supremacist capitalist patriarchy."[50] In other words, how are assignments, grading, and in-class participation designed to maintain my control and comfort in the classroom?

HOW WE WORK TOGETHER: PRACTICES

In all my courses, research on antiracist intersectional equity has led to ongoing change. A simple, yet urgent, modification arose from Erica Chu's

192   TEACHING DIFFICULT TOPICS

research, which provides tools to normalize discussion and promote learning about gender and pronouns.[51] This breaks the silence about cisgender identity being the norm. It also challenges the assumption that only transgender persons need to identify their gender, name, and pronouns. In syllabi I write: "My name is John Spilker-Beed. You can call me Dr. Spilker-Beed. The pronouns you should use when you speak about me are: he/him/his/his/himself." I also verbally state this information to the class on the first day to come out to them about my gender and model gender-affirming communication about names and pronouns. As part of an online survey for me to learn about the students and their goals, each person fills out the following information: "My name is _____. The name you should use when you speak to me/email me is: _____. The pronouns you should use when you speak about me are: _____." For the final question, students select from a list of pronouns in Chu's article.[52] By seeing the entire list, along with the option to provide pronouns not listed, everyone learns some of the current options for pronouns.

I created a handout, "Fostering Our Learning Community," that we read and discuss on the second day of class to co-create our ways of learning in community. The handout comprises quotes from two essays: "From Safe to Brave Spaces" by Brian Arao and Kristi Clemens and "Uncomfortable Learning" by Jasmine L. Harris.[53] The primary rationale for the handout comes from Harris's work. First, our learning environment needs "boundaries . . . that [provide] for a broadening of understandings and a challenging of preconceptions. . . ."[54] Second, throughout the semester, I want us to co-facilitate a learning environment where we "create a space for questions, rather than agreements, allowing openness around [our] hidden 'isms' (racism, sexism, classism, heterosexism, etc.), and encouraging [ourselves] to grow, rather than to change."[55] To encourage accountability, we discuss the ways we can rely on each other to remember and apply guidelines during discussions throughout the semester.[56] After students read the document, we discuss these questions: What are you glad to see, and why? What are you concerned or uncomfortable about? What do you have questions about? To foster community, we sit in a circle to be fully present with each other. This discussion allows us to see and hear each other and seek clarification. It sets a tone that we will honestly confront and learn about systems of privilege and oppression, because they form the foundation of all our institutions and ideologies. Many scholars remind us that neutral spaces do not exist.[57] The final question for our conversation reinforces the co-construction of learning: "How do we demonstrate respect to each other in the context of our learning work?"

Before they answer, we unsettle the concept of respect to eschew performances of niceness that protect privilege and comfort, shut down difficult conversations, and maintain status quo. I record the student responses for us to refer back to throughout the semester.

Administered five to seven weeks into previous semesters, an anonymous survey provides an opportunity for students to co-construct teaching and learning through their observations and feedback. My institution's Margaret J. Prouty Teaching Award comprises nine criteria, adapted from Arthur W. Chickering and Zelda F. Gamson's "Seven Principles for Good Practice in Undergraduate Education."[58] After winning the award in 2017, I wanted to continually survey my students to see how they felt I was performing using a Likert scale to evaluate these questions:

> Does this teacher... communicate high expectations,... encourage intellectual curiosity within and/or across disciplines,... encourage students to do their best work,... hold students accountable,... engage students in the class,... encourage collaboration/discussion among students,... engage diverse ways of thinking, learning, and knowing,... encourage faculty-student interaction,... use teaching methods beyond lecture?

Quantitative information did not tell me what students were experiencing or their ideas. Thus, for each question above, I added two free-response follow-up questions to contextualize the likert scale rating: "What ways do you see the professor do this in order to help student learning? Do you have specific suggestions for other ways the professor could do this in order to help student learning?" These changes invite students into anonymous dialogue with me to use the scholarship of teaching and learning to co-construct our work together. Rather than assuming that I'm the only person who knows how to interpret and apply this knowledge, the students tell me what they see me doing that they believe supports this scholarship and they recommend other possibilities. Our dialogue around the survey results involves acknowledging and working to dismantle the ways in which systems of domination inform definitions of best work, high expectations, student engagement, or holding students accountable.

By listening to students, and working to resist my socialization into white supremacy and the professoriate, I continue to discover less oppressive ways of teaching. These often revolve around owning that I have used grades as a cudgel to make them work. In fact, through my research on antiracist equity in teaching and learning, I have come to accept that my detailed rubrics for

194   TEACHING DIFFICULT TOPICS

each assignment reinforce Tema Okun's features of "white supremacy culture" under the guise of excellence and high-quality work.[59] Students have shared with me that in all of their classes their behavior and work is influenced by their fear of how they will be graded. I have forgotten how that felt, in part because I found success in that system during college. Even when faculty are highly transparent, students share during class conversations that they and their friends have experienced final grades that don't always match up to what's reflected in the grading system, and they would never dream of filing a grade appeal, often because they will have that professor again, or because they view all faculty as connected to each other and thus they worry about retribution from another faculty member who is friends with that professor. Embracing this culture of fear around grades, I wanted to create a space where students felt free to take risks that center the joy and freedom of intellectual inquiry.

I used to assign a daily score for in-class participation based on a rubric. I learned this method from a faculty mentor in graduate school. In my mind, it was ideally systematic, to my students, the practice felt suffocating. As a graduate student, this method taught me that I was capable of accomplishing much more than I thought possible. Therefore, I wanted my students to stretch their expectations and capacity for growth. But I had forgotten, through what unexamined privilege did I achieve success, and at what cost to my emotional health? After researching race, I could see how my method of grading participation reinforced white supremacy culture.[60] Participation and preparation are now documented and evaluated in a research journal, developed in consultation with the students. It anchors their research work that occurs before, during, and after each class meeting. In addition, four reflection essays document learning connected to course learning objectives, overarching concepts, and the development of twenty-first century career skills.[61]

Previously, students were expected to prepare a detailed outline of the assigned content for each class period, to reinforce their research skills. Theoretically, this expectation of student preparation used to work. Class discussions appeared to be enlivened with facts and analysis from the students' detailed notes. It was likely a figment of my imagination that students actually had the time or desire to do this. It was no longer working. Students shared that as they prepare for class, they take notes for class discussion by selecting quotes that speak to their interests, the semester-long class project, or fascinating things they are learning in other courses. Since I had recently been studying race, a topic about which I knew very little, I empathized with their experiences. Therefore, new preparation instructions ask students to document four quotes in their research journal and explain how they relate to larger concepts in the course and why you find them significant and helpful to your work in this course. During class, students add to their research journal at least two quotes from peer discourse. Thus, we collaboratively research using the assigned reading.

To alleviate grade-based fear as the primary motivating force, I designed a new grading system for assignments.[62] In an effort to simulate a pass/fail system, students earn an A for adequate work or a C for inadequate work; in rare cases, a D or F if the work is severely lacking. As part of the process, students must explain what grade they believe the assignment deserves and why, based on these criteria: specific & detailed, depth of thought, thoroughly explained, supported with evidence, revised, and follows the instructions (unless they want to articulate a compelling and/or creative reason they chose not to follow them). If I disagree and they do not earn an A, students can earn back points by submitting a response to this prompt: "For each grading criteria, write two to four sentences discussing the strengths and weaknesses in your assignment, and what needs to be improved for next time." I have also removed late penalties, because it only adds anxiety and/or demotivation to a situation that is already highly stressful.

To further lower the pressure for students and honor their complexities of living, working, and studying, I have designed extra credit assignments as a form of grade insurance. Thus, they can breathe, let go of fear, focus on their learning process and goals, and take risks that support hooks's notion of "education as the practice of freedom." Students can attend and submit notes on campus workshops to improve their learning skills. For diversity-instructive courses students can attend and submit notes on campus events to learn about diversity topics. Finally, they can meet with a professor and seek out feedback and strategies about their blind spots, then write about their plans to work on growth.

During 2020, university administrators urged the need for flexibility and understanding with students due to the COVID-19 pandemic. As fall 2021 commenced and the Delta variant raged, administrators and faculty have made it clear that care and struggle are no longer on the table as they forced a return to normal. Yet, as Sonya Renee Taylor points out, this would undercut equity. She urges,

> "We will not go back to normal. Normal never was. Our pre-corona existence was never normal other than we normalized greed, inequity, exhaustion, depletion, extraction, disconnection, confusion, rage, hoarding, hate and

196   TEACHING DIFFICULT TOPICS

lack. We should not long to return, My friends. We are being given the opportunity to stitch a new garment. One that fits all of humanity and nature."[63]

If we want equitable, supportive learning environments, students (and faculty) will always need care, understanding, and flexibility. Beyond the COVID-19 pandemic, this adaptive problem remains: "Figuring out how to help students learn, when I recognize that their learning approaches are changing and they differ from my content-specific training and socialization into the professoriate." Higher education research discusses ways we can adapt to foster transparency and support, and refrain from blaming the students.[64] Multiple sources address the urgent connection between equity and new modes of teaching and learning.[65] Based on Paulo Freire's concepts and approaches in *Pedagogy of the Oppressed*, the solutions should come from the students and their lived experiences, and not be imposed by me.[66] My work should be rooted in the scholarship of teaching and learning and done in collaboration with students and colleagues. However, this begins with the fundamental beliefs that people want to learn and they have knowledge and experience that should be valued in the learning process.

CONCLUSION

I have begun my honest reckoning with my racisms, patriarchy, classism, and ableism. When I arrived at NWU in 2011, I was presented with the opportunity to teach "African American Music." Instead, I created "Film Music" and the course has not been offered again. I argued that another course titled "American Music" should feature an integration of music from white, Indigenous, and black American cultures. What really occurred in 2011? I now understand the ways in which my response was rooted in my racisms, white supremacy, and desire to remain in segregated white spaces, ignorant about black lives. I didn't accept the invitation presented by a music course. However, I'm struck how things have come full circle, albeit from a different path. Through my work in gender studies applied to music, I chose to learn about racism and antiracism, which culminated in a music history course informed by my transdisciplinary teaching on racial injustice. How can I apply this experience to let go of control and domination and allow my students to have different paths and ways of working to arrive at a final project that may not look like either of us had expected?

The following statement in my syllabus and course calendar page explains my commitment to antiracist equity, which I view as the foundation of intersectional equity work. In our learning management system, this information will also headline each of the courses I teach.

> **"Black lives matter! Black, brown, and Indigenous lives are a human rights issue, not a partisan political debate. What can we do together to take the next step to address the legacy of racisms and white supremacy, heal ourselves, and transform our communities?** History is not a thing of the past. It built the present. It thrives today. I pledge to take action to achieve equity through policy change. I pledge to learn from and follow the antiracist leadership of people of color. I'm learning how to see and disrupt: 1. my racisms, 2. my active participation in and complicity with 'white supremacy culture' (a culture that privileges white people), 3. my socialization and choices to remain in segregated white spaces established by U.S. law, and 4. the debilitating and deadly impact of the 'imperialist capitalist white-supremacist patriarchy' (interlocking systems of oppression). Lifelong learning, uncomfortable inner work, and accountability can help me recover from my incentivized historical, social, and political illiteracy and deeply embedded dominance. Together, we can decenter whiteness and focus on black voices, experiences, perspectives, and achievements."

After much hand wringing, I decided that I didn't want to rely on statements from administrators or the institution. I should speak on my behalf about equity and education. This statement makes me feel stronger as a teacher and it keeps me accountable to myself and my students. I share this with students on the second day of class each semester. Together with the "Fostering Our Learning Community" handout, it sets the stage for how and why we work together.

I attended a writer's meeting in which gender studies colleagues offered helpful feedback about my abstract for this chapter. A white colleague in the history department at NWU remarked, "You sound defensive about the inclusion of black perspectives and racial justice in a music history course. American history is black history." My defensive posture, a product of internalized dominance, foremost relates to the ways in which I benefit from white supremacy and patriarchy. Through trauma therapy and education, I continue noticing and working through defensiveness, which is partly a trauma-based response. It also relates to my internalizing the hegemony of conservatory-based music education, and the hostility and employment precarity we experience when we don't fulfill the expectations of maintain-

198   TEACHING DIFFICULT TOPICS

ing white supremacy and patriarchy in music departments.[67] And, given my white segregated life, which I benefited from maintaining, I had more learning to do in order to fully understand what she meant. In *Stamped from the Beginning*, Kendi unpacks how Transatlantic Euro-American colonial history is black history. Additionally, Nikole Hannah-Jones's *1619 Project* illuminates the ways in which black lives are inextricably linked to our past and present.[68] Since forced black labor built these colonial white empires, black perspectives, experiences, and achievements should be thoroughly represented in our curricula. To maintain its stronghold on American minds and values, white supremacy has dictated otherwise. Given the deliberate erasure of racial injustice in our re-segregated K-12 schools, current university students need to learn this information so they can contribute to the common good of their communities and our tattered democracy.[69] The content of antiracism and racial justice can transform all aspects of our current courses and pedagogy and even lead to the creation of new courses and teaching practices. An honest reckoning with our nation's past and present of domination will equip students to successfully navigate and contribute to the work of intersectional equity.

Notes

1. Kristin Boudreau and Derren Rosbach offer helpful definitions to distinguish between multidisciplinary, interdisciplinary, and transdisciplinary approaches. "In a multidisciplinary approach, different disciplinary perspectives are incorporated in an investigation, but always in the exclusive service of the home discipline. . . . An interdisciplinary approach alternates between two disciplinary lenses, each retaining its own methods and concepts even as the disciplines unite to answer a question. . . . A transdisciplinary approach differs from both these other models in aiming at the unity of knowledge beyond disciplines with the goal of understanding the world in its messy complexity." See "The Value of a Transdisciplinary Approach," in *Project-Based Learning in the First Year: Beyond All Expectations*, ed. Kristin Wobbe and Elisabeth A. Stoddard (Sterling, VA: Stylus Publishing, 2019), 35.

2. I used this course title during the Spring 2021, Spring 2022, and Spring 2023 semesters. The hostile national landscape around equity, created by civil servants, understandably foments fear and confusion for citizens. To ameliorate any possible tension, and meet students where they are at in Nebraska, I have changed the course title effective spring 2024 to "Music History 2: Racial Equity." While the course remains committed to antiracist liberation, this change will hopefully invite more students into the course who may hold concerns, reservations, or anxieties around the word "antiracist."

3. See https://www.aacu.org/trht-campus-centers. A few sources on equity in higher education include: Kelly A. Hogan and Viji Sathy, *Inclusive Teaching: Strategies*

for Promoting Equity in the College Classroom (Morgantown: West Virginia University Press, 2022); Tia Brown McNair, Estela Mara Bensimon, and Lindsey Malcom-Piqueux, *From Equity Talk to Equity Walk: Expanding Practitioner Knowledge for Racial Justice in Higher Education* (San Francisco: Jossey-Bass, 2020); Frank Tuitt, Chayla Haynes, and Saran Stewart, eds., *Race, Equity, and the Learning Environment: The Global Relevance of Critical and Inclusive Pedagogies in Higher Education* (Sterling, VA: Stylus Publishing, 2016); Cia Verschelden, *Bandwidth Recovery: Helping Students Reclaim Cognitive Resources Lost to Poverty, Racism, and Social Marginalization* (Sterling, VA: Stylus Publishing, 2017); Badia Ahad-Legardy and OiYan A. Poon, eds., *Difficult Subjects: Insights and Strategies for Teaching About Race, Sexuality, and Gender* (Sterling, VA: Stylus Publishing, 2018); Lisa M. Landreman, ed., *The Art of Effective Facilitation: Reflections from Social Justice Educators* (Sterling, VA: Stylus Publishing, 2013); Maurianne Adams and Lee Anne Bell, eds., *Teaching for Diversity and Social Justice*, 3rd edition (New York: Routledge, 2016).

4. See Bryan Stevenson's interview with Terry Gross, *"Just Mercy* Attorney Asks U.S. to Reckon with Its Racist Past and Present," *NPR Fresh Air*, January 20, 2020, https://www.npr.org/2020/01/20/796234496/just-mercy-attorney-asks-u-s-to-reckon-with-its-racist-past-and-present. See EJI's video "Why Build a Lynching Memorial?," https://www.youtube.com/watch?v=x-0FGYdTR7g. All accessed July 9, 2020.

5. Equal Justice Initiative, https://eji.org/, 2023.

6. See Equal Justice Initiative, "Bryan Stevenson Joins Wynton Marsalis for Jazz at Lincoln Center Special Performance," May 17, 2021, https://eji.org/news/bryan-steven son-joins-wynton-marsalis-for-jazz-at-lincoln-center-special-performance/; Wynton Marsalis, "Jazz at Lincoln Center Presents 'Freedom, Justice, and Hope' Performed by The Jazz at Lincoln Center Orchestra with Wynton Marsalis With Special Guest Bryan Stevenson," https://wyntonmarsalis.org/news/entry/freedom-justice-and-hope-per formed-jazz-at-lincoln-center-orchestra-with-wynton-marsalis-special-guest-bryan -stevenson, accessed May 29, 2023; Jazz at Lincoln Center, "Wynton Marsalis and Bry-an Stevenson on the Value of Art and Identity," YouTube, February 25, 2021, https://www.youtube.com/watch?v=AvWQCF_iTdo

7. Equal Justice Initiative, "EJI Brings Classical Musicians Together to Engage with History of Racial Inequality," May 25, 2023, https://eji.org/news/eji-brings-classical -musicians-together-to-engage-with-history-of-racial-inequality/

8. Equal Justice Initiative, *The Legacy Museum: From Enslavement to Mass Incarcer-ation*, https://museumandmemorial.eji.org/museum, accessed June 30, 2023.

9. Lin-Manuel Miranda, *Hamilton: An American Musical* (Atlantic Records, 2015), MP3.

10. "'Education Leads to Liberation,' Nikole Hannah-Jones on The 1619 Project & Teaching Black History," *Democracy Now!*, May 26, 2023, https://www.democracynow .org/2023/5/26/spike_lee_nikole_hannah_jones_malcolm

11. Philip Dray, *At the Hands of Persons Unknown: The Lynching of Black America* (New York: The Modern Library, 2002), 230–31.

12. Amy Louise Wood, *Lynching and Spectacle: Witnessing Racial Violence in America, 1890–1940* (Chapel Hill: University of North Carolina Press, 2009).

13. Dray, *At the Hands of Persons Unknown*, 390, 391, 388–94 inclusive, 408. Robeson was part of a 1951 delegation that presented the United Nations with the report *We Charge Genocide: The Historic Petition to the United Nations for Relief from a Crime of the United States Government Against the Negro People.*

14. David M. Oshinsky, *Worse Than Slavery: Parchman Farm and the Ordeal of Jim Crow Justice* (New York: Free Press, 1997).

15. W. E. B. Du Bois, *The Souls of Black Folk* (New York: Signet Classics, 2012).

16. Du Bois, *The Souls of Black Folk*, "Of the Coming of John." To show how the past has built the present, this chapter could be paired with conductor Brandon Keith Brown's 2020 article about racialized violence in the concert hall. See Brandon Keith Brown, "When Black Conductors Aren't Comfortable at Concerts, Classical Music Has a Real Problem," *Level*, February 1, 2020, https://level.medium.com/black-concert-tra uma-5fa0459e5b3

17. Two conversations within opera communities, for example, include Philip Kennicott, "Can Opera Ever Meet Twenty-First-Century Standards of Political Correctness? Should It Even Try?" *Opera News* 80, no. 8 (February 2016), https://www.oper anews.com/Opera_News_Magazine/2016/2/Features/Discomfort_Zone.html and Charlotte Smith, "Soprano Angel Blue Cancels Arena di Verona Debut in Response to Anna Netrebko Blackface Scandal," *BBC Music Magazine*, July 15, 2022, https://www.cl assical-music.com/news/soprano-angel-blue-cancels-arena-di-verona-debut-in-resp onse-to-anna-netrebko-blackface-scandal/

18. As I continue to develop and revise this course, I look forward to studying these new sources that have emerged as this collection heads to press. Philip Ewell, *On Music Theory, and Making Music More Welcoming for Everyone* (Ann Arbor: University of Michigan Press, 2023); Horace Maxile, Jr. and Kristen Turner, *Race and Gender in the Western Music History Survey: A Teacher's Guide* (New York: Routledge, 2022); Ayana O. Smith, *Inclusive Music Histories: Leading Change through Research and Pedagogy* (New York: Routledge, 2024).

19. Wobbe and Stoddard, *Project-Based Learning in the First Year.*

20. See https://eji.org/, accessed January 30, 2021.

21. *Slavery in America: The Montgomery Slave Trade* (Montgomery: Equal Justice Initiative, 2018), https://eji.org/wp-content/uploads/2019/10/slavery-in-america-rep ort.pdf; *Reconstruction in America: Racial Violence after the Civil War, 1865–1876* (Montgomery: Equal Justice Initiative, 2020), https://eji.org/wp-content/uploads/2020/07 /reconstruction-in-america-report.pdf; *Lynching in America: Confronting the Legacy of Racial Terror* (Montgomery: Equal Justice Initiative, 2017), https://lynchinginamerica .eji.org/report/; *Segregation in America* (Montgomery: Equal Justice Initiative, 2018), https://segregationinamerica.eji.org/report/. Additional EJI reports include *Race and the Jury: Illegal Discrimination in Jury Selection* (Montgomery: Equal Justice Initiative, 2021), https://eji.org/report/race-and-the-jury/; *The Transatlantic Slave Trade* (Mont-

gomery: Equal Justice Initiative, 2023), https://eji.org/reports/transatlantic-slave-tra
de-overview/

22. Chris Burbach, "Hundreds Gather for Ceremony at Omaha Courthouse on Anniversary of 1919 Lynching and Riot," *Omaha World-Herald*, September 29, 2019, https://omaha.com/archives/hundreds-gather-for-ceremony-at-omaha-courthouse-on-ann
iversary-of-1919-lynching-and-riot/article_e08298ba-580b-5a77-9960-b7ebb2ea03e6
.html

23. James Potter, "'Wearing the Hempen Neck-Tie': Lynching in Nebraska, 1858–1919," *Nebraska History* 93 (2012): 138–53.

24. Paul Hammel, "Nebraskans Vote Overwhelmingly to Restore Death Penalty, Nullify Historic 2015 Vote by State Legislature," *Omaha World-Herald*, November 9, 2016, https://omaha.com/state-and-regional/nebraskans-vote-overwhelmingly-to-restore
-death-penalty-nullify-historic-2015-vote-by-state-legislature/article_38823d54-a5df
-11e6-9a5e-d7a71d75611a.html

25. Todd Cooper, "Most Nebraskans Voted to Abolish Slavery as Criminal Punishment. But 32% Voted to Keep It," *Omaha World-Herald*, November 6, 2020, https://omaha.com/news/state-and-regional/govt-and-politics/most-nebraskans-voted-to-abol
ish-slavery-as-criminal-punishment-but-32-voted-to-keep-it/article_69dbba59-11b6
-5f29-b56e-8bc7d6097865.html

26. Currently we read select chapters from Robin DiAngelo, *White Fragility: Why It's So Hard for White People to Talk about Racism* (Boston: Beacon Press, 2018); Ibram X. Kendi, *How To Be An Antiracist* (New York: One World, 2019); Derald Wing Sue, *Race Talk and the Conspiracy of Silence: Understanding and Facilitating Difficult Dialogues on Race* (Hoboken, NJ: Wiley, 2016); Resmaa Menakem, *My Grandmother's Hands: Racialized Trauma and the Pathway to Mending Our Hearts and Bodies* (Las Vegas: Central Recovery Press, 2017); Isabel Wilkerson, *Caste: The Origins of Our Discontents* (New York: Random House, 2020); Joseph Barndt, *Understanding and Dismantling Racism: The Twenty-First Century Challenge to White America* (Minneapolis: Fortress Press, 2007).

27. See Collaborative for Academic, Social, and Emotional Learning (CASEL), https://casel.org/, 2023; Sara Rimm-Kaufman, Michael Strambler, Kimberly Schonert-Reichl, eds., *Social and Emotional Learning in Action: Creating Systemic Change in Schools* (New York: Guilford Press, 2023); Nancy Frey, Douglas Fisher, Dominique Smith, *The Social-Emotional Learning Playbook: A Guide to Student and Teacher Well-Being* (Thousand Oaks, CA: Corwin Press, 2022).

28. See John Spilker, "Integrating Well-being and Intersectional Equity across a Revised Music History and Culture Curriculum," in *Sound Pedagogy: Radical Care in Music*, ed. by Colleen Renihan, John Spilker, and Trudi Wright (Urbana: University of Illinois Press, 2024), 76–96. In this chapter, I discuss assigned well-being reading to foster the connections between intellectual and emotional development. Drs. Rachel Pokora and Patty Hawk, NWU Communications Studies faculty, provided discourse instruction training and faculty support.

29. Marshall Rosenberg, *Nonviolent Communication: A Language of Life*, 3rd edition (Encinitas, CA: PuddleDancer Press, 2015).

30. Nikole Hannah-Jones, "Episode 3: The Birth of American Music," *1619* (podcast), September 6, 2019, https://www.nytimes.com/2019/09/06/podcasts/1619-black-ame rican-music-appropriation.html

31. Loren Kajikawa, "The Possessive Investment in Classical Music: Confronting Legacies of White Supremacy in U.S. Schools and Departments of Music," in *Seeing Race Again: Countering Colorblindness across the Disciplines*, ed. Kimberlé Williams Crenshaw, Luke Charles Harris, Daniel Martinez HoSang, and George Lipsitz (Berkeley: University of California Press, 2019): 155–74.

32. Henry Louis Gates, Jr., *Reconstruction: America After the Civil War*, Public Broadcasting System, 2019, https://www.pbs.org/weta/reconstruction. The documentary is based on Henry Louis Gates, Jr., *Stony the Road: Reconstruction, White Supremacy, and the Rise of Jim Crow* (New York: Penguin Books, 2019).

33. Mellonee V. Burnim and Portia K. Maultsby, *African American Music: An Introduction* (New York: Routledge, 2014). Other suggested resources include: Samuel Floyd, Jr., *The Power of Black Music: Interpreting Its History From Africa to the United States* (New York: Oxford, 1999); Samuel Floyd, Jr., Melanie Zeck, Guthrie Ramsey, Jr., *The Transformation of Black Music: The Rhythms, the Songs, and the Ships of the African Diaspora* (New York: Oxford, 2017); Guthrie Ramsey, Jr., *Who Hears Here?: On Black Music, Pasts and Present* (Berkeley: University of California Press, 2022).

34. See Kajikawa, "Possessive Investment."

35. See Carol Anderson, *White Rage: The Unspoken Truth of Our Racial Divide* (New York: Bloomsbury Publishing, 2016); Lawrence Glickman, "How White Backlash Controls American Progress," *The Atlantic*, May 21, 2020, https://www.theatlantic.com/ide as/archive/2020/05/white-backlash-nothing-new/611914/

36. Teo Armus, "Sen. Tom Cotton wants to take 'The 1619 Project' out of classrooms. His efforts have kept it in the spotlight." *Washington Post*, July 27, 2020, https://www.washingtonpost.com/nation/2020/07/27/tom-cotton-1619-project-slavery/; Michael Crowley and Jennifer Schuessler, "Trump's 1776 Commission Critiques Liberalism in Report Derided by Historians." *New York Times*, January 18, 2021, https://www.nytimes.com/2021/01/18/us/politics/trump-1776-commission-report.html

37. Jennifer Schuessler, "Bans on Critical Race Theory Threaten Free Speech, Advocacy Group Says," *New York Times*, November 8, 2021, https://www.nytimes.com/2021/11/08/arts/critical-race-theory-bans.html; Tim Craig and Lori Rozsa, "In His Fight Against 'Woke' Schools, DeSantis Tears at the Seams of a Diverse Florida," *Washington Post*, February 7, 2022, https://www.washingtonpost.com/nation/2022/02/07/desant is-anti-woke-act/; Anemona Hartocollis and Eliza Fawcett, "The College Board Strips Down Its A.P. Curriculum for African American Studies," *New York Times*, February 1, 2023, https://www.nytimes.com/2023/02/01/us/college-board-advanced-placem ent-african-american-studies.html; Keith E. Whittington, "DeSantis's Terrifying Plot Against Higher Ed," *Chronicle of Higher Education*, February 27, 2023, https://www.chr onicle.com/article/desantiss-terrifying-plot-against-higher-ed

38. William Cheng, *Just Vibrations: The Purpose of Sounding Good* (Ann Arbor: University of Michigan Press, 2016).

39. See Colleen Renihan, John Spilker, and Trudi Wright, eds., *Sound Pedagogy: Radical Care in Music* (Urbana: University of Illinois Press, 2024).

40. bell hooks, *Understanding Patriarchy* (Louisville Anarchist Federation Federation and No Borders: Louisville's Radical Lending Library, no date). See https://imaginenoborders.org/pdf/zines/UnderstandingPatriarchy.pdf, accessed May 20, 2020. hooks discusses this concept throughout her three teaching books. See bell hooks, *Teaching to Transgress: Education as the Practice of Freedom* (New York: Routledge, 1994); bell hooks, *Teaching Community: A Pedagogy of Hope* (New York: Routledge, 2004); bell hooks, *Teaching Critical Thinking: Practical Wisdom* (New York: Routledge, 2010).

41. Cheng, *Just Vibrations.*

42. William Cheng, *Loving Music Till It Hurts* (New York: Oxford University Press, 2020), 2.

43. Formulations and applications of critical and inclusive pedagogies are outlined in the essays of Frank Tuitt, Chayla Haynes, and Saran Stewart, eds., *Race, Equity, and the Learning Environment: The Global Relevance of Critical and Inclusive Pedagogies in Higher Education.* For a definition of and framework for critical and inclusive pedagogies, see Frank Tuitt, "Inclusive Pedagogy 2.0: Implications for Race, Equity, and Higher Education in a Global Context," in *Race, Equity, and the Learning Environment,* 205–21.

44. Dorinda J. Carter Andrews and Bernadette M. Castillo, "Humanizing Pedagogy for Examinations of Race and Culture in Teacher Education," in *Race, Equity, and the Learning Environment,* 126.

45. Carter Andrews and Castillo, "Humanizing Pedagogy," 126.

46. Carter Andrews and Castillo, "Humanizing Pedagogy," 126.

47. Lee Anne Bell, "Theoretical Foundations for Social Justice Education," in *Teaching for Diversity and Social Justice,* 3. For her description of power and domination, Bell cites Seth Kreisberg, *Transforming Power: Domination, Empowerment, and Education* (Albany: State University of New York Press, 1992).

48. Bell, "Theoretical Foundations for Social Justice Education," 3. In formulating the components of her definition of justice, Bell cites these sources for "distribution of resources": John Rawls, *A Theory of Justice* (Cambridge, MA: Harvard University Press, 1999); John Rawls, *Justice as Fairness: A Restatement* (Cambridge, MA: Harvard University Press, 2001); and these sources for "social processes": Iris Marion Young, *Justice and the Politics of Difference* (Princeton: Princeton University Press, 1990); Iris Marion Young, *Responsibility for Justice* (New York: Oxford University Press, 2011).

49. Bell, "Theoretical Foundations for Social Justice Education," 4.

50. bell hooks, *Understanding Patriarchy.*

51. Erica Chu, "'The Least We Can Do': Gender-Affirming Pedagogy Starting on Day One," in *Difficult Subjects: Insights and Strategies for Teaching about Race, Sexuality, and*

204   TEACHING DIFFICULT TOPICS

Gender, ed. Badia Ahad-Legardy and OiYan A. Poon (Sterling, VA: Stylus Publishing, 2018), 158–77.

52. Chu, "The Least We Can Do," 171.

53. Brian Arao and Kristi Clemens, "From Safe to Brave Spaces: A New Way to Frame Dialogue Around Diversity and Social Justice," in *The Art of Effective Facilitation: Reflections from Social Justice Educators*, ed. Lisa M. Landreman (Sterling, VA: Stylus Publishing, 2013), 135–50. Earlier in this volume, Kelsey Klotz also calls this work into action (see Chapter 3, fn 16). Jasmine L. Harris, "Uncomfortable Learning: Teaching Race Through Discomfort in Higher Education," in *Difficult Subjects*, 248–66. My handout "Fostering Our Learning Community" is found in Spilker, "Integrating Well-being and Intersectional Equity" in *Sound Pedagogy*.

54. Harris, "Uncomfortable Learning," 254.

55. Harris, "Uncomfortable Learning," 255.

56. Harris, "Uncomfortable Learning," 255.

57. Regarding so-called "neutral spaces," a few helpful sources readily come to mind. Comprising chapters 11 through 14, Part Three of *Difficult Subjects* is titled "Radical Pedagogy in 'Neutral' Places." See also Bianca C. Williams, "Radical Honesty: Truth-Telling as Pedagogy for Working Through Shame in Academic Spaces," in *Race, Equity, and the Learning Environment*, 71–82.

58. Arthur W. Chickering and Zelda F. Gamson, "Seven Principles for Good Practice in Undergraduate Education," *American Association for Higher Education Bulletin* 39, no. 7 (1987), 3–7. The article is available online: https://aahea.org/articles/sevenprinciples1987.htm, accessed July 8, 2020.

59. The original document is Tema Okun, "White Supremacy Culture," *Dismantling Racism Works*, https://www.dismantlingracism.org/uploads/4/3/5/7/43579015/okun_-_white_sup_culture.pdf, accessed July 4, 2020. The author presented an updated version, Tema Okun, "White Supremacy Culture–Still Here," May 2021, *White Supremacy Culture*, https://www.whitesupremacyculture.info/, accessed July 8, 2023.

60. See Okun, "White Supremacy Culture" and "White Supremacy Culture–Still Here."

61. For information on education and career skills, see Hart Research Associates, "Fulfilling the American Dream: Liberal Education and the Future of Work," July 2018, https://www.aacu.org/sites/default/files/files/LEAP/2018EmployerResearchReport.pdf; Hart Research Associates, "It Takes More Than a Major," Liberal Education 99, no. 2 (Spring 2013), https://www.aacu.org/publications-research/periodicals/it-takes-more-major-employer-priorities-college-learning-and

62. Since designing this grading system, I learned about several resources for further development. Susan D. Blum, ed., *Ungrading: Why Rating Students Undermines Learning (and What to Do Instead)* (Morgantown: West Virginia University Press, 2020); Monica Vesely, "The ICE model: An Alternative Learning Framework," *Centre for Teaching Excellence Blog*, University of Waterloo, https://cte-blog.uwaterloo.ca/5282/, accessed Dec 1, 2021; Asao B. Inoue, *Labor-Based Grading Contracts: Building Equity*

and Inclusion in the Compassionate Writing Classroom (Boulder: University Press of Colorado, 2019).

63. Sonya Renee Taylor, Instagram, April 2, 2020, https://www.instagram.com/p/B-fc3ejAlvd/?hl=en

64. Tia Brown McNair, Susan Albertine, Michelle Asha Cooper, Nicole McDonald, Thomas Major, Jr., *Becoming A Student-Ready College: A New Culture of Leadership for Student Success* (San Francisco: Jossey-Bass, 2016); Mary-Ann Winkelmes, Allison Boye, and Suzanne Tapp, eds., *Transparent Design in Higher Education Teaching and Leadership* (Sterling, VA: Stylus Publishing, 2019); Sean Michael Morris and Jesse Stommel, *An Urgency of Teachers: The Work of Critical Digital Pedagogy* (Hybrid Pedagogy, 2018), https://criticaldigitalpedagogy.pressbooks.com/

65. These sources have been cited in footnotes throughout. I would add Cia Verschelden, *Bandwidth Recovery*; Kevin Gannon, *Radical Hope: A Teaching Manifesto* (Morgantown: University of West Virginia Press, 2020); Cyndi Kernahan, *Teaching about Race and Racism in the College Classroom: Notes from a White Professor* (Morgantown: University of West Virginia Press, 2019).

66. See Paulo Freire, *Pedagogy of the Oppressed* (New York: Penguin Books, 1970).

67. See Kajikawa, "Possessive Investment."

68. Nikole Hannah-Jones led the project with her interactive online article, "Our Democracy's Founding Ideals Were False When They Were Written. Black Americans Have Fought to Make Them True." *New York Times Magazine*, August 14, 2019, https://www.nytimes.com/interactive/2019/08/14/magazine/black-history-american-democracy.html. The print version of the *1619 Project* is found in *New York Times Magazine*, August 14, 2019. It can be accessed online at https://www.nytimes.com/interactive/20 19/08/14/magazine/1619-america-slavery.html; Nikole Hannah-Jones, 1619, *New York Times Podcast*, August 23, 2019, https://www.nytimes.com/column/1619-project; Nikole Hannah-Jones, *The 1619 Project: A New Origin Story* (New York: One World, 2021); Nikole Hannah-Jones, *The 1619 Project*, Hulu documentary, 2023, https://press.hulu .com/shows/the-1619-project/

69. Regarding school resegregation see Beverly Daniel Tatum, *Can We Talk About Race? And Other Conversations in an Era of School Resegregation* (Boston: Beacon Press, 2007); Beverly Daniel Tatum, *Why Are All the Black Students Sitting Together in the Cafeteria?* (New York: Basic Books, 1997). The equity initiatives and publications of the Association of American Colleges and Universities seeks to equip students to contribute to the public good. See https://www.aacu.org/diversity-equity-and-stude nt-success

Works Cited

Adams, Maurianne, and Lee Anne Bell, eds., *Teaching for Diversity and Social Justice*, 3rd edition. New York: Routledge, 2016.

Ahad-Legardy, Badia, and OiYan A. Poon, eds. *Difficult Subjects: Insights and Strategies for Teaching about Race, Sexuality, and Gender*. Sterling, VA: Stylus Publishing, 2018.

206 TEACHING DIFFICULT TOPICS

Anderson, Carol. *White Rage: The Unspoken Truth of Our Racial Divide*. New York: Bloomsbury Publishing, 2016.

Arao, Brian, and Kristi Clemens. "From Safe to Brave Spaces: A New Way to Frame Dialogue Around Diversity and Social Justice." In *The Art of Effective Facilitation: Reflections from Social Justice Educators*, ed. Lisa M. Landreman, 135–50. Sterling, VA: Stylus Publishing, 2013.

Armus, Teo. "Sen. Tom Cotton wants to take 'The 1619 Project' out of classrooms. His efforts have kept it in the spotlight." *Washington Post*, July 27, 2020. https://www.was hingtonpost.com/nation/2020/07/27/tom-cotton-1619-project-slavery/

Barndt, Joseph. *Understanding and Dismantling Racism: The Twenty-First Century Challenge to White America*. Minneapolis: Fortress Press, 2007.

Bell, Lee Anne. "Theoretical Foundations for Social Justice Education." In *Teaching for Diversity and Social Justice*, 3rd edition, ed. by Maurianne Adams and Lee Anne Bell, 3–26. New York: Routledge, 2016.

Blum, Susan D., ed. *Ungrading: Why Rating Students Undermines Learning (and What to Do Instead)*. Morgantown: West Virginia University Press, 2020.

Boudreau, Kristin, and Derren Rosbach. "The Value of a Transdisciplinary Approach." In *Project-Based Learning in the First Year: Beyond All Expectations*, ed. by Kristin Wobbe and Elisabeth A. Stoddard, 33–47. Sterling, VA: Stylus Publishing, 2019.

Brown, Brandon Keith. "When Black Conductors Aren't Comfortable at Concerts, Classical Music Has a Real Problem." *Level*, February 1, 2020. https://level.medium .com/black-concert-trauma-5fa0459e5b3

Burbach, Chris. "Hundreds Gather for Ceremony at Omaha Courthouse on Anniversary of 1919 Lynching and Riot." *Omaha World-Herald*, September 29, 2019. https:// omaha.com/archives/hundreds-gather-for-ceremony-at-omaha-courthouse-on -anniversary-of-1919-lynching-and-riot/article_e08298ba-580b-5a77-9960-b7ebb2 ea03e6.html

Burnim, Mellonee V., and Portia K. Maultsby. *African American Music: An Introduction*. New York: Routledge, 2014.

Carter Andrews, Dorinda J., and Bernadette M. Castillo. "Humanizing Pedagogy for Examinations of Race and Culture in Teacher Education." In *Race, Equity, and the Learning Environment: The Global Relevance of Critical and Inclusive Pedagogies in Higher Education*, ed. Frank Tuitt, Chayla Haynes, and Saran Stewart, 112–28. Sterling, VA: Stylus Publishing, 2016.

Cheng, William. *Just Vibrations: The Purpose of Sounding Good*. Ann Arbor: University of Michigan Press, 2016.

Cheng, William. *Loving Music Till It Hurts*. New York: Oxford University Press, 2020.

Chickering, Arthur W., and Zelda F. Gamson. "Seven Principles for Good Practice in Undergraduate Education." *American Association for Higher Education Bulletin* 39, no. 7 (1987): 3–7.

Chu, Erica. "'The Least We Can Do': Gender-Affirming Pedagogy Starting on Day One." In *Difficult Subjects: Insights and Strategies for Teaching about Race, Sexuality, and*

Gender, ed. Badia Ahad-Legardy and OiYan A. Poon, 158–77. Sterling, VA: Stylus Publishing, 2018.

Cooper, Todd. "Most Nebraskans Voted to Abolish Slavery as Criminal Punishment. But 32% Voted to Keep It." *Omaha World-Herald*, November 6, 2020. https://omaha .com/news/state-and-regional/govt-and-politics/most-nebraskans-voted-to-abol ish-slavery-as-criminal-punishment-but-32-voted-to-keep-it/article_69dbba59-11 b6-5f29-b56e-8bc7d6097865.html

Craig, Tim, and Lori Rozsa. "In His Fight Against 'Woke' Schools, DeSantis Tears at the Seams of a Diverse Florida." *Washington Post*, February 7, 2022. https://www.washin gtonpost.com/nation/2022/02/07/desantis-anti-woke-act/

Crowley, Michael, and Jennifer Schuessler. "Trump's 1776 Commission Critiques Liberalism in Report Derided by Historians." *New York Times*, January 18, 2021. https:// www.nytimes.com/2021/01/18/us/politics/trump-1776-commission-report.html

DiAngelo, Robin. *White Fragility: Why It's So Hard for White People to Talk about Racism.* Boston: Beacon Press, 2018.

Dray, Philip. *At the Hands of Persons Unknown: The Lynching of Black America.* New York: The Modern Library, 2002.

Du Bois, W. E. B. *The Souls of Black Folk.* New York: Signet Classics, 2012.

"'Education Leads to Liberation,' Nikole Hannah-Jones on The 1619 Project & Teaching Black History." *Democracy Now!*, May 26, 2023. https://www.democracynow.org/20 23/5/26/spike_lee_nikole_hannah_jones_malcolm

Equal Justice Initiative. "Bryan Stevenson Joins Wynton Marsalis for Jazz at Lincoln Center Special Performance." *Equal Justice Initiative*, May 17, 2021. https://eji.org/ne ws/bryan-stevenson-joins-wynton-marsalis-for-jazz-at-lincoln-center-special-per formance/

Equal Justice Initiative. "EJI Brings Classical Musicians Together to Engage with History of Racial Inequality." *Equal Justice Initiative*, May 25, 2023. https://eji.org/news /eji-brings-classical-musicians-together-to-engage-with-history-of-racial-inequal ity/

Equal Justice Initiative. *The Legacy Museum: From Enslavement to Mass Incarceration.* https://museumandmemorial.eji.org/museum, accessed June 30, 2023.

Equal Justice Initiative. *Lynching in America: Confronting the Legacy of Racial Terror.* Montgomery, AL: Equal Justice Initiative, 2017. https://lynchinginamerica.eji.org/re port/

Equal Justice Initiative. *Reconstruction in America: Racial Violence after the Civil War, 1865–1876.* Montgomery, AL: Equal Justice Initiative, 2020. https://eji.org/wp-conte nt/uploads/2020/07/reconstruction-in-america-report.pdf

Equal Justice Initiative. *Segregation in America.* Montgomery, AL: Equal Justice Initiative, 2018. https://segregationinamerica.eji.org/report/

Equal Justice Initiative. *Slavery in America: The Montgomery Slave Trade.* Montgomery, AL: Equal Justice Initiative, 2018. https://eji.org/wp-content/uploads/2019/10/slav ery-in-america-report.pdf

208 TEACHING DIFFICULT TOPICS

Floyd, Jr., Samuel. *The Power of Black Music: Interpreting Its History From Africa to the United States*. New York: Oxford, 1999.

Floyd, Jr., Samuel, Melanie Zeck, and Guthrie Ramsey, Jr. *The Transformation of Black Music: The Rhythms, the Songs, and the Ships of the African Diaspora*. New York: Oxford, 2017.

Freire, Paulo. *Pedagogy of the Oppressed*. New York: Penguin Books, 1970.

Frey, Nancy, Douglas Fisher, and Dominique Smith. *The Social-Emotional Learning Playbook: A Guide to Student and Teacher Well-Being*. Thousand Oaks, CA: Corwin Press, 2022.

Gannon, Kevin. *Radical Hope: A Teaching Manifesto*. Morgantown: University of West Virginia Press, 2020.

Gates, Jr., Henry Louis. *Reconstruction: America After the Civil War*. Public Broadcasting System, 2019. https://www.pbs.org/weta/reconstruction

Gates, Jr., Henry Louis. *Stony the Road: Reconstruction, White Supremacy, and the Rise of Jim Crow*. New York: Penguin Books, 2019.

Glickman, Lawrence. "How White Backlash Controls American Progress." *The Atlantic*, May 21, 2020. https://www.theatlantic.com/ideas/archive/2020/05/white-back lash-nothing-new/611914/

Gross, Terry. "*Just Mercy* Attorney Asks U.S. to Reckon with Its Racist Past and Present." *NPR Fresh Air*, January 20, 2020. https://www.npr.org/2020/01/20/796234496 /just-mercy-attorney-asks-u-s-to-reckon-with-its-racist-past-and-present

Hammel, Paul. "Nebraskans Vote Overwhelmingly to Restore Death Penalty, Nullify Historic 2015 Vote by State Legislature." *Omaha World Herald*, November 9, 2016. https://omaha.com/state-and-regional/nebraskans-vote-overwhelmingly-to-resto re-death-penalty-nullify-historic-2015-vote-by-state-legislature/article_38823d54 -a5df-11e6-9a5e-d7a71d75611a.html

Hannah-Jones, Nikole. *1619*. *New York Times* Podcast. August 23, 2019. https://www.nyt imes.com/column/1619-project

Hannah-Jones, Nikole. "1619 Project." *New York Times Magazine*, August 14, 2019. https://www.nytimes.com/interactive/2019/08/14/magazine/1619-america-slave ry.html

Hannah-Jones, Nikole. *The 1619 Project: A New Origin Story*. New York: One World, 2021.

Hannah-Jones, Nikole. *The 1619 Project*. Hulu documentary. 2023. https://press.hulu .com/shows/the-1619-project/

Hannah-Jones, Nikole. "Our Democracy's Founding Ideals Were False When They Were Written. Black Americans Have Fought to Make Them True." *New York Times Magazine*, August 14, 2019. https://www.nytimes.com/interactive/2019/08/14/mag azine/black-history-american-democracy.html

Harris, Jasmine L. "Uncomfortable Learning: Teaching Race Through Discomfort in Higher Education." In *Difficult Subjects: Insights and Strategies for Teaching about Race, Sexuality, and Gender*, ed. Badia Ahad-Legardy and OiYan A. Poon, 248–66. Sterling, VA: Stylus Publishing, 2018.

Transdisciplinary Antiracism Research and Teaching   209

Hart Research Associates. "Fulfilling the American Dream: Liberal Education and the Future of Work." July 2018. https://www.aacu.org/sites/default/files/files/LEAP/20 18EmployerResearchReport.pdf

Hart Research Associates. "It Takes More Than a Major." *Liberal Education* 99, no. 2 (Spring 2013). https://www.aacu.org/publications-research/periodicals/it-takes -more-major-employer-priorities-college-learning-and

Hartocollis, Anemona, and Eliza Fawcett. "The College Board Strips Down Its A.P. Curriculum for African American Studies." *New York Times*, February 1, 2023. https:// www.nytimes.com/2023/02/01/us/college-board-advanced-placement-african -american-studies.html

Hogan, Kelly A., and Viji Sathy. *Inclusive Teaching: Strategies for Promoting Equity in the College Classroom*. Morgantown: West Virginia University Press, 2022.

hooks, bell. *Teaching Community: A Pedagogy of Hope*. New York: Routledge, 2004.

hooks, bell. *Teaching Critical Thinking: Practical Wisdom*. New York: Routledge, 2010.

hooks, bell. *Teaching to Transgress: Education as the Practice of Freedom*. New York: Routledge, 1994.

hooks, bell. *Understanding Patriarchy*. Louisville Anarchist Federation Federation and No Borders: Louisville's Racial Lending Library, no date. https://imaginenoborders .org/pdf/zines/UnderstandingPatriarchy.pdf, accessed May 20, 2020.

Inoue, Asao B. *Labor-Based Grading Contracts: Building Equity and Inclusion in the Compassionate Writing Classroom*. Boulder: University Press of Colorado, 2019.

Jazz at Lincoln Center. "Wynton Marsalis and Bryan Stevenson on the Value of Art and Identity." *YouTube*, February 25, 2021. https://www.youtube.com/watch?v=AvW QCF_iTdo

Kajikawa, Loren. "The Possessive Investment in Classical Music: Confronting Legacies of White Supremacy in U.S. Schools and Departments of Music." In *Seeing Race Again: Countering Colorblindness across the Disciplines*, ed. by Kimberlé Williams Crenshaw, Luke Charles Harris, Daniel Martinez HoSang, and George Lipsitz, 155– 74. Berkeley: University of California Press, 2019.

Kendi, Ibram X. *How To Be An Antiracist*. New York: One World, 2019.

Kennicott, Philip. "Can Opera Ever Meet Twenty-First-Century Standards of Political Correctness? Should It Even Try?" *Opera News* 80, no. 8 (February 2016). https:// www.operanews.com/Opera_News_Magazine/2016/2/Features/Discomfort_Zo ne.html

Kernahan, Cyndi. *Teaching about Race and Racism in the College Classroom: Notes from a White Professor*. Morgantown: University of West Virginia Press, 2019.

Landreman, Lisa M., ed. *The Art of Effective Facilitation: Reflections from Social Justice Educators*. Sterling, VA: Stylus Publishing, 2013.

Marsalis, Wynton. "Jazz at Lincoln Center Presents 'Freedom, Justice, and Hope' Performed by The Jazz at Lincoln Center Orchestra with Wynton Marsalis With Special Guest Bryan Stevenson." https://wyntonmarsalis.org/news/entry/freedom-justice -and-hope-performed-jazz-at-lincoln-center-orchestra-with-wynton-marsalis-spe cial-guest-bryan-stevenson

McNair, Tia Brown, Estela Mara Bensimon, and Lindsey Malcom-Piqueux. *From Equity Talk to Equity Walk: Expanding Practitioner Knowledge for Racial Justice in Higher Education.* San Francisco: Jossey-Bass, 2020.

McNair, Tia Brown, Susan Albertine, Michelle Asha Cooper, Nicole McDonald, Thomas Major, Jr. *Becoming A Student-Ready College: A New Culture of Leadership for Student Success.* San Francisco: Jossey-Bass, 2016.

Menakem, Resmaa. *My Grandmother's Hands: Racialized Trauma and the Pathway to Mending Our Hearts and Bodies.* Las Vegas: Central Recovery Press, 2017.

Miranda, Lin-Manuel. *Hamilton: An American Musical.* Atlantic Records, 2015. MP3.

Morris, Sean Michael, and Jesse Stommel. *An Urgency of Teachers: The Work of Critical Digital Pedagogy.* Hybrid Pedagogy, 2018. https://criticaldigitalpedagogy.pressbooks.com/

Okun, Tema. "White Supremacy Culture." *Dismantling Racism Works.* https://www.dismantlingracism.org/uploads/4/3/5/7/43579015/okun_-_white_sup_culture.pdf, accessed July 4, 2020.

Okun, Tema. "White Supremacy Culture–Still Here." *White Supremacy Culture,* May 2021. https://www.whitesupremacyculture.info/, accessed July 8, 2023.

Oshinsky, David M. *Worse Than Slavery: Parchman Farm and the Ordeal of Jim Crow Justice.* New York: Free Press, 1997.

Potter, James. "'Wearing the Hempen Neck-Tie': Lynching in Nebraska, 1858–1919." *Nebraska History* 93 (2012): 138–53.

Schuessler, Jennifer. "Bans on Critical Race Theory Threaten Free Speech, Advocacy Group Says." *New York Times,* November 8, 2021. https://www.nytimes.com/2021/11/08/arts/critical-race-theory-bans.html

Smith, Charlotte. "Soprano Angel Blue Cancels Arena di Verona Debut in Response to Anna Netrebko Blackface Scandal." *BBC Music Magazine,* July 15, 2022. https://www.classical-music.com/news/soprano-angel-blue-cancels-arena-di-verona-debut-in-response-to-anna-netrebko-blackface-scandal/

Ramsey, Jr., Guthrie. *Who Hears Here?: On Black Music, Pasts and Present.* Berkeley: University of California Press, 2022.

Renihan, Colleen, John Spilker, and Trudi Wright, eds. *Sound Pedagogy: Radical Care in Music.* Urbana: University of Illinois Press, 2024.

Rimm-Kaufman, Sara, Michael Strambler, Kimberly Schonert-Reichl, eds. *Social and Emotional Learning in Action: Creating Systemic Change in Schools.* New York: Guilford Press, 2023.

Rosenberg, Marshall. *Nonviolent Communication: A Language of Life,* 3rd edition. Encinitas, CA: PuddleDancer Press, 2015.

Spilker, John. "Integrating Well-being and Intersectional Equity across a Revised Music History and Culture Curriculum." In *Sound Pedagogy: Radical Care in Music,* ed. by Colleen Renihan, John Spilker, and Trudi Wright, 76–96. Urbana: University of Illinois Press, 2024.

Sue, Derald Wing. *Race Talk and the Conspiracy of Silence: Understanding and Facilitating Difficult Dialogues on Race.* Hoboken, NJ: Wiley, 2016.

Tatum, Beverly Daniel. *Can We Talk About Race? And Other Conversations in an Era of School Resegregation.* Boston: Beacon Press, 2007.

Tatum, Beverly Daniel. *Why Are All the Black Students Sitting Together in the Cafeteria?* New York: Basic Books, 1997.

Tuitt, Frank. "Inclusive Pedagogy 2.0: Implications for Race, Equity, and Higher Education in a Global Context." In *Race, Equity, and the Learning Environment: The Global Relevance of Critical and Inclusive Pedagogies in Higher Education*, ed. by Frank Tuitt, Chayla Haynes, and Saran Stewart, 205–21. Sterling, VA: Stylus Publishing, 2016.

Tuitt, Frank, Chayla Haynes, and Saran Stewart, eds. *Race, Equity, and the Learning Environment: The Global Relevance of Critical and Inclusive Pedagogies in Higher Education.* Sterling, VA: Stylus Publishing, 2016.

Verschelden, Cia. *Bandwidth Recovery: Helping Students Reclaim Cognitive Resources Lost to Poverty, Racism, and Social Marginalization.* Sterling, VA: Stylus Publishing, 2017.

Vesely, Monica. "The ICE model: An Alternative Learning Framework," Centre for Teaching Excellence Blog. University of Waterloo. https://cte-blog.uwaterloo.ca/5282/, accessed Dec 1, 2021.

Whittington, Keith E. "DeSantis's Terrifying Plot Against Higher Ed." *Chronicle of Higher Education*, February 27, 2023. https://www.chronicle.com/article/desantiss-terrifying-plot-against-higher-ed

Williams, Bianca C. "Radical Honesty; Truth-Telling as Pedagogy for Working Through Shame in Academic Spaces." In *Race, Equity, and the Learning Environment: The Global Relevance of Critical and Inclusive Pedagogies in Higher Education*, ed. by Frank Tuitt, Chayla Haynes, Saran Stewart, 71–82. Sterling, VA: Stylus Publishing, 2016.

Wilkerson, Isabel. *Caste: The Origins of Our Discontents.* New York: Random House, 2020.

Winkelmes, Mary-Ann, Allison Boye, and Suzanne Tapp, eds. *Transparent Design in Higher Education Teaching and Leadership.* Sterling, VA: Stylus Publishing, 2019.

Wobbe, Kristin, and Elisabeth A. Stoddard, eds. *Project-Based Learning in the First Year: Beyond All Expectations.* Sterling, VA: Stylus Publishing, 2019.

Wood, Amy Louise. *Lynching and Spectacle: Witnessing Racial Violence in America, 1890–1940.* Chapel Hill: University of North Carolina Press, 2009.

CHAPTER 12

Discussing White Nationalist Music in the Shadow of the Christchurch Mosque Shootings

The Importance of Reflecting on Race and Racism with Students in Aotearoa New Zealand

Olivia R. Lucas

On March 15th, 2019, a white supremacist terrorist attacked Muslims at Friday prayer in two Christchurch mosques, killing 51 and injuring 49 more. In a nation hitherto sheltered from the phenomenon of mass shootings, the event shattered New Zealand's sense of innocence.[1] That semester, I was teaching an elective undergraduate seminar titled "Extreme Sounds, Extreme Listening," that considered transgressive elements, moments and movements in popular music. Difficult topics in the course included, among others, music as torture in the US military detainment camps, white nationalist music, and violent misogyny in music. Given the course's subject matter, links to the Christchurch mosque shootings were inevitable and the event arose regularly in class discussion. This chapter reflects on my experience teaching this seminar in the aftermath of an historic tragedy. I explore the conflicts that arose among my personal teaching philosophy, cultural awareness, and University structures, and triangulate these issues toward reaffirming the significance of building classroom communities in which productive discussion of difficult topics is possible. I further reflect on my experiences as a white, US-American woman teaching in Aotearoa New Zealand,[2] where the politics of race and indigeneity play out in a post-colonial environment dissimilar to the one I was raised in.

Beyond the confines of my experience, this chapter deals with the fact that hard stuff—both personal and global—will always happen, and explores the reparative pedagogical potential of listening, discussion, and creation. Trauma and tragedy will occur in the lives of students, teachers, and their communities. Pain is a part of living, but healing can be a part of it, too. These realities are an important part of Cheng's call for a "reparative" musicology.[3]

My experience teaching musicology in the weeks and months immediately following the Christchurch mosque shooting allowed me to see that discussion of difficult topics that *feel* more distant to students—whether temporally or geographically—can help them to process events that feel closer to them. This technique unfolds one of the core activities of the humanities classroom: using (sometimes distant) texts to understand the human condition, both as it was and as it is. Although this pedagogical process is often fundamental to what we do, it is important not to overlook its reparative potential.

In Aotearoa, the academic year begins in early March, coinciding with the onset of meteorological autumn. March 2019 marked the beginning of my third academic year at Victoria University of Wellington—Te Herenga Waka, where I taught music theory and humanities electives in popular music. The terrorist attack took place on the Friday of the second week of classes. In the days following the attack, the University Vice-Chancellor and Provost sent numerous messages to both the entire University community as well as specifically to teaching staff restating the University's commitment to diversity and inclusivity, and highlighting counseling and other resources that were available to community members. No classes were canceled, but teaching staff were asked to be understanding of student absences and generous with extensions. A sample script for acknowledging the attacks in the classroom was disseminated on the 18th of March.[4] None of the students enrolled in my classes that semester were directly impacted by the attack but all felt its effects; the students' emotional processing of the event reminded me of mine and my peers' processing of the terrorist attacks of September 11, 2001, as high schoolers.

The readings for the third week of my seminar included Suzanne Cusick's work on music as torture in US detention centers.[5] I chose not to alter my teaching plan, knowing that Cusick's discussion of Islamophobia would likely cause Christchurch to arise in conversation. By the time Tuesday's class (19 March—five days after the shooting) arrived, discussion of the shooter's livestream of the attack, including its curated soundtrack of white supremacist music, was widespread.[6] Predictably, these chilling facts of the terrorist's development of a playlist for his attack—music to accompany terrorism—arose naturally in course of a class discussion about the systematic use of music to torture (typically Muslim) detainees. We did not linger on the specific topic of Christchurch, as the students were clearly hesitant to delve deeply into something so harrowing and still developing. At the same time, discussing Cusick's work on a related but more distant (to them) situation gave them language for processing the grief that accompanies a music lover's

214   TEACHING DIFFICULT TOPICS

first realization that music can be used for evil. Cusick's articles felt relevant to the violence to which Aotearoa had so recently been introduced, while simultaneously having the distance of specifically addressing atrocities committed by Americans in the early 2000s.

Later that week, on 21 March, the Provost's office sent another message to all teaching staff that read in part:

> "I would also like to reiterate some of the advice provided on Monday around teaching, which is to acknowledge what has happened in Christchurch and that students and staff have been deeply affected by it. We have support and resources available for students here [link removed]. I attach some information on coping with grief and distress following critical incidents that could be useful.
>
> **With many of us still feeling distressed, it is not the right time to discuss the events that happened in Christchurch in the classroom or use them as case studies or for class discussions. Please refrain from doing this.**" [emphasis added]

Although I would not consider my previous class discussion a "case study," by the time I received this message, I had already disobeyed it. And while I never walked into my seminar with a plan to focus on Christchurch or "use" the attacks for teaching, I continued to allow discussion of it whenever it arose, and guided these conversations as sensitively as I could.

At the end of April, students presented songs they had written and recorded. The students had enormous creative latitude with the project; I gave them a minimum duration and asked that the song interface with the themes of the class in some way. (I also provided numerous tips and resources for those new to songwriting, and encouraged creative risk-taking.) Responding to class discussions of how transgressive music can help process the inescapable cruelty of the world, two students teamed up and created "Lyre Bird," a musical video that paired footage of the Lyrebird, an Australian bird species known for its mimicry, with footage of New Zealand Prime Minister Jacinda Ardern and other leaders speaking to the nation following the attack. In their video, the Lyrebird's mimicry of anthropogenic sounds like sirens and cameras represented the way in which all of nature was bound up in humanity's folly and violence, and therefore the interconnectedness of all life on earth. In presenting their video to the class, the creators dedicated it to the victims, a small gesture that for them gave the project meaning beyond the fulfillment

Discussing White Nationalist Music 215

of course requirements, making it a component of two young people's real-time processing of a tragic event.

That instructors were forbidden from discussing the attacks beyond "acknowledgement" angered me, and conflicted with my beliefs that the humanities classroom is precisely where the ugliness and brutality of humanity should be confronted. Students noticed that their instructors said nothing of substance about the attacks. One morning in late March, I overheard a young woman on campus say that she was taking a class on "religion and violence," in which the terrorist attack—which was directed against Muslims at prayer—had not once been acknowledged, let alone discussed, which she found "creepy and upsetting." The stipulated classroom silence was not simply a space for reflection and processing, but a gag order that prevented those very activities. Just before the mid-term break in April, my own seminar students reflected on how acknowledgement of the attacks had come to feel domain-specific; certain times and spaces were designated for this purpose (typically via public memorials gatherings and support fora), but other aspects of university life had continued on as if nothing had happened. In a matter of weeks, the attacks had been safely contained where they could not contaminate quotidian University business such as learning and teaching.

In the process of writing this chapter, I reached out to Provost Larner to learn more about her reasoning behind requesting pedagogical silence. She replied that "The request that the shootings not be used as the basis of classroom activities was only relevant for the days immediately after the attacks." (No follow-up message was ever sent that indicated a relaxation of these strictures.)

She continued (excerpted):

> Turning the tragedy into a pedagogical exercise while the hurts were still very raw and the University was working through immediate issues like getting people to Christchurch for funerals was simply not appropriate. What did happen in the days immediately after the shooting was that many classes and university meetings started with a moment of silent reflection.
>
> As a country I think we have been very lucky (and were well led). Nearly a year on there has been good academic and public commentary (you may have seen, for example, the special issue of New Zealand Psychology [link removed] and I expect many classes in a wide range of disciplines now use the Christchurch shootings as a learning opportunity (Wendy Larner, email to author, January 20, 2020).

216   TEACHING DIFFICULT TOPICS

The journal issue Larner mentions was published on 15 April 2019—exactly one month after the attacks. The publication's brief turnaround demonstrates that New Zealand's academics began processing the event through the lenses of their respective fields almost immediately. The titles of the issue's articles (e.g., "Understanding the Terror Attack: Some Initial Steps" by Margaret Wetherell and "A screening instrument for assessing psychological distress following disasters: Adaptation for the March 15th, 2019 mass shootings in Christchurch, New Zealand" by Martin J. Dorahy and Neville M. Blampied) reflect the immediacy and present-ness of the events, striving for insights that could assist with initial responses and the provision of the best possible care to affected communities. A year later, the journal issue also serves as a historical document of these early reactions themselves, and presents a microcosm of how the nation as a whole turned its attention to the attacks, their aftermath, and the process of healing. Were these academics merely using the attacks as a case study or research "exercise"? Or were they using their fields of expertise to process a difficult event in a way that was productive for both themselves and their communities? The University administration's position seemed to indicate that immediately processing the shootings was appropriate for researchers, but not for students.

Furthermore, I would not describe discussions about the shootings that arose in my seminar in the ways that the provost did. Although I did "discuss the events that happened in Christchurch in the classroom" (Wendy Larner, email to Victoria University of Wellington teaching staff, March 21, 2019), I did not "use them as case studies" (same email) or "turn the tragedy into a pedagogical exercise" (Wendy Larner, email to author, January 20, 2020). I agree with the position that using recent terrorist attacks to achieve pre-existing pedagogical goals would be irresponsible. I also appreciate that allowing instructors and students to discuss the attacks in class comes with a non-zero risk that someone could say something insensitive or even hateful, either intentionally or unintentionally. I further acknowledge that in her role as Provost, it is her job to try to protect the University and that many Provosts would have made the same decision. My critique of the Provost's positions points less to her as an individual, and more to the way current university administrations tend to prioritize minimizing risk and avoiding controversy above promoting thoughtful pedagogy.

The administrative logic of the Provost's messages treats pedagogy as if it were timeless, static, and unresponsive. In this model of pedagogy, there are containers like "case study" into which any topically relevant event can be poured to produce the desired pedagogical outcome. Such pedagogy is a consumable that can be reliably produced and re-produced year after year, and sold to students. If this model represented how I conduct upper-level humanities instruction in a seminar context, then the Provost would be right that discussing the attacks would be inappropriate. However, in a classroom environment with a dozen students, where the core content involves questions of moral ambiguity surrounding music, use of music, and creators and performers of music, and in which students are routinely asked to weigh in with their personal thoughts, feelings, and ideas about these issues, it seems conversely irresponsible to forbid them from speaking about the worst mass shooting in their country's history.

The University's position on pedagogy seems to further suggest that the classroom can be isolated from the external events of the world, and that events of enormous significance—such as a terrorist attack—can be emotionally contained through the use of moments of silence, extra-curricular events and extension of assignment deadlines, while the pedagogical environment itself remains sterile. This sterility silences desires, suppresses emotions, and obstructs self-knowledge. The idea that the university classroom remains unimpacted by external events in the world is not only patently false, but also produces the very grounds upon which the humanities remain under attack by university administrations. Whereas the social and political respect afforded to STEM fields arises from their perceived direct link to employment, which in turn confers the ability to produce and receive "real-world" value, humanities academics often argue that their fields confer on students the skill of "critical thinking," or more colloquially, the skill of *dealing* with the "real world." Asking faculty to remain silent about traumatic current events may not impact the delivery of job skills, but it can make a course on "religion and violence" seem awfully out of touch and irrelevant.[7] In short, the University's request that the classroom remain unsullied by difficult real-world events ends up buttressing the argument that humanities study does not produce "real-world skills."

Even before the onset of the global Covid-19 pandemic and its impacts on our classrooms and teaching, numerous non-traumatic events amply demonstrate the impact of the "real world" on the university classroom. For example, Louisiana State University canceled the first two days of spring semester 2020 for students to attend (and recover from) the National Championship football game.[8] Severe weather, routine illness and transportation issues impact everyone's participation in university life at some point or another. I regularly grant extensions to students grieving relatives, pets, and breakups, or celebrating weddings and christenings; my students and my classrooms

218   TEACHING DIFFICULT TOPICS

exist within the constraints of real-world events. Enabling my students to discuss the attacks when they arose naturally due to pre-existing course content was my way of inviting the confluence of real-world events, my students' real-time reactions to those events, and the ideas we were studying. From this perspective, learning is a human process that cannot be separated from the student's humanity, and course content becomes a conduit to understanding the lived humanity of others.

In the middle of May, my seminar read Benjamin Teitelbaum's work on racism and white nationalism in music.[9] Here, again, although none of the readings or listenings dealt directly with the Christchurch shootings, they naturally loomed large over our discussion. By this point in the semester, the students knew each other well and conversations flowed naturally in class. Students were divided on whether or not exposing white nationalist music to the light of discussion productively raised awareness of its problematic prevalence or validated a phenomenon that it was more effective to ignore. The discussion became unavoidably personal. Students of color shared their experiences of growing up feeling excluded from mainstream New Zealand identities. Some of them additionally felt that discussing white nationalist music was important for helping white students understand that the ability to distance themselves from discussions of race was itself racial privilege. Some white students felt that since white nationalist music would never convince *them*, or any "reasonable" person, to become a racist, such music was better off ignored and starved of attention.[10] The specter of the white nationalist who had attacked Christchurch just two months earlier surfaced repeatedly in the conversation, as he embodied this question of whether white supremacists were better treated as isolated, deranged individuals or as the product of a networked and resourced political structure. The students also discussed the role of the internet in radicalization of not only white supremacists, but other groups such as self-identified "incels," or Islamic State recruits, and how social media algorithms can quickly take someone feeling normal adolescent emotions of loneliness, insecurity, and alienation down a dark path to groups that offer belonging in exchange for ideological loyalty.[11] Again, I did not set out to "use" the Christchurch attacks to teach my students something, but I did create a discussion environment in which reactions to current events could augment, illustrate, and help evaluate the problems posed by the course readings.

Beyond the messages sent out by the Provost in the aftermath of the terrorist attacks, the issue of discussing difficult events in the classroom was under general discussion in University committees. At the time, I represented the School of Music on the Faculty of Humanities and Social Sciences Learning, Teaching and Equity Committee. The University had tasked each faculty with drafting a document around teaching difficult topics. To help us get started, our committee studied the memorandum that the Faculty of Law had already drafted on this topic for their own use.

The Faculty of Law memorandum (version dated 21 June 2018) took the form of a list of suggestions for teaching staff, and acknowledged that there would necessarily be a diversity of reasonably held opinions on the topic, and indeed that arriving at a definition of "sensitive material" that is universally applicable is impossible.[12] It also acknowledged that in studying law, particularly criminal law, students would inevitably have to come face to face with negative aspects of humanity; course content would necessarily have to address rape, abuse, hate crimes, and other difficult topics from a legal perspective. Despite the centrality of violent and traumatic crimes to certain kinds of legal study, the memorandum nevertheless advised caution in the teaching of such material, encouraging instructors to give students specific content warnings, allow students to avoid content that they found troubling, and to avoid including difficult content unless academically necessary.

The approach taken in the faculty of humanities and social sciences to drafting the required document differed in that it approached teaching difficult topics as an important shared mandate of our disciplines. It was felt that the humanities classroom was, of all the parts of the university, the place where students could be equipped with the tools needed to deal with difficult topics not only in the classroom, but in a world full of events that are challenging to take in and process.

I agreed with my colleagues that any such memorandum should be written not from the perspective of: "*should* difficult topics be necessary to a course, we recommend the following steps to ameliorate the harm they could do to students . . . ," but from the perspective of: "As humanities scholars and teachers, it is our duty to help students prepare themselves for a challenging world; *when* difficult topics arise in a course, here are some tips and resources to assist in undertaking this important responsibility." Our committee largely shared a sense of bewilderment as to what the humanities and social sciences would have to offer if not ways of understanding all aspects of the human condition, and were frustrated by what felt like the University's assumption that difficult topics by default posed a risk of harm to students.

A large part of what goes on in the humanities seminar is asking students to react to readings or other texts. But what is the point of having students react to readings, if they're not allowed to react to real-world events? A read-

220   TEACHING DIFFICULT TOPICS

ing only matters insofar as it is read by actual people who are real-world entities. This is the only way for a text to be present in the real world. If we want students to believe texts matter in the world, we have to act like the world itself matters. Choosing not to discuss an ongoing event, no matter how traumatic, implies distance from it. By holding classes yet forbidding discussion of the terror attack, the University administration suggested it was far away and not relevant. It seemed they simultaneously believed it might negatively impact students, but wanted those impacts kept out of the classroom.

My own position as an outsider with insider privileges demanded that I take seriously the possibility that my resistance to the University's position manifested a lack of cultural understanding on my part. I was not a New Zealand citizen, but as a white woman with English as a native language and a career in an international institution that employed numerous foreign staff, I did not stick out, and I did not have a particularly hard time connecting with students. As a U.S.-American, my views on race and its role in the classroom are inextricably shaped by my understanding of the lingering effects of slavery, segregation, and Jim Crow on the U.S. education system. My two and a half years in Aotearoa New Zealand were a lengthy learning process, as I gradually absorbed the realities of its postcolonialism. In 2018, Māori people were approximately 16% of the population, with people of other Pacific ethnicities making up another 8%.[13] Inclusion of Māori language, culture, and governance in University life was a high priority at Victoria, with classes offered for staff to gain competence in these areas. Due to these and other quantifiable efforts at post-colonial reparation, many New Zealanders proudly consider their nation "bicultural," and tend to consider racism a much more serious problem for other countries, such as Australia and the U.S. When discussing issues of imperialism and race, the United States was a common scapegoat for students; it was easy for students to agree on the injustice of using rap lyrics as courtroom evidence, in part because they already understood the U.S. criminal justice system to be racist.[14] Similarly, they quickly leapt from the inherent moral reprehensibility of using music as torture to the fact that this was an atrocity committed by the U.S. military, which they already understood as a problematically imperialistic institution. Dealing with Christchurch forced students to confront violent racism on their own shores, rather than speak of it primarily as a distant problem that other countries have.

Given the extent to which my personal teaching philosophy prizes openness and direct conversation, when I first arrived in New Zealand, I was unprepared for the extent to which my Aotearoa students were slow to open up and preferred to approach difficult issues indirectly. In the process of adapting, however, I found that by directly addressing issues like white nationalist music in my syllabus, I had inadvertently provided a path for students to indirectly address a national trauma in a more comfortable way. Amidst a University environment that took an anxious and avoidant approach to students' relationship with the challenges of the real world, it felt important to discover a way to help students deal with difficult events in a way that felt comfortable for them. The methods themselves turned out to be classic—reading, listening, and discussion—the key was choosing classroom texts that enabled discussion at first from a distance, and allowing students to relate the discussion to their own reality at their own pace.

William Cheng's *Just Vibrations: The Purpose of Sounding Good* further develops Eve Kosofsky Sedgwick's idea of "paranoid" and "reparative" readings, considering how they might be brought to bear on musicological work. Cheng's book explains, supports and defends the possibilities of a reparative musicology, but in his "Coda," he advocates for a balance, saying, "the reparative and the paranoid are not locked in a zero-sum game. A rule of thumb would be to pursue repair where possible and to rely on paranoia when necessary."[15] The seminar at the center of this chapter sought to balance both of these perspectives. Although the course explicitly addressed several difficult issues, it also dealt with joy and pleasure. One aspect of the course celebrated the intensity, rebelliousness, and aesthetic pleasures of extreme music. We celebrated how pushing past socially constructed ideas of musicality (or "sounding good" in Cheng's terms) could give voice to marginalized communities. We discussed how continuous technological innovation energizes new creativity in soundmaking. However, we also critiqued the ways that marginalized musical communities could cultivate hate, and relied on "the paranoid's belief in the power of exposure and demystification" to address the reality that music can be used for evil.[16] Students contemplated how the line between loudness as pleasure and loudness as pain is razor-thin, and the role consent plays in shaping sonic experiences. This balancing of paranoid and reparative engagement with course materials cooperates with the way that "distant" case studies provided tangential frameworks for close, contemporary issues. Reparative engagement meant that students didn't have to have it all figured out, as reactions could be messy and spontaneous. Students had the option to focus their attention on traditional "paranoid" readings of course materials, or to draw "reparative" connections with their own experiences and current events. Suzanne Cusick argues that balancing these positions promotes "psychological and spiritual health," as it involves both attending to experience (mindfulness) and developing understanding of that experience.[17] Inasmuch as Cheng's book exhorts an ethic of care, this kind of pedagogy has the power to not only build traditional skills such as critical thinking and listening, but also actively rehearse skills for the maintenance of wellbeing.

Reflecting on her reaction to the re-election of George W. Bush as President of the United States in 2004, Toni Morrison wrote:

> There is no time for despair, no place for self-pity, no need for silence, no room for fear. We speak, we write, we do language. That is how civilizations heal. I know the world is bruised and bleeding, and though it is important not to ignore its pain, it is also critical to refuse to succumb to its malevolence. Like failure, chaos contains information that can lead to knowledge—even wisdom. Like art.[18]

Morrison's exhortation addresses artists, but her emphasis on the simple acts of speaking, writing, and "doing language" as a path to societal healing are fundamental to the purpose of the music-centered humanities classroom. "Doing language" about problematic art becomes a way to simultaneously "do language" about urgent social wounds that require healing. World events are not containable items to be re-packaged for pedagogical use, but the fluid reality to which our course materials can and should be applied. By allowing and enabling my students to speak about the Christchurch mosque shootings, I hope in some small way to have shown them that such a wound cannot be healed by silencing or isolating it, but only through thoughtful acceptance of it into the fabric of one's existence.

Notes

1. Details about the attack, its aftermath, and the victims can be found in *Stuff*'s "The End of Our Innocence" project: https://interactives.stuff.co.nz/2019/03/end-of-our-innocence/. Just over a year after the attack, on March 26, 2020, the perpetrator pled guilty to 51 counts of murder, 40 counts of attempted murder, and 1 count of terrorism. See Blair Ensor and Sam Sherwood, "Christchurch Mosque Attacks: Gunman Pleads Guilty to Murder, Attempted Murder and Terrorism," *Stuff*, March 26, 2020, accessed July 24, 2023, https://www.stuff.co.nz/national/crime/120565800/christchurch-mosque-attacks-accused-pleads-guilty-to-murder-attempted-murder-and-terrorism

2. "Aotearoa" is the Indigenous Māori name for New Zealand. The nation's two names are often used interchangeably or combined, as in "Aotearoa New Zealand."

3. William Cheng, *Just Vibrations: The Purpose of Sounding Good* (Ann Arbor, MI: University of Michigan Press, 2016), 9–10.

Discussing White Nationalist Music   223

4. The sample script was sent out by the Provost's office, in an email that included other suggestions, such as taking a minute's silence and acknowledging that students might not feel up to talking in class. The sample script read, "Before we start [class], I would like to acknowledge the terrible terrorist attack perpetrated against New Zealanders, targeted at Muslims at prayer, in Christchurch. I know that things feel different now, and that you may be feeling shocked, or scared, or sad, or any number of other emotions. So we need to be aware of these feelings, and try to look after each other as we continue with our studies and in our lives. And as time goes on, we should think about how we could help to prevent this kind of thing happening again, and of ways we can support the Muslim community in New Zealand and here at the University" (Wendy Larner, email to Victoria University of Wellington teaching staff, March 18, 2020).

5. Suzanne G. Cusick, "Music as Torture/Music as Weapon." *Trans: Revista Transcultural de Música* 10 (2006): https://www.sibetrans.com/trans/article/152/music-as-torture-music-as-weapon; Suzanne G. Cusick, "'You are in a place that is out of the world . . .': Music in the Detention Camps of the 'Global War on Terror.'" *Journal of the Society for American Music* 2/1 (2008): 1–26.

6. Within a week of the attack, possession and/or distribution of the terrorist's livestream and manifesto were made illegal in New Zealand by Chief Censor David Shanks (see Radio New Zealand, "Christchurch Mosque Shootings: 'Manifesto' Deemed Objectionable," March 23, 2019, accessed July 24, 2023, https://www.rnz.co.nz/news/national/385399/christchurch-mosque-shootings-manifesto-deemed-obje ctionable). However, discussions of the manifesto's and livestream's content remained available in international media. See, for example, Gerry Doyle, "New Zealand Mosque Attacker's Plan Began and Ended Online," *Reuters*, March 15, 2019, accessed July 24, 2023, https://www.reuters.com/article/us-newzealand-shootout-internet/new-zea land-mosque-attackers-plan-began-and-ended-online-idUSKCN1QW1MV and Lisa Martin and Ben Smee, "What Do We Know about the Christchurch Attack Suspect?" *The Guardian*, March 15, 2019, accessed July 24, 2023, https://www.theguardian.com /world/2019/mar/15/rightwing-extremist-wrote-manifesto-before-livestreaming-ch ristchurch-shooting

7. This silencing has become more explicit and widespread in the United States, in states where legislatures have banned the teaching of certain topics, most commonly those related to systemic racism.

8. Mark Ballard, "LSU Cancels Classes for National Championship; Make-Up Days are Likely, School Says," *The Advocate*, January, 10, 2020, accessed July 24, 2023, https:// www.theadvocate.com/baton_rouge/sports/lsu/article_6c347bac-33d1-11ea-9393 -0f245d8f6970.html

9. Benjamin Teitelbaum, "Saga's Sorrow: Femininities of Despair in the Music of Radical White Nationalism." *Ethnomusicology* 58, no. 3 (2014): 405–30.

10. Issues of free speech played less of a role in these discussions than they might have in a U.S. classroom. Because of the First Amendment, protection of free speech

224   TEACHING DIFFICULT TOPICS

is much stronger in the U.S. than in New Zealand, where hate speech is banned by the Human Rights Act of 1993 (sections 61 and 131).

11. For more on social media and extremism, see, for example, Brendan Koerner, "Why ISIS is Winning the Social Media War" *Wired*, April 2016, accessed July 24, 2023, https://www.wired.com/2016/03/isis-winning-social-media-war-heres-beat/, Katherine J. Wu, "Radical Ideas Spread Through Social Media. Are the Algorithms to Blame?" *Nova*, March 28, 2019, accessed July 24, 2023, https://www.pbs.org/wgbh/nova/article/radical-ideas-social-media-algorithms/, and *Homeland Security Newswire*, "White Supremacist Groups Thriving on Facebook" May, 29, 2020, accessed July 24, 2023, http://www.homelandsecuritynewswire.com/dr20200529-white-supremacist-groups-thriving-on-facebook

12. It is worth noting that the majority of Law students in Aotearoa New Zealand are undergraduates.

13. Statistics New Zealand, "2018 Census Population and Dwelling Counts," September 23, 2019, accessed July 24, 2023, https://www.stats.govt.nz/information-releases/2018-census-population-and-dwelling-counts

14. Brendan O'Connor, "Why Are Rap Lyrics Being Used as Evidence in Court?" *Noisey*, November 3, 2014, accessed July 24, 2023, https://www.vice.com/en_us/article/rdaba6/rap-lyrics-as-evidence

15. Cheng, *Just Vibrations*, 101

16. Cusick, "You Are in a Place That is Out of the World," par. 22

17. Cusick, "You Are in a Place That is Out of the World," par. 24

18. Toni Morrison, "No Place for Self-Pity, No Room for Fear: In Times of Dread, Artists Must Never Choose to Remain Silent," *The Nation*, March 23, 2015, accessed July 24, 2023, https://www.thenation.com/article/archive/no-place-self-pity-no-room-fear/

Works Cited

Ballard, Mark. "LSU Cancels Classes for National Championship; Make-Up Days are Likely, School Says." *The Advocate*. January, 10, 2020. https://www.theadvocate.com/baton_rouge/sports/lsu/article_6c347bac-33d1-11ea-9393-0f245d8f6970.html

Cheng, William. *Just Vibrations: The Purpose of Sounding Good*. Ann Arbor: University of Michigan Press, 2016. https://doi.org/10.3998/mpub.9293551

Cusick, Suzanne G. "Music as Torture/Music as Weapon." *Trans: Revista Transcultural de Música* 10 (2006). https://www.sibetrans.com/trans/article/152/music-as-tortur e-music-as-weapon

Cusick, Suzanne G. "'You are in a place that is out of the world . . .': Music in the Detention Camps of the 'Global War on Terror.'" *Journal of the Society for American Music* 2/1 (2008): 1–26.

Dorahy, Martin J., and Neville M. Blampied. "A Screening Instrument for Assessing Psychological Distress Following Disasters: Adaptation for the March 15th, 2019 Mass Shootings in Christchurch, New Zealand." *New Zealand Journal of Psychology* 48, no. 1 (2019): 23–28. https://www.psychology.org.nz/wp-content/uploads/NZJP-Vol-48-No-1-DRAFT-v2-1.pdf

Discussing White Nationalist Music 225

Doyle, Gerry. "New Zealand Mosque Attacker's Plan Began and Ended Online." *Reuters*. March 15, 2019. https://www.reuters.com/article/us-newzealand-shootout-in ternet/new-zealand-mosque-attackers-plan-began-and-ended-online-idUSKCN1 QW1MV

Ensor, Blair, and Sam Sherwood. "Christchurch Mosque Attacks: Gunman Pleads Guilty to Murder, Attempted Murder and Terrorism." *Stuff*. March 26, 2020. https://www.stuff.co.nz/national/crime/120565800/christchurch-mosque-attacks-accus ed-pleads-guilty-to-murder-attempted-murder-and-terrorism

Hartevelt, John, ed. "The End of Our Innocence." *Stuff*. March 29, 2019. https://interact ives.stuff.co.nz/2019/03/end-of-our-innocence/

Homeland Security Newswire. "White Supremacist Groups Thriving on Facebook." May, 29, 2020. http://www.homelandsecuritynewswire.com/dr20200529-white-suprema cist-groups-thriving-on-facebook

Koerner, Brendan I. "Why ISIS is Winning the Social Media War." *Wired*, April 2016, https://www.wired.com/2016/03/isis-winning-social-media-war-heres-beat/

Martin, Lisa, and Ben Smee. "What Do We Know about the Christchurch Attack Suspect?" *The Guardian*. March 15, 2019. https://www.theguardian.com/world/2019 /mar/15/rightwing-extremist-wrote-manifesto-before-livestreaming-christchurch -shooting

Morrison, Toni. "No Place for Self-Pity, No Room for Fear: In Times of Dread, Artists Must Never Choose to Remain Silent." *The Nation*. March 23, 2015. https://www.the nation.com/article/archive/no-place-self-pity-no-room-fear/

New Zealand Department of Justice. "Human Rights Act 1993." http://www.legislation .govt.nz/act/public/1993/0082/latest/DLM304212.html

O'Connor, Brendan. "Why Are Rap Lyrics Being Used as Evidence in Court?" *Noisey*. November 3, 2014. https://www.vice.com/en_us/article/rdaba6/rap-lyrics-as-evid ence

Radio New Zealand. "Christchurch Mosque Shootings: 'Manifesto' Deemed Objectionable." March 23, 2019. https://www.rnz.co.nz/news/national/385399/christchurch -mosque-shootings-manifesto-deemed-objectionable

Statistics New Zealand. "2018 Census Population and Dwelling Counts." September 23, 2019. https://www.stats.govt.nz/information-releases/2018-census-population -and-dwelling-counts

Teitelbaum, Benjamin. "Saga's Sorrow: Femininities of Despair in the Music of Radical White Nationalism." *Ethnomusicology* 58, no. 3 (2014): 405–30.

Wetherell, Margaret. "Understanding the Terror Attack: Some Initial Steps" *New Zealand Journal of Psychology* 48, no. 1 (2019): 4–7. https://www.psychology.org.nz/wp -content/uploads/NZJP-Vol-48-No-1-DRAFT-v2-1.pdf

Wu, Katherine J. "Radical Ideas Spread Through Social Media. Are the Algorithms to Blame?" *Nova*, March 28, 2019. https://www.pbs.org/wgbh/nova/article/radical-ide as-social-media-algorithms/

CHAPTER 13

Don't You Cry for Me

A Critical-Race Analysis of Undergraduate Music Theory Textbooks

Philip Ewell and Megan Lyons

INTRODUCTION

Textbooks are authoritative sources that outline the foundations of a discipline. Instructors and students alike rely on the depth and accuracy of the materials presented in their classrooms, thus textbooks are carefully chosen with respect to past traditions, current trends, and future possibilities.[1] However, when examining contemporary music theory textbooks in the United States, one questions whether the traditions, trends, and possibilities presented truly represent the country for which these textbooks are intended. In fact, 98% of the musical examples from seven representative textbooks were written by white persons. In pointing this out, we highlight one of the most pressing and current aspects of music theory education in the United States: systemic and structural racism.[2] We will show that music theory, in its presentation of what music is, represents a system that excludes those who are not white. This system, in turn, represents a structure, one of racial exclusionism.

In this chapter we, a black cisgender man and a white cisgender woman, examine seven of the most common undergraduate music theory textbooks to demonstrate how race and music theory textbooks intersect. More specifically, we look at their musical examples and how they reflect or do not reflect current trends. These textbooks are representative of what we call "music theory's white racial frame,"[3] which contains many "racialized structures" that reliably benefit whites while disadvantaging nonwhites.[4] Furthermore, because whiteness has worked hand in glove with maleness in shaping the music theory curriculum represented in these textbooks, we also consider gender representation in these textbooks. Finally, we will highlight the presence of white-supremacist and blackface-minstrelsy composer Ste-

226

phen Foster in our analysis. The inclusion of such a composer, and especially his "Oh! Susanna (Don't You Cry for Me)," shows music theory's remarkable insensitivity with respect to racial matters, and points to our general inability to understand how whiteness has shaped the study of music theory in the United States.

We begin with a lengthy discussion of the data that we culled from these textbooks, which includes data on the race and gender of all musical examples from the books. This discussion gives way to a consideration of the musical examples by Foster, which in turn leads to a breakdown of the different races of composers of color represented in the textbooks, with special attention given to Asian composers. After a brief turn to popular music examples and how they fit into our critical-race analysis, we offer an example of how one might introduce some of these data and ideas into the classroom, while we reflect on how all of this might be relevant not just outside of the music theory classroom, but to other parts of the university writ large. At the very end we offer six appendices that give information for all musical examples by composers of color and women composers from the six textbooks that included them—one textbook had none—including the title of the piece, the measure numbers, the chapter and page number in which the examples appear, and the music theory topic being discussed. It is our hope that this discussion will provide a catalyst for further action in terms of racial and gender inclusivity in the music theory classroom, which has become something of a bellwether for higher education.

DATA ANALYSIS

Seven textbooks, as seen below in Table 13.1, account for roughly 96% of the market share of music theory textbooks.[5] Of the 3039 musical examples presented in the seven textbooks, only 61 (2.01%) were written by composers of color, while 98 (3.22%) of the examples were composed by women.[6] Two textbooks—by Aldwell/Schachter/Cadwallader and Laitz—contained a total of only two examples by composers of color, while containing a total of 1015 examples.[7] For these two textbooks, only 0.2% of the examples were written by composers of color, while they account for roughly 13% of the market share of American music theory textbooks. These two textbooks also had the fewest examples by women, with a total of two examples for only 0.2% of their total examples.

Unsurprisingly, a small number of white-male composers account for

228 TEACHING DIFFICULT TOPICS

Table 13.1: Musical examples by composers of color and women in the most common music theory textbooks

Textbook	Percentage of market share	Total # of examples	# of examples by composers of color	% of examples by composers of color	# of examples by women composers	% of examples by women composers
Aldwell, Schachter, and Cadwallader, 4th ed. (2011)	5	465	0	0%	0	0%
Benward and Saker, 9th ed. (2015)	13	333	8	2.40%	7	2.10%
Burstein and Straus, 2nd ed. (2019)	11	413	13	3.15%	35	8.48%
Clendinning and Marvin 3rd ed. (2016)	25	504	15	2.98%	14	2.78%
Kostka, Payne, and Almén, 8th ed. (2018)	29	370	10	2.70%	10	2.70%
Laitz, 4th ed. (2015)	8	550	2	0.36%	2	0.36%
Roig-Francoli, 2nd ed. (2010)	5	404	13	3.22%	30	7.43%
TOTALS	96	3039	61	2.01%	98	3.22%

many of the examples in all textbooks. Table 13.2 shows the percentages for the three most common composers, Johann Sebastian Bach, Ludwig van Beethoven, and Wolfgang Amadeus Mozart. In the Benward/Saker, for instance, 33% of the examples were by Bach alone, while 46% of its examples were composed by these three composers. In the Aldwell/Schachter/Cadwallader, exactly half of the musical examples were written by these three composers, while the Burstein/Straus, at 28%, saw the lowest usage of these composers. Clearly, an overwhelming number of examples in the seven textbooks were written by an extremely small group of white-male composers, which points to music theory's inability to envision a music theoretical world beyond whiteness and maleness. In a feedback loop, the concepts covered in these textbooks stem from the works of composers such as Bach, Beethoven, and Mozart. In turn, the theories discussed are based on these few composers' compositions, which limits the musical examples included from composers outside of so-called "canonic" composers.

Table 13.2: Percentages of musical examples by Bach, Beethoven, and Mozart

Textbook	% Examples in Text by J.S. Bach	% Examples in Text by Beethoven	% Examples in Text by Mozart	TOTALS
Aldwell, Schachter, and Cadwallader, 4th ed. (2011)	20%	11%	19%	50%
Benward and Saker, 9th ed. (2015)	33%	5%	8%	46%
Burstein and Straus, 2nd ed. (2019)	12%	8%	8%	28%
Clendinning and Marvin 3rd ed. (2016)	14%	3%	13%	30%
Kostka, Payne, and Almén, 8th ed. (2018)	16%	9%	14%	39%
Laitz, 4th ed. (2015)	5%	13%	14%	32%
Roig-Francoli, 2nd ed. (2010)	19%	7%	11%	37%

Table 13.3: Racial and gender data of composers for the most common music theory textbooks

Textbook	Percentage of market share	Total # of composers	# of composers of color	% of composers of color	# of women composers	% of women composers
Aldwell, Schachter, and Cadwallader, 4th ed. (2011)	5	41	0	0%	0	0%
Benward and Saker, 9th ed. (2015)	13	90	7	7.78%	7	7.78%
Burstein and Straus, 2nd ed. (2019)	11	128	10	8.00%	29	23%
Clendinning and Marvin 3rd ed. (2016)	25	110	12	10.91%	9	8.18%
Kostka, Payne, and Almén, 8th ed. (2018)	29	94	10	10.64%	3	3.19%
Laitz, 4th ed. (2015)	8	90	2	2.22%	1	1.11%
Roig-Francoli, 2nd ed. (2010)	5	98	6	6.12%	17	17.35%
TOTALS	96	651	47	7.20%	66	10.14%

TEACHING DIFFICULT TOPICS

Table 13.4: Burstein/Straus first edition and second edition data

	1st ed. (2016)	2nd ed. (2019)
Total # Composers	51	128
Total # Women Composers	4 (8%)	29 (23%)
Total # Composers of Color	1 (2%)	10 (8%)
Total # Musical Examples	304	413
Total # Examples by Women Composers	5 (1.6%)	35 (8%)
Total # Examples by Composers of Color	1 (.3%)	13 (3%)
% Examples Bach	17%	12%
% Examples Beethoven	12%	8%
% Examples Mozart	13%	8%
% Total Examples Bach, Beethoven, Mozart	42%	28%

Considering the abundance of examples by white-male composers, it is worth calculating the content of the textbooks by the number of *composers* with respect to race and gender, and not the number of musical examples. Table 13.3 shows these calculations. The table shows that the textbook by Aldwell/Schachter/Cadwallader has the fewest distinct composers, 41, while the textbook by Burstein/Straus has the most, 128. Clendinning/Marvin had the greatest number of composers of color at 12. Also noteworthy were the high number of women composers, 17 (17.35% of total composers), contained in the textbook by Roig-Francoli, and 29 (23% of total composers) in the Burstein/ Straus. Finally, when viewing composers, and not examples, 7.20% of the composers represented in all textbooks were composers of color, and 10.14% of the composers represented in all texts were women. These are higher numbers than those of musical examples, but we still note that the excessive amount of attention dedicated to white-male composers does not allow for much of an expansion of composers who do not identify as such.

The Burstein/Straus textbook presents a unique case study, as our data collection began with the 2016 first edition and has since been updated to include the 2019 second edition. The data in Table 13.4 shows how the diversity of musical examples increased between the two editions. Most drastically, the number of distinct composers increased by 250%. In the first edition, nearly half of the examples were composed by Bach, Beethoven, and Mozart alone. The second edition featured more examples by a more diverse group of composers.

In a moving piece on the African American woman composer Florence Price, *New Yorker* music critic Alex Ross touches on our dependence on white male composers, calling it "lazy":

Don't You Cry for Me 231

The adulation of the master, the genius, the divinely gifted creator all too easily lapses into a cult of the white-male hero, to whom such traits are almost unthinkingly attached. . . . To reduce music history [and music theory of course] to a pageant of masters is, at bottom, lazy. We stick with the known in order to avoid the hard work of exploring the unknown.[8]

Our dependence on white-male composers is also a result of white racial framing, as Ewell points out in "Music Theory and the White Racial Frame."[9] As a comparison, once textbook authors realized that there were virtually no women composers in our music theory textbooks, they began to include them. In similar fashion, the first solution authors turn to in order to solve the racial imbalance is to find more examples by Chevalier de Saint-Georges, William Grant Still, and Scott Joplin. But stocking our textbooks with musical examples by these black composers is not the sole solution to this problem, which is a result of framing western functional tonality as the only organizational force in music worthy of music theory's consideration in the music theory classroom. As the main musical organizational force that emerged from Europe in the seventeenth–nineteenth centuries, functional tonality is also racialized as "white," and a fine example of a racialized structure, which sociologist Eduardo Bonilla-Silva says is "*the totality of the social relations and practices that reinforce white privilege*)."[10] The fact that many of the ideas from functional tonality appear in so many of the world's musics is a direct result of the power of colonialism and hegemony.[11] Thus the problem in our music curricula concerns not only the racial and gender identity of the composers we study, but the music theories behind their music. This distinction between the whiteness of the musics and the whiteness of the music theories is of vital importance insofar as we in music theory can generally only envision one (expanding the western repertoire to include nonwhite/nonmale composers) and not the other (studying nonwestern/nonwhite music theory). The case of the two editions of the textbook by Burstein/Straus shown in Table 13.4 is a prime example of the additive activity of "diversity, equity, and inclusivity," which often serves as a cover for maintaining the racialized and gendered structures of music theory in the United States.

OH! FOSTER

The undergraduate textbooks by the following authors contain at least one example by Stephen Foster: Benward/Saker, Burstein/Straus, Clendinning/

232   TEACHING DIFFICULT TOPICS

Marvin, Kostka/Payne/Almén, Laitz, and Roig-Francolí. Foster was one of the most important names in nineteenth-century American blackface minstrelsy, and he himself wore blackface from time to time.[12] "Oh! Susanna" might be a good example of parallel phrase structure, but what about the second-verse lyrics, written by Foster himself: "I jumped aboard de telegraph and trabbled down de riber / De lectric fluid magnified, and killed five hundred nigger." Theory textbooks routinely include lyrics to songs, often in French, Italian, or German and in English translation, but Foster's are obviously excluded. Note the absurd caricatured "negro" dialect of the blackface minstrel, who did so much to dehumanize blacks in the buffoonish subhuman practice of black-face minstrelsy. In "Race, Blacksound, and the (Re)Making of Musicological Discourse," Matthew Morrison explains how blackface led to exclusionist practices in musicology (2019); the same could be said for music theory. The inclusion of a white supremacist composer like Foster in our music theory textbooks represents the extraordinary insensitivity of music theory's white frame—and of the textbook publishers we hasten to add—with respect to racial matters. It also points to our inability to recognize how whiteness has shaped the field. In "Dinah, Put Down Your Horn: Blackface Minstrel Songs Don't Belong in Music Class," Katya Ermolaeva (2019) speaks of the harmful legacy of including these racist songs in children's songbooks.[13] Further, she speaks of the objectification and dehumanization that blackface entailed, and links these harmful elements to the music classroom. Most important, she speaks of how these minstrel songs and their lyrics often conditioned whites to believe that blacks were somehow impervious to pain, and of how the legacy of blackface has a legacy that we still have not come to terms with today: "The normalization of violence against African Americans has reper-cussions that are still felt today, as Black Americans are less likely than White Americans to receive medical treatment for pain, and young Black males are up to 13 times more likely to die from homicide than non-Hispanic White males."[14]

Table 13.5 shows all the examples by Stephen Foster in the seven text-books we examined. In total, eleven examples by Stephen Foster are found in the six textbooks that had at least one (Aldwell/Schachter/Cadwallader had none). The majority of the examples illustrate a type of form, whether it be a type of period or binary form, and the remainder demonstrate introductory concepts such as notating meter or a predominant chord. However, none of the textbooks contextualize the songs or Stephen Foster within the history of minstrelsy. A more careful curation of musical examples could eliminate the need for these problematic examples, replacing them with music by compos-

Table 13.5: Stephen Foster examples in the most common music theory textbooks

Textbook	Page #	Chapter	Piece	Topic
Aldwell, Schachter, and Cad-wallader, 4th ed. (2011)	N/A	N/A	N/A	N/A
Benward and Saker, 9th ed. (2015)	41	2	"Oh! Susanna"	Pentatonic Scale
	125	6	"Camptown Races"	Parallel Period
Burstein and Straus, 2nd ed. (2019)	148	15	"Annie, my own love"	Cadential 6/4
	322	36	"Oh! Susanna"	Period and its cadences
Clendinning and Marvin 3rd ed. (2016)	368	18	"Oh! Susanna"	Parallel Period
Kostka, Payne, and Almén, 8th ed. (2018)	336	20	"Oh! Susanna"	Rounded Binary
Laitz, 4th ed. (2015)	280	12	"Beautiful Dreamer"	Pre-Dominant
Roig-Francoli, 2nd ed. (2010)	279	11	"Gentle Annie"	Parallel Period
	283	11	"Jeanie with the Light Brown Hair"	Modulating Period
	27	B	"Oh! Susanna"	Notating meter

ers of color and/or women composers. But this is one of the most important parts of white framing, ignoring inconvenient facts if they harm the overall message of whiteness. In *The White Racial Frame: Centuries of Racial Framing and Counter-Framing*, sociologist Joe Feagin says:

The dominant racial frame has sharply defined inferior and superior racial groups and authoritatively rationalized and structured the great and continuing racial inequalities of this [American] society. In a whitewashing process, and most especially today, this dominant framing has shoved aside, ignored, or treated as incidental numerous racial issues, including the realities of persisting racial discrimination and racial inequality.[15]

Clearly, ignoring or "treating as incidental" racial inequality and racial issues has been the case with Stephen Foster, whose examples remain a constant reminder of our virulent racist past in the United States. We argue here that it is time to remove these racist reminders—these music-theoretical Confederate monuments—from music theory textbooks as well.

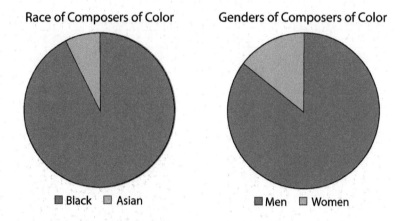
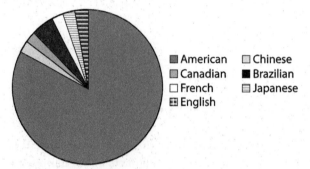

Figure 13.1: Composers of Color in the most common music theory textbooks

COMPOSERS OF COLOR IN TEXTBOOKS

In the textbooks that contained examples by composers of color, there were 41 distinct composers of color (Aldwell/Schachter/Cadwallader had none). Figure 13.1 shows the race, nationality, and gender of these composers. Of these 41 composers, only two were not Black (African descent)—Chen Yi (Chinese woman, b. 1953) and Tōru Takemitsu (Japanese man, 1930–1996). Thus, our music theory examples are, from a critical-race perspective, black and white, and nothing else. By focusing all efforts, minimum though they are, to diversify race based solely on Blackness (again, African descent), we music theorists entirely marginalize and erase nonblack (non-African) people of color, which is extremely common in the U.S. It should go without saying that contributions from nonblack people of color deserve music theory's consideration at all levels: classrooms, conferences, publications, and the racial/ethnic makeup of governing structures. In the seven most common music theory textbooks, which represent 96% of the market share, only two examples from 3039 total examples were written by Asian composers, and those two examples appear in just one textbook, that by Clendinning/Marvin.

Genre is another important aspect of the musical examples from these textbooks. While most are from the classical genre, popular music examples are the next most important. We define popular music genres here as they appear in the textbooks: jazz, rock, blues, musical theater, and popular American ballads of the early-mid twentieth century. While the inclusion of popular music examples could be seen in itself as diversifying the classical curriculum, the racial breakdown of composers tells a familiar tale. Table 13.6 shows the data for pop music examples in the textbooks, while Table 13.7 shows the data for pop composers. Of the 3039 total musical examples, only 175 (5.76%) could be classified as popular. (74.28% of those examples were composed by white persons.) Of the 651 total composers, only 130 (19.97%) could be classified as popular. (73% of those composers were white persons.) This is a marked difference from the white/nonwhite breakdown of all examples in the texts. This can be attributed to jazz examples by black composers, which account for a high number of popular examples. 42.7% of the composers in the textbook by Clendinning/Marvin were classified as popular. This seems to be a high number, but can easily be explained since "composers" often include singers, producers, and writers, among others. That is, for one musical example there may be multiple names listed. At a rather low number, only ten (8%) of the total pop composers were women, both white and nonwhite, which is surprising considering the immense number of well-known pop artists who are women.

STARTING THE CONVERSATION: INSIDE AND OUTSIDE
THE CLASSROOM

It is challenging to bring this topic of academic representation and problematic history into an undergraduate classroom. The most important part of including this difficult topic into the classroom is to create a safe and welcoming environment for all students, including those whose beliefs may differ from those of traditional music theory. By letting all students know that their ideas will be valued, no matter what their personal beliefs, and by ensur-

Table 13.6: Popular music examples from the most common music theory textbooks

Textbook	# of musical examples	# of "pop" examples	# of "pop" examples as percentage	# of "pop" examples by white composers	% of "pop" examples by white composers	# of "pop" examples by composers of color	% of "pop" examples by composers of color	# of "pop" examples by women composers	% of "pop" examples by women composers
Aldwell/Schachter/Cadwallader, 4th ed., 2011	465	0	0.00%	0	0.00%	0	0.00%	0	0.00%
Benward/Saker, 9th ed., 2015	333	20	6.01%	13	65.00%	7	35.00%	1	5.00%
Burstein/Straus, 2nd ed., 2019	413	5	1.21%	4	80.00%	1	20.00%	0	0.00%
Clendinning/Marvin, 3rd ed., 2016	504	72	14.29%	52	72.22%	20	27.78%	9	12.50%
Kostka/Payne, 8th ed., 2018	370	20	5.41%	9	45.00%	11	55.00%	1	5.00%
Laitz, 4th ed., 2015	550	8	1.45%	6	75.00%	2	25.00%	0	0.00%
Roig-Francoli, 2nd ed., 2010	404	50	12.38%	46	92.00%	4	8.00%	1	2.00%
TOTALS	3039	175	5.76%	130	74.28%	45	25.72%	12	6.86%

Table 13.7: Popular music composers from the most common music theory textbooks

Textbook	# of composers	# of "pop" composers	# of "pop" composers as percentage	# of white "pop" composers	% of white "pop" composers	# of "pop" composers of color	% of "pop" composers of color	# of women "pop" composers	% of women "pop" composers
Aldwell/Schachter/Cadwallader, 4th ed., 2011	41	0	0.00%	0	0.00%	0	0.00%	0	0.00%
Benward/Saker, 9th ed., 2015	90	18	20.00%	12	66.67%	6	33.33%	1	5.56%
Burstein/Straus, 2nd ed., 2019	128	4	3.12%	3	75.00%	1	25.00%	0	0.00%
Clendinning/Marvin, 3rd ed., 2016	110	47	42.73%	35	74.47%	12	25.53%	7	14.89%
Kostka/Payne, 8th ed., 2018	94	20	21.28%	9	45.00%	11	55.00%	1	5.00%
Laitz, 4th ed., 2015	90	7	7.78%	5	71.43%	2	28.57%	0	0.00%
Roig-Francoli, 2nd ed., 2010	98	34	34.69%	31	91.18%	3	8.82%	1	2.94%
TOTALS	651	130	19.97%	95	73.01%	35	26.92%	10	7.69%

238   TEACHING DIFFICULT TOPICS

ing that the environment for airing these ideas will be respectful and collegial, we as educators can initiate the difficult discussions that our students so crave surrounding issues of marginalized identities in the music classroom. Here is a sample project that can begin these discussions:

1. Designate a music theory example to be studied that was written by someone whose views, musical or otherwise, could be considered offensive. Do not tell the students of the offensive material; rather, focus on the music-theoretical topic to be discussed in the example. Focus on a specific type of identity discrimination.
   a. Racism: examples by Stephen Foster ("Oh! Susanna," Verse 2), Percy Grainger, John Powell, among others; depictions in music theater or opera; topics and themes in songs; the inclusion of a genre like "the blues" as tokenism; etc.
   b. Antisemitism: examples by Richard Wagner, Peter Tchaikovsky, Igor Stravinsky, or Anton Webern; depictions in music theater or opera (*The Death of Klinghoffer*); topics and themes in songs; the existence of antisemitic tropes such as "globalism" or Hollywood, which can relate to the music industry, and how that relates to the given example; etc.
   c. Sexism/misogyny: Franz Schubert's "Heidenröslein" and Goethe's text suggesting violence against women; depictions in music theater or opera; topics and themes in songs; etc.
2. Once the music theory topic is finished, tell the students about the offensive material and get initial reactions. Then, assign a response paper that allows the students to explore how the context might be important and how the offensive material may have influenced the work, the artists, the reception, etc. At this point it is useful to offer a short piece of pop-culture writing that takes up the "separating the art from the artist" debate. Four notable examples are Cheng 2019, Ermolaeva 2019, Friedman 2014, and Hess 2017.[16] Also, the concept of gatekeeping, and "who gets to decide" what counts as music theory, will be a natural outgrowth of such personal reflection and eventual group discussion.
3. When handing the response papers back, spend the entire class period discussing the offensive material, how and why white frameworks have generally whitewashed this material, and how they, the students, might move forward in planning a music theory curriculum.
4. Choose 3–5 such interventions during the course of the semester, and

have the students write short biographies for given composers, trying to find traces of those things that we find problematic today. Have students suggest other composers or examples that avoid the offensive topic altogether, stressing the work of those who do not identify as both white and male.

5. Finally, have the students search for an example outside of the western canon that can somehow relate to the topic of discussion, and that might be offered as a supplement to the topic at hand.

CONCLUSION

There can be no question that the global coronavirus pandemic, in conjunction with the ensuing worldwide reaction to the killing of George Floyd and so many others, has raised race and race relations to a level not seen since the 1960s in the United States. We hardly need to write that raising issues surrounding race in the music theory classroom is a worthy goal. And insofar as this is happening on the heels of the #MeToo movement, it is clear that both structural racism and structural sexism need to be reexamined in-depth. This type of structural realignment is happening everywhere in institutions of higher learning, and focusing our attention on core textbooks allows others to see how music is addressing these issues, which will allow music to be part of a broader academic conversation. Though we have focused primarily on issues of representation with respect to music examples and composers, revamping and expanding topics normally taught in core music theory classes is also important. We in music theory lag behind other fields like History, Classics, or Political Science, which are themselves still behind other fields like African American or Women's and Gender Studies. Such realignments often lead to interdisciplinary activities, which are part and parcel of deconstructing whiteness and deconstructing maleness.

Importantly, we do not suggest eliminating basic works of the western canon by composers such as Bach or Mozart. Rather, we suggest a serious reconsideration of the number of examples from such composers in relation to other previously undervalued figures who did or do not identify as both white and male. We also recommend presenting composers like Bach and Mozart as examples of good music for its time, yet not somehow better than other musics of the world composed at the same time. And in certain rare cases, yes, we suggest removal, as with the white-supremacist blackface-minstrelsy composer Stephen Foster, unless adequate contextualization

240 TEACHING DIFFICULT TOPICS

can accompany such a composer. Expanding the breadth of composers in our basic textbooks will expand our understanding of race and gender and convey to our students that music is more than just white and male. Finally, such expansion supports the antiracist idea that all racial groups are equals in all of their apparent differences, as well as the antisexist idea that all genders are equals in all of their apparent differences. We should all seek to hold ourselves accountable as we forge new paths in our music curricula together.

APPENDIX 13.1: WOMEN COMPOSERS AND COMPOSERS OF COLOR IN BENWARD AND SAKER, 9TH ED. (2015)

Throughout these tables, composer names in bold indicate composers of color, while italicized composer names indicate women composers (within the composers of color tables). This helps highlight overlap between identity categories. For example, Chen Yi's name appears in bold in a list of women composers, to highlight that she is a woman of color; her name is italicized in a list of composers of color to highlight that she is a woman.

Musical Examples by Composers of Color

Composer	Piece	Measures	Chapter	Page #	Topic
Coltrane, John	Mr. P.C.	mm. 1–12	4	85	Lead Sheet Symbols
Davis, Roquel	"I'd Like to Teach the World to Sing"	mm. 1–8	14	299	Secondary Dominant
Johnson, Robert	"Sweet Home Chicago"	mm. 1–12	10	221	Blues Progression
Joplin, Scott	Maple Leaf Rag	mm. 77–80	11	240	Dominant Seventh Chord—resolving in circle progression
Kinney, L. Viola	"Mother's Sacrifice"	mm. 15–21	11	240	Dominant Seventh Chord—resolving in circle progression
Parker, Charlie	Au Privave	mm. 1–4	1	14	Syncopation
Parker, Charlie	Au Privave	mm. 1–3	11	239	Circle Progressions
Taylor, Billy	Taylor Made Piano	p.158, B	7	146	Thick Texture

Musical Examples by Women Composers

Composer	Piece	Measures	Chapter	Page #	Topic
Harrison, Annie	"In the Gloaming"	mm. 9–16	6	144	Phrase Structure; Scale Degrees; Tonic triad chord members

Jacquet de la Guerre, Élisabeth	Sarabande from Suite in D Minor	mm. 21–28	12	259	Leading Tone Chords in the Baroque Era
Kinney, L. Viola	Mother's Sacrifice	mm. 15–21	11	240	Dominant Seventh Chord—resolving in circle progression
Owens, Carol	"Freely, Freely"	mm. 26–32	7	150	Homorhythmic (chordal) texture
Reichardt, Louise	"Die Blume der Blumen"	mm. 1–4	11	236	Dominant Seventh Chord
Schumann, Clara	Prelude II in B-flat Major Op. 16	mm. 48–52	14	310	Secondary Chords
Szymanowska, Maria Wolowska	Nocturne in B-flat Major	mm. 1–5	14	297	Secondary Dominant and Secondary Leading Tone

APPENDIX 13.2A: WOMEN COMPOSERS AND COMPOSERS OF COLOR IN BURSTEIN/STRAUS (2016)

Musical Examples by Composers of Color

Composer	Piece	Chapter	Page #	Topic
Joplin, Scott	"The Easy Winners"	23	224	Arpeggiated 6/4 Chord

Musical Examples by Women Composers

Composer	Piece	Chapter	Page #	Topic
Dussek, Sophia	Harp Sonata No. 3, II	14	147	Subdominant Harmonies
Jacquet de la Guerre, Élisabeth-Claude	Suite in D Minor	29	280	Picardy Third
Lang, Josephine	"Gott sei mir Sunder gnadig"	21	205	ii6 functioning as V
Reichardt, Louise	"Poesie von Tieck"	7	87	Non-Chord Tones
Reichardt, Louise	"Vaters Klage"	31	292	Italian Augmented Sixth

APPENDIX 13.2B: WOMEN COMPOSERS AND COMPOSERS OF COLOR IN BURSTEIN/STRAUS (2019)

Musical Examples by Composers of Color

Composer	Piece	Chapter	Page #	Topic
Chen Yi	*Northern Scenes*	44	401	Transposition
Handy, WC	"Joe Turner Blues"	32	288	Common-Tone Chromatic Chords
Joplin, Scott	"The Easy Winners"	23	214	Arpeggiated 6/4

242   TEACHING DIFFICULT TOPICS

Nunes Garcia, JM	*Matinas e encomendação de defuntos*	13	129	Dominant Passing Chords
Nunes Garcia, JM	*Matinas e encomendação de defuntos*	14	140	Subdominant Harmonies
Nunes Garcia, JM	Memento I, Kyrie	10	107	V 8–7
Pinto, Luis Alvares	"Lições de Solfejo 1"	5	66	Contrapuntal Motion
Sancho, Ignatius	Minuet Book II, No. 2	35	320	Sentence
Sawyer, Jacob	"All the Rage"	18	174	Subdominant Harmonies
Sawyer, Jacob	"Welcome to the Era"	32	286	Augmented I Chord
Smith, Hale	*Three Brevities* for Solo Flute, No. 2	44	406	Set Theory Transformations
Tan Dun	*Elegy: Snow in June*	40	362	Pentatonic Collections
White, José Silvestre	"Zamacueca"	23	213	Passing 6/4

Musical Examples by Women Composers

Composer	Piece	Chapter	Page #	Topic
Bartholomew, Ann	"Hodderson"	5	56	Voice Leading
Beauharnais, Hortense de	"Reine Berthe"	25	233	Secondary Dominants
Casson, Margaret	"The Cuckoo"	23	212	Pedal 6/4
Cecil, Theophania	"St. Jerome's"	19	178	vi chords
Chaminade, Cécile	"Rêve d'un soir"	32	285	Augmented V chord
Chen Yi	*Northern Scenes*	44	401	Transposition
Crawford Seeger, Ruth	*Diaphonic Suite*, No. 1, i	47	441	Sentence
Crawford Seeger, Ruth	"In Tall Grass"	45	416	Wedge Progression
Crawford Seeger, Ruth	"Rat Riddles"	45	421	Inversional Symmetry
Cuthbert, Elizabeth	"Howard"	16	161	IV Chords
Dussek, Sophia	Four Favorite Airs for Harp, No. 5	21	198	VII Chords
Dussek, Sophia	Harp Sonata, Op. 2, No. 3, ii	14	137	Harmonic Progressions
Hill, Mildred and Patty	"Good Morning to All"	35	320	Sentence
Jacquet de la Guerre, Élisabeth	Suite in D Minor	29	267	Picardy Third
Lang, Josephine	"Gott sei mir Sünder gnädig"	21	195	iii6 chords
LeBrun, Francesca	Sonata for Keyboard and Violin, Op. 1, No. 1, iii	35	320	Sentence
Leonarda, Isabella	*Magnificat*	25	229	Secondary Dominants
Leonarda, Isabella	*Salmi Concertati*	24	218	Neighbor Chord

Lutyens, Elisabeth	Two Bagatelles, Op. 48, No. 1	44	411	Set Class Transformations
Lutyens, Elisabeth	Two Bagatelles, Op. 48, No. 1	46	425	Serialism
Lutyens, Elisabeth	Two Bagatelles, Op. 48, No. 1	46	429	Serialism
Lutyens, Elisabeth	Two Bagatelles, Op. 48, No. 1	46	431	Serialism
Lutyens, Elisabeth	Two Bagatelles, Op. 48, No. 1	46	434	Serialism
Mamlok, Ursula	*Panta Rhei*	41	368	Hexatonic Collection
Montgeroult, Hélène	Etude No. 5	12	121	V4/2 Chords
Montgeroult, Hélène	Etude No. 15	18	172	ii7 Chords
Pinottini, Maria Teresa	Keyboard Sonata in E♭	10	104	V7 Chords
Ployer, Barbara	second-species counterpoint	8	88	Second Species Counterpoint
Ran, Shulamit	*Verticals*	43	389	Pitch Class
Reichardt, Louise	"Vaters Klage"	31	277	Italian Augmented 6th
Saariaho, Kaija	*L'amour de loin*	40	360	Pentatonic Collection
Saariaho, Kaija	*Sept papillons* (for solo cello)	41	368	Hexatonic Collection
Schröter, Corona	"Der Brautschmuck"	13	133	Parallel Fifths
Schumann, Clara	*Einfache Praeludium für Schüler*	32	287	Neapolitan Chords
Scott, Alicia	"Annie Laurie"	36	322	Period
Tourjee, Lizzie	"Wellesley"	12	121	V6/5 Chords
Tower, Joan	*Vast Antique Cubes*	41	373	Octatonic Collection
Troschke, Wilhelmine von	Thema con Variazioni	6	68	PAC and IAC
Zwilich, Ellen Taaffe	Chamber Concerto for Trumpet and Five Players	42	378	PLR Transformations

APPENDIX 13.3: WOMEN COMPOSERS AND COMPOSERS OF COLOR IN CLENDINNING/MARVIN (2016)

Musical Examples by Composers of Color

Composer	Piece	Measures	Chapter	Page #	Topic
Basie, Count	"Splanky"	mm. 1–12	29	603	Blues Scale
Chen Yi	"Shan Ge"	mm. 6–13	40	864	Western + Non-Western
Davis, Hal	"I'll Be There"	mm. 5–8	7	143	Lead-Sheet Notation
Dozier, Lamont	"Baby Love"	Lyrics	29	606	Simple Verse Form
Gordy, Berry	"I'll Be There"	mm. 5–8	7	143	Lead-Sheet Notation

244 TEACHING DIFFICULT TOPICS

Holland, Brian	"Baby Love"	Lyrics	29	606	Simple Verse Form
Hutch, Willie	"I'll Be There"	mm. 5–8	7	143	Lead-Sheet Notation
Joplin, Scott	"Pine Apple Rag"	opening	2	22	Beat
Joplin, Scott	"Pine Apple Rag"	mm. 1–4	2	36	Syncopation
Joplin, Scott	"Pine Apple Rag"	mm. 5–12	20	417	Secondary Dominants to V
Joplin, Scott	"Solace"	mm. 1–4	1	13	Grand Staff
Joplin, Scott	"Solace"	mm. 21–24	21	18	Dynamics
Joplin, Scott	"Solace"	mm. 9–12	2	37	Syncopation
Joplin, Scott	"Solace"	mm. 61–65	21	434	Harmonic Momentum
West, Bob	"I'll Be There"	mm. 5–8	7	149	Lead-Sheet Notation

Musical Examples by Women Composers

Composer	Piece	Measures	Chapter	Page #	Topic
Chen Yi	"Shan Ge"	mm. 6–13	40	864	Western + Non-Western
Hensel, Fanny Mendelssohn	"Nachtwanderer"	mm. 3–6	4	71	Rhythm in Compound Meters
Hensel, Fanny Mendelssohn	"Nachtwanderer"	mm. 34–39	27	565	Less Common Augmented Sixth Chords
Hensel, Fanny Mendelssohn	"Neue Liebe, neues Leben"	mm. 1–4, 73–77	2	39	Rhythm in Simple Meters
Hensel, Fanny Mendelssohn	"Neue Liebe, neues Leben"	mm. 1–4	19	399	Pachelbel Sequence
Hensel, Fanny Mendelssohn	"Neue Liebe, neues Leben"	mm. 69–71	19	406	Ascending Parallel 6/3 Chords
Hensel, Fanny Mendelssohn	"Neue Liebe, neues Leben"	mm. 26–30	30	621	Descending Chromatic Bass
King, Carole	"You've Got A Friend"	Lyrics	29	608	AA'BA'
Matson, Vera	"Love Me Tender"	mm. 5–8	20	412	Secondary Dominant
Parton, Dolly	"I Will Always Love You"	mm. 1–5	3	55	Key Signatures
Robinson, Vicki Sue	"Turn the Beat Around"	Chorus	28	596	Minor pentatonic progressions
Schumann, Clara	*Drei Romanzen,* Op. 21, No. 1	mm. 1–8	22	453	Pivot Chord Modulation
Schumann, Clara	*Drei Romanzen,* Op. 21, No. 1	mm. 1–26	33	700	Large Ternary
Schumann, Clara	"Liebst du um Schönheit"	Lyrics	28	581	Rhyme-scheme analysis

Don't You Cry for Me   245

APPENDIX 13.4: WOMEN COMPOSERS AND COMPOSERS OF COLOR IN KOSTKA/PAYNE/ALMÉN (2018)

Musical Examples by Composers of Color

Composer	Piece	Measures	Chapter	Page #	Topic
Adderley, Julian	Sermonette	mm. 1–9	3	48	Lead Sheet Symbols and Triad Notation
Hampton, Lionel	Red Top	Part of Chorus	12	202	Lead Sheet suspensions and delayed resolution
Hendricks, Jon	Sermonette	mm. 1–9	3	48	Lead Sheet Symbols and Triad Notation
Joplin, Scott	Fig Leaf Rag	mm. 61–68	24	433	Common-Tone diminished seventh chords
Kynard, Ken	Red Top	Part of Chorus	12	202	Lead Sheet suspensions and delayed resolution
Parker, Charlie	Thriving from a Riff	mm. 1–8	24	432	Common-Tone diminished seventh chords in lead sheet symbols
Richie, Lionel	Hello	Opening stanza	7	98	Sequence using Circle of Fifths
Silver, Horace	The Preacher	mm. 8–16	24	437	Circle of fifths sequence
Watts, Mayme	Alright, Okay, You Win	mm. 1–12	20	337	12-bar blues
Wyche, Sid	Alright, Okay, You Win	mm. 1–12	20	337	12-bar blues

Musical Examples by Women Composers

Composer	Piece	Measures	Chapter	Page #	Topic
Hensel, Fanny Mendelssohn	Auf der Wanderung	mm. 11–14	22	390	German Augmented Sixth Chord
Hensel, Fanny Mendelssohn	Beharre	mm. 11–16	24	434	Common-Tone diminished seventh chords
Hensel, Fanny Mendelssohn	Von dir, mein Lieb, ich scheiden muss	mm. 5–9	17	288	Secondary Dominants of chords other than V
Payne, Dorothy	Skipping	mm. 1–14	26	490	Tonal Center, Accompaniment, Melodic Phrasing
Schumann, Clara Wieck	Beim Abschied	mm. 15–18	15	239	ii4/2 chord as passing
Schumann, Clara Wieck	Concert Variations Op. 8, Var. 2	mm. 1–2	24	430	Common-Tone diminished seventh chords
Schumann, Clara Wieck	Papillons Op. 2, No. 12	mm. 70–88	16	265	Secondary Dominants

246 TEACHING DIFFICULT TOPICS

Schumann, Clara Wieck	Piano Trio Op. 17 IV	mm. 56–59	21	360	Borrowed ii-half-diminished-7
Schumann, Clara Wieck	Polonaise Op. 6, No. 6	mm. 1–5	22	395	Resolving Augmented-Sixth Chords
Schumann, Clara Wieck	Romance Op. 5, No. 3	mm. 26–29	15	248	I7 chord

APPENDIX 13.5: WOMEN COMPOSERS AND COMPOSERS OF COLOR IN LAITZ (2015)

Musical Examples by Composers of Color

Composer	Piece	Measures	Chapter	Page #	Topic
Coltrane, John	"Giant Steps"	mm. 1–15	29	714	Sequential Progressions
Pinkard, Maceo	"Sweet Georgia Brown"	mm. 21–33	28	670	Off-tonic beginning

Musical Examples by Women Composers

Composer	Piece	Measures	Chapter	Page #	Topic
Schumann, Clara	"Andante espressivo" Quatre pieces fugitives, Op. 15, No. 3	mm. 1–7	19	464	Tonicization and back-relating dominant
Schumann, Clara	"Les Ballet des Revenants" from Quatre pièces caractéristiques, Op. 5	mm. 44–47	5	174	Tonic and Dominant Chords as tonal pillars

APPENDIX 13.6: WOMEN COMPOSERS AND COMPOSERS OF COLOR IN ROIG-FRANCOLI (2010)

Musical Examples by Composers of Color

Composer	Piece	Measures	Chapter	Page #	Topic
Dett, Nathaniel	In the Bottoms	mm. 1–8	29	676	Appoggiatura Chords
Dett, Nathaniel	Enchantment "Song of the Shrine"	mm. 1–4	27	648	Altered Triads, Augmented 6th Chords, Common Tone Diminished Seventh Chords
Ellington, Duke	"I Let a Song Go Out of My Heart"	final cadence	23	543	Minor Subdominant used as a pre-dominant

Don't You Cry for Me 247

Ellington, Duke	"Satin Doll"	final cadence	24	567	Neapolitan Chord as dominant substitution
Price, Florence	Fantasie Negre	mm. 141–148	7	223	Types of 6/4 Chords
Saint-Georges, Chevalier	Adagio	mm. 21–29	9	256	Tonic and Dominant Prolongation
Saint-Georges, Chevalier	Ernestine "O Clemangis, lis dans mon ame"	mm. 90–101	26	618	Pivot Chord Modulation
Saint-Georges, Chevalier	Sonata II for Violin and Piano	mm. 13–16	8	240	Neighbor 6/4 and V6/5 as Prolongation
Saint-Georges, Chevalier	Sonata II for Violin and Piano	mm. 1–10	18	421	Secondary Dominants of II
Saint-Georges, Chevalier	Sonata III for Violin and Piano	mm. 69–72	25	575	Augmented Sixth Chords
Saint-Georges, Chevalier	Symphonie Concertante in AM, Op. 10, No. 2	mm. 1–16	11	288	Phrase/Period Structure
Strayhorn, Billy	"Satin Doll"	final cadence	24	567	Neapolitan Chord as dominant substitution
Williams, Mary Lou	Nite Life	mm. 5–9	29	674	Nondominant Extended Tertian Chords

Musical Examples by Women Composers

Composer	Piece	Measures	Chapter	Page #	Topic
Beach, Amy	"Barcarolle" from Three Pieces, Op. 28, No. 1	mm. 1–6	15	355	Seventh Chords— Voice Leading and Doubling Guidelines
Beach, Amy	Sous les étoiles, Op. 65, No. 4	mm. 11–18	29	695	Chromatic Sequence
Farrenc, Louise	Trio in Em, Op. 45, I	mm. 113–121	26	609	Modulation using Augmented Sixth Chords
Farrenc, Louise	Trio in Em, Op. 45, I	mm. 133–148	27	631	Modulation using Common Tone—Keys related by a third
Heckscher, Celeste	Valse Bohème	mm. 77–84	25	586	French Augmented Sixth resolving to Cadential 6/4
Hensel, Fanny Mendelssohn	Six Songs, Op. 7, No. 4 "Du bist die Ruh"	mm. 26–32	23	544	Modal Mixture
Jacquet de la Guerre, Élisabeth	Suite in Am, Sarabande	mm. 1–8	9	257	Passing viio6 chord

Lang, Josephine	Früzeitiger Frühling	mm. 5–11	19	450	viio7 chords
Lang, Josephine	"Gott sei mir Sünder gnädig"	mm. 5–10	13	310	Harmonic Rhythm
Lang, Josephine	"Ich gab dem Schicksal dich zurück"	mm. 59–68	24	564	Neapolitan Chord appearing with other borrowed chords
Mahler, Alma	Five Songs "Ekstase"	mm. 15–23	27	635	Altered Triads
Mahler, Alma	Five Songs "In meines Vaters Garten"	mm. 126–129	29	672	Eleventh and Thirteenth Chords
Martinez, Marianne	Sonata in AM	mm. 1–2	9	250	Passing viio6 chord
Martinez, Marianne	Sonata in AM	mm. 4–5	12	295	Intervallic Expansion and Contraction
Paradis, Maria Theresia von	Sicilienne	mm. 7–10	24	561	Neapolitan Chord
Price, Florence	Fantasie Negre	mm. 141–148	7	223	Types of 6/4 Chords
Reichardt, Louise	From Ariel's Revelation "Frühlingsblumen"	mm. 1–8	11	276	Phrase Structure
Reichardt, Louise	From Ariel's Revelation "Frühlingsblumen"	mm. 9–17	15	375	Diatonic Seventh Chords and their functions
Schumann, Clara	"Ich stand in dunklen Träumen"	mm. 6–13	20	471	Modulation to V
Schumann, Clara	Trio in Gm, Op. 17	mm. 269–270	15	360	Diatonic Seventh Chords and their functions
Schumann, Clara	Trio in Gm, Op. 17	mm. 1–9	17	409	Secondary Dominants of IV
Schumann, Clara	Trio in Gm, Op. 17	mm. 22–32	20	492	Modulation to Closely Related Keys
Schumann, Clara	Vier Stücke aus Soirees Musicales, Op. 2 "Notturno"	mm. 1–6	27	635	Altered Triads
Scott, Clara	Twilight Fancies	mm. 1–8	18	421	Secondary Dominants of II
Sloman, Jane	"La Favorite" Etude-Mazurka	mm. 1–8	18	423	Secondary Dominants of VI
Szymanowska, Maria	Nocturne in B♭ Major	mm. 17–19	4	171	Tonic Prolongation
Szymanowska, Maria	Nocturne in B♭ Major	mm. 53–55	15	364	ii7 Chords and Voice Leading
Szymanowska, Maria	Nocturne in B♭ Major	mm. 27–31	19	460	Secondary Leading-Tone Chords

Viardot-Garcia, Pauline	"Die Beschworung"	mm. 1–3	7	211	Types of 6/4 Chords
Williams, Mary Lou	Nite Life	mm. 5–9	29	674	Nondominant Extended Tertian Chords

Notes

1. For further reading on how textbooks shape student perception of history, see James Loewen's *Lies My Teacher Told Me: Everything Your American History Textbook Got Wrong* (New York: The New Press, 2018). For further background information on the western canon's influence on music curricula, see Cora Palfy and Eric Gilson's "The Hidden Curriculum in the Music Theory Classroom," in the *Journal of Music Theory Pedagogy* 32 (2018): 79–110, https://digitalcollections.lipscomb.edu/jmtp/vol32/iss1/5/

2. While we only use "United States" in this chapter, and while the seven textbooks we examine were in fact all produced and authored in the United States, we realized that most aspects of our textbook analysis can apply to Canada as well insofar as Canadian music theory closely resembles U.S. music theory. But we only wish to speak about U.S. music theory since we are both U.S. citizens who trained in the U.S. Further, we refrain from using "North America" as a stand-in for "the United States and Canada," insofar as North America extends down to the Panama-Colombia border and includes many countries, each with its own music theory tradition, aside from the U.S. and Canada.

3. Philip Ewell, "Music Theory and the White Racial Frame," in *Music Theory Online* 26, no. 2 (September 2020), https://mtosmt.org/issues/mto.20.26.2/mto.20.26.2.ewell.html

4. Eduardo Bonilla-Silva, *Racism without Racists: Color-Blind Racism and the Persistence of Racial Inequality in America* 5th ed. (Lanham, MD: Rowman & Littlefield, [2003] 2018). For more on white racial framing see Joe Feagin, *The White Racial Frame: Centuries of Racial Framing and Counter-Framing* (New York: Routledge, [2009] 2013).

5. According to Justin Hoffman, Senior Acquisitions Editor at Oxford University Press, formerly of W. W. Norton & Company. Email correspondence with Philip Ewell, May 24, 2019.

6. Of the possible overlap between these two groups there were six composers who were both women and a composer of color: Chen Yi, L. Viola Kinney, Florence Price, Vicki Sue Robinson, Maymie (also spelled "Mayme") Watts, and Mary Lou Williams.

7. Aldwell, Schachter, and Cadwallader have since released a fifth edition (2019), which was not published at the time of data collection for this study.

8. Alex Ross, "The Rediscovery of Florence Price," in *The New Yorker* (January 29, 2018), https://www.newyorker.com/magazine/2018/02/05/the-rediscovery-of-florence-price

250   TEACHING DIFFICULT TOPICS

9. Ewell, "Music Theory and the White Racial Frame."

10. Bonilla-Silva, *Racism without Racists*, 9.

11. For an example of this power, see Kofi Agawu's "Tonality as a Colonizing Force in Africa," in *Audible Empire: Music, Global Politics, Critique*, edited by Ronald Radano and Tejumola Olaniyan (Durham: Duke University Press, 2016).

12. See https://black-face.com/stephen-foster.htm

13. Katya Ermolaeva, "Dinah, Put Down Your Horn: Blackface Minstrel Songs Don't Belong in Music Class" (October 30, 2019), https://gen.medium.com/dinah-put-down -your-horn-154b8d8db12a

14. Ermolaeva, "Dinah, Put Down Your Horn."

15. Feagin, *The White Racial Frame*, 22.

16. William Cheng, "Gaslight of the Gods: Why I Still Play Michael Jackson and R. Kelly for My Students," in *The Chronicle of Higher Education* (Sep. 15, 2019): https:// www.chronicle.com/article/Gaslight-of-the-Gods-Why-I/247120#comments-anchor; Ermolaeva, "Dinah, Put Down Your Horn"; Michael Friedman, "Can't Escape Stephen Foster," in *The New Yorker* (March 10, 2014): https://www.newyorker.com/culture/cul ture-desk/cant-escape-stephen-foster; Amanda Hess, "How the Myth of the Artistic Genius Excuses the Abuse of Women," in *New York Times* (Nov. 10, 2017): https://www .nytimes.com/2017/11/10/arts/sexual-harassment-art-hollywood.html

Works Cited

Agawu, Kofi. "Tonality as a Colonizing Force in Africa." In *Audible Empire: Music, Global Politics, Critique*. Edited by Ronald Radano and Tejumola Olaniyan. Durham: Duke University Press, 2016.

Aldwell, Edward, Carl Schachter, and Allen Cadwallader. *Harmony and Voice Leading*. 4th ed. Boston: Schirmer, 2011.

Benward, Bruce, and Marilyn Saker. *Music in Theory and Practice*. Ninth edition. 2 vols. New York: McGraw Hill, 2015.

Bonilla-Silva, Eduardo. *Racism without Racists: Color-Blind Racism and the Persistence of Racial Inequality in America*. 5th ed. Lanham, MD: Rowman & Littlefield, [2003] 2018.

Burstein, L. Poundie, and Joseph N. Straus. *Concise Introduction to Tonal Harmony*. 2nd ed. New York: W. W. Norton & Company, 2019. First published 2016 by W. W. Norton & Company.

Cheng, William. "Gaslight of the Gods: Why I Still Play Michael Jackson and R. Kelly for My Students." *The Chronicle of Higher Education*, Sep. 15, 2019. https://www.chro nicle.com/article/Gaslight-of-the-Gods-Why-I/247120#comments-anchor

Ermolaeva, Katya. "Dinah, Put Down Your Horn: Blackface Minstrel Songs Don't Belong in Music Class." October 30, 2019. https://gen.medium.com/dinah-put-do wn-your-horn-154b8d8db12a

Ewell, Philip. "Music Theory and the White Racial Frame." *Music Theory Online* 26, no. 2. September 2020. https://mtosmt.org/issues/mto.20.26.2/mto.20.26.2.ewell.html

Feagin, Joe. *The White Racial Frame: Centuries of Racial Framing and Counter-Framing.* New York: Routledge, [2009] 2013.

Friedman, Michael. "Can't Escape Stephen Foster." *The New Yorker*, March 10, 2014. https://www.newyorker.com/culture/culture-desk/cant-escape-stephen-foster

Hess, Amanda. "How the Myth of the Artistic Genius Excuses the Abuse of Women." *New York Times*, Nov. 10, 2017. https://www.nytimes.com/2017/11/10/arts/sexual -harassment-art-hollywood.html

Hoffman, Justin. Email correspondence with Philip Ewell, May 24, 2019.

Kostka, Stefan, Dorothy Payne, and Byron Almén. *Tonal Harmony.* Eighth edition. New York: McGraw Hill, 2018.

Kuhn, Thomas. *The Structure of Scientific Revolutions.* Chicago: University of Chicago Press, 1962.

Laitz, Steven G. *The Complete Musician: An Integrated Approach to Theory, Analysis, and Listening. Fourth Edition.* Oxford: Oxford University Press, 2014.

Loewen, James W. *Lies My Teacher Told Me: Everything Your American History Textbook Got Wrong.* New York: The New Press, 2018.

Morrison, Matthew. "Race, Blacksound, and the (Re)Making of Musicological Discourse." *Journal of the American Musicological Society* 72, no. 3 (Fall 2019): 781–823.

Palfy, Cora S., and Eric Gilson. "The Hidden Curriculum in the Music Theory Classroom." *Journal of Music Theory Pedagogy* 32 (2018): 79–110. https://digitalcollections .lipscomb.edu/jmtp/vol32/iss1/5/

Rolg-Francoli, Miguel. *Harmony in Context.* Second edition. New York: McGraw Hill, 2010.

Ross, Alex. "The Rediscovery of Florence Price." *The New Yorker*, January 29, 2018. https://www.newyorker.com/magazine/2018/02/05/the-rediscovery-of-florence -price

CHAPTER 14

Stephen Foster and Slavery in Music Textbooks

A Case Study Outlining the Benefits of Using Class Time to Enrich Textbook Narratives about American Slavery

Christopher Lynch

For many years as an instructor of music history classes, I thought I possessed a strong basic knowledge of minstrel composer Stephen Collins Foster (1826–64) and was confident that the textbooks with which I taught contained brief but adequate content on him and his music. Probably owing much to my own privilege, I was too trusting of these narratives and lacked critical frameworks and life experiences that might have helped me question them. As a white man, learning to temper my own privilege in the classroom and in my writing is an ongoing, iterative process. But when I began working at the University of Pittsburgh Library System's Center for American Music, the principal library and archive of Foster's life and legacy, I found myself needing to quickly accelerate this process. As I delved into primary and secondary sources to prepare for instruction sessions, I soon discovered what many music history teachers have long known: textbooks are severely insufficient. As Joseph Byrd wrote in 2009, "Many textbooks on American music treat minstrelsy as almost a footnote. When they do discuss it, they restrict it to the small pre-1860 shows, often sweeping it under the rug of the Civil War. And they say nothing whatever of the huge popularity of sheet music editions of minstrel songs nor, of course, of the lingering racism that colored the rest of the 19th century and beyond."[1] Byrd's critique is still true today. Many of Foster's songs play with stereotypes of people of African descent as happy slaves, "uppity" free people who aspire to middle-class respectability, freed people who are nostalgic for slavery, and happy-go-lucky buffoons. But students who rely on textbooks alone for information about Foster are provided no frameworks for understanding these depictions. Instead, textbooks distort the historical record by overemphasizing Foster's achievements, cherry-picking musical examples

252

and biographical details, and downplaying racism in his songs, painting an overly heroic portrait and erasing a long, consequential debate about his music and its roles in American life.

The inadequacies of textbooks force educators to take it upon themselves to develop enhanced content for teaching about minstrelsy. In this chapter, I offer a critique of the assumptions underlying the most used American music and Western music history textbooks before suggesting freely available digitized materials in the Center for American Music's collections that can be utilized to expand textbook narratives. Whereas textbooks privilege the development of musical styles—chords, melodies, phrases, musical form, etc.—this chapter advocates teaching students primarily about social history to create a framework within which they can understand music, including but not limited to musical style, placing music in dialog with concepts taught in classes across the university. Rather than specific assignments or activities, I recommend guiding questions that can be asked of students in a variety of teaching situations to lead them through analyses of digitized early editions of Foster songs such as "Jeanie with the Light Brown Hair," "Oh! Susanna," and "Nelly Was a Lady." In addition to leading students to a richer understanding of Foster's place in American history, these questions help students understand knowledge as a social construct.

FOSTER'S MUSIC IN TEXTBOOKS

Although music history textbooks have greatly expanded their coverage in recent decades, little has been done to alter the underlying structure of tracing the development or "evolution" of musical genres and styles through time. Musical examples are chosen to "exemplify" the formal characteristics and musical devices common to a particular composer, location, time, and/ or genre.[2] With little space reserved for contextualization, textbooks almost entirely divorce music from sociology and economics, inadequately portraying how and why music was created and performed. Scant on context, textbooks exaggerate the achievements of composers, presenting them as inventors, perfecters, or exemplars, unmatched by peers.[3] In short, music history textbooks fail to adequately represent history.

Textbook presentations of Foster are not just brief but impeccably groomed, portraying the songwriter as a heroic "pioneer" of American history. For example, in *American Popular Music* Larry Starr and Christopher Waterman describe Foster as "probably the first person in the United States

254   TEACHING DIFFICULT TOPICS

to make his living as a full-time professional songwriter, surviving on the fees and royalties generated by sales of sheet music."[4] This statement fails to account for the social structures that helped him rise to the position of privilege from which he became a professional songwriter. In addition to his family's political connections to the upper echelon of the conservative Democratic Party, Foster benefited from slavery—directly from slave labor and indirectly from wealth earned through enslavement and the racial hierarchy established by the institution.[5] He also benefited from the ways in which copyright laws enabled white authors to profit off black music.[6] But textbooks provide no indication that Foster's talent as a songwriter was not the only reason for his achievements. Nor do they sufficiently describe his success. He certainly sold more sheet music than any previous American composer, but it is debatable whether he really earned a living as a songwriter. Although sheet-music sales earned him a decent income for a few years in the 1850s, he lived with his brothers and parents for most of his life. Shortly after his parents' deaths in 1855, his brothers cut off support, leading to a period of financial precarity exacerbated by his growing dependence on alcohol and, beginning in 1861, the disruptions of the Civil War. Around the beginning of the war, Foster's wife, Jane, took a job as a telegrapher. When he died in 1864 at the age of 37, the thirty-eight cents in his pocket was all he had. Textbooks build up Foster as a hero, but there is a richer story to be told about the nascent music industry, whom it was set up to benefit, and the limits of those benefits.

In their choice of musical examples and construction of song taxonomies, textbook authors conceal racism and distance Foster from white supremacy. *A History of Western Music*, for instance, acknowledges the racism of minstrelsy but avoids delving into Foster's racial caricatures by selecting as its only musical example "Jeanie with the Light Brown Hair," in which a white man nostalgically remembers the white Jeanie (her race is indicated in the cover art, shown in Figures 14.4 and 14.5).[7] Largely bypassing issues of race, the textbook's music anthology emphasizes the song's expression of "sentiments of love, loss, and regret," the AABA form of the verses, and "subtle elements [that] make the melody especially poignant and memorable." The anthology further distances Foster from racism by incorrectly stating that "by 1854, when he wrote 'Jeanie with the Light Brown Hair,' he had stopped writing minstrel songs and was concentrating his efforts on parlor songs."[8] In truth, Foster merely temporarily abandoned songs in which the lyrics specify the race of the singing persona and characters. In 1860 he again began explicitly indicating black personas.[9] Even in the interregnum, Foster's songs such as "Ellen Bayne" and "Old Dog Tray" were originally published with minstrel performer Edwin P. Christy's name emblazoned across the covers.[10] Clearly, then, even in these years Foster knowingly wrote songs for performances by *both* amateurs in the parlor and minstrel professionals who sang the songs while wearing blackface and mocking African Americans on stage. Textbooks' song taxonomies, which separate parlor and minstrel songs, function to improperly distance Foster from racism. In reality, the hard distinction between minstrel and parlor songs is an artificial construct.

In *An Introduction to America's Music*, Richard Crawford and Larry Hamberlin acknowledge that "race was fundamental to the minstrel show" and that "there is no evidence that white minstrels shared profits with the black Americans whom they imitated." But they also write that "neither racism . . . nor economic exploitation fully explains minstrelsy's impact,"[11] which leads to a long discussion emphasizing everything about minstrelsy except race. In their lopsided analysis, they obfuscate Foster's portrayal in "Camptown Races" of the stereotype of happy-go-lucky free people of African descent who gamble away their money at the horse track by describing the song only as "jaunty and tuneful."[12] They portray "Old Folks at Home" as a song that conveys a message less about race than universal human emotions that stem from isolation: "The song . . . reaches into new expressive territory. The persona, a displaced slave, sings of loneliness and longing, having no apparent plan to return to the home for which he yearns. Together the words and tune convey the emotional weariness that isolation can bring."[13] The authors do not acknowledge the song's flirtation with the stereotype of the freed man who longs to return to slavery. The character sings that he's "still longing for de old plantation," yet Crawford and Hamberlin merely state that he longs for "home." The authors reserve the most space for "Jeanie with the Light Brown Hair," a discussion of which spans three pages and covers the concepts of AABA form, arpeggio, fermata, and cadenza.[14]

In *Music in the Nineteenth Century*, Walter Frisch's limited contextualization of primary sources misrepresents Foster as progressive. He describes minstrelsy as a genre in which white artists "poked fun—often maliciously—at African-American life" and romanticized enslavement. But he claims that Foster did not intend to "domesticate" or "falsify" "for white consumption what was certainly a degrading, dehumanizing existence" for enslaved people. He writes,

> Foster, who would side with the North in the Civil War and was generally sympathetic to black Americans, saw things differently. He wrote to Christy in 1852: "I find that by my efforts I have done a great deal to build up taste for the

256 TEACHING DIFFICULT TOPICS

Ethiopian song among refined people by making the words suitable to their taste, instead of the trashy and really offensive words which belong to some songs of that order. Therefore I have concluded to pursue the Ethiopian business without fear or shame."[15]

Frisch's assertion that Foster sided with the North is true but misleading. Foster, like every member of his family, was a member of Abraham Lincoln's opposition: he was a Democrat. Throughout his life he publicly campaigned and wrote campaign songs for Democratic political candidates who opposed abolition and supported states' rights to choose to be slave states but not to choose to harbor escaped slaves as refugees. During the Civil War, Foster supported Abraham Lincoln in the sense that he supported the fight to quash the rebellion and preserve the Union, but as far as is known he never embraced emancipation or any radical elements of Republicanism, aligning himself with the faction of Democrats known as War Democrats.

Frisch fails to acknowledge that Foster's war songs such as "We Are Coming, Father Abraam, 300,000 More" and "That's What's the Matter" contain no suggestions that Foster ever broke from the Democratic party, only supporting the war as a means of saving the nation and never even mentioning slavery. Frisch also does not acknowledge that Foster's only song to address the issue, the minstrel song "A Soldier in the Colored Brigade," expresses the desire to preserve slavery, saying that people in power had "better let him [the slave] be." The lyrics were written by Foster's close friend George Cooper, who later reminisced that "Foster disliked the war as, to my mind, he scorned to see the disruption of the ties that held the negroes to their masters & of which he had written so many songs."[16] By omitting these facts and simply stating that Foster "would side with the North," Frisch creates the false impression for the average reader that Foster sided with Lincoln and emancipation.

Frisch portrays Foster's letter to Christy as indicating that he disagreed with minstrelsy's dehumanizing depictions of black people. But scholars have pointed out that Foster does not express this opinion in the letter. As Steven Saunders writes,

It is something of a leap from accepting Foster's phrases about "suitable" lyrics and "eliminating trashy and really offensive words," to attributing an idealistic social mission to his songwriting. In fact, Foster's famous letter is not primarily about a utopian vision of racial harmony, or even principally about money, title pages, or his negotiations with Christy. Another clear concern emerges in several phrases of the letter that use remarkably similar locutions, all linking the first person possessive, "my," with various styles of popular song[.] . . . Foster's string of "mys" suggests that something other than race is at issue: namely, his reputation, his sense of self as a composer, and his desire to project the proper image in the marketplace.[17]

Foster was just embarking on his attempt to support himself through songwriting alone when he wrote this letter. It makes much more sense that his concerns were aimed at appeasing commonly held sentiments of white consumers rather than converting those consumers to a progressive sociopolitical worldview.

In sum, music history textbooks exhibit the same tendencies that James W. Loewen has identified in his analysis of high school American history textbooks: "Faced with unpleasantries, textbooks—old and new—wriggle to get the hero off the hook."[18] Many of us have had enough. Because of Foster's dehumanizing depictions of people of African descent, Philip Ewell recently called into question his centrality in music theory textbooks, a call that he and Megan Lyons repeat in this volume (see chapter 13). While critiquing music theory's white racial frame, Ewell observes that "theory textbooks routinely include lyrics to songs, but Foster's are obviously excluded" because of their overt racism. Noting that Foster "did so much to dehumanize blacks in the buffoonish subhuman practice of blackface minstrelsy," Ewell questions "why we in music theory would want to honor a figure who did so much to dehumanize blacks in the first place. The inclusion of a white supremacist composer like Foster in our music theory textbooks . . . represents a remarkable insensitivity on the part of the white racial frame."[19] Ewell suggests discarding from theory textbooks Foster's music altogether, not merely the lyrics, when teaching concepts such as parallel phrase structure. Not only could the same concepts be taught with non-racist examples, but well-chosen replacements could also lead theory pedagogy to embrace new theoretical frameworks.

Although music history textbooks contain more context than theory textbooks, their focus on musical form and style limits discussion of social history. In the case of Foster, his music could easily be removed and replaced, as Ewell advocates, and the same musical concepts could be introduced with less controversial examples. Music history textbooks do need to make space for the inclusion of composers and musics that are more representative of historical contexts. But music history can also be so much more than a study of form and style.

258   TEACHING DIFFICULT TOPICS

FOSTER'S MUSIC IN THE CLASSROOM

More and more, instructors are making the difficult but informed choice to remove Foster from their curricula. While I support these efforts to make room for traditionally underrepresented composers and musics, compelling reasons remain for continuing to include Foster in curricula that address racism and national myth-making. His career was singular during a formative stage in the history of the US music industry. He became a professional songwriter when printed sheet music by (mostly white) American composers, newly protected by copyright law, was first rapidly disseminated through a network of merchants to (mostly white) middle-class consumers who performed the music in their homes, which were increasingly furnished with newly mass-produced pianos.[20] In this context, Foster became the first American to write many songs that quickly spread across the globe and remain widely known today. Refocusing pedagogy on social and economic history can help portray "canonical" composers like Foster less heroically and shed light on the mechanisms that enabled the creation and popularization of their music. Such an approach can help students understand much of Foster's music as belonging to the category of "contemptible collectibles," a category of historical cultural products that performed reprehensible cultural work but that can be studied to adequately understand the past.[21]

Rather than avoid Foster's contemptible collectibles by choosing only a "parlor song," educators who decide to teach about Foster should at the very least select a representative example of each of the three song types that account for most of the songs Foster composed: comic minstrel songs, sentimental songs, and sentimental minstrel songs.[22] Intended as humorous to their primarily white target audience, Foster's comic minstrel songs depict disparaging stereotypes of people of African descent. Reinforced by melodies and accompaniments filled with musical stereotypes, often using the upbeat and bouncy styles of the polka and dances of the British isles, comic minstrel songs typically portray their characters as simple and happy. Usually, the lead singer sings the verses and is joined by a rousing male chorus in harmony, which would have been performed by the entire line of "blacked up" performers in a minstrel show (see Figure 14.1). These songs were incredibly popular in the theater, but as sheet music they did not sell well because their lewdness violated the codes of behavior that governed social interactions in the Victorian home.[23] Foster earned almost all his income from the sale of sheet music since he was not a performer himself and copyright law did not allow him to collect royalties from performances by other performers. Out of financial

Table 14.1: Well-Known Examples of Foster's Songs

Comic Minstrel Songs	Sentimental Ballads	Sentimental Minstrel Songs
Oh! Susanna (1848)	Jeanie with the Light Brown Hair (1854)	Uncle Ned (1848)
Nelly Bly (1850)	Come Where My Love Lies Dreaming (1855)	Nelly Was a Lady (1849)
De Camptown Races (1850)	Gentle Annie (1856)	Old Folks at Home (1851)
Ring, Ring de Banjo! (1851)	Slumber, My Darling (1862)	Massa's in de Cold Ground (1852)
	Beautiful Dreamer (1862)	My Old Kentucky Home (1853)
		Old Black Joe (1860)

necessity, once he committed himself to making a career out of songwriting, his output veered away from lewd comedy toward sentimentality. His publishers nudged him in this direction, urging him shortly after signing his contracts in 1849 "to compose only such pieces as are likely both in the sentiment & melody to take the public taste."[24] Foster's sentimental songs exhibit the ideals and etiquette of middle- and upper-class homes, and they give voice to emotions associated with courtship, love, and loss.[25] They are slower and more lyrical than comic minstrel songs, and they occasionally exhibit the influence of Italian *bel canto* opera. The sentimental songs with black personas, which I call sentimental minstrel songs, combine these conventions with the stereotypes of people of African descent found in comic minstrel songs.

The four songs on which Foster's fame primarily lies—"Old Folks at Home," "Massa's in de Cold Ground," "My Old Kentucky Home," and "Old Black Joe"—are sentimental minstrel songs.[26] In these songs Foster devised a formula for appealing to a broad cross section of predominantly white sheet-music consumers. Not only were the songs simultaneously suitable for blackface performance on the minstrel stage and performances in middle- and upper-class homes, they were also constructed with open meanings designed to "take the public taste" by speaking to people with different political opinions. These songs almost never openly embrace anti- or pro-slavery messages but contain coded messages fashioned to be deciphered differently by different listeners across the political spectrum.[27] These gestures are similar to what Ian Haney López refers to as "dog whistles," or coded rhetoric employed by politicians that "operates on two levels: inaudible and easily denied in one range, yet stimulating strong reactions in another."[28] Because of these characteristics, Foster reception was divided in his day, selling across the anti- and pro-slavery divide.

260   TEACHING DIFFICULT TOPICS

It has been no less divided since his death, with different listeners hearing his sentimental minstrel songs as racist, anti-racist, and neutral.

The collections of the Center for American Music include all known early editions and arrangements of Foster's songs, which have been digitized to facilitate study and classroom use.[29] Early editions of Foster's published songs can help students understand their original commercial, social, and political contexts. Guiding student analyses of editions by starting with questions with easily identifiable answers—*Who published this piece? Where? When? How much did it cost? What instruments is it written for?*—can help prepare students for questions that inspire higher level thinking. By analyzing the engraved or lithographed publication information, students can see that music was printed in cities like New York, Boston, Baltimore, and Cincinnati. Dealer stamps indicate the music shops to which publishers shipped music across the country, where it was sold to consumers. The covers also indicate that the cost of sheet music was relatively expensive. As indicated in the examples in Figures 14.2 and 14.3, an individual piece usually cost $0.25. If students plug that into an inflation calculator, they will see that $0.25 is about the equivalent of $8.50 in 2020 dollars, a good sum for a single piece that would quickly add up to a considerable amount of money for an entire collection.[30] (Some covers from the period feature the number "2 ½," which meant that the piece cost two-and-a-half dimes, or $0.25.) Turning to the first page of the score, students will see that most songs were written for voice and piano or, less frequently, voice and guitar. These initial questions lay the groundwork for pondering what the materials tell us about who might have purchased them. Ask students: *Based on this information about cost and the skills and instruments required to play the pieces, whom do you think publishers targeted as consumers?* Students will see that this music was created for middle- and upper-class consumers. Although Candace Bailey has documented cases of African Americans purchasing sheet music and participating in musical customs historians have traditionally associated with middle-class whiteness, we know that Foster thought of his middle and upper-class consumers as white.[31] In early 1853, one prominent music publisher insisted to him that his blackface songs did not appeal to white consumers and urged him to write only "White men's music."[32] For the next seven years, Foster did as he was told.

Close reading of the materiality of the sheet music, particularly the evidence of the laborious and relatively costly art of publishing, deepens students' understandings of its cost and, therefore, the target audience. Figures 14.2 and 14.3 reveal that some covers still have indentations showing the shape of the lithographic stone that the printer physically pressed onto the page over 150 years ago. Ask students questions that inspire them to figure out what these indentations are: *What made these indentations? Do they tell us anything about how this sheet music was printed?* Students can also compare different copies to see different gradations of ink that resulted from printers using stones and engraved plates multiple times, resulting in prints being successively lighter before the ink was reloaded. To help them figure out why the darkness of the ink varies, ask students: *What happens when your computer printer is running out of ink?* Early prints of "Jeanie with the Light Brown Hair" reveal that at some point during the printing of the first edition of the piece, the publisher hired someone to redo the lithographic cover, perhaps because the original stone had broken. The artist closely copied Napoleon Sarony's original art, but close examination reveals differences: the facial features are quite different, the pendant on the necklace is higher on the original than on the copy, below the necklace the number of visible lace crossings is different, the leafy borders are different, "Foster's" signature in the bottom right is not the same, etc. After analyzing the traces of the printing process with students, ask: *How do the visible traces of the printing process enhance your understanding of the cost of sheet music? Was printing easy and cheap?*

Understanding that the music was created primarily for middle- and upper-class white consumers is foundational to understanding the characters in the songs and the messages they convey. To help students understand the portrayal of the character in "Oh! Susanna," have them read and listen to the first verse and ask them: *How is the character's intelligence portrayed?* The singer in "Oh! Susanna" is portrayed as buffoonish and unintelligent. In the first verse, the character is hardly capable of stringing together two thoughts that do not contradict each other:

I come from Alabama with my banjo on my knee
I'se gwine to Lou'siana
My true lub for to see.
It rain'd all night de day I left,
De wedder it was dry;
The sun so hot I froze to def,
Susanna, dont you cry.

If students struggle to understand this aspect of the song, ask them a more specific question: *Where does the character contradict himself, and what does that say about his intelligence?*

262   TEACHING DIFFICULT TOPICS

The second verse, rarely performed or included in new editions today, is almost always unknown to students. In my experience, students have trouble immediately grasping the nuances of the verse, but often they are visibly uncomfortable with the use of the N word and lack of respect for black lives:

> I jump'd aboard the telegraph
> And trabbled down de ribber,
> De lecktrick fluid magnified,
> And kill'd five hundred Nigga.
> De bulgine bust and de hoss ran off,
> I really thought I'd die;
> I shut my eyes to hold my bref
> Susanna dont you cry.

Most students will need carefully crafted questions to lead them through the meaning of these words. *What technologies are referred to in this verse? What is a bullgine (also known as a "bull engine")? Were these technologies new in the 1840s? Does the character fully understand these technologies?* As they ponder these questions, they will hopefully come to realize that this verse pokes fun at the difficulties of keeping apace of the mid-nineteenth century's new technologies: the telegraph, the steamboat, and the railroad. The character's confusion is conveyed through his incorrect statements that telegraphs use electricity and magnetism, and that electricity is a fluid. He confuses an actual telegraph with a steamboat named *The Telegraph*, and he is also confused about engines. A steamboat did not run on a bull engine, which was an engine for a locomotive, and since bull engines generated their horsepower by burning coal, there would not have been horses to run off when the engine malfunctioned. These elements of the verse can help students understand another stereotype portrayed in the song. Ask students: *What is the character's reaction to the horrible events of the second verse?* Unphased by tragedy, he is portrayed as a perpetually happy buffoon. The portrayal of the happy black man or woman who sings joyfully despite life's difficulties was standard in pro-slavery and white supremacist propaganda.

Foster wrote "Oh! Susanna" no later than 1848, and it is representative of the kind of music from which he veered away after he signed his contracts in 1849. Ask students: *Why might middle- and upper-class white consumers have been put off by "Oh! Susanna"? What might have been viewed as inappropriate for informal home performances with women, children, and guests present?* A sentimental song like "Jeanie with the Light Brown Hair" can help students understand what was widely viewed as more appropriate for such settings. In most of Foster's sentimental ballads with white characters, white femininity is construed by the character in whose voice the song is written, usually a white man. Asking students to examine emotions, images, and metaphors associated with these songs' male and female characters can be a valuable entry point for discussions of historical constructions of gender: *What emotions are expressed in the song?* Students can easily identify that the male persona of the singer in "Jeanie with the Light Brown Hair" is mournful as he nostalgically remembers his absent love, Jeanie, who has presumably died. Ask students to dig deeper: *How does the singer describe Jeanie? What metaphors does he employ? In what types of settings does he remember her?* Typical of these types of songs, Jeanie is described in natural settings and characterized through nature metaphors: Her spirit is "borne like a vapor on the summer air," she frolics "where the bright streams play," she is "happy as the daisies," she sings with the "blithe birds," and she has a "day-dawn smile." Explain to students that the song was written in the 1850s as Pittsburgh experienced rapid industrialization, and ask them: *In the context of industrialization, why might "Jeanie with the Light Brown Hair" use nature metaphors for its deceased title character?* This question might inspire students to see that Jeanie's absence can be seen as a symbol of a commonly perceived danger of the day: the loss of nature and the agrarian lifestyle to urban expansion and modern living.[33]

Juxtaposing "Oh! Susanna" and "Jeanie" with the sentimental minstrel song "Nelly Was a Lady" helps students understand the ambiguity of the latter genre. On the one hand, it can be interpreted as a progressive song. To inspire students to understand this interpretation, explain to them that in the period African Americans—even free African Americans—were denied citizenship and typically dehumanized in popular culture. Ask students: *In this context, what might be the significance of calling Nelly a lady? How can this be heard as challenging the common stereotypes of the day?* Since "lady" was a term reserved for middle- and upper-class white women, the song could be interpreted as suggesting that both white and Black women could be ladies in a gesture toward equality.[34] Since "Jeanie with the Light Brown Hair" also portrays a lady, you might ask the students to compare the portrayals of Nelly and Jeanie: *Besides being referred to as a "lady," how else does the song portray Nelly as a lady, like Jeanie?* Students will notice that the song describes Nelly with almost the same nature metaphor used in "Jeanie with the Light Brown Hair": Jeanie had a "day-dawn smile," and Nelly's smile "seem'd like de light ob day a dawning." Ask students: *Do the songs also dignify their male charac-*

264   TEACHING DIFFICULT TOPICS

ters? Students will observe that the singers in both songs—Nelly's mournful husband and Jeanie's regretful companion—are portrayed as feeling deep, human emotions, perhaps another gesture toward equality.

Explain to students that these progressive gestures are dog whistles, for there is nothing explicitly progressive about the song. Asking them to compare "Nelly Was a Lady" and "Oh! Susanna" can reveal that "Nelly Was a Lady" has other dog whistles that enable it to be heard in a very different way. Ask students: *Despite the positive aspects of their portrayals, what could still be seen as offensive about the characters in "Nelly Was a Lady"?* Students might note the use of dialect, which could be interpreted as signifying the characters are "simple" or "buffoonish," like the character in "Oh! Susanna." Ask students about the caricature of the happy slave: *How does "Nelly Was a Lady" gesture toward the stereotype of the "happy slave" that we saw in "Oh! Susanna"?* Students might note that in the fifth verse of "Nelly Was a Lady" the singer laments the end of his "happy days":

Down in de meadow mong de clober,
Walk wid my Nelly by my side;
Now all dem happy days am ober,
Farewell my dark Virginny bride.

These words can be interpreted in different ways. On the one hand, the character might simply be expressing sadness because he had been happy with his wife, and now she's gone. But since the "happy slave" stereotype was commonly deployed in pro-slavery propaganda in the years leading to the Civil War, this was a dog whistle aimed at people with pro-slavery leanings, who could have heard the enslaved character's reference to his "happy days" as part of that tradition.

Given the similarities to "Oh! Susanna," ask students: *Do you think "Nelly Was a Lady" was intended as a serious song or a comic song?* Hopefully students will realize that there is no straightforward answer to this. On the one hand, since the song has no overt jokes at the expense of its characters, a "serious" performance of it with a progressive intent can easily be imagined. But calling Nelly a lady is also another dog whistle, for the song was written for both home performance as well as blackface performance in minstrel shows, where the character of Nelly would have been performed in drag for comic effect. In minstrelsy, the Black "lady" was a longstanding trope, an imagined type of person mocked as "uppity," that is, as aspiring to middle-

Stephen Foster and Slavery in Music Textbooks   265

class respectability shown as naturally incompatible with Black woman-hood.[35] Such mockery is shown in the centerpiece on the sheet-music cover for "Oh! Susanna" in Figure 14.1. The "woman" wears clothes and performs a dance associated with middle-class whiteness, and the "manly" qualities of the performer in drag underscores the purported incongruities between blackness and white middle- and upper-class sensibilities and activities.

Regarding the question of comedy, Foster's intentions are somewhat questionable. In 1851 he wrote to the minstrel performer Edwin P. Christy about the performance of his song "Oh! Boys Carry Me 'long," instructing him that it "should be sung in a pathetic, not a comic style."[36] Some scholars point to this letter as suggesting that Foster did not intend his songs as racist, and that minstrels contorted them into racist caricatures against his wishes.[37] Given his political opinions and overt racism in songs like "Oh! Susanna" and "A Soldier in the Colored Brigade," and because performances filled with "pathos" are known to have been laughed at by audiences in Foster's day,[38] it is impossible to draw such a conclusion. Foster may have wanted the pathos to be the joke, at least sometimes. All that can be known for sure is that when songs like "Nelly Was a Lady" were interpreted as part of the tradition mocking black upward mobility, they conveyed the common white supremacist message that black women could never be ladies. When they were performed straight in the parlor, they may have been received as politically neutral or even progressive. In such songs, Foster managed to say this, that, and the other without saying much of anything at all.

CONCLUSION

When I introduce students to Foster, I want them to learn to understand his music in the way that it was understood by one of the most famous abolitionists of Foster's time, Frederick Douglass. In an 1855 address to an anti-slavery society that was reprinted in his autobiography that year, Douglass stated,

> It would seem almost absurd to say it, considering the use that has been made of them, that we have allies in the Ethiopian songs .... They are heart songs, and the finest feelings of human nature are expressed in them ... "Old Kentucky Home," and "Uncle Ned," can make the heart sad as well as merry, and can call forth a tear as well as a smile. They awaken the sympathies for the slave, in which anti-slavery principles take root, grow and flourish.[39]

266   TEACHING DIFFICULT TOPICS

Douglass was certainly inspired to say this by the regular insertion of some of Foster's sentimental minstrel songs into theatrical adaptations of Harriet Beecher Stowe's abolitionist novel *Uncle Tom's Cabin*.

Matthew Shaftel suggests that Douglass's words are evidence that Foster's songs "reinforced a new understanding of slaves and slave life, allowing Stephen Foster to add his musical support to the anti-slavery movement."[40] Douglass's speech, however, was less one-sided than Shaftel makes it out to be. Douglass knew in 1855 what historians have only recently recovered and what students can learn if given the proper tools. He understood that Foster's songs did not merely lend "support to the anti-slavery movement," for the ambiguities of some of them allowed them to be put to competing uses. Given Douglass's speech's audience of anti-slavery activists, it is understandable that he emphasized the antislavery uses of the songs, but his disparaging words about "the use that has been made of them" also acknowledges their use in white-supremacist theater and pro-slavery activism. As Douglass would have known, in their day the songs' ambiguities allowed them to dignify and mock, to be performed in blackface minstrel shows and anti-slavery rallies, and to be inserted into anti-slavery and pro-slavery adaptations of *Uncle Tom's Cabin*.[41] Foster was a commercial songwriter. He wrote songs to sell songs, and he created a formula for selling more music than any of his competitors in an exceptionally divisive and racist era.

In the end, Foster's songs can inspire students to think critically about primary and secondary sources. Embracing original sources gives students the opportunity to see what choices the authors of their textbooks made—what historical figures they include, omit, and center in their text; what musical examples they choose; and how they frame their subjects. Guiding students through analysis of original sheet music engages students with the processes of historiography. As Erin Conor observes, "Historiography helps students see that: a) the nature of a discipline as well as the questions it asks change over time, and, b) information is not a fixed artifact but rather it continually shifts in relation to ongoing struggles for voice and representation."[42] Primary sources can expose students to the processes of knowledge creation and the construction of history. They can show students that the representations of race in Foster's songs were shaped by powerful commercial, ideological, and social forces. They can also show that similar forces shape textbook narratives and the ways in which we read them.

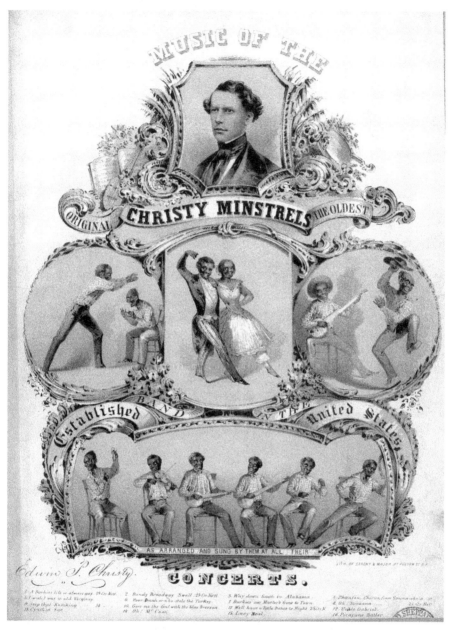

Figure 14.1: The cover art for this early edition of "Oh! Susanna" shows Edwin P. Christy, founder of the Christy Minstrels, at the top of the page and scenes from a minstrel show—including the whole line of performers—below. At the bottom of the page is a list of songs performed by Christy's troupe.

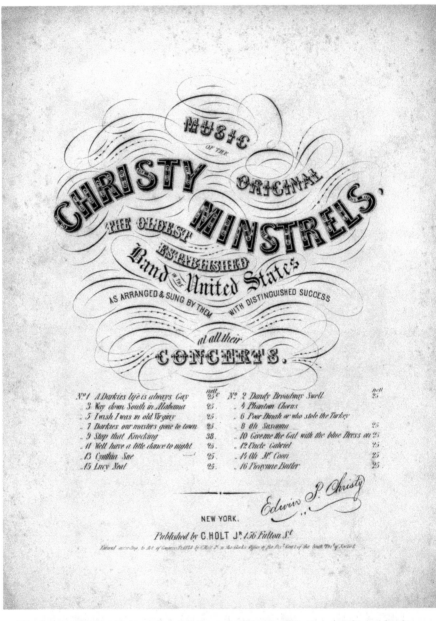

Figure 14.2: The imprint is still visible from the lithographic stone used to make the covers of these two nearly identical early printings of "Oh! Susanna." (See Figure 14.3 for the other printing.) The ink on the copy in Figure 14.3 is much lighter, indicating that it was made after other copies were made and not long before the ink was probably reapplied to the stone.

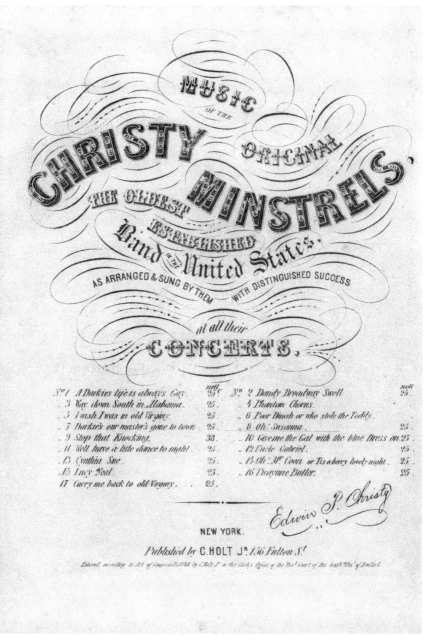

Figure 14.3: The imprint is still visible from the lithographic stone used to make the covers of these two nearly identical early printings of "Oh! Susanna." (See Figure 14.2 for the other printing.) The ink on this copy is much lighter, indicating that it was made after other copies were made and not long before the ink was probably reapplied to the stone.

Figure 14.4: An early print of "Jeanie with the Light Brown Hair," published by Firth, Pond & Co. This lithographic cover is one of the earliest prints of the piece. Besides the cover, the print in Figure 14.5 is identical to this one; all of the inside pages were printed from the same engraved plates. For an unknown reason Firth, Pond & Co. had to have the cover redone. The lithographic artist copied the original as closely as possible (see Figure 14.5).

Figure 14.5: Remake of the cover to an early print of "Jeanie with the Light Brown Hair," published by Firth, Pond & Co. Besides the cover, this print is identical to the original; all of the inside pages were printed from the same engraved plates. For an unknown reason Firth, Pond & Co. had to have the cover redone. The lithographic artist copied the original (see Figure 14.4) as closely as possible.

Notes

1. Joseph Byrd, "Whitewashing Blackface Minstrelsy in American College Textbooks," *Popular Music and Society* 32, no. 1 (February 2009): 82.

2. For an overview of the complex set of values that has shaped traditional musical examples in music history courses, see Mark Evan Bonds, "Selecting Dots, Connecting Dots: The Score Anthology as History," *Journal of Music History Pedagogy* 1, no. 2 (Spring 2011): 77–91.

3. The ramifications of musicology's disciplinary boundaries have been criticized from a variety of angles. See David Hunter, "Music and the Use of the Profits of the Anglo-American Slave Economy (ca. 1610–c. 1810)," in *The Oxford Handbook of Economic Ethnomusicology*, ed. Anna Morcom and Timothy D. Taylor (New York: Oxford University Press, 2021); Tamara Levitz, "Decolonizing the Society for American Music," *Bulletin of the Society for American Music* 43, no. 3 (Fall 2017): 1–13; William Cheng, *Just Vibrations: The Purpose of Sounding Good* (Ann Arbor: University of Michigan Press, 2016), 6–8; Phil Ford, "Disciplinarity (Or, Musicology is Anything You Can Get Away With)," *Dial M for Musicology*, June 28, 2015, https://dialmformusicology.wordpress.com/2015/06/28/disciplinarity/; and Georgina Born, "For a Relational Musicology: Music and Interdisciplinarity, Beyond the Practice Turn," *Journal of the Royal Musical Association* 135, no. 2 (2010): 205–43.

4. Larry Starr and Christopher Waterman, *American Popular Music: From Minstrelsy to MP3*, 5th ed. (New York: Oxford University Press, 2018), 52.

5. Christopher Lynch, "Stephen Foster and the Slavery Question," *American Music* 40, no. 1 (Spring 2022).

6. Matthew D. Morrison, "Blacksound," in *The Oxford Handbook of Western Music and Philosophy*, ed. Tomás McAuley, Nanette Nielsen, Jerrold Levinson, and Ariana Phillips-Hutton (New York: Oxford University Press, 2020), 558. See also Morrison, "Race, Blacksound, and the (Re)Making of Musicological Discourse," *Journal of the American Musicological Society* 72, no. 3 (Fall 2019): 781–823.

7. J. Peter Burkholder, Donald Jay Grout, and Claude V. Palisca, *A History of Western Music*, 9th ed. (New York: W. W. Norton, 2014), 605. For similar treatments of Foster, see Mark Evan Bonds, *A History of Music in Western Culture*, 4th ed. (New York: Pearson, 2013), 413 and 416; and Richard Taruskin and Christopher H. Gibbs, *The Oxford History of Western Music*, College Edition (New York: Oxford University Press, 2013), 631.

8. J. Peter Burkholder and Claude V. Palisca, *Norton Anthology of Western Music*, vol. 2, *Classic to Romantic*, 7th ed. (New York: W. W. Norton, 2014), 375.

9. For a deconstruction of the myth that Foster converted to progressivism in the early 1850s, see Jennie Lightweis-Goff, "'Long Time I Trabble on de Way': Stephen Foster's Conversion Narrative," *Journal of Popular Music Studies* 20, no. 2 (June 2008): 150–65.

10. For original covers, see Deane L. Root and Steven Saunders, *The Music of Stephen

C. Foster: A Critical Edition, vol. 1, *1844–1855* (Washington, DC: Smithsonian Institution Press, 1990), 262 and 372.

11. Richard Crawford and Larry Hamberlin, *An Introduction to America's Music*, 3rd ed. (New York: W. W. Norton, 2018), 113.

12. Crawford and Hamberlin, *America's Music*, 118.

13. Crawford and Hamberlin, *America's Music*, 122.

14. Crawford and Hamberlin, *America's Music*, 125–27.

15. Walter Frisch, *Music in the Nineteenth Century* (New York: W. W. Norton, 2013), 203–4.

16. George Cooper to Vincent Milligan, July 2, 1917, Foster Hall Collection, Center for American Music, University of Pittsburgh Library System. For more on Foster's Democratic politics, see Lynch, "Stephen Foster and the Slavery Question.

17. Steven Saunders, "The Social Agenda of Stephen Foster's Plantation Melodies," *American Music* 30, no. 3 (Fall 2012): 279–80. For more on how Foster's sentimental minstrel songs do not reflect progressive values, see Jabari Asim, *The N Word: Who Can Say It, Who Shouldn't, and Why* (New York: Houghton Mifflin, 2007), 80–82.

18. James W. Loewen, *Lies My Teacher Told Me: Everything Your American History Textbook Got Wrong* (New York: The New Press, 2018), 17.

19. Philip A. Ewell, "Music Theory and the White Racial Frame," *Music Theory Online* 26, no. 2 (September 2020).

20. For copyright law, see Jason Lee Guthrie, "America's First Unprofessional Songwriter: Stephen Foster and the Ritual Economy of Copyright in Early American Popular Music," *Journal of the Music & Entertainment Industry Educators Association* 19, no. 1 (2019): 37–72. For pianos, see Richard Crawford, *America's Musical Life: A History* (New York: W. W. Norton, 2001), 234–35; and Cynthia Adams Hoover and Edwin M. Good, "Piano," *Grove Music Online, Oxford Music Online*, January 31, 2014, www.oxfordmusico nline.com, accessed November 24, 2021.

21. The term "contemptible collectible" was coined by Patricia A. Turner. See Turner, *Ceramic Uncles and Celluloid Mammies: Black Images & Their Influence on Culture* (Charlottesville: University of Virginia Press, 2002). It is also frequently used by museum curators, including David Pilgrim at the Jim Crow Museum. See Pilgrim, *Understanding Jim Crow: Using Racist Memorabilia to Teach Tolerance and Promote Social Justice* (Oakland, CA: PM Press, 2015). Jennifer Forness recommends that K–12 educators take a similar critical approach. See Forness, "Reconsidering the Role of Stephen Foster in the Music Classroom," *Music Educators Journal* 103, no. 2 (December 2016): 58–63.

22. William W. Austin refers to these song types as comic Ethiopian songs, poetic ballads, and pathetic plantation songs. William W. Austin, *"Susanna," "Jeanie," and "The Old Folks at Home": The Songs of Stephen C. Foster from His Time to Ours*, 2nd ed. (Urbana: University of Illinois Press, 1987).

23. Petra Meyer Frazier's analysis of mid-nineteenth-century women's music revealed that minstrel songs were almost completely absent. See Petra Meyer Frazier,

274   TEACHING DIFFICULT TOPICS

"American Women's Roles in Domestic Music Making as Revealed in Parlor Song Collections: 1820–1870," PhD diss., University of Colorado, 1999, 189 n. 13. Other studies, however, have shown that some women's collections display a tolerance for the inclusion of sentimental minstrel songs. See Katherine Preston, "Music in the McKissick Parlor," in *Emily's Songbook: Music in 1850s Albany*, ed. Mark Slobin, James Kimball, Katherine K. Preston, and Deane Root (Middleton, WI: A-R Editions, 2011), 17–18. See also Stephanie Elaine Dunson, "The Minstrel in the Parlor: Nineteenth-Century Sheet Music and the Domestication of Blackface Minstrelsy," PhD diss., University of Massachusetts Amherst, 2004.

24. Firth, Pond & Co. to Stephen Foster, September 12, 1849, FHC, C916.

25. For a contextualization of Foster's music in the parlor, see JoAnne O'Connell, *The Life and Songs of Stephen Foster* (Lanham, MD: Rowman & Littlefield, 2016), 129–47 and 171–83.

26. The enduring popularity of these songs into the late 1800s and beyond is due in large part to their continued insertion into stage adaptations of *Uncle Tom's Cabin*. See Austin, *"Susanna," "Jeanie," and "The Old Folks at Home"*, 235. These four songs were also among the most recorded Foster songs in the early period of recorded sound. See George R. Creegan, "A Discography of the Acoustic Recordings of Stephen C. Foster's Music," PhD diss., University of Pittsburgh, 1987.

27. Lynch, "Stephen Foster and the Slavery Question."

28. Ian Haney López, *Dog Whistle Politics: How Coded Racial Appeals Have Reinvented Racism and Wrecked the Middle Class* (New York: Oxford University Press, 2014), 3.

29. Each digitized edition of Foster's songs held in the Center for American Music's collection can be found in the University's online catalog (Pittcat): www.library.pitt .edu

30. I recommend www.measuringworth.com for inflation calculations. For this calculation, I adjusted the amount using the Consumer Price Index.

31. Candace Bailey, "Music and Black Gentility in the Antebellum and Civil War South," *Journal of the American Musicological Society* 74, no. 3 (Fall 2021): 600–610.

32. Richard Storrs Willis, ed., "Pittsburgh," *Musical World and New York Musical Times* 5, no. 5 (January 29, 1853): 75.

33. See Susan Key, "'Forever in Our Ears': Nature, Voice, and Sentiment in Stephen Foster's Parlor Style," *American Music* 30, no. 3 (Fall 2012): 290–307; and Key, "Sound and Sentimentality: Nostalgia in the Songs of Stephen Foster," *American Music* 13, no. 2 (Summer 1995): 145–66.

34. For this interpretation, see Deane L. Root, "Music and Community in the Civil War Era," in *Bugle Resounding: Music and Musicians of the Civil War Era*, ed. Bruce C. Kelley and Mark A. Snell (Columbia: University of Missouri Press, 2004), 45–46.

35. Dunson, "Minstrel in the Parlor," 120–25.

36. Stephen Foster to Edwin P. Christy, June 12, 1851, FHC, C999.

37. See Matthew Shaftel, "Singing a New Song: Stephen Foster and the New American Minstrelsy," *Music & Politics* 1, no. 2 (Summer 2007): 21; and Deane L. Root, "The

'Mythtory' of Stephen C. Foster or Why His True Story Remains Untold," *American Music Research Center Journal* 15 (2005): 11–12.

38. See Julia J. Chybowski, "Blackface Minstrelsy and the Reception of Elizabeth Taylor Greenfield," *Journal of the Society for American Music* 15, no. 3 (August 2021), 307–10.

39. Frederick Douglass, "The Anti-Slavery Movement, Lecture Delivered before the Rochester Ladies' Anti-Slavery Society, March 19, 1855," in *Frederick Douglass: Selected Speeches and Writings*, ed. Philip S. Foner (Chicago: Lawrence Hill Books, 2000), 329; and "The Anti-Slavery Movement," in *My Bondage and My Freedom* (New York: Miller, Orton & Mulligan, 1855), 462.

40. Shaftel, "Singing a New Song," 27.

41. For adaptations of *Uncle Tom's Cabin*, see Sarah Meer, "Minstrel Variations: 'Uncle Toms' in the Minstrel Show," in *Uncle Tom Mania: Slavery, Minstrelsy & Transatlantic Culture in the 1850s* (Athens: University of Georgia Press, 2005), 51–72; and John L. Brooke, "Transforming Culture: Commercializing Anti-Slavery," in *"There Is a North": Fugitive Slaves, Political Crisis, and Cultural Transformation in the Coming of the Civil War* (Amherst and Boston: University of Massachusetts Press, 2019), 170–210.

42. Erin Conor, "Re-envisioning Information Literacy: Critical Information Literacy, Disciplinary Discourses, and Music History," *Journal of Music History Pedagogy* 9, no. 1 (February 2019): 38.

Works Cited

Archives

Foster Hall Collection. Center for American Music, University of Pittsburgh. Pittsburgh, Pennsylvania.

Secondary Sources

Asim, Jabari. *The N Word: Who Can Say It, Who Shouldn't, and Why*. New York: Houghton Mifflin, 2007.

Austin, William W. *"Susanna," "Jeanie," and "The Old Folks at Home": The Songs of Stephen C. Foster from His Time to Ours*, 2nd ed. Urbana: University of Illinois Press, 1987.

Bonds, Mark Evan. "Selecting Dots, Connecting Dots: The Score Anthology as History." *Journal of Music History Pedagogy* 1, no. 2 (Spring 2011): 77–91.

Bonds, Mark Evan. *A History of Music in Western Culture*, 4th ed. New York: Pearson, 2013.

Born, Georgina. "For a Relational Musicology: Music and Interdisciplinarity, Beyond the Practice Turn." *Journal of the Royal Musical Association* 135, no. 2 (2010): 205–43.

Brooke, John L. *"There Is a North": Fugitive Slaves, Political Crisis, and Cultural Transformation in the Coming of the Civil War*. Amherst and Boston: University of Massachusetts Press, 2019.

276   TEACHING DIFFICULT TOPICS

Burkholder, J. Peter, Donald Jay Grout, and Claude V. Palisca. *A History of Western Music*, 9th ed. New York: W. W. Norton, 2014.

Burkholder, J. Peter, and Claude V. Palisca. *Norton Anthology of Western Music*, vol. 2, *Classic to Romantic*, 7th ed. New York: W. W. Norton, 2014.

Byrd, Joseph. "Whitewashing Blackface Minstrelsy in American College Textbooks." *Popular Music and Society* 32, no. 1 (February 2009): 77–86.

Cheng, William. *Just Vibrations: The Purpose of Sounding Good.* Ann Arbor: University of Michigan Press, 2016.

Chybowski, Julia J. "Blackface Minstrelsy and the Reception of Elizabeth Taylor Greenfield." *Journal of the Society for American Music* 15, no. 3 (August 2021): 305–20.

Conor, Erin. "Re-envisioning Information Literacy: Critical Information Literacy, Disciplinary Discourses, and Music History." *Journal of Music History Pedagogy* 9, no. 1 (February 2019): 28–43.

Crawford, Richard. *America's Musical Life.* New York: W. W. Norton, 2001.

Crawford, Richard, and Larry Hamberlin. *An Introduction to America's Music*, 3rd edition. New York: W. W. Norton, 2018.

Creegan, George R. "A Discography of the Acoustic Recordings of Stephen C. Foster's Music." PhD diss., University of Pittsburgh, 1987.

Douglass, Frederick. *Frederick Douglass: Selected Speeches and Writings.* Edited by Philip S. Foner. Chicago: Lawrence Hill Books, 2000.

Douglass, Frederick. *My Bondage and My Freedom.* New York: Miller, Orton & Mulligan, 1855.

Dunson, Stephanie Elaine. "The Minstrel in the Parlor: Nineteenth-Century Sheet Music and the Domestication of Blackface Minstrelsy." PhD diss., University of Massachusetts Amherst, 2004.

Ewell, Philip A. "Music Theory and the White Racial Frame." *Music Theory Online* 26, no. 2 (September 2020).

Ford, Phil. "Disciplinarity (Or, Musicology is Anything You Can Get Away With)." *Dial M for Musicology*, June 28, 2015, https://dialmformusicology.wordpress.com/2015/06/28/disciplinarity/

Forness, Jennifer. "Reconsidering the Role of Stephen Foster in the Music Classroom." *Music Educators Journal* 103, no. 2 (December 2016): 58–63.

Frazier, Petra Meyer. "American Women's Roles in Domestic Music Making as Revealed in Parlor Song Collections: 1820–1870." PhD diss., University of Colorado, 1999.

Guthrie, Jason Lee. "America's First Unprofessional Songwriter: Stephen Foster and the Ritual Economy of Copyright in Early American Popular Music." *Journal of the Music & Entertainment Industry Educators Association* 19, no. 1 (2019): 37–72.

Hoover, Cynthia Adams, and Edwin M. Good. "Piano." *Grove Music Online, Oxford Music Online*, January 31, 2014, www.oxfordmusiconline.com, accessed November 24, 2021.

Hunter, David. "Music and the Use of the Profits of the Anglo-American Slave Economy (ca. 1610–c. 1810)." In *The Oxford Handbook of Economic Ethnomusicology*, ed. Anna Morcom and Timothy D. Taylor. New York: Oxford University Press, 2021.

Key, Susan. "'Forever in Our Ears': Nature, Voice, and Sentiment in Stephen Foster's Parlor Style." *American Music* 30, no. 3 (Fall 2012): 290–307.

Key, Susan. "Sound and Sentimentality: Nostalgia in the Songs of Stephen Foster." *American Music* 13, no. 2 (Summer 1995): 145–66.

Levitz, Tamara. "Decolonizing the Society for American Music." *Bulletin of the Society for American Music* 43, no. 3 (Fall 2017): 1–13.

Lightweis-Goff, Jennie. "'Long Time I Trabble on de Way': Stephen Foster's Conversion Narrative." *Journal of Popular Music Studies* 20, no. 2 (June 2008): 150–65.

Loewen, James W. *Lies My Teacher Told Me: Everything Your American History Textbook Got Wrong.* New York: The New Press, 2018.

López, Ian Haney. *Dog Whistle Politics: How Coded Racial Appeals Have Reinvented Racism and Wrecked the Middle Class.* New York: Oxford University Press, 2014.

Lynch, Christopher. "Stephen Foster and the Slavery Question." *American Music* 40, no. 1 (Spring 2022).

Meer, Sarah. *Uncle Tom Mania: Slavery, Minstrelsy & Transatlantic Culture in the 1850s.* Athens: University of Georgia Press, 2005.

Morrison, Matthew D. "Blacksound." In *The Oxford Handbook of Western Music and Philosophy*, ed. Tomás McAuley, Nanette Nielsen, Jerrold Levinson, and Ariana Phillips-Hutton. New York: Oxford University Press, 2020.

Morrison, Matthew D. "Race, Blacksound, and the (Re)Making of Musicological Discourse." *Journal of the American Musicological Society* 72, no. 3 (Fall 2019): 781–823.

O'Connell, JoAnne. *The Life and Songs of Stephen Foster.* Lanham, MD: Rowman & Littlefield, 2016.

Pilgrim, David. *Understanding Jim Crow: Using Racist Memorabilia to Teach Tolerance and Promote Social Justice.* Oakland, CA: PM Press, 2015.

Preston, Katherine. "Music in the McKissick Parlor." In *Emily's Songbook: Music in 1850s Albany*, 14–21. Edited by Mark Slobin, James Kimball, Katherine K. Preston, and Deane Root. Middleton, WI: A-R Editions, 2011.

Root, Deane L. "Music and Community in the Civil War Era." In *Bugle Resounding: Music and Musicians of the Civil War Era*, 37–53. Edited by Bruce C. Kelley and Mark A. Snell. Columbia: University of Missouri Press, 2004.

Root, Deane L. "The 'Myth-Story' of Stephen C. Foster, or Why His True Story Remains Untold." *American Music Research Center Journal* 15 (2005): 1–18.

Root, Deane L., and Steven Saunders. *The Music of Stephen C. Foster.* 2 vols. Washington, DC: Smithsonian, 1990.

Shaftel, Matthew. "Singing a New Song: Stephen Foster and the New American Minstrelsy." *Music & Politics* 1, no. 2 (Summer 2007): 1–26.

Starr, Larry, and Christopher Waterman. *American Popular Music: From Minstrelsy to MP3*, 5th ed. New York: Oxford University Press, 2018.

Taruskin, Richard, and Christopher H. Gibbs. *The Oxford History of Western Music, College Edition.* New York: Oxford University Press, 2013.

Turner, Patricia A. *Ceramic Uncles and Celluloid Mammies: Black Images & Their Influence on Culture.* Charlottesville: University of Virginia Press, 2002.

CHAPTER 15

The Jazz of a Black Ethnographer

A Memoir of Pedagogy, Improvisation, and Reflexivity at a Liberal Arts College

Whitney Slaten

This chapter considers how students' engagement with reflexivity and improvisation offer new pedagogies for ethnographic research within the liberal arts classroom and a graduate seminar. Improvisation, central to jazz performance, enables students to acknowledge their own being and becoming, amid their analyses of how people theorize the social contexts of music. To swing in such ways, to syncopate between times of studying oneself and others, suggests a paradigm of research that honors the social sciences of musicians, audiences, and their allies who have negotiated jazz in ways that have formed specific ontological, epistemological, and hegemonic understandings and assertions. Through the example of leading the ethnomusicology program at Bard, the author details the curriculum, examples of student work, and the importance of the relationship between teaching and research when teaching difficult topics. This chapter calls for a disciplinary reawakening, enabling music studies to respond to the contemporary moment through connecting ethnographic learning with student agency.

FINDING ETHNOMUSICOLOGY

Donald Byrd was the only one to ask who I was and listen to the answer. He was among the most important jazz musicians and trumpet players of his generation. I was an undergraduate student of jazz performance and sound engineering at William Paterson University when he was a visiting artist-in-residence in 2004. Byrd had seen me walking on the campus and he invited me to talk in his office, which was at some distance from the music building. He told me that he was on his way to Teterboro Airport, where his plane was. After establishing that he was among the few of his contemporaries to have

278

an earned doctorate as a jazz musician, he wanted to know about what led me to college, and to talk about my future.

I told him about my father's sound engineering business, the strength of my high school jazz program, and my matriculation at Hampton University, a historically Black university in Virginia, where I had hoped to study jazz performance. As I began to describe my involvement in the marching band from the summer through the fall of my first year, and the turn toward classical training in music throughout the spring semester, his head started to nod slowly, as if to gesture that he knew where my story was heading. I told him that in addition to me, roughly a dozen of my classmates who could improvise decided to transfer to music programs throughout the country that offered a degree in jazz. These classmates and I recorded audition tapes in secret, not wanting to tell anyone our plans, and we all eventually admitted that we felt some level of guilt about the decision to leave Hampton. Some amount of guilt and regret for leaving stayed with me not only at that moment talking with Byrd, but would also extend into the future. However, I did not have to characterize those feelings to him. He then told me about what seemed to be his evangelical mission to establish jazz studies in the curricula of a number of historically Black colleges and universities since the 1970s. He seemed to know about specific aspects of this at Hampton, but never detailed them to me. Byrd helped me understand how certain Black colleges discouraged the curricular study of jazz as a protective measure to guard students against economic investments in the industrially exploitative negotiations with popular culture, even though he and I, in our different times, wished there could be some engagement with the music and its intellectual legacy. Then our conversation became future facing. Byrd wanted to know what I wanted to find in jazz. It took some time for my 20-year-old self to articulate my answer to this, but I eventually characterized my desire to study the processes of jazz and its Africanist intellectual foundations, particularly in what would contribute to an anti-essentialist discourse about Black expressive culture. The example I had been working with at the time was a research project about harmonic systems in pre-colonial sub-Saharan Africa. This piqued his interest. He recommended that I read works by Kwabena Nketia and Kofi Agawu, and to eventually meet them someday. Donald Byrd was the first to recommend that I study ethnomusicology in graduate school.

During my time at William Paterson, I had the privilege to learn from James Williams about his insistence on the exploration of Black spiritualism within the inner voices of tonal harmony. Donald Braden possessed and taught me vertical and horizontal melodic virtuosity. Kenny Garrett

280   TEACHING DIFFICULT TOPICS

impressed upon me the import of developing vibrato. Clark Terry's theorizations of linguistics in phrasing fundamentally changed my improvisations. Babatunde Olatunji taught me the power of the voice within the context of modes and polyrhythms, and he led me to feel even closer to John Coltrane than I thought I was beforehand. These experiences, as well as the singular act of mentorship by Donald Byrd, brought me to study ethnomusicology at Columbia University.

Heeding the lesson of protection by Hampton University, while also considering the paradigmatic aspirations of the Columbia ethnomusicology program at that time, I thought strategically about my selection of a research topic. Through my background in sound engineering, I pursued ethnographic research on practices of live sound reinforcement engineering at world music, jazz, and music theater concerts and productions in New York City. This work responded to a sound studies discourse that emerged from perpetuations of mediation as a framework rooted in linguistic analysis. Studies of mediation sought to de-essentialize the ontology of music within post-structuralist discourses in cultural anthropology and ethnomusicology. However, ethnographic fieldwork continually reminded me of how strategic my choice to use the discourses of sound and technology in music was. Here was a way to gain expertise as a researcher while protecting the cherished intellectual foundations of Black processes in the making of expressive culture that wield both craft and art, and everything between techne and episteme.

I belong to a small, disparate, and dispersed group of black people, following Zora Neale Hurston, who trained as ethnographers at Columbia University. Questioned in different ways by our white contemporaries, who famously fought white supremacy, ever since such advocacy by Franz Boas, many of us always felt and knew of the dangerous intimacies of this supremacy; nevertheless, we have each conducted serious fieldwork, wielding method and concept with rigor, care and protection. Hurston was watchful of science. She witnessed the shift of consensus about the culture concept in Boas's anthropology, as well as the tenuous notion that such scientific racism would not persist in the ethnographic method. At some distance from anthropology, her pursuit of narrative, and its revelations, predate the discipline's eventual realizations of "ethnoscience" in the 1970s, or the partial embrace of reflexivity and thick description in the "writing cultures" turn in the 1980s.

Throughout graduate school, I realized a greater freedom to develop these ideas of method and concept in my teaching as an adjunct or a term professor. I develop syllabi dedicated to considering the cross-talk between ethnography, technology, and improvisation. In my roles as a professor of music history, music technology, music theory, and ethnomusicology, the needs and the talents of my students at Columbia, William Paterson University, Seton Hall University, and The New School not only honed productive course work over the years, but ways to develop important colloquia set within a number of important campus events. In particular, the progression of such events that had been developed in fieldwork and in the classroom, from Columbia University to Bard College, has helped to converge my earlier experiences, the operations on jazz by Black life in Harlem, and the contemporary paradigmatic aspirations of sound studies, on how I have shaped ethnomusicology at Bard College.

PUBLIC ENGAGEMENT ON CAMPUS

I have found most success teaching difficult topics when research and public engagement inform my pedagogy. Thinking and connecting with the Bard community, the surrounding campus community, and intellectual communities throughout the academy have been crucial in remaining attuned to how scholarship can speak to the stakes of the moment, and how to best engage and teach students foundations in ethnomusicology with an immediacy about contemporary social life. Below are a few examples of how public work impacts the pedagogical, conceptual, and methodological approaches that I will discuss in the subsequent sections.

In the podcast titled "A Discussion on the influence of Military Music on the American Sound, from Reconstruction to the Roaring Twenties" with the West Point Music Research Center, including Jonathan Crane and Kristina Teuschler, I drew from my work on early American music, early jazz, and my experience as a band performer, discussing the concept of military music in the United States and introducing the centers of influence during the reconstruction period following the Civil War. This flowed into addressing the relationships between religious and military ritual practices to detail how movement, both physical and spiritual, is a critical part of these musical engagements. We concluded with a discussion about the imbalance between the study of musics that influence American culture, particularly related to Wiley Hitchcock's "cultivated" versus "vernacular" debate and the association of bands to "high" and "low" culture.

During the 2020 Bard Music Festival "Out of the Silence," I wrote program notes for two concerts featuring the works of Edward Duke Ellington and Samuel Coleridge-Taylor, drawing on my work on historic performance

282   TEACHING DIFFICULT TOPICS

style. Within a virtual discussion, "The Life of Joseph Bolonge," by invitation of Boston's *A Far Cry* Chamber Orchestra, I contextualized this historic figure in the contemporary climate of reckoning with black male life, mapping my research about the presence of the African Diaspora in Europe and the cultural contributions therein. In a pre-performance conversation about the emergence of black composers in the 21st century, considering Florence Price's Symphony No. 1 in E minor, I detailed "The Juba like the Scherzo: The Social Commentary of a Symphony's Third Movement," framing form as central in understanding cultural significance in symphonic music.

"A Conversation with Marcus Roberts" in October 2020, an online, public event that introduced him to the Bard community and engaged Roberts's biography, jazz history, and his performance practice provided space for students to connect material from my *Jazz Histories of Sound and Communication* course to the artistry of a leading contemporary jazz musician. The event also constructed a broader interdisciplinary point of contact for music studies across programs and divisions of the College. Students of history and American studies were interested in the role of migrations between the southern and northern United States in shaping musical aesthetics. Anthropology students were fascinated to know about the practices of observation that jazz musicians enact in performance. Philosophy students explored matters of dependency and generosity in practices of improvisation. Literature students inquired about the ways that jazz improvisers form narrative. Conservatory students were interested in how performance practices represent histories of style.

In fall 2019, I produced "1619: A Commemoration in Sound," at the Bard Fisher Center, convening students, faculty, and administrators from across the College as well as convening residents of the Hudson Valley. The event was a remembrance marking the 400th anniversary of the first arrival of enslaved people from Africa in the North American British Colonies—the beginning of slavery in dominant histories of the United States of America. I invited jazz artist T.K. Blue, choreographer Souleymane Badolo, and illustrator James Ransome to participate in the program that offered an exploration of history, memory, legacy, and gestures between the U.S. and Africa. I share the details of the event's development to trace how producing this public event gave me tools in teaching difficult topics in *Jazz Histories of Sound and Communication*. Fielding questions from students, faculty, administrators, and other stakeholders revealed the terrain of reception to Nikole Hannah-Jones's *1619 Project*,[1] as well as ways to connect it to Black performing arts.

In conjunction with the Center for Jazz Studies at Columbia University and Jazzmobile, Inc., I organized an event entitled "Jazzmobile, Community, and the Harlem Soundscape" to engage how Jazzmobile constructs community and the soundscape in the midst of Harlem's changing milieu. Jazzmobile has presented free, live jazz concerts continuously for over fifty years, through which audiences, production teams, organizers and musicians sound and listen to amplified jazz at historical sites in Harlem's outdoors. The program featured performances by Jazzmobile all-stars, my keynote address interrogating Jazzmobile as cultural repatriation, and a roundtable discussion with Jazzmobile audience members. Students in attendance were able to see the interrelation among scholarship, musicianship, and ethnography between their own community at Columbia and a historically underrepresented, though geographically adjacent one in Harlem.

Most recently, I hosted a private seminar of senior scholars affiliated with the Columbia University Center for Jazz Studies Study Group. Literary theorists, art historians, musicologists, and musicians from across the American and European academies comprise this group that meets annually to explore and develop new approaches in the study of jazz music and culture. The session centered on my work with jazz and technology and expanded the discourse about jazz and science, a central theme in my approach to teaching difficult topics that fuses the humanities and the sciences.

Producing public events not only distributes my ideas, but also feeds back into my scholarship and teaching at Bard. In the course design of a graduate seminar about Black composers and an upper level undergraduate course, *Musicology Among Enslaved Americans*, for example, as well as reinforcing my approach to teaching courses like *Jazz Histories of Sound and Communication* and *Improvisation as Social Science*, I drew on the lessons from these public events in my approach to pedagogy. Additionally, these events generated fora for my students to engage their coursework beyond the classroom, which is a key component to the ethnomusicology concentration at Bard, where I prioritize ethnographic fieldwork and music ethnography.

ETHNOMUSICOLOGY CONCENTRATION AT BARD

Both my teaching and research focus on how the social positions of musicians and audiences shift, in moments when sound becomes music. This analysis of time and resonance in music and society contributes to the discourses of ethnomusicology, jazz studies, technology studies, the philosophy of music, and the sociology of art. The relationship between my teaching and

284   TEACHING DIFFICULT TOPICS

research guides my pedagogical approach when teaching difficult topics. To detail this approach, I overview the ethnomusicology concentration at Bard College, the coursework offered, and examples of student work to show how reflexivity and improvisation guide ethnomusicological pedagogy at a liberal arts college. By teaching students the intellectual history of poststructuralism in ethnography since the 1980s, as led by James Clifford and George Marcus (1986), I raise awareness about reflexivity through contextualizing the social milieu of our readings and problematizing the transparency and opacity of power that ethnographers and interlocutors negotiate. Students engage scholarship about improvisation while considering examples that reveal the collective choices of individuals and groups who pursue various opportunities in time. I guide each student to acknowledge the interactive improvisivity of both social actors and structures.[2]

I have ensured that new ethnomusicology students at Bard College consider ethnographic fieldwork in terms much less accepted by their graduate student counterparts at research universities: it is as much a chance to experiment with their own being and becoming, as it is a time to explore how people theorize their lifeworlds in the social contexts of music. Bard's participation in the liberal arts model encourages interdisciplinary course readings that students ethnographically engage. However, their analytical juxtapositions of such scholarship with theory from the field frame their ethnographic writing such that it becomes not only a *bildungsroman* for themselves but also one about the experience of their fellow students. Beyond the introductory course, students pursue special topics courses in ethnomusicology that often emphasize critical improvisation studies, jazz, and American musics. The ways in which musical and extramusical improvisation suggest a social science of comparable potentials for social agents and structures, as well as how the confluence of oppression, cultural generosities, and tactics of resistance associated with becoming and being free in the United States equally inform new frameworks through which students encounter the field again. I posit that improvisation and ethnographic reflexivity can construct a specific liberal arts pedagogical model for college students.

The concentration in ethnomusicology encourages students to pursue coursework across social science and humanities divisions across the College, in addition to their studies within the Music Program. Core courses such as *Introduction to Ethnomusicology, Ethnographies of Music and Sound,* and *Field Methods in Ethnomusicology* grounds these interdisciplinary experiences. In addition, Bard ethnomusicology students take a range of special topics courses. These include *The Social Life of Loudspeakers, Sound Studies and Critical Listening, Improvisation as Social Science, Musicology Among Enslaved Americans*, as well as *Jazz Histories of Sound and Communication*. This coursework directly informs Moderation, a Bard tradition in which second-year students present projects to a board of three faculty members for consideration of a student's acceptance to the Upper College. This work also informs their senior ethnographic fieldwork projects.

CORE COURSES

The core courses introduce students to the intellectual history of ethnomusicology, focusing on the emergence, disappearances, and perpetuation of key concepts and methods across the field. In anticipation of students' final paper, Moderation, and senior project ethnography, the core courses often depict modern cosmological realms in which their interlocutors might encounter the individual, the group, as well as usual sites of structure and agency. These are helpful to students who seek methods of first producing imagery (Becker 1998) for the projects they propose;[3] however, class discussions also regularly problematize the efficacy of such depictions in representing the fluidity and complexities of social positions in practices of producing, circulating, and consuming music. These pictures also stimulate class conversations about the students' reflexive engagements in their projects, further developing their expectations of field encounters based on the consideration of their emic or etic (insider or outsider) perspectives, from moment to moment during their ethnographic inquiry. In the transitions from fieldwork to write-up, students realize a more musical and rhythmic experience of a reflexivity than the Writing Culture Turn in anthropology may have originally imagined.[4]

Working on final paper projects that normally describe campus-based musical gatherings, students often engage in participant-observations of the activities and friends with whom they are familiar. During my office hours, students comment on how these matters of balancing representations of themselves and their friends can be a gratifying challenge, and how it provides them a space to grapple with difficult topics in their everyday life.

SPECIAL TOPICS COURSES

I also design special topics courses that foreground examples of how musical people negotiate comparable dynamics in their representations of self

286   TEACHING DIFFICULT TOPICS

and other. My design is done in close conjunction with my own research and public expressions to the campus community about jazz, music, culture, and African American life. These courses suggest that there are ethnographers everywhere, reminding students to appreciate this as they grow to become increasingly collaborative with friends in the field who already theorize their cultural context.

All of the collective engagement in the field encounter anticipates reflexive ethnographic representation, and students' collaborations foreground such interactionism. As they are doing fieldwork on campus, the matter of subject position becomes complex. Bard students are conducting ethnographic research where they have already become participants—in clubs, as leaders of student organizations, members of bands, rappers, producers, and influencers. For as much as core courses work to show the various positions of ethnographer and interlocutor, what many students encounter are intimacies and shifts between the researcher and the researched. This is the substance of the Bard field encounter, and it overdetermines a richness in the description of the ethnographer's expression in the writing encouraged by special topics courses. Students often tell me that they find solace within the special topics courses. The juxtaposition of their seeking to understand musical culture on and off campus to these courses' acknowledgment that musicians and audiences of the past had negotiated a similar practice, strengthens and affirms students' resolve in their work as they pursue larger projects in ethnomusicology.

Improvisation as Social Science

One such course is *Improvisation as Social Science*. It asks the following questions: How does improvisation operate as social research? What does it mean to improvise? How do not only musicians, but also people in everyday life, and broader social structures, improvise with one another? How can critical improvisation studies shift our recognition of the phrase "jazz studies" from a noun to a declarative statement? This course provides an introduction to improvisation studies both within and beyond music. Students read, present, and discuss scholarship about improvisation while considering examples that reveal the collective choices of individuals and groups who pursue various opportunities over time. Lectures and demonstrations focus on how such examples outline "new" methodologies for qualitative social research, culminating in a paper that explores how improvisational techniques in music can inform poststructural ethnographic research and outline "new" methodologies for qualitative social research.

One important course text is Tracy McMullen's "The Improvisative" in the *Oxford Handbook of Critical Improvisation Studies.* An anthropology major enrolled in the course identified the following feature:

> McMullen writes about the improvisative as a conceptual framework missing from contemporary cultural theory. She points out the ways in which Butler, Derrida, and Hegel's concepts of performativity emphasize a distinct self/other binary that inherently leans towards prioritizing the other. While with McMullen's concept of the improvisative 'one focuses on how to give to the situation without a concern for how one is read or if one is legible.'[5] As a responsive rather than reactive mode of performance, focus is shifted towards a different form of 'other' that exists in a single isolated moment. McMullen presents various forms of situating the self in time, identifying modes through which our understanding of time has the capacity to influence the relationship to self.[6]

This improvisative function for a student of ethnography begins to reveal the epistemological expectations between the interlocutor and the ethnographer, as well as the temporality of these expectations. This course culminates in a paper that explores how improvisational techniques in music can inform ethnographic research.

Jazz Histories of Sound and Communication

Another special topics course is *Jazz Histories of Sound and Communication.* It asserts that Jazz history is plural. Beginning as histories of expressions by African descendants in the New World, their sounds and social positions have both attracted and resisted the participation of allies and oppressors in the construction of jazz as American culture. Histories such as these foreground assertions of jazz as both an American sound and the sound of something broader. The various lifeworlds of jazz—local and global, past and present—lead to questions about the music's folk, popular, and art music categorization. Through a framework of exploring the history of jazz through specific sounds and surrogate communications, this course surveys the development of musical aesthetics set within specific social contexts that reveal how improvisation wields the production and reception of sounds and

288   TEACHING DIFFICULT TOPICS

communications within and beyond the bandstand. Students in the survey course read, present, and discuss writing about jazz and its periods. Lectures situate specific media examples of performances across folk, popular, and art contexts, in ways that also foreground the significance of individual and group agency. Examples of race, gender, class, nationality, generation, and their intersections in jazz music are the focus of the final research paper assignment.

One text that explores the multi-modal agency of a jazz musician is Robert O'Meally's "Checking Our Balances: Louis Armstrong, Ralph Ellison, and Betty Boop" in *Uptown Conversation*. In response to it, an ethnomusicology major noted the discussion of how some African American performers hide with the use of humor as masks. The student cited O'Meally's reference of Armstrong and Boop cartoons, where this kind of masking held power over racist oppressors. For Armstrong, the student noted, the use of performative smiling subverted his oppressor's power. Through a framework of exploring the history of jazz through specific sounds and surrogate communications like Armstrong's smile, this course surveys the development of musical aesthetics set within specific social contexts that reveal how improvisation wields the production and reception of sounds and communications within and beyond the bandstand.

After years of success, this course led to the development of *Musicology Among Enslaved Americans*. In this seminar, we study the music of African Americans as foundational to musical culture within the United States, and continually symbolic of notions of American exceptionalism around the world. Negotiating a gruesome exploitation that would fund the wealth of the nation, enslaved Americans of African descent expressed features of what this music would become, with great care. Scholars frequently categorize the musicality of the enslaved into sacred and secular forms, mainly the blues and the spirituals. They debate matters of authenticity, meaning, survival, and beauty. However, this course asks the following question: What was the hermeneutical music discourse among enslaved African Americans? This question marks the beginning of a proper ethnomusicological inquiry, as it expects an assertion of a people's own theorizations of music's social and cultural contexts to challenge or confirm the extant literature of related scholarship. How would they respond to the contrast between W. E. B. DuBois and Zora Neale Hurston regarding what she called "neo-spirituals?" How could their expressions about precursors to blues and jazz differently engage Amiri Baraka and Gunther Schuller? Led directly by examples of slave narratives, other course readings include autobiography, as well as the accounts of abolitionists and Union officers. Lectures and demonstrations focus on how such examples relate to twentieth and twenty-first century discourses.

One example that we examined in both *Jazz Histories of Sound and Communication* and *Musicology Among Enslaved Americans* was the work of saxophonist Kenny Garrett and his ensemble. Garrett, one of the important saxophonists of John Coltrane's lineage, asserts forms of African cultural retentions through his improvisations. In his music, such as the album *Standard of Language*, one might hear the near vocal expressions of pentatonic and diatonic scales in ways that both put forward a linguistic example of a modal and impressionistic speech surrogacy, as well as an almost dramatic portrayal of an African descendant's virtuosic negotiations with Western tonality. Amid the driving and dialogic syncopations inserted by the members of the ensemble, the often richly complex harmonic accompaniment of Garrett's melodies further emotionally contextualizes the listener's encounter with the challenges and triumphs that his improvisations conjure. For example, moments of extended repetition and exclamation evoke the practice of the ring shout that took place in settings such as the Jamestown Settlement extending late into the period of the American Civil War. These choreographed circular movements and repeated musical accompaniment were a practice by which Africans experimented with transitions from polytheism or Islam to Protestant Christianity in the Americas. Garrett's example of improvisation and human agency form a significant facet of social life in contemporary jazz.

SENIOR PROJECT EXAMPLES

Students have incorporated approaches that they learned in core and special topics courses into their required senior projects, and I offer examples from the spring 2019, 2020, and 2021 semesters to exemplify students' varied engagements with concept and method in their independent work. All senior projects at Bard are cataloged within the College's library, which is available to the public. The excerpts below are taken from three students' published projects, and used with their permission. I mean to portray how teaching difficult topics during these semesters of intense, wide-ranging global reckonings inspired this student research. I have observed that the ethnographic work of ethnomusicology students map values for reflexivity and improvisation from their coursework in distinct ways.

TEACHING DIFFICULT TOPICS

Maia Kamil, Spring 2019

Maia Kamil drew from her coursework in shaping her senior project. In "Why The Scared Sing: 'Stage-Fright' as a Rite of Passage," Kamil studied stage fright in indie rock performance to "... begin deconstructing the cultural structures that define and perpetuate fear on stage in [an] attempt to avoid its elimination. Through reframing our understanding of stage-fright and looking at new shared understandings of what musical performance is, fear no longer has to be seen as crippling but a crucial phenomenon in the process of performance and life." Her analysis goes on to consider the following:

> In conversing with my interlocutors, it has become evident that—recalling Arthur van Gennep's framework—the majority of them have yet to fully cross through either the separation, or in some cases, the liminal stages of their individual rites of passage. Although each encompasses a sincere urge to sing and exhibit their musical talent—in varying ways—they have found themselves almost trapped within overwhelming feelings of alienation whereby as a result they delegitimize themselves as singers. It seems as though the participants, especially those from marginalized backgrounds, are consumed in the whirlwind of performance-based fears and have as of yet to share their truest musicality—by which I mean the musical self most representative of themselves—with others. This sense of panic and foreboding become amplified to the point of no longer being mere hindrances, but full-on obstructions that cyclically perpetuate their reluctances to perform. Many of the informants I have spoken to who experience stage-fright find themselves almost incapable of piercing through the walls of the second and third stage of van Gennep's model: (a) they remain in either the separation phase, where they undergo an alienation from their social body, or (b) embody this sense of liminality and thus are never entirely steadfast and confident in their musical capabilities.[7]

Kamil's analysis of stage fright ethnographically juxtaposes Arnold van Gennep's studies of rites of passage and Victor Turner's liminality in relation to Thomas Turino's consideration of Bourdieu's habitus and De Certeau's tactics. These were topics that we discussed in the Bard ethnomusicology core course *Ethnography: Music and Sound.*

Zoë Peterschild Ford, Spring 2020

Zoë Peterschild Ford's senior project showcases concepts and methods from Improvisation as Social Science. In "The Ethos of the Blues: An Ethnography of Blues Singers and Writers" Peterschild Ford studied a blues singer based in Montreal, tracing what she theorizes as a "blues ethos." She wrote, "What I call the 'ethos of the blues' refers to a blues spirit that exists not only in music, but in literature, and in everyday life," and Peterschild Ford argues that this singer's ". . . practice reveals that blues is a music that values protective, generous, and exploratory narrative." Her extended overview is as follows:

> This paper addresses, through the example of Dawn Tyler Watson, the symbiosis of literature and music, structural constraints and agentive outlets in the popular music industry, and the construction of musical narratives, both improvised and not. In the first chapter I will describe the trip I took to Montreal during which I first encountered Dawn, and I will discuss Tracy McMullen's themes of improvisation and generosity in jazz. In the second chapter I will address the second concert, a disco-oriented dance music set, as it relates to Phillip Auslander and expressions of personhood. In the third chapter I will talk about the third concert, a performance of Dawn's original music with an eight piece blues band, and Robert O'Meally's work on the connection between music and literature.
>
> When I first engaged this project the only thing I knew for sure was that it would connect with the blues. And it could have gone many ways. The first time I went to Montreal explicitly for this project, I had no idea of what I would find and what I would and could make of it. But Dawn and a highfalutin' handful of scholars and writers and professors helped me along the way. This is how it unfolded. My project itself is an improvisation within a world of improvisation—the world of the blues.[8]

As Peterschild Ford's project developed, I observed how she discussed reflexivity and improvisation in her analysis. For example, she wrote:

> As I consider Dawn and the ways in which a blues singer must wrestle with the frustrations of structure, I wonder about the way I'm writing this ethnography, too. The negotiations of structure and agency, as a blues singer in Quebec or as an ethnomusicology student in New York, are as opaque as genre or improvisation. What of this writing is fabrication for the sake of satisfying the institution and the reader and what are the words that I really can't keep

292 TEACHING DIFFICULT TOPICS

off the page. How could anyone (even me) parse it out? Part of the irony of performance is that no one person can ever truly know which permutation of a performer exists at any given time on a stage or a page.[9]

The importance of agency emerged in Peterschild Ford's ethnographic study of improvisation. Among people in the music industry, artists, and journalists, she articulated how blues performance constructed a way for this artist to navigate industry and assert her autonomy.

Matice Maino, Spring 2021

Matice Maino's senior project, "Hip-Hopping Over the Great Firewall of China" explores how Chinese students studying at Bard interact with and participate in Chinese Hip Hop and what this participation reveals about ". . . class, race and regionalization in the age of digitized communication." He reflected:

> Up until writing this paper, I had blindly embraced the benefits of a technology that had irrefutably changed the social fabrics of my generation. . . . I am thus resolved to study ways in which the Internet serves as a pathway for the increasing globalization we are witnessing, and how younger generations' connections to the outside world have changed. . . . I decided to focus on the rise of Hip Hop within China, an ongoing phenomenon that has skyrocketed since 2017. As an avid musician and Hip Hop lover, I strongly gravitated to the area of study of Global Hip Hop and how culture has left its U.S. original home to serve as a platform of expression for youth around the world. Through the lenses of Hip Hop, we can trace ways in which youth around the world interact with global trends, and how senses of locality and globalization are navigated with the assistance of the Internet.[10]

This project followed Maino's coursework in *Ethnography: Music and Sound,* and our conversations about James Reese Europe and the globalization of jazz in Paris during World War I. Maino ethnographically observed how international Chinese students at Bard experience Chinese Hip Hop amid the genre's global popularity, especially how it relates to "marginalized youth identity" and digital censorship.[11]

THE ORCHESTRA NOW (TŌN) GRADUATE SEMINAR

My pedagogy also encourages graduate students to consider the autodidactic practices of the AACM. In addition to senior projects, my experiences teaching The Orchestra Now (TŌN) graduate seminar offered similar opportunities to draw upon reflexivity and improvisation. Members of *The Orchestra Now*, or TŌN, are professional orchestral musicians at Bard who earn a Master's degree through the development of projects that express curatorial engagements with music, history, performance life, contemporary practices of self-promotion, and social media representation. I encouraged students to consider the autodidactic approaches to the Association for the Advancement of Creative Musicians, as historicized by George Lewis in *A Power Stronger Than Itself*. The AACM's collective of musicians have never sought to conform to a singular style. They have maintained a community discourse that privileges and encourages its members and groups to define their own identities, paying special attention to tactics of avoiding constrictive industrial categorization.

Though TŌN is an entirely different ensemble with an entirely different set of goals and values, the course provided an opportunity to introduce TŌN musicians to groups like the AACM. The seminar encouraged independent research and communal discourse with a guiding principle to embrace interdisciplinarity. Students learned how the AACM members regard improvisation that engages musical and extramusical practices of self-representation, particularly in expressive contexts where AACM members seek to distinguish themselves.

This approach of TŌN calls attention to the growing matriculations of contemporary undergraduates into graduate programs. The ways that social generation or birth cohorts progress from elite liberal arts settings into advanced graduate study, and the collective experience of the Internet and new media lifeworlds, have a role in shaping intimacy between reflexivity and improvisation. Any sense of a collective sensibility about this intimacy will progress into the research institution setting where a similar pedagogical approach may be needed in ethnomusicological futures.

CONCLUSION

I continue to build upon this intellectual foundation, fusing undergraduate and graduate teaching and research. While my teaching is centered in music, its scope reaches throughout the humanities and social sciences. I have been

294   TEACHING DIFFICULT TOPICS

able to both appeal to students' interests in popular culture and attract them to classic paradigms and recent scholarship. At Bard, I have been intentional about not training future ethnomusicologists per se, but basing my pedagogical approach in a liberal arts exploration of paradigmatic tensions with academic studies of music's social context. My developments in critical pedagogy are in conversation with the current international racial reckoning. Facilitating studies of the rich intellectual foundations of expressive culture for Bard meets students where they are, and guides their intellectual growth, through reflexivity and improvisation.

Notes

1. Nikole Hannah-Jones, "1619 Project," *New York Times Magazine*, August 14, 2019, https://www.nytimes.com/interactive/2019/08/14/magazine/1619-america-slavery .html

2. This is informed by expressions of George Lewis and the ways that they are additionally explored in George Lewis and Benjamin Piekut, eds., *The Oxford Handbook of Critical Improvisation Studies, Volume 1* (Oxford: Oxford University Press, 2016).

3. Howard Becker, *Tricks of the Trade: How to Think about your Research While You're Doing It* (Chicago: University of Chicago Press, 2008 [1998]).

4. The Writing Culture volume challenged anthropology and related fields to consider the motivation, bias, and literary voice in ethnographic analysis. See James Clifford and George E. Marcus, eds., *Writing Culture: The Poetics and Politics of Ethnography* (Berkeley: University of California Press, 1986).

5. Tracy McMullen, "The Improvisative" in *The Oxford Handbook of Critical Improvisation Studies* Volume 1, edited by George E. Lewis and Benjamin Piekut (Oxford: Oxford University Press, 2016), 123.

6. Anonymous student paper.

7. Maia Kamil, "Why The Scared Sing: 'Stage-Fright' as a Rite of Passage" (Senior Projects Spring 2019), 30 https://digitalcommons.bard.edu/senproj_s2019/2

8. Zoë Emilie Peterschild Ford, 2020. "The Ethos of the Blues: An Ethnography of Blues Singers and Writers" (Senior Projects Spring 2020), 9. https://digitalcommons .bard.edu/senproj_s2020/218

9. Ford, "The Ethos of the Blues," 21.

10. Matice F. Maino, "Hip-Hopping Over the Great Firewall of China: Authenticity, Language and Race in the Global Hip Hop Nation" (Senior Projects Spring 2021), 1–2. https://digitalcommons.bard.edu/senproj_s2021/81

11. Maino, "Hip-Hopping Over the Great Firewall of China," 5.

Works Cited

Becker, Howard. *Tricks of the Trade: How to Think about your Research While You're Doing It.* Chicago: University of Chicago Press, 2008 [1998].

Clifford, James, and George E. Marcus, eds. *Writing Culture: The Poetics and Politics of Ethnography.* Berkeley: University of California Press, 1986.

Ford, Zoë Emilie Peterschild. "The Ethos of the Blues: An Ethnography of Blues Singers and Writers." Senior Projects Spring 2020. https://digitalcommons.bard.edu/senproj_s2020/218

Kamil, Maia. "Why The Scared Sing: 'Stage-Fright' as a Rite of Passage." Senior Projects Spring 2019. https://digitalcommons.bard.edu/senproj_s2019/2

Lewis, George E., and Benjamin Piekut, eds. *The Oxford Handbook of Critical Improvisation Studies, Volume 1.* Oxford: Oxford University Press, 2016.

Maino, Matice F. "Hip-Hopping Over the Great Firewall of China: Authenticity, Language and Race in the Global Hip Hop Nation." Senior Projects Spring 2021. https://digitalcommons.bard.edu/senproj_s2021/81

McMullen, Tracy. "The Improvisative." In *Oxford Handbook of Critical Improvisation Studies,* edited by George E. Lewis and Benjamin Piekut, Volume 1, 115–27. Oxford: Oxford University Press, 2016.

O'Meally, Robert G. "Checking Our Balances: Louis Armstrong, Ralph Ellison, and Betty Boop." In *Uptown Conversation: The New Jazz Studies,* edited by Robert G. O'Meally, Brent Hayes Edwards, and Farah Jasmine Griffin, 278–96. New York: Columbia University Press, 2004.

Contributors

Philip Ewell is a professor of music theory at Hunter College of the City University of New York. His specialties include Russian music theory, Russian opera, modal theory, set theory, rap and hiphop, and race studies in music.

Jessica Grimmer is a musicologist specializing in late 19th and 20th-century cultural history whose work centers on the relationships between music, institutions, and political discourse.

Kelsey Klotz is currently Assistant Professor of Musicology and Ethnomusicology at the University of Maryland, College Park, where she teaches courses in popular music and jazz. Her previously published work includes a book, *Dave Brubeck and the Performance of Whiteness*, and articles on Miles Davis, the Modern Jazz Quartet, Kenny G, and Dave Brubeck.

Olivia R. Lucas is currently Assistant Professor of Music Theory at Louisiana State University, where she teaches courses in music theory and popular music. She has previously published articles and chapters on metal music, concert light shows, and the music of Nicki Minaj.

As Head of the Theodore M. Finney Music Library, **Christopher Lynch** helps curate the University of Pittsburgh Library System's Stephen C. Foster museum and archive.

Megan Lyons is currently Assistant Professor of Music Theory at Furman University in Greenville, South Carolina where she teaches the core curriculum and upper-level theory electives. Beyond her work in music theory pedagogy, her research explores the alternate guitar tunings of Joni Mitchell and text-music interactions of female singer-songwriters.

Breana H. McCullough is a graduate student in the department of ethnomusicology at the UCLA, where she studies and works toward self-determination and sovereignty through the re-Matriation of cultural material pertaining

Contributors

to music and beyond. McCullough is an avid performer of the baroque and modern viola where she cultivates performance spaces that empower Indigenous ways of being, knowing, and understanding.

Sean M. Parr is Professor of Music at Saint Anselm College where he teaches music history and voice performance, as well as humanities courses in the core curriculum. His research interests focus on nineteenth-century opera, the operatic voice, dance, gender, and race, and he recently published his first book, *Vocal Virtuosity: The Origins of the Coloratura Soprano in Nineteenth-Century Opera* (Oxford University Press, 2021).

John Pippen teaches courses on music history and ethnomusicology at Colorado State University, where he is currently Assistant Professor of Music. His research applies theories of class and labor to contemporary classical music groups in Chicago.

As a Principal Lecturer at the University of North Texas, **April L. Prince** designs and teaches courses for non-majors. Her recent publications focus on the iconography of Clara Schumann and the music of early country music women, Roba Stanley and Rosa Lee Carson.

Laura Moore Pruett is Associate Professor of Music at Merrimack College in North Andover, Massachusetts, and has published on the life and music of Louis Moreau Gottschalk as well as transformational pedagogy. In her work both inside and outside the classroom, she seeks balance at the intersections of art, history, teaching, and reflection.

Colette Simonot-Maiello is currently Associate Professor of Musicology at the University of Manitoba in Winnipeg, Manitoba, Canada, where she teaches courses in musicology and ethnomusicology. Her scholarship includes presentations and publications on politics, gender, and religion in modern Canadian and French opera, and music history pedagogy.

Whitney Slaten is Associate Professor of Music at Bard College where he teaches ethnomusicological field methods and ethnography. Ethnographic participation in music festivals informs his scholarship that contributes to the discourses of ethnomusicology, the historiography of American music, sound and technology, and critical improvisation studies.

Contributors 299

Annalise Smith currently teaches courses in musical theatre, opera, and music history at Memorial University of Newfoundland and Labrador. She also serves as the Project Coordinator for the Research Centre for the Study of Music, Media, and Place.

Everette Scott Smith is Assistant Professor of Instruction in Double Reeds and Musicology at Southeastern Louisiana University. His publications and research center around the life and works of John Cage, and the published works of minoritized composers in 19th-century New Orleans.

John Spilker-Beed, Associate Professor of Music and affiliate faculty in gender studies and interdisciplinary studies at Nebraska Wesleyan University, has transformed the study of music history through a transdisciplinary case-study approach that prizes care pedagogy and intersectional equity. He is co-editor of *Sound Pedagogy: Radical Care in Music* (Univ. of Illinois Press, 2024), and his research on dissonant counterpoint and Henry Cowell has been published in *American Music* and the *Journal of the Society for American Music*.

Trudi Wright is an Associate Professor and the Music Program Director at Regis University where she investigates the relationship between music and culture with her students. Wright's most current research in teaching music history can be read in her co-edited essay collection, *Sound Pedagogy: Radical Care in Music* (University of Illinois Press, 2024).

Index

1619 Project. See Hannah-Jones, Nikole
20 Feet from Stardom (documentary), 47

Absher, Amy, 23
activism, 5, 7, 109, 113, 187, 266; extraactivism, 149, 158; opera as, 95
Adorno, Theodor, 41
Afzal-Khan, Fawzia, 105
agency, human, 191, 289; student, 9, 33, 37, 40, 45–46, 52–55, 59, 278, 285, 288, 291–92
American Alliance of Museums, 64
analysis, critical race, 227
Angola, 65
antiracist, 61–62, 185–87, 190–91, 193, 197–98, 240
anti-police, 67
antisemitism, 238
anxiety, 4, 54, 115, 128, 169, 195
Arao, Brian, 192
Ardern, Jacinda, 214
Arendt, Hannah, 41
arts entrepreneurship. *See* entrepreneurship, arts
assignment(s), 7, 47–48, 50, 52–53, 57n10, 57n13, 58n22, 62–63, 67–68, 70, 112–16, 118, 120, 122–25, 126n6, 185, 190–91, 194

Baamaaya, 65
Balatri, Filippo, 86
band, military, 66; President's Own, 66
Baraka, Amiri, 47, 56n7, 288
Barclay, Jennifer, 21

Barkley, Elizabeth, 113
Barnett, Pamela, 62, 73n28
Bartoli, Cecilia, 81
Baumgardner, Astrid, 15
Beeching, Angela Myles, 14, 24n5
bel canto, 259
Bell, Lee Ann, 190–91, 203n48
Bennett, Dawn, 19–20, 24n4
Berg, Maggie, 168–69, 178n6
Bizet, Georges, 84; *Les pêcheurs de perles*, 84
blackface, 21, 52–53, 55, 59n22, 66, 68, 112, 115, 117–19, 187, 200n17, 226, 232, 239, 255, 257, 259–60, 264, 266
Black Lives Matter, 41, 115, 121, 197
Black Power, 66, 189
Blampied, Neville M., 216
"Blurred Lines," 50
Bonilla-Silva, Eduardo, 231
Braiding Sweetgrass, 158
Bright, William, 148–49
Brown, Michael, 66–67
Brown, Will, 188
Browner, Tara, 154, 164n5
Bruenger, David, 17–18, 20–22
Burney, Charles, 86
Burney, Susan, 87
Burnim, Mellonee V., 189
Butler, Judith, 79, 287
Byrd, Donald, 278–80
Byrd, Joseph, 252

cabaletta, 83
Canada/Canadian, 7–8, 132–42, 249n2

302   *Index*

canon, 16, 22, 37, 61, 64, 95, 107, 112, 131, 143n2, 151, 161, 228, 239, 249n1, 258

capitalist/capitalism, 6, 13–14, 18–20, 158, 190–91, 197

capoeira, 65

castrato/castrati, 78–82, 84–88, 89n4

Champagne, Claude, 137; *Altitude*, 137

Chance, Michael, 81

Charlottesville (Virginia), 39–40. *See also* white supremacy

Chase, Claire, 14

Cheng, William, 5, 9n4, 189–90, 212, 221–2, 238, 272n3

Chicagou, Agapit, 154

Chicks, The (Dixie Chicks, The), 66

choice, creator, 105, 254, 258, 266, 280; student, 21, 52–54, 81, 96, 115, 120, 123–25, 132, 159–60, 173–74, 177, 197, 284, 286

choral, 168, 177n4

Chu, Erica, 191–92

Church, Catholic, 80, 169

Christofellis, Aris, 81

Christy, Edwin P., 255–56, 265, 267

cishetero, 96

classes, large-enrollment, 45–46, 49, 53, 56n1, 127n14

Clemens, Kristi, 192

climate, change of 1; political 66, 282

J. Cole, 54, 59n24

Coleridge-Taylor, Samuel, 281

Collier, Amy, 175

colonialism, post-colonialism, 132, 141

Commission, Truth and Reconciliation (TRC)

Compendium Musicae, 151

composers of color, 20, 227–30, 234, 236, 240–46

construct, social, 45, 71n9, 77–80, 85, 127n11, 153, 221, 253–54, 263, 266, 287, 291–92

contralto, 87; heroes *en travestie*, 82

Corelli, Franco, 83

Cornelius, Steven, 63, 65. *See also* Natvig, Mary

Cotton, Tom, 189

countertenor, 81

curriculum, 45, 64, 70, 116, 126n2, 127n8, 127n14, 128n18, 132, 134–36, 188, 226, 235, 238n3, 278

Crenshaw, Kimberlé Williams, 47, 153

criticism, 19, 99, 108n13, 128n21

Cross, K. Patricia, 113

Ice Cube, 172

culture, 6, 33, 35, 40–41, 61–64, 68–69, 95, 97–98, 106–7, 108n13, 285–8, 292, 294; African, 65; Brazilian, 65; Middle Eastern, 99; Muslim, 105–6, 108n8; South Asian, 105; Western, 106

Cusick, Suzanne, 98, 213–14, 221

Csikszentmihalyi, Mihaly, 169

Dagbamba, 65

David, Giovanni, 82

Davis, Lori Patton, 2

decolonize, 8, 112, 131–32, 134–35, 140, 142, 143n10, 144n13

Diamond, Beverley, 138, 144n16

DiAngelo, Robin, 61, 67, 69, 73n2

diversity, 45. *See also* inclusion

discussion, 2–3, 5, 7–9, 23n1, 33–38, 40–43, 45, 47–49, 52–53, 58n22, 62–63, 65–70, 73n34, 77, 79, 84–85, 89n2, 101, 104, 107n1, 107n6, 112–15, 118, 136–37, 141, 169, 172–73, 175, 178n7, 192–94, 212–24, 216, 218, 220–21, 223n6, 223n10, 227, 238–39, 255, 257, 263, 281–83, 285, 288

Donzelli, Domenico, 82

Dorahy, Martin J., 216

Douglass, Frederick, 62, 121, 265–66

Du Bois, W. E. B., 187

Duprez, Gilbert-Louis, 82–83

DWYL ("do what you love"), 14–17, 19. *See also* entrepreneurship, arts

education, 4–6, 9n4, 13, 15, 19, 22, 37, 46,
51, 56nn1–3, 57n10, 65, 67, 106, 112–3,
116, 126n2, 127n6, 127n8, 127n14, 134,
143n10, 144n11, 167, 178n6, 185–88, 190–
91, 195–97, 198n3, 204n61, 220, 226–27
Eidsheim, Nina Sun, 21
Ellison, Ralph, 47, 56n7, 288
Enlightenment, 82
enslavement, 254–55
entrepreneurship; arts,13–6, 18–22, 24n12
epistemology, 161–62
equity, 51, 56, 68, 70, 159, 185, 187, 189–91,
193, 195–98, 205n69, 219, 231
Ermolaeva, Katya, 232, 238
Estill, Adriana, 66
ethnographer, 9, 280, 284, 286–87
ethnomusicology, 136, 138–42, 144,
145n17, 145n20, 278–81, 283–86, 288–91
Eurocentric, 61, 64, 132–33, 138, 151, 159
Ewell, Phillip, 9, 200n18, 231, 249n5, 257
examen, 169–77, 178n9, 179n11, 179n14,
179n19
exercises, spiritual, 170–71

faculty, 57n11, 134–35, 144, 168–86

9, 171, 193–96, 217, 219, 282, 285; contingent, 15, 46; development of, 4; music,
186, 190; tenured, 5, 46
Faiz, 97, 100
falsetto, 81–82, 84
Farinelli; *Son qual Nave,* 86
Fassbaender, Brigitte, 81
Feagin, Joe, 62, 233
feedback, 41, 49–50, 52, 54, 56, 61, 68–69,
115, 120, 124, 128n21, 193, 195, 197, 228
Feldman, Martha, 82, 89n4
feminine/femininity, 79, 81, 84, 108, 152,
263
Florida, Richard, 18
flow, 169
Foster, Stephen, 9, 227, 231–33, 238–

39, 252–63, 265–66, 272n7, 272n9,
273nn16–7, 274nn25–6, 274n29
fragility, 2; white, 69
Big Freedia, 65
Freitas, Roger, 81
Franklin, Aretha, 53
Frisch, Walter, 143n2, 255–56
Fussell, Peter, 18

G-Unit, 67
Gannon, Kevin M., 175, 179n27
Gardner, Eric, 67
Garrett, Kenny, 279, 289
Gates, Jr., Henry Louis, 189
Gedda, Nicolai, 84
gender, 1–5, 7, 15, 21, 47–50, 61–62, 64–65,
67–69, 77–81, 84–86, 88, 96, 112, 114–15,
123, 131, 141, 152–53, 192, 196–97, 226–27,
229, 230–31, 234, 239–40, 263, 288
genocide, 39, 42–3, 133, 149, 185
Ghana, 65
ghetto, 34, 42
Gibney, Shannon, 68, 73n36
Giddens, Rhiannon, 53, 114, 118–19
globalization, 167–8, 175, 292
Gordon, Bonnie, 101
Graña, César, 18
gypsy, 37

Haggard, Merle, 52, 59
Hannah-Jones, Nikole, 186; *1619 Project,*
282
Harding, Charlie, 47, 49
Harris, Jasmine L., 192
Harris, Luke Charles, 71n5
health, mental, 35, 41, 59n22, 115
hegemony, 61, 189, 197, 231
Hendrix, Jimi, 66
heteropatriarchy, 152
Hill, Lauryn; "Black Rage," 67
Hispanic, 114. *See also* Latinx
historiography, 136, 138–39, 141–42, 266

304   *Index*

Hoefnagels, Anna, 138–39
Holiday, Billie, 49; "Strange Fruit," 114
Holocaust, 3, 6, 33–42
homophobia, 1
hooks, bell, 195
Horne, Marilyn, 81–82
Hurston, Zora Neale, 22, 280, 288
hybrid, 138
hypermasculinity, 65

identity, 2–3, 41, 47, 50, 56n3, 65, 70, 71n9,
    78, 81, 85, 89n2, 123, 137–38, 152, 189–92,
    231, 238, 240, 292
Ignatius (of Loyola), 170–71
improvisation, 9, 278, 280, 282, 284, 286–
    89, 291–94
incarceration, 186
inclusion, 9, 47–48, 52, 61, 66, 69–70, 143,
    161, 197, 220, 227, 232, 235, 238, 257, 274.
    See also diversity
Inclusive Museum Project, The, 64
Indigenous, 8, 132–41, 143n2, 143n8,
    144n11, 148–64, 186, 196–97, 222n2,
    298
individual, 1–2, 13–17, 20–23, 36, 38, 40,
    45–46, 53–55, 63, 65, 69, 108n13, 112–13,
    127n11, 131, 138, 140, 148–49, 153, 164,
    169–70, 190–91, 216, 218, 260, 284–86,
    288, 290
industrialization, 263
Islamophobia, 213

Jaroussky, Philippe, 81–82
jazz, 42, 47, 57n9, 64, 131, 185, 199n6, 235,
    278–92
Jesuit(s), 155, 167, 169–71, 174–75, 177n2,
    178n9, 179nn10–1, 179n18
Jewish, 39, 41, 43, 44n2
justice, 5, 7, 46, 95, 98–99, 109n19, 114–15,
    121, 133–34, 143n10, 185–91, 198, 199n6,
    200–201n21, 203n48, 204n53, 220
Joplin, Scott, 20–23; *Treemonisha,* 22

Kahn, Coppélia, 96
Kajikawa, Loren, 62, 71n5, 71n9, 188–89
Kernahan, Cyndi, 69
kinship, 149–50, 153, 162–63
Koskoff, Ellen, 139.
Ku Klux Klan, 63

labor, 1, 6, 13–23, 25n23, 26n29, 26n34, 52,
    143n4, 198, 254
language, 40, 46, 50, 67, 97, 105, 116, 133–
    34, 143n10, 148, 152–53, 213, 220, 222
Larner, Wendy, 215–16, 223n4
Laqueur, Thomas, 80
Latinx, 39, 107n7. *See also* Hispanic
learning, 1–2, 7, 9, 20, 34, 36–37, 48–49, 52,
    56n1, 57n10, 58n21, 61–64, 67–70, 96,
    101, 112–16, 119, 126n6, 148–49, 151–52,
    157–58, 167, 169, 175, 179n17, 185, 188,
    190–98, 201n27, 215, 218–19, 239, 252,
    278
Leoncavallo, Ruggero; *Pagliacci,* 100
Levine, Adam, 83
Levine, James, 109n17
Levitz, Tamara, 132, 141
LGBTQIA+, 131, 152, 170
López, Ian Haney, 259
Louisiana State Penitentiary, 65
Loewen, James W., 249n1, 257
lynching, 49, 186–88
lyrebird, 214

Mai, Mukhtar, 95–101, 106, 107n6, 108n11
Major, Claire Howell, 113
Maniaci, Michael, 81
Martin, Henry, 188
Martin, James, 170–72, 175, 179n19
Martin, Trayvon, 67
Marsalis, Wynton, 185
masculine/masculinity, 77–79, 81–82,
    84–85, 96, 152
Maultsby, Portia K., 189
Mercure de France, 156–57

Index 305

methods, field, 284–85; improvisational, 291; research, 148, 152, 198n1; teaching, 113, 134, 193, 221

Mexico City, 167

mezzo-soprano, 85

McGill, Anthony, 185

middle-class, 3, 13–14, 252, 258, 260, 265

Mintz, Steven, 116

Minstrelsy. *See* songs

Miranda, Lin-Manuel, 186

modality, 45

Monáe, Janelle, 47, 49–50, 52, 55, 59; *Dirty Computer*, 55

Moore, Leonard, 66

Moreschi, Alessandro, 81–82

Morrison, Beth, 104, 107n6

Morrison, Matthew, 232

Morrison, Toni, 222

mosque, 212–13, 222

movement, Civil Rights, 2, 23

Movement, #MeToo, 95, 106, 239

Movement, Rhodes Must Fall, 132

Mozart, Wolfgang Amadeus, 228–30, 239; *Abduction from the Seraglio, The*, 97; *Don Giovanni*, 96, 107n1; *Marriage of Figaro, The*, 99

Music Appreciation (class), 7, 61–64, 69, 72n17, 112, 127n8

music, American; Canadian; degenerate, 34, 42; nineteenth-century, 16, 21, 80, 82–85, 114–21; popular, 136–44; protest, 53, 66, 118–19

musici, 80, 86

musicking, 114, 126n4, 128n21, 190

myth, 43, 81, 108n14, 258, 272n9

narrative, 2, 8–9, 15, 19, 22, 61, 64, 109n22, 113–14, 119, 126n3, 131, 136–41, 144n14–15, 145n16, 157, 160–61, 186, 188, 252–53, 266, 280, 282, 288, 291

nationalism, 66, 218; multicultural, 138; transnationalism, 138

Napoléon, 82

Natvig, Mary, 63, 65

neoliberalism, 13–14, 20

neo-Nazi, 39

Nettl, Bruno; *Heartland Excursions*, 62

New Orleans, 20, 64, 69, 72n18, 127n14; Bounce music, 65

Nicolás, Adolpho, 167, 177n2

Nicolas, Louis, 155

Nicholls, Thomas C., 64, 72n18

NWA, 169

Nytch, Jeffrey, 14, 16

Okun, Tema, 194

Oluo, Ijeoma, 65

O'Malley, John W., 170

opera, 7, 20, 22, 42, 77–86, 89n2, 89n10, 95–101, 104–7, 108n10, 114, 116, 151, 154, 159–60, 187, 200n17, 238, 259

oppression, 1, 19, 23, 62, 65, 67, 70, 112, 152–53, 191–92, 197, 284

Order, Catholic, 169

von Otter, Anne Sofie, 81

Pakistan, 95, 98–100, 105–6, 108n11, 110n24

pandemic, 1, 51–52, 54, 56n1, 57n8, 57n10, 57n12–13, 58n22, 59n24, 167–68, 177n4, 195–96, 217, 239

Papal States, 80

paranoid, 221

Parton, Dolly, 53, 244

passaggio, 83

pedagogy, 4–5, 8, 51, 54, 57n11, 66, 126n4, 136, 140, 158–60, 178n6, 179n11, 179n17, 190, 196, 198, 216–7, 222, 257–58, 281, 283–84, 293–94 (Ignatian)

People, Spirit, 157–58

Picca, Leslie Houts, 62

Pittsburgh New Music Ensemble, 14

Potter, Will, 287

power(s), 5–7, 18, 20–23, 50, 53–54, 66, 82, 87, 89n10, 101, 106, 113, 119, 126n4, 138, 140, 143n4, 152, 158–60, 170, 172, 186, 189–91, 203n47, 221–22, 231, 250n11, 256, 280, 284, 288; dynamics, 5, 7

Powers, Ann, 64, 117

Price, Florence, 230, 247–48, 249n6, 282

privilege(s), 2, 13, 45, 62, 67, 69, 139–40, 189, 192–94, 197, 218, 220, 231, 252–54, 279, 293

publishing, sheet music, 252, 254, 258, 260–61

queer, 4, 50, 55, 65, 190

Quintanilla-Pérez, Selena, 53

Quran, 106

Rabideau, Mark, 16–17, 19

race/racism, 2, 4–5, 7, 15, 20–22, 23n1, 45, 47–48, 50–51, 61–63, 65–66, 68–69, 71n6, 73n36, 123, 141, 153, 161, 194, 212, 218, 220, 226–27, 230, 234, 239–40, 254–55, 257, 266; critical studies of, 5–6, 8–9, 15, 190; unconscious, 61; backstage, 62, 70n5

Radano, Ronald, 21, 250n11

rally, 39–40

Rameau, Jean-Phillipe, 151, 154–55, 160; Galentes, Les Indes, 154, 157, 162–63; Savages, Les, 159, 164n5

Rap, 54, 65, 220, 286

rape, 7, 95–101, 103–7, 107n7, 108n11, 109n22–109n23, 219

Rape of Lucretia, 100

Reclamation Project, The, 112, 115–16, 127n6, 128n21

reflection, 3–5, 35, 40, 46, 53, 58n22, 115–16, 122, 125, 148, 151, 154, 159–60, 168–77, 178n6, 194, 215, 238n2

reflexivity, 9, 278, 280, 284–85, 289, 291, 293–94

remix, 7, 113, 115, 120, 123–25

Remix Project, The, 113–14, 122, 127n6

representation, 50, 72n16, 88, 98, 101, 109n21, 115–16, 156, 159–61, 226, 235, 239, 266, 285–86, 293

reparative, 186–87, 212–13, 221

resilience, 5, 8, 153

resistance, 34, 43, 62, 66, 97

Re-write, Re-right, re-rite, 164

Romani/Roma, 37

rondeau, 154

Ross, Jen, 175, 180n27

Rousseau, Jean-Jacques, 85

safety, 4, 51, 54, 79, 168

Sancho, Ignatius, 242

Sankaram, Kamala, 7, 95, 100

Scharff, Christina, 15

science, social, 34, 143n10, 219, 278, 283–86, 291, 293

Sedgwick, Eve Kosofsky, 221

Seeber, Barbara K., 168–69, 178n6

segregation, 22, 186, 188, 205n69, 220

seminar, 5–6, 33, 35–36, 41–42, 78, 82, 186, 212–19, 221, 278, 283, 288, 293

settler, 132, 134, 136–39, 142n1, 144nn10–1, 152–53, 161, 169

sexuality, 2, 47–48, 50, 61–62, 64–65, 78, 81, 131; heterosexuality, 152; pansexuality, 55

shooting, 1, 6, 39, 49–50, 212–13, 215–18, 222

Simone, Gail, 97, 108n9

Simone, Nina, 47

Sims, John, 114, 118

slavery, 160, 185–88, 220, 252, 254–56, 259, 262, 264–66, 282

Sloan, Nate, 47, 49

slow (pedagogy), 167–69, 171–72, 175, 177, 178n6

Smart, Elizabeth, 106

Smith, George, 188

Smith, Hale, 242

social justice, 5, 46, 115, 143n10, 190–91

songs, 43, 87, 112, 115, 117, 119–22, 128n23,

137, 149, 151, 155, 162, 164, 214, 238, 246–48, 265, 273n22; blackface, 260; minstrel, 118, 187, 232, 252–60; parlor, 118, 187, 273n17, 232, 252–60, 267; protest, 53

Sound of Music, The, 67

sovereignty, 149, 153, 161, 164

space, 1–4, 8, 33–36, 39–41, 45, 48, 51, 53–54, 57n12, 58n22, 65, 69, 97, 99, 101, 104–5, 113–14, 132, 139–42, 149–50, 152–53, 160, 162–64, 168–9, 171–74, 177, 192, 194, 196, 197, 204n57, 215, 253, 255, 257, 282, 285, 298; brave, 46, 51; safe, 33, 42, 46, 51, 55, 66, 68

Spotify, 14

von Stade, Frederica, 81

Starr, Larry, 253

stereotype, 21–22, 53, 65, 105, 115, 128n19, 157, 162–63, 252, 255, 258–59, 262–64

Stevenson, Bryan, 185, 199n4

storytelling, 160

success, 13, 15, 17–18, 20–23, 33, 52, 55, 56n5, 66, 70, 134, 159, 173, 189, 194, 254, 281, 288

supremacy, white. *See* white supremacy

Switched on Pop, 47, 49

Taylor, Sonya Renee, 195

teaching, 1–9, 16, 19–20, 22–23, 35–36, 41, 45–46, 49–52, 54–55, 56n1, 56n5, 57n13, 61–64, 68, 70, 78, 95–96, 99–101, 105, 114, 127n14, 134, 138, 140, 142, 158, 164, 167–68, 170, 172, 178n6, 179n17, 185, 187, 189–90, 193, 196, 198, 203n40, 212–17, 219–20, 223n4, 223n7, 253, 257, 278, 280–84, 289, 293

technique, 8, 35, 95, 101, 168, 213; improvisational, 286; pedagogy, 6, 8, 112; vocal, 82–84

Teitelbaum, Benjamin, 218

tenor, 78, 81–85, 89n10

terrorism, 185, 213, 222n1

Terry, Clark, 280

textbook(s), 9, 41, 47, 61, 63, 131, 136, 138, 143n2, 145n16, 186, 226–40, 249nn1–2, 252–55, 257, 259, 266

theory, music, 3–4, 9, 213, 226–29, 231–9, 249n2, 257, 281

Thumbprint, 7, 95–6, 98–101, 103, 104–7; Opera Ithaca production of, 95

Timberlake, Justin, 83

tokenism, 135, 238

transdisciplinary, 185–87, 189, 196, 198n1

transgender, 65, 84–85, 192

transphobia, 1

trauma, 2–3, 9, 33–36, 39, 41, 55, 59, 97, 101, 104, 106, 151, 197, 212, 217, 219–21

Tree of Life Synagogue, 33, 39

tribe, 159; Karuk, 148; Mastoi, 96; Mitchigamea, 151, 154, 161, 164n5

Tuck, Eve, 132, 143n10

Turino, Thomas, 113, 169, 290

Unite the Right, 39

university, 6, 49, 57n13, 63, 134, 167–68, 195, 198, 212, 218–21, 227, 253, 273n16, 274n29; Bard College, 281; Brown, 117, 126nn2–3; Cape Town, 132; Colorado, 16; Columbia, 280–83; Cornell, 95; Jesuit, 179n11; DePauw, 16; Emory, 58n14; Georgetown, 172; Hampton, 279–80; HBCU; Harvard, 3; Iowa, 3; Louisiana State, 3, 217; Loyola New Orleans, 127n14; Manitoba, 133; Michigan, 33, 44n6; New School, The, 281; North Carolina at Charlotte, 46; Nebraska Wesleyan, 185; North Carolina, 117; North Texas, 114, 127n6, 127n8, 127n14; Ohio State, 17; Oklahoma City, 127n14; Pittsburgh, 252; Regis, 170–71, 179n17; Seton Hall, 281; Vanderbilt, 58n15; Victoria of Wellington, 3, 213, 215–17, 223; Washington in St Louis, 58n14; William Paterson, 278, 281

308   *Index*

value, 7, 13–14, 16–20, 26n34, 52, 70, 101, 106–7, 109n17, 110n25, 116, 122, 137, 139, 141, 143, 186, 198, 217, 272n2, 273n17, 289, 291, 293

Verdi, Giuseppe; *Requiem*, 82; *Il trovatore*, 83

violence, 1, 3, 6–7, 39, 41, 68, 79, 95–101, 104–5, 107, 108n10, 109n22, 133, 149, 152, 158–59, 161, 187–88, 200n16, 214–5, 217, 232, 238

Vox, 47

voix mixte, 84

Waka, Te Herenga, 3, 213

Walker, Margaret, 126n3, 132, 141–42, 143n4

Waterman, Christopher, 253

Way, Good, 150–51, 153, 158

Wetherell, Margaret, 216

whiteness, 4, 57n17, 61, 63, 69, 71n9, 185, 189, 197, 226–28, 231–33, 239, 260, 265

white racial frame, 67, 226, 231, 233, 257

white supremacy, 4, 62, 71n5, 164, 186, 188–89, 193–94, 196–98, 254, 280. *See also* racism

Williams, Bert, 53

Williams, James, 279

Williams, Mary Lou, 247, 249, 249n6

Wilson, Darren, 66

Wilson, Shawn, 148

Witmer, Robert, 138

Woodstock, 66

woman, adult, 80; African-American, 230; American, 212; Black, 262, 265; Chinese, 234; cisgender, 3–4, 79, 81, 96–9, 104, 106, 109n22, 137, 226; of color, 240; heterosexual, 114; Karuk, 150; Pakistani, 95; trans, 85; white, 58n17, 105, 220, 226; young, 51, 215

xenophobia, 1, 5, 38

Yancy, George, 62, 71n6

Yankowitz, Susan, 7, 95–97

Yang, K. Wayne, 132, 142n1

Zia-ul-Haq, 103, 110n24

Zima, 156, 159–60